Labour Law in the Netherlands

Labour Law in the Netherlands

Third Edition

Antoine T.J.M. Jacobs

This book was originally published as a monograph in the International Encyclopaedia of Laws/Labour Law and Industrial Relations.

Founding Editor: Roger Blanpain
General Editor: Frank Hendrickx
Volume Editor: Frank Hendrickx

Wolters Kluwer

Published by:
Kluwer Law International B.V.
PO Box 316
2400 AH Alphen aan den Rijn
The Netherlands
E-mail: international-sales@wolterskluwer.com
Website: lrus.wolterskluwer.com

Sold and distributed in North, Central and South America by:
Wolters Kluwer Legal & Regulatory U.S.
7201 McKinney Circle
Frederick, MD 21704
United States of America
Email: customer.service@wolterskluwer.com

Sold and distributed in all other countries by:
Air Business Subscriptions
Rockwood House
Haywards Heath
West Sussex
RH16 3DH
United Kingdom
Email: international-customerservice@wolterskluwer.com

ISBN 978-94-035-2115-2

e-Book: ISBN 978-94-035-2141-1
web-PDF: ISBN 978-94-035-2195-4

The Author

Dr Antoine T.J.M. Jacobs is Emeritus Professor in Labour Law, Social Security Law and Social Policy at the University of Tilburg, the Netherlands.

Born on 30 April 1946, in Vaals (the Netherlands), he took his Master's (*cum laude*) in Law at Leyden University, 1973. Later he studied in Düsseldorf, Paris, Cambridge, Canterbury and Brussels.

He was deputy-secretary on social affairs at the Dutch Merchant Shipping Council (1968–1974) and lecturer in Labour Law and Social Security Law at Tilburg University (1976–1982). In 1986 he obtained his doctorate (*cum laude*) at Tilburg University in Tilburg on the right of collective bargaining from a European and comparative perspective.

He has written books and articles on Dutch labour and social security law in general, the right to work, the right to strike, discrimination and employment, the direct effect of international norms on Dutch labour and social security law, the influence of International Labour Organization (ILO) norms on Dutch social security law, labour law and social policy of the European Communities, labour law in the German Federal Republic, labour law, employment law and social security law in the United States (US), Dutch collective labour law, the Dutch law on dismissals and flexible workers, actual developments in Dutch social security law, the Constitution of the European Union (EU), etc.

He held the chair of Professor in Labour Law, Social Security Law and Social Policy at Tilburg University from 1987 until 2011. After his retirement he continued teaching there as well as at the State University of Milan.

He has been a visiting professor in Glasgow (1990), Montpellier (1993), Bari (1995), Nantes (1996), Leuven (1998), Padua (2010), Moscow (2013) and Pavia (from 2014); has given papers on comparative labour law at international conferences on labour law in Cologne, Frankfurt, Komintini (Greece), Fontevreau (France), Tokyo, Barcelona, Johannesburg, Montreal, Paris, etc., cooperated with colleagues in other European countries on comparative work and has advised the European Commission and social partners in the Netherlands on matters of labour law and social security law.

He is a member of the Research Network on transnational trade union rights of the European Trade Union Institute.

The Author

Table of Contents

Table of Contents

List of Abbreviations

AAC	*Advies- en Arbitrage Commissie* (Advisory and Arbitration Committee)
ABU	*Algemene Bond van Uitzendondernemingen* (Federation of Temporary Work Agencies)
ACA	Act on Collective Agreements (*Wet op de Collective Arbeidsovereenkomst*)
ADV	*Arbeidsduurverkorting* (Reduction of Working Hours)
AECA	Act on the Extension of Collective Agreements (*Wet op het algemeen verbindend en onverbindend verklaren van bepalingen van collectieve arbeidsovereenkomsten*)
AEIA	Allocation of Employees by Intermediaries Act (*Wet allocatie arbeidskrachten door intermediaires*)
AETAW	Act on Equal Treatment Based on Age at Work (*Wet gelijke behandeling op grond van leeftijd bij arbeid*)
AETHCI	Act on Equal Treatment Based on Handicap or Chronic Illness (*Wet gelijke behandeling op grond van handicap of chronische ziekte*)
AETMW	Act on Equal Treatment of Men and Women (*Wet Gelijke Behandeling van Mannen en Vrouwen*)
AMW	Act on Minimum Wages and Minimum Holiday Allowances (*Wet Minimumloon en Minimum vakantiebijslag*)
AOW	*Algemene Ouderdomswet* (General Old Age Pensions Act)
ARAR	*Algemeen Ambtenarenreglement* (General Regulation for the Civil Service)
AREP	Act on the Regulation of Executive Pay (*Wet Normering Topinkomens*)
ASEC	Act on the Social-Economic Council (*Wet op de Sociaal-Economische Raad*)
AWVN	*Algemene Werkgevers Vereniging Nederland* (Cross-Industry Employers' Association)
BA	Bankruptcy Act (*Faillissementswet*)

List of Abbreviations

CC	Civil Code (*Burgerlijk Wetboek*)
CDA	*Christen Democratisch Appèl* (Christian Democratic Appeal)
CEO	Chief Executive Officer (*Voorzitter Raad van Bestuur*)
CJEU	Court of Justice of the EU
CNV	*Christelijk Nationaal Vakverbond* (Protestant Trade Union Confederation)
CWI	*Centrale Organisatie voor Werk en Inkomen* (Central Organization for Work and Income)
DR	Dismissal Regulation (*Ontslagregeling*)
EC	European Community (*Europese Gemeenschap*)
ECLI	European Case Law Identifier
EEA	European Economic Area
EEC	European Economic Community (*Europese Economische Gemeenschap*)
ERB	Employee Representative Body (*Personeelsvertegenwoordiging*)
ESC	European Social Charter
EU	European Union (*Europese Unie*)
EUPWA	EU Posted Workers (Terms and Conditions of Employment) Act (*Wet arbeidsvoorwaarden gedetacheerde werknemers in de Europese Unie*)
EWCA	European Works Councils Act (*Wet op de Europese Ondernemingsraden*)
FLA	Foreigners Labour Act (*Wet Arbeid Vreemdelingen*)
FNV	*Federatie Nederlandse Vakbeweging* (General Trade Unions Confederation)
FWA	Flexible Working Act (*Wet Flexible Werken*)
GAET	General Act on Equal Treatment (*Algemene Wet gelijke Behandeling*)
GDP	Gross Domestic Product (*Bruto Nationaal Product*)
GDPR	General Data Protection Regulation (*Algemene Verordening Gegevensbescherming*)
HR	*Hoge Raad* (Dutch Supreme Court)
HRM	Human Resources Management (*Afdeling Personeelsaken*)
HSA	Health and Safety at Work Act (*Arbeidsomstandighedenwet*)
IJCLLIR	International Journal of Comparative Labour Law and Industrial Relations
ILLR	International Labour Law Reports
ILO	International Labour Organization (*Internationale Arbeidsorganisatie*)

IT	Information and Technology
JAR	*Jurisprudentie Arbeidsrecht* (a Dutch Labour Law Cases Review)
LIV	Low Income Advantage (*Lage Inkomens Voordeel*)
LTO-Nederland	*Land- en Tuinbouw Nederland* (Farmers' Confederation)
MHP	*Middelbaar en Hoger Personeel* (Confederation of White-Collar unions)
MKB-Nederland	*Midden en Klein Bedrijf Nederland* (Confederation of Small and Medium Sized Enterprises)
MNC	Multinational Company (*Multinationale Onderneming*)
NAS	Nationaal Arbeids Secretariaat
NCDA	Notification of collective dismissals Act (*Wet Melding Collectief Ontslag*)
NJ	*Nederlandse Jurisprudentie* (a General Dutch Cases Review)
NL	*Nederland* (the Netherlands)
NVV	Nederlands Verbond van Vakverenigingen
OECD	Organization of Economic Cooperation and Development (*Organisatie van Economische Samenwerking en Ontwikkeling*)
OIA	Organization of Industry Act (*Wet op de Bedrijfsorganisatie*)
P&P Service	*Arbodienst*
PW	*Participatiewet* (Participation Act)
SER	*Social Economische Raad* (Social and Economic Council)
SNB	Special Negotiating Body (*Bijzondere Onderhandelingsgroep*)
Stb.	Staatsblad (*Official Journal of the Netherlands*)
Stcrt.	Staatscourant (*Official Gazette of the Netherlands*)
SUWI Act	*Wet Structuur Uitvoeringsorganisatie Werk en Inkomen* (Act on the Structure of the Administration for Work and Income)
SZW	*Ministerie van Sociale Zaken en Werkgelegenheid* (Ministry of Social Affairs and Employment)
UBA	Unemployment Benefits Act (*Werkloosheidswet*)
UK	United Kingdom
UN	United Nations (*Verenigde Naties*)
US	United States
UWV	*Uitvoeringsinstituut Werknemersverzekeringen* (Employees' Social Security Administration)
VAR	*Verklaring Arbeidsrelatie* (Declaration on the Status of Independent Contractor)
VCP	*Vakcentrale voor Professionals* (Confederation for Professionals)

List of Abbreviations

VNO-NCW	Main Dutch Employers Confederation
VUT	*vervroegd uittreden* (Early Retirement)
WAA	Wages Allowances Act (*Wet tegemoetkomingen Loondomein*)
Wajong	Incapacity Insurance (Young Disabled Persons) Act
WCA	Works Councils Act (*Wet op de Ondernemingsraden*)
WDA	Wage Determination Act (*Wet op de Loonvorming*)
WIA	Work and Income (Capacity for Work) Act
WTA	Working Time Act (*Arbeidstijdenwet*)
ZZP-ers	*zelfstandigen zonder personeel* (Independent Contractors without Personnel)

General Introduction

Chapter 1. General Background

§1. Geography, Population and Economy

1. The Netherlands is a small country of around 17.3 million people occupying 37,000 sq.km in the heart of north-western Europe, on the continental shores of the North Sea between Germany, France and the United Kingdom (UK), a stone's throw from the capital of Europe, Brussels. Easy access from the North Sea has made the delta of the rivers Rhine, Maas and Scheldt the gateway to Europe and, as a result, a major centre of economic activity.

Apart from a small hilly area in the south-east, the country is flat. As about one-third of the country lies below sea level, the dykes are of vital importance. For over a thousand years, the land has been saved and reclaimed by building and maintaining dykes. The struggle against the water of the sea and the rivers is a permanent task.

The western part of the country (called: Holland) has traditionally been the most densely populated and this is where the three main cities are situated: Amsterdam, capital of the Netherlands; Rotterdam, one of the largest ports in the world; and The Hague, seat of the government. The Netherlands is a democratic monarchy (*see* paragraph 11) with a strong emphasis on the rule of law. It ranks among the highest countries in the world as regards the effectiveness of its legal system[1] and the freedom of the press.[2] It is the no. 8 on the world list of less corrupt countries.[3] Dutch universities rate highly in prestigious rankings such as those of the *Times Higher Education Supplement.*

The Netherlands' economy is noted for its stability, high skilled workforce and developed infrastructure. The establishment of the European Economic Community (EEC) – now the European Union (EU) – has given a new dimension to the Netherlands' function as an economic link. The Netherlands comprises a small area but is densely populated and has an impressive economy. It ranks eighteenth in the

1. *See* the Rule of Law Index of The World Justice Project, 2013.
2. Freedom House Report, 2014.
3. Transparency International, 2014.

world in terms of total Gross Domestic Product (GDP) (2012)[4] and is the fifth-largest economy in the Euro Zone. The country ranks sixth on the list of most competitive countries in the world[5] and it is among the top five countries in terms of labour productivity. The Netherlands is the no. 4 in Europe as regards its attractiveness for foreign investments.[6] Thanks to its good infrastructure and attractive business climate, the Netherlands is well positioned as the 'gateway to Europe'. The port of Rotterdam is the largest port in Europe and the third busiest in the world. Schiphol airport ranks fourth among the European airports. The Netherlands is now considered to be the world's third-best country for trade.[7] It is the world's eighth-largest exporting country and the third-largest exporter in the region. As the Dutch economy is to a large extent dependent on foreign trade and derives more than 65% of GDP from both port activities and merchandise exports, the Dutch economy is also quite vulnerable. Therefore the degree of international competitiveness of the Netherlands is a prime indicator of its economic health. It is evident that the Dutch performance is also very fragile. The Dutch Prime Minister Mark Rutte recently called the Netherlands: 'a tender vase'. The preservation of this fragile structure is the fundamental concern of Dutch political and social forces. It explains why the Dutch government was always so involved in the determination of wages in the private sector, even if currently it intervenes in the private sector by persuasion and indirect pressure rather than by direct intervention (*see* Part II, Chapter 3).

2. The country's main mineral wealth used to be natural gas (which is actually decreasingly exploited), but the national income is mostly generated by intensive agriculture, industry and services. One of the most striking features of this small, densely populated country is its agricultural performance. It is the second largest exporting country of agrarian products (after the United States (US)) – USD 110 billion yearly. More obvious are the area's transit functions and related service activities. The delta has become a favourite location for internationally oriented industries in the areas of oil, chemical, metal, heavy machinery, foodstuffs and electronics. Due, above all, to the presence of major industrial multinational companies (MNCs) within the country, the Netherlands is the world's fifth-largest source of direct investment. And it is the sixth biggest destination of foreign direct investment in the world (unfortunately to some extent in mailbox companies, such as Fiat-Chrysler and Airbus!).

Although there are not many pure 'Dutch' MNCs left – most of them are nowadays predominantly held by foreign investors – the Dutch still like to consider a number of them as Dutch multinationals as these companies still have their roots and headquarters in the Netherlands (*see* Table 1):[8] Royal Dutch Shell (petroleum and chemicals), Unilever (foodstuffs, detergents), Philips (consumer electronics, healthcare and lighting) and Akzo Nobel (man-made fibres, plastics, fertilizers, pharmaceuticals, pesticides) are among the largest corporations in Europe in their

4. Figures of the Center for Economic and Business Research, 2013.
5. *See* The Global Competitiveness Index of the World Economic Forum, 2018.
6. *See* research 2018 of the Accountancy and Consultancy firm EY.
7. World Economic Forum, Enabling Trade Index, 2014.
8. Royal Dutch Shell and Unilever have headquarters in both the Netherlands and the UK.

fields. Other internationally renowned Dutch enterprises are DSM (chemicals), Heineken (beer), Ahold (food retail), KLM (airlines), Rabobank, ING and ABN AMRO (banking) and Achmea, Aegon and Nationale Nederlanden (insurance).

Table 1 Global Ranking of 'Dutch' Enterprises in 2018[9]

	Company	*Global Rank*	*Revenues (Million USD)*
1	Royal Dutch Shell (oil)	5	3,118
2	Aegon (life insurance, pensions and asset management)	139	654
3	Unilever (food)	153	605
4	ING (banking)	171	563
5	Louis Dreyfus (food)	173	554
6	Lyondell Basell Industries (plastics, chemicals)	338	245
7	Royal Philips Electronics	423	281
8	Randstad (temporary agency work)	450	262
9	Heineken Holding (beer)	475	248
10	Rabo Bank	492	238

Although since the 1970s these companies have substantially reduced their direct share in the Dutch labour market (*see* Table 2), it may be argued that their presence in the Netherlands is an indirect source of employment of ten thousands of workers (via the contracting out of all sorts of services and manufacturing – *see* Table 3).

Table 2 Decrease of Jobs in the Netherlands in Purely 'Dutch' MNCs

	1980	*2013*
Philips	80,000	13,000
Shell	23,000	8,000
DSM	23,000	6,000
Akzo Nobel	23,000	5,000
Unilever	14,000	3,000
Heineken	7,000	4,000

9. Fortune Global.

Table 3 The Largest Dutch Employers – In Terms of Numbers of Full-Time Jobs – In 2017

Police	62,000	Tax authorities	29,000
Military	60,000	KLM	26,000
Rabobank	39,000	ING	25,000
Post NL	31,000	Dutch Railways	23,000
Justice	30,000	ABN AMRO	19,000
Ahold	30,000	Employees' Social Security Administration (UWV)	17,000

The main drawback of the economic strength of the Netherlands is the Dutch contribution to pollution. The Netherlands ranks fourth in the EU as regards the greenhouse gas emission per capita.

§2. Economic Growth and Employment

3. The Dutch economy has experienced an almost uninterrupted expansion since World War II, with real national income more than doubling in the period from 1961 to 1982. One of the reasons why the Netherlands has been able to finance its welfare system may be found in the efficient organization of its production. The labour costs per unit of production in the Netherlands used to be among the lowest in the EU. The productivity of the Dutch worker used to be 1.5 times that of the Japanese worker. This favourable relationship between the price and quality of its products explained how the Netherlands sustained its competitiveness for the first three decades after World War II.

However, following the first oil crisis of 1973–1974, the pace of the economy slowed down noticeably (*see* Table 4).

Table 4 Growth Rates of GDP – Annual Percentage Change in Volume

1970	6.2	1980	1.3	1990	4.2	2000	3.9	2010	1.6
1971	4.3	1981	-0.8	1991	2.4	2001	1.9	2011	1.0
1972	2.5	1982	-2.1	1992	1.7	2002	0.1	2012	-1.0
1973	2.8	1983	2.1	1993	1.3	2003	0.3	2013	0
1974	4.3	1984	3.1	1994	3.0	2004	2.2	2014	1.4
1975	0	1985	2.6	1995	3.1	2005	2.0	2015	2.0
1976	4.6	1986	2.8	1996	3.4	2006	3.4	2016	2.2
1977	2.5	1987	1.9	1997	4.3	2007	3.9	2017	2.9
1978	2.7	1988	3.4	1998	3.9	2008	1.8	2018	2.8
1979	2.0	1989	4.4	1999	4.7	2009	-3.7		

The low economic growth in the Netherlands at the beginning of the 1980s resulted in a drop in employment and consequently an increase in the unemployment rate. In the first half of the 1980s employment fell by 1.5% annually, which was a sharper drop than in most other EU countries. The standardized unemployment rate peaked in 1983 (11.4%). During the 1980s many observers saw little to admire in the various aspects of the Dutch economy and the Dutch government became increasingly aware that it had to tackle the costs of its welfare system as well as the low level of participation on the labour market. There was a large gap between net and gross wages (which economists call 'the tax wedge on labour'). With gross wages about twice as high as net wages, the Dutch gap was an EU record. It was caused by the extensive system of public services and social protection in the Netherlands. The welfare system of the Netherlands, i.e., gross public expenditure on social security, was almost a third of its GDP each year. Most of this had to be paid for out of taxation and social security contributions.

In the second half of the 1980s rates of GDP growth were higher. The improved general economic condition since the mid-1980s increased employment. The new jobs were mainly filled by school-leavers and housewives re-entering the labour market. That is why the unemployment rates (around 9% in 1990) as well as the proportion of long-term unemployment showed only a moderate decrease.

At the beginning of the 1990s economic growth and employment growth stagnated again, but after 1993 economic growth surged to a relatively high level where it stayed until 2000. In those years 150,000–200,000 new jobs were created each year. Although these jobs have primarily benefited new entrants to the labour market, they also benefited the long-term unemployed: long-term unemployment decreased from 50% of the unemployed in 1995 to around 42% in 2000 (*see* Table 5).

Table 5 Unemployed Labour Force and Registered Unemployment as Percentage of the Labour Force, 1997–2018

Year	*Unemployment*	*%*	*Year*	*Unemployment*	*%*
1997	448,000	6.6	2008	300,000	3.8
1998	354,000	5.1	2009	377,000	4.8
1999	301,000	4.3	2010	426,000	5.4
2000	270,000	3.8	2011	419,000	5.4
2001	252,000	3.5	2012	507,000	6.4
2002	302,000	4.1	2013	650,000	7.,0
2003	396,000	5.4	2014	700.,000	7.,1
2004	476,000	6.4	2015	600.,000	6.,5
2005	482,000	6.5	2016	500.,000	5.,3
2006	410,000	5.5	2017	400.,000	4.,3
2007	344,000	4.5	2018	350.,000	3.,6

4. In 2001 the Dutch unemployment rate was back to the level prevailing in the 1970s: 3.5%, the lowest of the EU. Thanks to an economic upswing some 1 million new jobs were created during the 1990s and the percentage of unemployed dropped to about 3.5% in 2001, which was extremely favourable as compared to the 7.3% of the EU as a whole. In the eyes of foreign observers the Netherlands has fared relatively well in these years. Economic growth was above the European average and the government budget was in balance.

These robust successes attracted much interest from abroad. From having been considered 'the sick man' of Europe in the early 1980s, the Dutch economy had emerged as one of Europe's strongest, with consistently robust economic growth and job creation in the 1990s. Much of the success had been ascribed to the so-called Dutch *poldermodel* (*see* paragraphs 14 et seq.). Apparently the Dutch had managed to make their economy better performing without substantially reducing the level of labour law and social security legislation. On the contrary, Dutch government officials were eager to emphasize that good social legislation is essential to ensure smooth processes of adaptation. A well-designed social policy, one which contributes towards social cohesion and invests in training and education, acts as a kind of lubricant in a dynamic economy. The 'Welfare State as an Economic Performer' was the slogan of the social democratic wing of the coalition government that ruled the Netherlands between 1994 and 2002. Apparently the high labour standards in the Netherlands carry some longer-term benefits along with their immediate costs. Such benefits may lie in the high productivity rate of most Dutch employees, the loyalty and willingness of well-protected workers to contribute to innovation, and the better overall stability and infrastructure of a country with high employment protection levels. All this should not conceal the fact that many aspects of Dutch labour law and social security law have been changed in these years; not by wholesale reforms but by subtle piecemeal changes in labour law, social security and the tax system, which have made it more flexible and somewhat less burdensome for employers. Very important also was the voluntary wage restraint of the trade unions. Between 1982 and 1997 collectively agreed pay rises were well below those of the Netherlands' main competitors.

Unavoidably this economic success created new problems. In 2000 strong economic growth had led to a tight labour market. Dutch businesses had difficulties finding suitable staff. This fuelled wage growth (since 1997 exceeding that of the main competitors of the Netherlands) and pushed up inflation to 4.5% in 2001, the highest level since 1977. The rise in productivity had fallen below the EU average.

The world economy and also that of the Netherlands was severely hit by the events of 9/11 2001 in the US, so after the year 2001 economic growth slowed down considerably and the beginning of 2003 saw the sharpest rise in unemployment since the 1970s. The slowdown of Western economies after 2000 pushed the Dutch economy to the brink of a recession. In July 2003 unemployment had risen to 5.4% (*see* Table 6). This prompted the Dutch government to initiate new rounds of changes in the Dutch system of social security and tax law, which has become an ongoing process until today. The economic situation improved by 2006–2007, but in 2008 the Netherlands was – like most EU Member States – hit by the banking crisis. Initially the consequences were less grave than in other EU Member States. With an unemployment figure of ca. 5% (2009–2011) the Netherlands ranked among the best performing economies of the EU. Many a Dutch company managed to cope with the crisis, notably in the sectors of chemicals, chip manufacturers, lorry- and bus-builders. However, in the course of 2011 the Dutch also had to bow to the crisis and the unemployment rate strongly increased to around 7% in 2014.

Table 6 Unemployment Rates in % of the Active Population

	2010	*2011*	*2012*	*2013*
The Netherlands	5.4	5.4	6.4	7.0
Germany	7.6	6.5	5.6	5.4
France	9.9	9.6	9.9	10.8
UK	7.9	7.7	8.2	7.8
EU average	9.6	9.5	10.1	11.0

Taboos faltered as a result of the banking crisis. More drastic reforms in the old-age pension schemes, the disablement benefit schemes and social assistance could be realized. In 2015 also a more comprehensive reform of the rules of the labour market was brought about (*see* paragraph 195). As a result of the economic crisis since 2008 the average income from work of a Dutch active person (both employees and independent workers) has fallen from EUR 25.50 an hour in 2012 to EUR 24.60 in 2014.

In these years some productivity advantages have disappeared because of above-average wage increases. The hourly labour costs (wages/salaries and other costs) in the Netherlands were at EUR 34, well over the EU average, but on the average of its main trade partners (Germany, Belgium, France and the UK). Nevertheless, other research showed that Dutch workers were still among the most productive in the world.[10] The 'average tax wedge on labour' in the Netherlands decreased from 40.5% to 32.0% between 1995 and 2012. However, to some extent this figure is misleading because it partly results from the fact that many costs of statutory social security schemes have been shifted to employers (privatized arrangements, *see* for instance paragraph 151). They are no less of a burden for employers!

As national systems of labour law and social protection impose direct labour costs on enterprises, it may pay for companies to relocate manufacturing and jobs to countries with weak labour standards ('offshoring'). This relocation has certainly taken place in the Netherlands during the last fifty years, but in some sectors more than in others. And it still continues: in 2019 Philips announced the relocation of 230 jobs to Poland. However, according to government researches this relocation has been made good by at least the same number of newly created jobs, notably in the service sector. Recent years have also seen some cases of 'reshoring' (companies bringing their production sites back to the Netherlands). This trend may be enforced by further robotization of the Dutch economy (*see* paragraph 6).

In the course of 2014 it appeared that the most recent economic recession in the Netherlands was over. Economic growth had resumed (*see* Table 4) and the level of

10. PwC research, 2014.

unemployment decreased accordingly. Actually (April 2019) it has reached the low figure of ca. 3.6% (350,000 persons) (*see* Table 5). The main problem of the Dutch labour market is now the shortages of labour! There are – 2019 – 250,000 job vacancies, which apparently cannot be filled by the 350,000 formally unemployed persons. This is either because – in the eyes of employers – these unemployed workers do not have the competences or – in the eyes of the workers – they for whatever reason do not want to fill these vacancies. This now inspires employers, politicians and scholarly writers to come forward with all sorts of creative solutions (*see* paragraph 6).

5. It should be noted that in the Netherlands different types of unemployment figures are released. Some of the figures produced by Statistics Netherlands are the lowest because unemployment is defined as registered unemployed people actively seeking employment of at least twelve hours a week and who are immediately ready to accept a job. However, Statistics Netherlands also produces figures which are higher as they count all unemployed people who in theory should be ready to enter the labour market and so comprise people looking for a job of less than twelve hours a week.

There is a case for saying that unemployment in the Netherlands is even higher than the official figures, as there is still much 'hidden' unemployment among people on sick pay, in disablement benefits schemes and in early retirement (VUT) schemes (*see* paragraph 165).

As far as unemployment is concerned comparison of the Netherlands to other Organization of Economic Cooperation and Development (OECD) countries reveals that (i) there is a large share of long-term unemployed workers; (ii) youth employment rates are high relative to older workers but low relative to other OECD countries; (iii) there are many partially disabled persons unemployed, and in particularly handicapped youth; (iv) labour force participation is relatively high, only for older workers the labour force participation is still low; (v) Dutch workers work relatively few hours (*see* paragraph 116) and (vi) Dutch spending on active labour market programmes is quite high.

Table 7 Unemployment in Age Categories (%)

15–25 years	10
25–35 years	5.5
35–45 years	4
45–55 years	4.5
55–65 years	5

In Table 7, these figures show that in the Netherlands the elderly workers are not substantially overrepresented in the unemployment figures. Youth unemployment is more serious. It must, however, be emphasized that elderly workers are overrepresented as regards long-term unemployment. The unemployment among elderly workers tends to be much more protracted than in other age categories. Only 9% of the 55–65-year-old unemployed find a job within one year.

Finally, as has been mentioned, there are also several segments of the Dutch labour market with shortages of labour and further shortages are expected in future. The ageing of the population is one of the contributors to this because in the sector care the need for new jobs is due to rise each year until 2030 by 1.2%. In this sector, however, the factor of financing is the main problem. This sector cannot expand incessantly as there is much pressure to keep government spending and healthcare contributions as low as possible.

For some people this is a motive to open the borders more for migrants. Immigration from EU countries was low until ca. 2000, but since then it has risen to ca. 200,000 yearly as a result of the expansion of the EU into Central Europe. The number of workers with a non-Dutch ethnic background has been steadily growing. Persons with a non-Western origin are accounting for about 12% of the population (*see* paragraph 92). Most of them are from Turkey, Morocco, Surinam and the Dutch Antilles. The unemployment rate in this category is constantly twice or three times the number of persons with a Dutch-ethnic background. There are various laws to ensure that the labour market is an inclusive labour market. They include the General Equal Treatment Act, other anti-discrimination laws (*see* paragraphs 87 et seq.) and reintegration provisions in the Participation Act (PW), the Unemployment Benefits Act (UBA), the Work and Income (Capacity for Work) Act (WIA) and the Incapacity Insurance (Young Disabled Persons) Act. Special attention is devoted to ensuring access to these schemes for groups that are less self-reliant or cannot automatically benefit from the measures, and to avoid distinctions between insiders and outsiders.

Attention should also be paid to the demographic factor. In the Netherlands the population is ageing at a rapid pace. Not so much as in Germany, but more rapidly than for instance in the US. In the year 2050 the number of 65+ persons as a percentage of the entire population will have risen as opposed to the year 2010:

Germany	from	20.4%	to	31.5%
Netherlands	from	15.3%	to	25.1%
Denmark	from	16.3%	to	23.8%
US	from	13.1%	to	20.2%

The ageing of the population will have heavy consequences in the foreseeable future. The pension system is at risk and also the prognosticated increase in the care costs of old people as a result of the ageing of the population is worrying as the long-term main economic indicators are uncertain for the Netherlands (*see* Table 8).

Table 8 Some Comparative Economic Indicators in 2017 (in %)

	Netherlands	*Germany*	*France*	*UK*
Real GDP Growth	2.9	1.8	1.2	0.5
General government deficit/surplus	-0.8	-0.1	+0.2	1.0
National debt (in GDP)	58	62	98	82

6. Nevertheless most observers are optimistic about the long-term perspectives of the Dutch labour market. As a matter of fact in recent years, the number of unemployed has decreased, not only because of the economic upswing but also because of the exodus of the baby-boom generation (the ageing factor) and the decreasing influx of youngsters (dejuvenation) and this development has in the year 2019 created many shortages on the Dutch labour market. This worries the government as shortages may easily push up wages and so cause inflation and a deterioration of the competitiveness of Dutch business. Therefore the government is trying to maximize the unutilized potential in the Dutch labour market. This is not easy, because with employment participation at around 76% (2017) there is not much unutilized potential left, as it is much more difficult to find employment on the labour market for the remaining theoretical potential. That explains why this debate has been dominated by the call for flexibility, pressure on those who are not working or only part-time working and smoother transitions from one job to another.

The impact of further automatization, digitalization and robotization[11] remains an uncertain factor for the future of the Dutch labour market. A 2017 research established that the Netherlands is in the top group of countries as regards the application of new technologies.[12] Up till now robotization in the Netherlands is already above the average of the OECD countries (107 industrial robots on 10,000 workers), although it is much lower than in South Korea and Japan.[13] In an OECD study of April 2018, the Netherlands figures low on the list of countries at risk of job losses through further robotization. In other research, it is assumed that further robotization in the Netherlands may destroy 1.3 million jobs but at the same time shall create 1.4 million new jobs.[14] The Dutch government refrains from drawing optimistic or pessimistic prognoses but intends to focus on various aspects of its policies to prepare the Dutch society for coping with the consequences of automatization, digitalization and robotization.[15]

11. *See* E. Brynjolfsson & A. McAgee, *The Second Machine Age*.
12. McKinsey research, 2017.
13. International Federation of Robotics (FR), 2018.
14. McKinsey research, 2017.
15. Parliamentary Papers no. 29544-773.

§3. The Composition of the Labour Force

7. In 1983 the economically active population consisted of about 4.3 million wage earners, 0.6 million self-employed (their co-working family members included), and 0.7 million unemployed. In 2010 the economically active population consisted of about 6.4 million wage earners, 0.7 million self-employed, and 1.4 million unemployed people. In 2018 the Netherlands had an economically active population of about 8.7 million people and 0.35 million unemployed. The number of self-employed has risen to 1.1 million, which is now 12% of the economic active population. The so-called labour force participation rate had gradually risen from 60% in 1996 to 76% in 2017 (*see* Table 9).

Table 9 Labour Force Participation Rate (2017)

	Netherlands	*UK*	*Germany*	*France*
Total	76	74	75	65
Male	80	78	78	68
Female	72	69	71	62

Again, there may be different figures in this field which show a higher degree of labour participation as they also include very small part-time jobs.

The increase in the participation rate has been largely caused by the increased participation of women in the labour market. It has risen from 47% in 1995 to actually 72%. A second factor is the participation of elderly persons (over 55 years). After 1980 growing numbers of elderly workers deserted the labour market, but this process has come to a halt and in recent years the labour force participation rate of elderly workers (55–65 years) has recovered substantially from 31.8% in 1997 to 63%, which is certainly not bad, but could be higher. In Sweden this figure stands at 75% and this is a goal the Dutch government would like to equal. Also the number of people still working beyond the age of 65 is rising. In 2002 it was 3.4% of persons between 65 and 70, in 2010 it was 7.2%. In category 70–74 these figures are 1.4% in 2002 and 3.4% in 2010. Since then the increase continued: in 2013 there were 182,000 65+ persons at work as against 85,000 in 2009.

8. The labour force is distributed over different branches of the economy. They are employed by some 1,400 employers with over 250 workers and by 420,000 employers with 2–250 workers. About 73% are employed in the private sector and 12% in the public sector and 15% in the semi-public sector.

In 2011 2.3% of the active population were engaged in agriculture, 18.9% in industry and energy and 77.8% in services. Job creation since the 1990s has predominantly been in the service sector. Although employment also increased in the manufacturing sector and agriculture, it did not do so in relative figures.

The rising proportion of the service sector in total employment (66.4% in 1985 and 77.8% in 2011) in the Netherlands is, after Luxembourg, the highest in the EU, while the proportion of employment in manufacturing industry in total employment is one of the lowest and is steadily decreasing at an annual rate of about 2.5%. It is now at a level of about 15% of total employment, creating 17% of GDP. Although this is comparable with, for instance, US figures, Dutch policymakers are worried about the steadily decreasing share of manufacturing industry in the Dutch economy, which once used to account for 75% of the exporting capacity of the Dutch economy, now 63%.

During the 1980s *part-time jobs* were the dominant source for employment growth in the Netherlands. Between 1987 and 1994 two-thirds of Dutch employment growth was in part-time jobs, while between 1994 and 1999 half of the net employment growth was in part-time jobs. Moreover, 20% of new jobs were small part-time (less than twelve hours) jobs occupied by women and youngsters. The proportion of part-time jobs in total employment increased from around 17% in 1980 to 51% in 2014, the highest in the OECD. The EU average is only 18%. The growth of part-time employment is to a certain extent supply-side driven. More than in other EU countries, in the Netherlands the wishes of employees as regards temporary jobs play an important role. In the Netherlands working part-time is regarded as a normal and desired type of employment, illustrated by the high number of part-time workers who report that they voluntarily work in this type of employment. They seem satisfied with part-time work. Only 10% would like to work more (in the EU: 28%).[16] Especially women are working part-time (76% of women, 27% of men; *see* paragraph 119). A large number of part-time workers explain the low average number of hours of Dutch workers: only 1,419 hours a year (*see* paragraph 118).

In recent decades the most typical Dutch family model is the one-and-a-half model: in households with two partners and half-grown children, the male partner typically has a full-time job and the female partner a part-time job (*see* Table 10).

Table 10 Families with Children up to 12 years (%)

	1995	*2008*	*2013*
With only one working parent	50	26	23
With 1.5 working parent	31	54	54
With 2 working parents	4	8	8

9. Since the beginning of the 1980s also the volume of *temporary jobs* (fixed-term contracts, 'on-call' contracts, temporary agency work, freelance contracts) has strongly increased. The proportion of temporary employment in total employment rose from 6% in 1983 to over 15% in 2000 and to actually 35%, one of the highest proportions in the EU. Almost half of the recent employment growth has been in temporary jobs.

This 35% temporary work is a considerable figure and a further rise of this figure is probable. Although many workers newly offered flexi-work contracts after some

16. Eurostat, 2017.

time manage to find permanent employment, great numbers of flexi-workers stay on in flexi-work. Less than 30% of flexi-workers have found permanent work after two years (*see* Table 11).

Table 11 Workers on Non-standard Employment Contracts

In Age Categories (%)			*In Types of Flexible Contracts (In Millions (Full-Time))*		
Age	*2003*	*2018*	*2003*	*2018*	
15–25	47	45			
25–35	19	23	0.6	1.0	Fixed-term contracts
35–45	12	11	0.3	0.7	On-call/zero-hours contracts
45–55	10	11	0.2	0.3	Temporary agency work
55–65	8	7	0.6	1.0	Self-employed
65–75	4	3			

Among workers on flexible contracts the largest numbers are those working on fixed-term contracts and on-call contracts (about 375,000). Also temporary agency work became more widespread than in any other EU country. In the past temporary agency work was mainly offered in unskilled or semiskilled jobs. Nowadays many temporary work firms are providing highly specialist workers, such as Information and Technology (IT) employees, opticians and lawyers. In the past temporary work businesses specialized in providing workers, engaged for a short period. In recent years the Netherlands has seen the emergence of staff-leasing arrangements – notably experts engaged for an indefinite period by intermediaries to place them in user companies – and payroll firms (*see* paragraph 66).

Finally, there is an increase in freelance workers and workers in independent entrepreneurship without personnel (ZZP-ers). In 2011 16% of enterprises were operated with the involvement of such ZZP-persons; in 2013 the figure was 31%. A total of 35% of the ZZP-ers is working full-time, 65% on part-time basis. One out of seven ZZP-persons is earning less than the official Dutch poverty-line income (about EUR 1,040 a month for a single person). The large number of ZZP-ers is partly to be explained by the tax concessions to these persons, which can go up as high as EUR 22,000 a year. The European Commission is critical about the growth of the ZZP-sector in the Netherlands (2017). It sees it as a menace to the Dutch system of social security, which is only partially financed by contributions of ZZP-persons.

Experience has taught that as soon as the Dutch economy recovers, the expansion of the labour force will be first in the area of flexi-workers and not in standard employment contracts. And as soon as the economy goes into a recession flexi-workers are the first to be made redundant. This experience became very painful in 2008/2009. And in those days it was criticized that the most important government measure to help to overcome the crisis (short-time working, *see* paragraph 133) was not useful for flexi-workers, but only for the permanent workforce.

The strong increase in the number of flexi-contracts has revealed that the Dutch labour market to a large extent has become a two-tier labour market. Although there exists a number of labour law rules promising temporary workers equal treatment with permanent workers in several aspects of employment conditions (*see* paragraphs 66 and 100), the realities are different. Statistics show that flexible workers are earning 15% to 30% less than comparable persons on standard employment contracts. They do not enjoy equal treatment in the termination of the contract, are (in practice) exposed to greater health risks and devoid of training and are more often unemployed. Consequently many temporary workers have a second class position in society. For instance they have difficulties in obtaining a mortgage, which is very unpleasant as renting social housing is equally difficult. The actual government is committed to reducing the share of flexi-work on the labour market, *inter alia* by fighting the abuse of this kind of employment by outlawing bogus constructions (*see* paragraphs 51 and 149).[17]

Finally, as in all countries, there is the so-called informal economy. Like everywhere estimations about its size are varying largely, but the average comes down to about 10% of the economy. It is concentrated in sectors like pubs and restaurants, agriculture and food, taxi services, delivery, engineering and clothing (*see* Table 12).

Table 12 Estimates of the Extent of the Informal Economy (in % of GDP)

Netherlands	10	Germany	14
UK	11	EU average	18.5
France	11	Italy	21

§4. Wealth and Poverty

10. The Netherlands belongs to the most prosperous countries in the world. It ranks fourth on the World list. It also ranks fourth on the list of net financial assets of its inhabitants with an average of EUR 96,000 per inhabitant.[18] The number of 'high net worth' families (more than EUR 1 million assets) is about 200,000, which

17. Parliamentary Papers no. 17050/447.
18. Global Wealth Report of Allianz, 2018.

is a density of 2.6% (15th on the world list).[19] The richest 1% is holding 26% of the assets of the Netherlands, the richest 5% 42%[20] the richest 20%: 80%.

These last figures illustrate already that the richness of the Dutch is very unevenly distributed. Certainly the working population only gets a small share in this richness. This may be illustrated by the figures on the labour share in the national income. In the Netherlands this share stood at its peak ca. 1980. It was 81% in 1995 and has meanwhile dropped to 73% in 2017.

Among the wage earners, however, the situation in the Netherlands is more compact than that in other Western European states. The Netherlands ranks first in Europe on the list of the countries with less unequal income distribution.[21] The highest wages are lower and rarer than those earned across Europe. In contrast, the lowest wages are higher than those paid elsewhere in Europe but much more widespread. However, in recent years, the gap between executive pay and the other wages is growing and leads to worries and measures (*see* paragraph 288). From these figures it may be inferred that in the Netherlands inequality in assets is quite large, whereas inequality of income is comparatively small. Foreigners are often struck by the fairly low level of poverty in the Netherlands and its relative, though not exceptional, wealth. Compared to other EU Member States, the number of people facing the risk of poverty and social exclusion is relatively small in the Netherlands. This is mainly due to the comprehensive social security system in the Netherlands.[22] The main schemes are: the General Old Age Pensions Act (AOW) providing a basic income for the all the elderly; the General Surviving Dependants' Act compensating with a basic income the loss of income due to the death of a breadwinner; there are the UBA and the WIA, compensating employees for loss of income due to the unemployment and for incapacity for work; there is the obligation on employers to continue the payment of salary during two years for employees who are unable to work due to illness (*see* paragraph 151). Finally, there is the PW for all residents with insufficient income or capital to support themselves and who do not qualify for other benefits.

The amount of the minimum benefit under all these schemes is linked to the minimum wage (*see* paragraph 140), which is automatically linked to the average rise in workers' pay. All this has created a system in which the prosperity of benefit recipients rises in line with that of working people. Although this linkage could not be maintained during the recession years of the 1980s, it has always played the role of a 'shibboleth' in Dutch social politics and was restored in the 1990s. Due to this linkage and the activating nature of the system, the percentage of the population with a low income has fallen from 16% in the mid-1990s to 7.9 in 2016. The official statistics agency in 2017 has put the so-called living wage or the poverty line this (2017) at EUR 1,040 a month for a single person, EUR 1,380 for a single parent with one child and EUR 1,980 for a couple with two children (*see* paragraph 142). This means that the Dutch minimum wage, which is ca. EUR 1,653 a month,

19. Figures of the Boston Consulting Group, 2013.
20. University of Bamberg, 2014.
21. Ifo Institute München, July 2018.
22. *See* F. Pennings, Monograph on The Netherlands in the *International Encyclopedia for Social Security Law*.

is for most people well above the 'living wage' or the 'poverty line'. However about ca. 180,000 persons for one reason or another do not earn such an income and are therefore living under the poverty line. So, despite the country's relatively good score in EU terms, the risk of poverty in the Netherlands has returned during the most recent financial crises and still demands attention.

Chapter 2. The Political Background

§1. General Observations

11. After the French occupation (1795–1813) the Netherlands emerged as a unitary state (kingdom) with a centralized administration in 1814, replacing the Dutch Republic of the United Provinces (1581–1795), which was a confederation of various, relatively autonomous provinces.

The legislative power rests with the government and Parliament together; the executive power formally rests with the government alone, but it is under the permanent scrutiny of Parliament and the judiciary. The judicial power rests with the courts.

The government consists of the king and his ministers (the Cabinet) together. The king is 'immune', which means that only the ministers are responsible. Successive constitutional reforms over the last 150 years have left the king with almost no political power and made his function merely ceremonial. Parliament is composed of the *Eerste Kamer* (Senate, 75 seats) and the *Tweede Kamer* (House of Representatives, 150 seats). Of the two, the *Tweede Kamer* is the most important. It can, for instance, amend a Bill, whereas the *Eerste Kamer* can only endorse or veto a Bill. The *Tweede Kamer* and not the *Eerste Kamer* controls the exercise of the executive power by the government. A Cabinet or an individual member of the Cabinet who has lost the confidence of the majority of the *Tweede Kamer* has to resign.

The various political parties are represented in Parliament on the basis of proportional representation. Their candidates for the *Tweede Kamer* are directly chosen by all men and women aged 18 or over. Members of the *Eerste Kamer* are chosen by the Provincial Councils which in their turn are directly chosen by all men and women aged 18 or over.

§2. Political Parties, Coalition Cabinets

12. It should be recalled that the Netherlands is a country of religious and political minorities. This fact has dominated its history. In the nineteenth century, in contrast to other countries, such as the UK and Germany, the emancipation of the working class was preceded by an emancipation of religious minorities, namely orthodox Calvinists and Roman Catholics. Their struggle was mainly concerned with the control of education and the claim for government subsidies for denominational schools; labour and social problems were of only secondary importance.

As a result of this struggle, the denominational parties emerged as the main opponents of the liberals and conservatives by the end of the nineteenth century. The socialists arrived on the scene somewhat later, merely becoming a minority among the other minorities of Protestants, Catholics and liberals.

After World War I each minority continued to construe its own segment of society. This ideological segregation (in Dutch called *verzuiling* – 'pillar'-like divisions in society) encompassed political parties, schools, trade unions and employers' associations, mass media, healthcare, welfare, sports clubs, etc. This situation revived after World War II, but since the 1950s religious influence has gradually diminished. Most of the old dividing lines have vanished since then.

The decline of religious influence can be illustrated by the vicissitudes of the denominational parties. In 1956 the three Christian parties held in total 77 of the 150 seats in the *Tweede Kamer*. In 1977, when the three parties joined forces to form a new party, the Christian Democratic Appeal (CDA), their number of seats was down to 49. It now has only 19 seats (2017 elections).

Another example of the decline of religious influence is manifested in the world of social partners. In 1977 the Catholic Trade Union gave up its identity by merging with the social democratic trade unions confederation into the General Trade Unions Confederation (FNV) (*see* paragraph 269). In the 1990s all denominational structures on the employer's side disappeared (*see* paragraph 274).

No single political party has ever had the prospect of governing the country alone. The Netherlands has always been governed by a coalition cabinet. The Christian democratic parties were most of the time the backbone of those Cabinets, sometimes sharing the power with the social democrats, sometimes with the liberals. Only between 1994 and 2002 and between 2012 and 2017 did social democrats and liberals shared power, sending the Christian Democrats into opposition. The actual government consists of two liberal and two Christian parties. During the last decade the Netherlands have seen the growth of 'populist' parties on the right and the left, which has made the political situation more complicated than before.

13. Legislative power and socio-economic policies in our welfare states have become unthinkable without dialogue with the social partners: this is often described as 'the economy of concertation' (or consensus economy). In the Netherlands this situation is shaped by delicate political relationships, which attach much importance to social consensus. Attempts are always made to avoid severe public confrontations both on the part of the government and on the part of the social partners.

The public authorities scrupulously avoid taking the side of one or the other of the social partners (in contrast with the traditional UK case of the intimate relationship between the Tories and business and between Labour and the unions), although it stands to reason that in the Netherlands a centre-left government is preferred by the unions, while a centre-right government will be more sensitive to employers' aspirations. However, all governments have formally kept an equal distance from both social partners.

Before World War II the picture was somewhat different. Social Democrats and liberals were much more in favour of one extreme or the other. However, it was the preponderance of the Christian Democrat political and social forces that ensured a balanced development. Christian Democrat policies were in this respect heavily inspired by the social teachings of the Roman-Catholic and Protestant churches, which favour a middle-of-the-road approach to economic problems.

One of the proposals of Christian social teachings has been to establish joint institutions of workers' and employers' representatives. These representatives should solve their differences in close cooperation and promote mutual interests and also the interests of the community. This idea, often called 'corporatism', was rejected by liberals as well as socialists and, elsewhere in Europe abused under fascist dictatorships. In a democratic form, however, it had become widespread in various Western European states not least in the Netherlands (*see* paragraphs 279 et seq.). This tendency to 'neo-corporatism' is frequently criticized as it makes social-economic structures less transparent and rather inert. But despite these criticisms the idea still flourishes, today less so in a formal way, more in an informal way.

The overall effect is that the social development in the Netherlands is never a stop-go process as it is in France or a periodical swing of the pendulum as it is in the UK. It is more a steady evolution rather than a revolution with labour law and social security law undergoing many, but unspectacular, adaptations from year to year.

As a product of the processes outlined above, Dutch labour law can be characterized as a middle-of-the-road law, on the one hand protecting the weak and giving workers a say in socio-economic governance, while at the same time not overburdening enterprises and leaving ample scope for managerial decision-making. Of course there is a constant tug-of-war about increasing managerial freedom and as a result a reduction of the protection of workers or vice versa. Although there are always discussions regarding minor adaptations, none of the major political parties, trade unions or the employers' associations proposes a major overhaul of the existing socio-economic system.

Chapter 3. The System of Industrial Relations

14. The history and the various aspects of the system of industrial relations in the Netherlands will be described in detail in Part II. It may suffice for this introduction to point at one of the main characteristics of this model: the rather harmonious character of this relationship. Employers and employees' organizations adopt a strategy of conflict avoidance. A climate of industrial peace is predominant. Compared with many other countries employees in the Netherlands and their unions only rarely resort to the strike weapon. In the sophisticated, harmonious system of industrial relations of the Netherlands the trade union movement is weak in numbers, moderate in its positions and therefore well regarded in the eyes of the public, the politicians and the employers. In times of slack business the trade unions are prepared to renounce of substantial pay claims and to cooperate in the restructuring of enterprises.

Employers are not hostile to trade unions. Attitudes like 'union-bashing' are completely unknown in the Netherlands and would not be accepted by the courts and public opinion. Most employees are individualistic and not very strike prone. Discussion and bargaining over problems and antagonistic interests in order to reach a consensus are widely preferred. Therefore forums of discussion have been established at all levels of the economy – at the cross-sector level (the bipartite *Stichting van de Arbeid* and the tripartite *Sociaal-Economische Raad* (*see* paragraphs 290 et seq.)), at sector level in various kinds of joint bodies and collective bargaining practices, and at enterprise level, in works councils. Key decisions on socio-economic disputes are in the hands of the courts, which tend to leave management ample space for manoeuvre but bind it rigorously to the procedural rules of the game.

The principal change made to the Dutch system of industrial relations in reaction to the various challenges was the one made during the 1980s and the 1990s: the near-total abolition of all instruments of state control on wage formation (*see* paragraphs 281 et seq.). Only auxiliary forms of state intervention, such as the statutes on collective agreements, minimum wages and equal pay remained on the statute book (*see* paragraph 24). Ever since the system has been characterized by a number of voluntary practices providing for consensus building at all levels in the socio-economic area. It was then labelled with the buzz-word *poldermodel* (after the typical Dutch landscape *polder* – low, flat areas behind dykes).[23]

The system of collective bargaining is strongly supported by two Acts of Parliament. The first act provides for a legalized system of collective agreements and the second ensures a wide coverage of this system. Finally, the Works Councils Act (WCA) guarantees the priority of collective agreements over agreements between employers and works councils (*see* paragraph 391).

Sector collective agreements are still widely extended *erga omnes* (*see* paragraph 324) so that employers cannot extract themselves from the binding force of a collective agreement. The employers' organizations are very positive and cooperative in requesting the Ministry for such extensions *erga omnes*.

---

23. M. Keune (ed.), *The Polder Model, Still a Dutch Miracle* (2015).

The Dutch still believe very much in the idea that employers should compete with each other on quality and not on wage costs. Even employers are inclined to prefer the rigidities of collective agreements over the social unrest that could result from a breakdown of the system of sector collective bargaining. Therefore in the Netherlands social partners still struggle to keep alive the many sector collective agreements and to reach some flexibility by giving the collective agreements a framework character.

MNCs are thought to be a major source of pressure for supplanting sector-level collective agreements by enterprise-level agreements. However, MNCs operating in the Netherlands are still partly covered by sector-level agreements. Most MNCs seem to have no problem with the Dutch system of industrial relations, except some MNCs based in the US and Japan, which try to keep the unions out and have concluded some kind of labour agreement with their works councils.

Current developments in industrial relations call for less detailed regulation, and many new labour law statutes mirror this trend by giving more responsibility for determining employment conditions to management and labour.

15. The various characteristics of the Dutch system of industrial relations may perhaps be best highlighted by contrasting them to neighbouring Germany. It may strike foreign observers that both countries have in common:

- an orderly, comprehensive and legalized system of collective agreements;
- a dual system of workers' representatives (unions and works councils);
- a very low strike record and interventionist control of strikes by the courts.

However, the Netherlands and Germany differ from each other, in that:

- the instrument of extension *erga omnes* of collective agreements is much more used in the Netherlands than in Germany;
- in the Netherlands there is no direct representation of the workers in the Supervisory Councils of the large enterprises as in Germany; the works councils in the Netherlands have only indirect influence;
- in the Netherlands there exists a stronger linking of wage developments in the private sector to that in the public and semi-public sector and to social security benefits than in Germany;
- in the Netherlands the idea of the autonomy of the social partners is much more weakly developed than in Germany; the government is not so reluctant to intervene in the process of collective bargaining as in Germany;
- in the Netherlands collective bargaining at national cross-sector level is much more important than in Germany;
- in the Netherlands collective bargaining at enterprise level is less developed than in Germany;
- in the Netherlands unions are weaker in membership and therefore more moderate and prepared to compromise than in Germany. Also Dutch employers are more union-friendly and inclined to compromise with the unions than their German colleagues;

- in the Netherlands unions and employers seem to be more creative in finding solutions to the dilemma of mitigating high labour costs and at the same time maintaining the high level of social protection than the unions and employers in Germany.

A final major difference in the legal framework of collective wage formation until 2014 was the absence in Germany of any effective statutory minimum wage. This difference, however, has largely disappeared as from 2015, now that Germany has created a statutory minimum wage at about the same level as the Netherlands. In the Netherlands there has been a statutory minimum wage since the 1950s (*see* paragraphs 139 et seq.). This minimum wage may be considered as a safety net for the weakest categories of workers (poorly qualified workers, casual workers, immigrants, and so on).

Chapter 4. General Aspects of Labour Law

§1. Origins, Functions and Prospects of Labour Law

16. Modern labour law in the Netherlands dates back to the last part of the nineteenth century when it emerged as a set of rules to restrain the almost unlimited 'freedom of trade' that had existed since about 1800. During the first three-quarters of the nineteenth century the Netherlands, like other European nations, was firmly in the grip of the economic and legal concepts associated with the 'Enlightenment movement' (Smith, Rousseau, Ricardo et al.). The state refrained from bridling entrepreneurship and from interfering on the labour market, and the legal system was accordingly inspired by the belief in the equality of individuals with 'freedom of contract' forming the basis of their mutual relationships.

These two concepts paved the way for economic and technological growth, which only gained momentum in the Netherlands after the French-German War of 1870–1871. However, this unfettered growth also created extensive social misery in all industrial areas of Europe. This prepared the ground for the seeds of socialism, which soon threatened the existing political order. The ruling classes gradually realized that economic freedom and its legal expression, the freedom of contract, had to be regulated and limited.

So, modern labour law could emerge. In 1872 the existing penal provisions against the freedom to strike were abolished. In 1874 the first Act prohibiting child labour was adopted, and in 1889 this Act was extended to give some protection to the working times of women and young persons as well. The first Health and Safety at Work Act – *Arbeidsomstandighedenwet* (HSA) came into being in 1895. The contract of employment was extensively regulated in the Civil Code (CC) in 1907. These new provisions brought about more fairness and certainty in the employment relationship, but as far as crucial issues (wages, job security) were concerned their impact was rather meagre.

As a result of the social turmoil in Europe at the end of World War I the Dutch government changed from being a more or less passive bystander to being a rather more active participant in the industrial relations system. In the legal field a start was made with the Labour Act of 1919, which more severely and comprehensively regulated the maximum working day and maximum working week. A mechanism for enquiry and mediations in labour disputes was put on the statute book in 1922 and collective agreements were statutorily regulated by Acts of 1927 and 1937. Furthermore, the government began to stimulate the establishment of bipartite bodies at sector and national cross-sector level (*see* paragraphs 279 et seq.).

In the period following World War II the Netherlands was rebuilt under a coalition of Christian Democrat and Social Democrat parties. Their governments maintained a tight control on wages and prices until far into the 1960s. This development was based on the theories of Keynes, which held sway over Dutch economic policies for several decades. According to these theories, public authorities should actively intervene in the economy in order to pursue a set of economic objectives, such as preserving the balance of payments, a sufficient level of investment, a stable price level, full employment, a reasonable redistribution of income, a state budget in balance and a stable currency.

Labour law was strengthened by a minimum wage legislation, acts about holidays with pay, improved dismissal protection, equal pay for men and women and employee involvement in the management of companies. A comprehensive system of social security schemes was set up, providing minimum protection against the risks of illness and disability, unemployment, old age and death, health costs, care costs and the costs of raising children. In the 1970s and 1980s, equality and non-discrimination were high on the agenda of the lawmakers.

The wages control policy was gradually dismantled after the mid-1960s to disappear completely in the 1980s/1990s. However, due to the long history of centralized wage control policy, the practice of institutionalized consultation and cooperation at all-industry level remained well developed. Several institutions, such as the Foundation of Labour and the Social and Economic Council (the SER), are its main offspring (*see* paragraphs 290 et seq.).

17. During the economic recession of the 1980s the Netherlands had difficulties in maintaining its labour and social security laws that had pushed labour costs to ever-higher levels. Large sections of the population failed to find work and remained unemployed for many years. This led economists and employers to assert that labour law in the Netherlands had gone too far and was jeopardizing the well-being of the very people for which it had originally been designed to protect. The ensuing debate ushered in a trend towards deregulation, which, however, has had only marginal results in the Netherlands. Legislators were not prepared to make wholesale departures from existing labour laws. Moreover, the trade union movement managed to fight off major changes in collective agreements but was prepared to cooperate with flexibility strategies of the management.

The difficulties encountered in changing labour regulations have engendered a change in management strategy; the flexible firm model is now the order of the day as it conveniently bypasses some of the existing labour regulations. In the 1980s, economic recession forced many firms to lay off thousands of workers. However, during recovery these firms did not re-expand their standard workforce to pre-recession levels, but instead new employment was mostly created by means of 'flexible contracts' – fixed-term contracts, labour on call, labour hired from temporary work agencies, labour on subcontracting, freelance contracts, quasi-independent homeworkers, etc. This trend has been called the Japanization of business. Quite often labour law as regards these peripheral workers is weaker than the labour law protecting the traditional standard workforce.

The most important legal cause for the rise in flexible labour has been attributed to the rigidities and cost-raising aspects of Dutch labour law, especially the Dutch law on dismissals. Indeed, the Dutch law in this field is somewhat tougher than elsewhere in Europe, because for each dismissal which occurs without the consent of the employee, an administrative permit or a judicial rescission of the contract is required (*see* paragraph 202). Courts became generous in imposing severance pay at the average rate of about one-and-a-half-month salary for every year of service. Most flexible contracts escaped this rigidity, which made the use of flexible labour very attractive to Dutch employers.

During the 1980s lawmakers were hesitating over how to deal with this new phenomenon. The economic, sociological and legal aspects of flexible labour were exhaustively studied, but despite the various critical assessments from most authors very little legislation was passed reviewing the legal position of flexible work in the Netherlands. This passivity could be explained by the fact that the government was under two contradictory pressures. On the one hand there was pressure from the employers to lift some of the tightest rules of labour law, notably the *ex ante* controls on dismissals. On the other hand the government was exposed to pressure from trade unionists and labour lawyers to improve the protection of flexible workers. In those years, the Netherlands was ruled by governments which favoured deregulation and for that reason were not anxious to issue new statutory labour law. They wanted to leave the issue of drawing up suitable arrangements by negotiation to business organizations, individuals and the social partners. The Netherlands was not alone in hesitating, though. At European level proposals as regards atypical labour relations were not successful either until the end of the 1990s!

It was finally in the mid-1990s that the Dutch legislator embarked on a clear compromise policy under the name 'flexicurity', a combination of flexibility and security. This concept aimed to combine a flexibilization of labour laws in certain areas with a consolidation and even a strengthening of the labour law protection in other areas (*see* paragraph 193). Further compromise strategies were pursued in the area of working time: employer calls for greater flexibility have been reconciled with demands from trade unions and other groups for measures to ensure a better work-life balance for employees (*see* paragraph 110).[24]

These compromises were embedded in a general situation of 'moderation'. Wage moderation is the essential element of the Dutch model. The trade unions were moderate in their pay claims and did not oppose employers' strategies for modernization and technological innovations.

With hindsight the voluntary wage restraint of the Dutch trade unions may be seen as 'tacit compromise' – the government restricting itself to only a minor reduction of the welfare state in exchange for a large self-restraint among the social partners. Obviously such a far-reaching compromise did not come like a bolt from the blue. It was in fact the fruit of a long history of 'consensus' in the Netherlands.

Since the 1990s, many Dutch labour law and social security Acts have been 'fine-tuned' to adapt them to the changing situations on the labour market. In several cases, this was done to implement the labour law rules of the EU.

18. The many changes in Dutch labour law and social security law[25] were not inspired only by political and economic motives. They were also inspired by changes in society. An example of this can be found in the modern Dutch system of social security which was set up on the basis of the traditional pattern of the family: two-parent families in which the man was considered the breadwinner, the woman working until marriage and then abandoning her job indefinitely to care for the upbringing of the children and doing the home chores. In the Netherlands of the 1950s and 1960s this was also considered the ideal type. The wage of the worker

24. T. Wilthagen & F. Tros, *The Concept of 'Flexicurity': A New Approach to Regulating Employment and Labour Markets*, *Transfer* Vol. 10, 166–186 (2004).
25. A. de Roo, *The Landscape of Dutch Labor Law*, in *Understanding Dutch Law* 335–339, 350–351 (Taekema, De Roo & Elion-Valter eds, The Hague: Bju 2011).

(including family allowances) should be sufficient to maintain a wife and children. It was not seen as an ideal to push married women with children to the labour market. However, all this changed during the 1960s and 1970s. The drive for equal treatment of men and women, supported by international norms, incited the legislator to make important changes in the Dutch labour law and social security (*see* paragraphs 87 et seq.)

The idea of flexible labour was appealing not only to the employers but also to the variety of people searching for employment. Many women preferred flexible or part-time work as it enabled them to combine child care with professional work. Youngsters just entering the labour market often prefer flexible labour because it enables them to browse around on the labour market before making a specific career decision, etc. Students and some elderly workers are often best served with flexible jobs.

Another fruit of the changes in society is the increased consideration in Dutch labour law for the non-professional interests of the employees (labelled *privétisering* by the leading Dutch labour lawyer Paul van der Heijden). This is most obvious in the changes in the law on working times and leave regulations (*see* Part I, Chapter 3).

Employers and employees might share a common interest on the offer of flexible labour, but at the same time, flexible labour, characterized by its more precarious status, will never fulfil the majority of the needs and aspirations both of the individual worker and of the labour force in general.

Flexible labour also seems at odds with the modern idea of equality. Numerous researchers have revealed that flexible contracts are most widespread among women, teenagers and ethnic minorities. As the quality of these contracts is assessed as being less favourable to the workers than regular contracts, this unequal distribution of flexible labour is seen as a kind of indirect discrimination.

Not surprisingly Dutch law, by implementing EU law, has recently put new emphasis on the need for equal treatment for these categories of employees (*see* paragraph 87). However, it is doubtful whether these provisions are able to really give equal treatment to the peripheral workers in the flexible firm.

Labour costs have gone up in the industrial world to such an extent that employers, forced to safeguard competitiveness, apparently see no other choice than to spend their money on labour as carefully as possible. It is for this reason that the concept of the 'flexible firm' has risen and is most unlikely to disappear in the foreseeable future.

However, the concept of the 'flexible firm' is undermining the very foundations of traditional labour and social security law. Employers nowadays are buying labour by the hour. This harks back to the nineteenth-century ideas in which labour was seen as a commodity. One day labour law had the aspiration of raising the worker from this status of a 'commodity' (see the preamble to the International Labour Organization (ILO) Constitution) and to treat him or her as a person, to the point of giving him/her the status of a 'citizen' of the enterprise. Yet employees, who are not regarded as 'core' personnel seem to be excluded from a real citizenship.

It stands to reason that labour law and social security law have enormous difficulties in finding new balances and structures in which the concept of the 'flexible' firm can be accommodated in a socially acceptable way. It is here that one of the main challenges for labour and social security lawyers for the twenty-first century lies.

The increase of flexible labour can be seen as one of the features of the trend of 'individualization' of our era, which erodes the old ideas of 'community' and 'solidarity'. Flexibility partly proceeds from individualization, which is a strong tendency of Western culture. At the same time individualization may well undermine the very concepts of labour law. Up until now these trends seem only to have affected the substantive rules of labour law and social security. Apparently procedural rules and structures – the system of industrial relations – seem to remain for the moment – but for how long?

Traditionally labour law emerged as a collective strategy against managerial power. It is rooted in strongholds of industrial productions, such as mining and factories, where solidarity between workers was easily forged.

On this solidarity trade unions were built, strikes could be organized and collective agreements concluded. The growing number of flexible workers is a strong handicap for the trade unions as it appears that flexible workers are less eager to organize and more difficult to mobilize. It also has a negative effect on industrial democracy. Flexible workers are less committed to the plight of the undertaking, and for that reason they are either ignored by or not interested in the operations of Dutch procedures of industrial democracy.

Are not all the structures of the inherited system of industrial relations at risk of decay if the concepts of the new firm, flexibilization and individualization of the workers march on?

From an academic point of view the late Professor Max Rood – Professor in Labour Law in Leyden – in 1999 sketched four challenges to Dutch labour law in general: the dominance, since the 1990s, of neoclassical economic theories, the rise of individualism in our society, the enormous diversification of jobs on the labour market and shrinking trust in the regulatory power of the national state.

§2. Definitions and Notions of Labour Law

19. Labour law (or social law as it is mostly called in the Netherlands) was recognized as a specialized area of academic study shortly before World War II. There exists, however, no uniform concept of its scope. Its boundaries are uncertain and parts of it overlap other academic subjects, such as private law, company law and administrative law. Nevertheless, all scholars agree that labour law comprises the legal rules which regulate the relationship between employer and worker and between their respective organizations.

This description includes workers and their organizations in the private sector as well as in the public sector. Traditionally the labour law and large parts of the social security law did not affect the public sector, as this sector was ruled by special regulations. However, for a number of years now there has been a tendency to apply common labour law also to employees in the civil service. This process, called 'normalization', is almost completed (*see* paragraph 54).

Social security legislation was originally linked to the concept of the contract of employment. That is, it protected workers against certain risks, such as old age, occupational hazards, illness and invalidity. In the years since World War II, however, a far more extensive social security system has been developed which, in many cases, extends its blessings not only to workers but also to all residents of the Netherlands. This extension has loosened the ties with labour law. Furthermore, the social security system has developed its own (very complicated) administrative machinery.[26]

All these facts taken together have promoted the recognition of social security law as an independent academic subject, although many links with labour have been preserved. Traditionally most universities have established chairs in 'social law', which embraces both labour law and social security law. Only in recent years some specialized chairs in social security have been established.

In this contribution, however, I will restrict myself to labour law. Social security is dealt with in the *International Encyclopaedia for Social Security Law*.

Labour law can be analysed in two main subdivisions:

(a) individual labour law, which focuses on the contract of employment, the rights and duties of the individual employer and worker, dismissal law and similar problems, pertaining to private law. In addition come the rules about the working environment in the enterprise, such as rules concerning maximum working hours, safety and health. These are rules of public law, i.e., they are backed up by criminal and administrative sanctions. All this is described in Part I;
(b) collective labour law, which includes trade union law, collective bargaining, collective agreements, strikes and institutional participation (i.e., the participation of workers' representatives by way of works councils and supervisory boards); this is described in Part II.

Individual labour law is a real mix between state legislation and regulation emanating from the social partners.

However, industrial relations in the Netherlands are largely ordered by the social partners' self-government. Therefore legislators have not needed to intervene in the area of industrial relations as intensively as, for example, in France or the UK. The prime exception is the idea of industrial democracy and notably the system of works councils, which is imposed on business through Acts of Parliament.

26. A. Eleveld, *A Critical Perspective on the Reform of Dutch Social Security Law* (2012).

Chapter 5. Sources of Labour Law

20. The sources of labour law in the Netherlands are:

(a) the relevant articles of the Constitution;
(b) international provisions;
(c) statutes (Acts of Parliament);
(d) royal decrees, general regulations of the administrative authorities, etc.;
(e) collective agreements;
(f) the individual contract of employment;
(g) the employer's managerial authority;
(h) company rules;
(i) custom and practice (usage);
together with the case law of the courts.

§1. CONSTITUTIONAL LAW

21. Constitutional law obviously determines the powers of the various public authorities. According to the constitutional structure, the heteronomous labour law of the Netherlands derives essentially from national power structures (the king, the government and Parliament), to the almost total exclusion of subordinate authorities such as provinces and municipalities.

The impact of fundamental rights was very limited in labour law in the Netherlands up to the end of 1960s, as the Dutch Constitution contained almost exclusively 'civil and political' fundamental rights. Since the 1960s, the Netherlands has ratified a growing number of international treaties, which contain fundamental 'social' rights. The Dutch Constitution was also updated in 1983 with a more extensive list of the various fundamental rights (Articles 1–23), including a few fundamental 'social rights'.

Although these rights are chiefly of a programmatic nature, this trend strengthened the impact of fundamental rights on labour law in the Netherlands. This is particularly true in the area of trade union freedom, the freedom to enter into collective bargaining, the right to strike, privacy, labour law litigation and equality of treatment as regards race, sex, religion, civil status, sexual orientation, etc.

§2. INTERNATIONAL LAW

22. Constitutional law also plays a crucial role in determining the impact of international law on Dutch law. In the Netherlands, international treaties come into force nationally following ratification, which has to be authorized by Parliament. In some cases the government simultaneously tables a Bill in which the terms of national law are brought into line with the international convention, which is to be ratified.

However, Dutch law follows the philosophy of monism. Even if national legislation has not been (sufficiently) amended, the terms of international treaties which have been duly ratified have priority over national laws, provided that their nature and content are appropriate for direct effect (Articles 93 and 94 of the Dutch Constitution).[27]

The Netherlands is a member of various international and supranational organizations, such as the ILO, the Council of Europe and the European Union. It has a tradition of great loyalty as regards the ratification of international treaties containing social regulations. Consequently, the vast majority of the conventions of the ILO and the 'social' treaties of the United Nations (UN) and the Council of Europe have been ratified by the Netherlands. If the conformity of Dutch law with international provisions is afterwards contested, the government is prepared to restore harmony, although the debate may take some time! A good example was the wages control policy. When in the 1970s and 1980s the Netherlands was criticized on that issue by the ILO, the wages control policy was finally changed to bring it into line with ILO standards on free collective bargaining (*see* paragraphs 281 et seq.).

Sometimes the Dutch courts do their bit in restoring the harmony between Dutch law and the ratified international norms. For instance, the Dutch courts have recognized the direct applicability of Article 6(4) of the European Social Charter (ESC) (the right to strike, *see* paragraphs 335 et seq.) and Article 26 of the UN Treaty on civil and political rights (the general prohibition of discrimination, *see* paragraph 87). However, these are exceptional cases. Most of the terms of international treaties are such that they do not lend themselves to direct application to individual legal relationships. This is all the more so with documents, such as resolutions and recommendations. Sometimes the applicability of these texts on contracts of employment is construed by the courts via the bona fides principle (*see* paragraphs 105 and 106).

23. Much stronger is the influence on labour law and social security of the law of the EU. In the first place the EU can take – and has taken – measures, which have a direct and binding effect on the citizens of the Member States, such as the regulation about the free movement of workers (*see* paragraph 78). In the second place, EU directives have led to important changes in national legislation. The Netherlands' Equal Pay and Equal Treatment legislation was enacted on the stimulus of the EU (*see* paragraph 93). In the Dutch law on health and safety numerous amendments were made to bring it in line with the prescriptions of the EU (*see* paragraphs 159 et seq.). EU rules on workers' rights in the case of transfer of undertakings (*see* paragraph 178) and on the information of the worker about the terms of his contract of employment (*see* paragraph 74) have undoubtedly inspired Dutch legislation and case law in these areas.

Finally mention should be made of the European Convention on Human Rights, which has some noticeable impact on the Dutch law, notably in the field of privacy in employment relationships (*see* paragraph 107).[28]

It is important to stress that in the Netherlands there is no specific High Court to test statutes against international law. All courts, also the lower ones, may perform

27. A.T.J.M. Jacobs, *Monism at Work*, in *Liber amicorum K. Lörcher*.
28. A. Jaspers & W. Roozendaal, *Dutch Labour Law and the European Convention on Human Rights*, in *Europäische Zeitschrift für Arbeitsrecht* 161–177 (2/2013).

this test, but in civil/criminal/tax law it is the Dutch Supreme Court – *Hoge Raad* (HR) that gives the ultimate judgment, in Social Security Law the Central Appeal Tribunal and in other Administrative Law the Administrative Bench of the Council of State (*see* paragraph 38). The fact, however, that already lower courts may pronounce about the compatibility of statutes with international law may easily create confusion about the applicability of an Act of Parliament.

§3. Legislation

24. In the Netherlands, in contrast to France, labour law and social security law, as set out in formal legislation, is not codified into a comprehensive Labour Law Code. Only the rules on the individual contract of employment have been codified as part of the Dutch CC, actually in Chapter 10 of Book 7 of this Code.[29] The other labour laws are scattered throughout Dutch legislation. The desire to amend or renew legislation comes in most cases from the Dutch government or Parliament (inspired by the aspirations of society). The desired changes are then submitted by the government to the social partners in order to receive their opinion via consultation requests to the *SER* or to the *Stichting van de Arbeid* (*see* paragraphs 290 et seq.) and – in recent years – also to public Internet consultation and subsequently may become Bills for formal statutes which have to be adopted by both Chambers making up the Dutch Parliament (*see* paragraph 11). They are finally signed and promulgated by the king. Sometimes the initiative for legislative changes is taken by the central organizations of employers and employees, who are concluding (compromise) agreements on changes in labour law legislation which they offer the government for turning them into statutory law.

The Netherlands Parliament may in principle legislate on any matter provided the fundamental rights set out in the Constitution and ratified international treaties are respected. Parliament has the task of verifying this conformity since, under the Constitution, promulgated laws are inviolable. Parliament may be guided on a Bill's conformity with the Constitution by taking advice from the Council of State, which is the supreme political and legal consultative body. There is, however, no Constitutional Court to verify the conformity of a statute with the Constitution after its promulgation. For this reason constitutional law has never played as dominant a role in labour law and social security in the Netherlands as it does in Germany. However, the courts may carry out a verification of whether a statute is in accordance with the provisions of international treaties ratified by the Netherlands as far as these provisions lend themselves to direct application (*see* paragraphs 22 and 23). This possibility has led in recent years to the cancellation, notably of some terms of Dutch statutes on social security by the courts because of their non-conformity with international regulations. Also the impact of fundamental rights on Dutch labour law has been growing in recent years.

29. Legislation Dutch Civil Code in English http://www.dutchcivillaw.com/civilcodebook077.htm.

25. Dutch statutory labour law is to a very large extent unitary labour law, encompassing all sorts of sectors of the private economy. Exceptions as to the size of enterprises are sometimes made (*see* paragraph 52).[30]

Sometimes Dutch Acts of Parliament – also in matters of labour law – only give basic regulatory principles. Detailed rules are contained in royal orders, ministerial decrees, ministerial circulars, policy rules, etc., issued by the government. Such decree or order can never temporarily be used as an alternative form of legislation as in Italy and Spain. Unlike in France, in the Netherlands there is no dispute as regards the distinction between the 'scope' of statutes and decrees.

Parliament in principle is not involved in these secondary rules issued by the government, but it is kept informed and retains the possibility of imposing its will where necessary through a censure motion. The social partners have no formal right of consultation during the formulation of decrees of the government. They are always consulted in practice, however, in the case of social measures. Royal orders, decrees, etc., of the government are subject to court supervision from the point of view of their conformity with legislation and the Constitution. Those which are illegal may be quashed under the common law of administrative contention.

§4. Collective Agreements

26. Next to statutory law, collective agreements are the major source of labour law. In fact, it can be argued that for the vast majority of workers (about 80% of the workforce are covered by a collective agreement) collective agreements are as important as statutory protection. In the first place this is because some of the most important conditions of employment are not at all covered by statute or only by way of minimum arrangements, and therefore largely depend on a collective agreement, such as the above-minimum wage, overtime compensation and occupational social security. Moreover, it should be noted that statutory law itself often is a product of collective bargaining. Normally a statute is only introduced when the problem in question has for some time already been regulated by collective agreements in the main industries. This happened, for instance, in the case of paid holidays, minimum wages, job protection and family allowances, which had all been regulated in various collective agreements long before they became part of statutory law. Finally there are several provisions in Dutch statutory labour law which are only relatively mandatory. They can be waived by a collective agreement (*see* paragraph 34), thus offering the social partners the possibility to adapt tight rules to the special conditions of a certain trade or industry.

The system of collective bargaining is strongly supported by two Acts of Parliament. The first act, the Act on Collective Agreements, 1927 (ACA) (*Wet op de Collective Arbeidsovereenkomst*), ensures the mandatory sway of the collective agreement over the contract of employment, and the second one, the Act on the

30. *See* S. Peters, *Verdund Sociaal Recht*, Deventer, 2006; on pp. 675–686 we find an English-language description and discussion of the differentiation according to company size as a frequent occurrence in the legislation and regulatory framework pertaining to labour law, with special attention to the fields of employee participation, sickness and dismissal.

Extension of Collective Agreements – *Wet op het algemeen verbindend en onverbindend verklaren van bepalingen van collectieve arbeidsovereenkomsten*, 1937 (AECA) – ensures a wider coverage of this system (*see* paragraph 324). In recent years some legal problems about these collective agreements came to the fore, which will be dealt with in Part II, Chapter 4. Cross-industry agreements in general have no binding force, but the courts may sometimes give them such force through the bona fides principle (*see* paragraph 103).

27. Some older provisions in Dutch statutory law provide for some public law instruments that may have similar binding effects on contracts of employment as collective agreements, viz. regulations drawn up by 'joint industrial boards' (*see* paragraph 282) or by the Minister for Social Affairs under the Wage Determination Act – *Wet op de Loonvorming* ((WDA), Articles 5 and 6, *see* paragraph 281). However, such regulations hardly exist in practice.

§5. Agreements with Works Councils, Company Rules and Rules Unilaterally Imposed by the Employer

28. Nowadays in the Netherlands a variety of agreements between the employer and the works council are increasingly entered into. However, there is no general concept about the legal status of such agreements. Some kinds of agreements between the employer and the works councils are specifically indicated:

- agreements on working time in the Working Time Act – *Arbeidstijdenwet* (WTA) (*see* paragraphs 115 et seq.) and on leave in the Work and Care Act (*see* paragraph 125);
- agreements on additional powers for the works council in the WCA (*see* paragraph 397).

All other kinds of agreement between the employer and the works councils are not specifically regulated; they have no other status than other unspecified agreements under the general law of contracts. They may bind the concluding parties (employer and works council) but not third parties. So, most of the times all these agreements are lacking direct effect on the contracts of employment. No such instrument as the German *Betriebsvereinbarung* exists in the Netherlands (*see* paragraph 401).

29. The contract of employment implies, by definition, a certain amount of scope for the employer to unilaterally issue binding rules (*see* paragraph 81). The scope of this prerogative may vary in each employment relationship. It may be restricted by statute and collective or individual agreement, by custom and practice and by the principle of bona fides (*see* paragraphs 102–103). It certainly under Dutch law does not have such an important status as it has, for instance, in Denmark. However, a certain degree of managerial authority has to be left to the employer; otherwise the contract cannot be considered to be a contract of employment (*see* paragraph 49). This 'managerial authority' gives the employer the possibility of unilaterally laying down enterprise regulations. Employers can also lay down regulations unilaterally while making them appear to be bilateral; they draft rules which are accepted by employees when they sign their individual contract of employment (incorporation).

As opposed to German legislation, under which the statutory rules on the so-called *Allgemeine Geschäftsbedingungen* (standard contract terms) have been declared applicable to contracts on employments, in the Netherlands contracts of employment as well as collective agreements are still explicitly exempted from the applicability of the Dutch rules on standard contract terms.

30. Company rules (*reglement* in Dutch: *règlement intérieur* in French), which contain directives relating to the internal order of the enterprise, predate the collective agreement. In the past they gave concrete shape to the employer's power unilaterally to issue a set of regulations specific to the enterprise.

In 1907 Parliament made the validity of company rules subject to the conditions that they had been properly published and that the employee had accepted them in writing. These provisions, however, were of little real significance, as employees in practice found it difficult to register their disagreement. So the unilateral setting of company rules has continued.

One might think that this unilateral nature was more forcefully suppressed in 1970 when the law stipulated that company rules required the approval of the works council. Yet, according to case law of the HR, company rules which were not properly published and not submitted for approval by the works council could retain their compulsory nature by way of incorporation by a clause in the individual contract of employment.

Amidst this confusing situation Parliament in 1998 abolished the provisions on company rules altogether! It replaced them by a sole statutory provision (Article 7:613 CC) on the binding force of clauses in the individual contract of employment about the modification of the incorporated company rules (*see* paragraph 173).

So, as opposed to countries like France and Belgium, in the Netherlands the establishment of company rules is not mandatory and nor does the law impose any regulation or limitation on the content of company rules.

It is mainly in the large enterprises that all sorts of company manuals are still in use. They may be issued unilaterally or with the consent of the works council. They may have binding force on the contract of employment because their rules may be regarded as a part of managerial power, inherent in the contract of employment (*see* paragraph 81), or because a clause in the contract of employment establishes their applicability, or because their rules are seen as 'custom and practice' (*see* paragraph 32).

§6. The Contract of Employment and Custom and Practice

31. The contract of employment is often reduced to a kind of 'entrance ticket', as rights and obligations are regulated by legal provisions set out in collective agreements and company rules. This means that in many cases employers and employees have only to agree on the duration of the contract, the date of entry into service, the function which will be carried out, the real wage as well as the ordinary working times.

Many employers and employees wish, however, to set out more precise arrangements in the contract of employment, for instance:

(a) to lay down rights which go beyond the minimum provisions of the law or the collective agreement;
(b) to settle issues which, due to waivers in the law or the collective agreement, may be settled by a (written) contract of employment;
(c) to settle issues for which laws or collective agreements do not make provision;
(d) to settle individual issues, such as working hours, or the number of hours or days of work to be provided if these differ from usual standards applicable in the enterprise.

Especially as regards jobs which are not subject to a collective agreement there are undoubtedly good reasons for entering into a detailed contract of employment. This often concerns higher management, but also certain occupational sectors and whole enterprises which have not entered into collective agreements because of the lack of organization of employers. Also the trend to make collective agreements less detailed (*see* paragraph 289) may require more substantial contents of the individual contract of employment.

32. 'Custom and practice' is the last and weakest source of the Dutch system of sources of labour law. It is part of the Dutch legal tradition to count custom as one of the sources of the law on contracts (Article 6:248 Dutch CC). For instance, the amount of the wage if it is not specified in other sources (*see* paragraph 137), the payment of a gratuity which is not based on a provision of the contract of employment, the collective agreement, etc., may be invoked on the basis of practice/usage (*see* paragraph 129). The same is true for the remuneration of overtime (*see* paragraphs 118/130). However, as far as labour law is concerned, most items nowadays are covered either by statute or by collective agreement. This means that the scope for custom and practice in labour relations is a narrow one. Only exceptionally statutes or court decisions refer to custom and practice in the branch of industry or in the enterprise (*see* paragraph 131/137 for examples). The trickiest problem raised by standards deriving from custom and practice is: proving their existence. Employers may contest the existence of custom and practice; they may also claim that employees did not immediately oppose the modification of a practice and that they therefore tacitly accepted the modification. A claim based on custom and practice will always fail if it conflicts with the provisions of legislation and collective agreements, sometimes even if these provisions are less favourable to employees than custom and practice. Consequently, custom and practice is somewhat neglected in Dutch labour law nowadays because it is the weakest source of labour law.

§7. Judge-Made Law

33. According to prevalent legal theory in the Netherlands the decisions of the courts are not officially regarded as a source of law. A court decision ends the dispute between the parties concerned but does not create a binding general legal rule. This – more or less – follows from the fact that there is no rule of *stare decisis*: a court is not de jure bound by precedents; it is neither bound by its own previous decisions, nor by those of a higher court. Nevertheless, de facto, the decisions of the courts often have far-reaching effects upon judges and citizens alike. Therefore, whatever legal theory may say about judge-made law, considered from the angle of legal practice, court decisions are undoubtedly an important and integral part of the legal system.

Court decisions are very often followed on the same footing as statutory law. This is particularly true as far as leading cases decided by the HR are concerned. By giving a new interpretation to statutory law the HR creates legal rules. And this also occurs whenever statute law is absent, i.e., in the field of strike disputes (*see* paragraphs 336 et seq.). In those cases the HR frequently not only decides the individual case but also provides guidelines for future cases. Thus, although in formal terms, the courts of first instance do not have to abide by the case law of higher courts, in practice they do. Courts of first and second instance have, however, been responsible for some modifications of labour law, derogating from outdated case law of the HR, for instance as regards the right to strike (*see* paragraph 335), the duty to provide work (paragraph 85), etc.

Nevertheless case law has only played a modest part in the development of labour law theory in the Netherlands. The Netherlands does not have a Constitutional Court and – in contrast to most EU Member States – does not have labour courts (*see* paragraphs 35 et seq.). The creation of judge-made labour law is largely due to common law courts. This type of case law is unlikely to bring about a specific doctrine of labour law. Courts merely interpret and apply the law. In the cases where courts are asked to fill in the gaps in the law, for instance as regards the right to strike, there is much reluctance to create spectacular new developments. The courts tend to follow the developments in mainstream legal scripture and in industrial practice.

As a general trend it can be seen that case law of the last fifty to sixty years has been characterized by a predominant social attitude. Courts tend to protect employees, using general legal principles, against employers who are considered to be more powerful, for instance in the law relating to proof, the law relating to damage caused by employees, etc. In Dutch this principle is called *ongelijkheidscompensatie* (compensation for inequality).

§8. The Conflict of Rules and the Hierarchy of Sources

34. In the Netherlands statutory law does not lay down a clear hierarchy of sources of labour law as is the case in Belgium. Under Dutch law the hierarchy of sources of labour law follows from general principles which apply under civil and public law: statutes have priority over contracts, treaties over statutes (provided they are directly applicable); collective agreements have priority over individual contracts. These principles provide us with the following order of priority:

(i) international regulations;
(ii) statutes, secondary legislation and case law;
(iii) collective agreements;
(iv) the individual contract of employment and company rules;
(v) custom and practice.

The hierarchical criterion is less easy to transpose to conflicts between agreements with the works council, the managerial and disciplinary authority of the head of the enterprise and company rules, individual contracts of employment and custom and practice; the same applies to the hierarchy of collective agreements entered into at more than one level. In this area there are many uncertainties in Dutch labour law.

The entire hierarchy of sources is also affected by the 'principle of the most favourable law', i.e., the idea that the regulations contained in a lower source of law may derogate from the regulations contained in a higher source if this is favourable to employees. The higher source is no more than a 'floor' for the regulations of a lower source to build upon and to provide additional advantages for employees in a particular branch of industry or enterprise. The principle of the most favourable law is indisputably applicable when a higher source of law uses terms such as 'at least'. But even if no such terms are used, the applicability of the principle of the most favourable law may be assumed most of the times. In some cases, however, the rules contained in a higher source are construed in such a way that they are to be seen as a standard or maximum, not allowing derogations in favour of the employees. They are a 'floor' and a 'ceiling' at the same time. This may also be the case with collective agreements, as opposed to, for instance, Germany, where collective agreements are always liable to derogations *in melius* (*see* paragraph 322).

Finally, as indicated above, there are also a few places in Dutch labour law in which a higher source of law allows derogations in lower sources, even if these are derogations *in peius*, less favourable to the employees (the so-called waivers). Some of these provisions allow derogations *in peius* only by way of collective agreements with the unions (in Dutch, *driekwartdwingend recht*; in German, *Tarifdispositives Recht*). Others allow derogations *in peius* also if it is with the approval of the works council (*vijfachtste* or *tweederde dwingend recht*). Still others allow derogations by way of individual contracts of employment, provided that this derogation is agreed in writing (in Dutch, *semi-dwingend recht*). And there are even some provisions in

Dutch statutory labour law which allow any agreed derogation and thus are only applicable if the issue is not settled otherwise (so-called default rules, in Dutch, *regelend recht*).[31]

31. *See* R. Houweling & L. Langedijk, *The End of Mandatory Rules in the Employment Contract Law*, in *Life Time Contacts* 223–242 (L. Nolger & U. Reifner eds, Hamburg, 2013).

Chapter 6. The Court System

§1. Introduction

35. Another characteristic of Dutch labour law is the prominent role played by the ordinary courts. The rights of Dutch employees have been strongly enshrined in statutory law; the courts may deal in full with labour law disputes without being subject to any substantive restriction; the existence of the summary proceedings and of subsidized legal aid have greatly facilitated employees' access to the courts; trade unions may also take action in the courts in the event of disputes relating to the interpretation and enforcement of a collective agreement to which they are a party (*see* paragraph 332). All this makes strikes in the Netherlands for 'conflicts of rights' (such as on a dismissal or non-payment of wages), as opposed to 'conflicts of interests' (such as on a desired wage increase) rare (*see* paragraph 345). Moreover, in conflicts of interests leading to strikes, the judges play a central role in containing the strikes (*see* paragraphs 337 et seq.). This contributes highly to the prevailing climate of social peace.

Finally, in the Netherlands more than elsewhere, judges are involved in the process of industrial democracy (*see* Part II, Chapter 6). Almost all managerial decisions are nowadays open for judicial appeal. The judges use this role not to intervene with the economic rationale of decision-making, but by forcing managers to play according to the procedural rules.

§2. The Ordinary Courts

36. The high profile of Dutch judges in labour law is all the more remarkable in view of the fact that the Netherlands – in contrast to most EU Member States – does not have specialized labour courts. All civil disputes connected with a contract of employment or a collective agreement come under the jurisdiction of the ordinary courts. These courts are staffed by professional judges, with laymen serving on the bench in some exceptional cases only (*see* paragraph 38). There are no juries in the Netherlands. These courts have been rather accessible thanks to a generous legal aid system and low procedural and financial thresholds, although in both aspects in recent years some deterioration can be reported. The courts generally show a high degree of 'social sensitivity', which, among other things, is illustrated by their readiness to occasionally shift the burden of proof to the employers' side, thereby bending employment rules in favour of the workers.

The ordinary courts are:

(a) the (11) District Courts (*Rechtbank*);
(b) the (4) Courts of Appeal (*Gerechtshof*);
(c) the *HR*.

In the past there used to be a larger variety of courts. In that situation the *unus iudex* court (*kantongerecht* or cantonal court or magistrate's court or lower court or subdistrict court) was the competent judge in first instance in most labour law cases, with the District Court as the Appeal Court. Since a reform of the Dutch judiciary in 2002 the *kantongerecht* has been integrated into the District Court. Although the 'cantonal judge' still exists as a function, the cantonal court no longer exists as an institution; it became a separate 'section' of the District Court. The ordinary Courts of Appeal became the ordinary appeal court for all labour law cases. A further reform of 2013 reduced the number of courts and cancelled the obligation to instal separate cantonal sections within each District Court.[32] Most managements of the District Courts now have created teams of judges dealing with and ruling on cantonal judges' cases. It is left to the management of the various District Courts to further organize the adjudication of cantonal judges' cases. There used to be subdistrict courts in about sixty-two towns all over the country; actually the number of places where cantonal judges are sitting is down to thirty-two.

However, these cantonal judges are no pure labour courts. Actually they deal with a variety of cases: besides all cases out of contracts of employment (irrespective of the value of the claim) these are: credit transactions, cases regarding contracts of commercial agents, hire purchase, consumer sales, lease and rental contracts – all irrespective of the value of the claim – and all other civil actions up to EUR 25,000, matters of guardianship as well as summary offences (Articles 42 et seq. Act on Judicial Organization).

Since 2002 a decision of the cantonal judge given in first instance is subject to the appellate jurisdiction of the Court of Appeal. This court normally sits with three judges. Decisions of the Courts of Appeal mostly are subject to 'appeal in cassation' to the HR. In contrast to the ordinary appeal procedures, the HR is bound by the facts as established by the lower courts and will only decide on questions of law. Nevertheless it often gives indications ('*gezichtspunten*') about what kind of facts lower courts must take into account in judgments on certain legal questions. The HR can either dismiss the appeal or quash the decision of the Appeal Court. In the latter case the HR may either remit the case to another Appeal Court or render final judgment itself. Normally the HR sits with a five-judge panel, but can also sit with a three-judge panel.

37. The procedure before the cantonal judge was originally intended to be simple, speedy and inexpensive. The Code of Civil Procedure contained a number of exceptions, especially for first instance labour law cases. Legal counsel was not obligatory, the fees to the clerk of the courts' office were low and procedures could be initiated by an informal request instead of by a writ of summons. A 2002 reform had deleted the last two facilities, but they were partly restored in 2015. Speed is still guaranteed for the proceedings on sick pay (*see* paragraph 151) and concerning the termination of employment which still are started with a petition (*see* paragraphs 211 et seq.). Other labour law cases take as much time as the normal procedures. This fact, in addition to the fact that the decisions of a District Court are often subject to appeal to a Court of Appeal and appeal in cassation to the HR, can make labour lawsuits prolonged and costly affairs.

32. *See* M.Y.H.G. Erkens, *Rechtspleging in arbeidszaken*, Deventer, 2013; on pp. 255–266 there is an English-language summary of the role of the subdistrict court in Dutch labour law.

In labour law cases the normal rules of civil procedure on the burden of proof are applicable: the party who asserts must prove, unless the statute says otherwise or the court reverses the burden of proof on the basis of bona fides (Article 150 Code of Civil Procedure). However, in a number of areas of labour law the courts (and sometimes also the legislator, *see* paragraph 90) have bend these rules somewhat in order to attain a better division of the burden of proof between the parties.[33]

Procedures must be brought to either the court of residence of the defending part or of the place where normally the work is performed (Articles 99–100 Code of Civil Procedure).

Trade unions have, besides the possibility to assist their members as council in court, the possibility to challenge employers actions in court in their own right (*see* paragraph 332).

If a quick decision is urgently needed, either the cantonal judge or a special judge of the District Court (*Voorzieningenrechter*) can give a summary decision. In principle these decisions are subject to (summary) appeal and appeal in cassation, but in practice often the summary decisions of the cantonal judge/*Voorzieningenrechter* act as a final judgment, as the parties renounce of appeal and of continuing the substantive proceedings. This summary procedure plays an important role in strike disputes, which, of course, normally have to be decided as quickly as possible (*see* paragraphs 337 et seq.).

§3. Special Courts

38. Three special courts should be mentioned here because of their connection with labour law.

In the first place, those parts of labour law which have an administrative law character – for instance working times, health and safety at work and the Foreign Labour Act – are handled in first instance by the District Courts, but in a special section ('Administrative Law') and then, in appeal, by the Administrative Law Bench of the Council of State.

In the second place reference should be made to proceedings about statutory social security cases and civil servants cases. They are also handled in first instance by the administrative law section of the District Courts, sitting mostly with one judge. No laymen are involved in these sections. A decision of the District Court in these matters is subject to the appellate jurisdiction of a special court, i.e., the Central Appeal Tribunal (*Centrale Raad van Beroep*) in Utrecht, sitting with a three-judge panel (no laymen either). However, litigation on occupational social security schemes is judged by the cantonal judge, with appeal to the Court of Appeal and further appeal 'in cassation' to the HR. The same used to be for civil-servant cases,

33. *See* C. Bosse, *Bewijslastverdeling in het Nederlandse en Belgische arbeidsrecht*, Deventer, 2003; on pp. 310–314 are an English-language description and discussion of the distribution of the burden of proof among employers and workers in the litigation on employment contracts in the areas of the existence of a contract of employment, equal treatment, wages, availability and illness, labour accidents and occupational diseases and dismissal.

but because of the process on 'normalisatie' (*see* paragraph 54) these cases as from 2020 will be dealt with by the ordinary courts.

Finally, attention should be drawn to the Companies Bench (*Ondernemingskamer*) of the Court of Appeal of Amsterdam. This division sits with three judges and two lay experts and has unique jurisdiction in first instance for the entire country in a number of cases resulting from industrial democracy legislation (*see* Part II, Chapter 6), with only appeal in cassation to the HR.

§4. Alternatives

39. The main alternative for the court system in the Netherlands is the involvement of the UWV (*Uitvoeringsorganisatie Werknemersverzekeringen* (Employees Social Security Administration)) in dismissal cases (*see* paragraphs 204 and 251). If dismissals are based on economic reasons or long-lasting illness of the employee, this organization is the first instance to give a judgment whether or not to deliver the so-called dismissal permit. Only in second instance parties can turn to the cantonal judge to challenge the decision of the UWV (*see* paragraphs 204 et seq.).

The Foundation of Labour in 1990 recommended the social partners at sectoral and enterprise level to promote the establishment of alternative dispute resolution, and this recommendation has been implemented in several collective agreements. However, research has shown that these facilities are not widely used in the Netherlands.[34]

Only in a few sectors, such as professional soccer, private education and the churches are mediation and arbitration panels functioning.

More prominent is the Human Rights Board, formerly called Equal Treatment Commission, which handles in a prejudicial phase complaints about unequal treatment (*see* paragraphs 87 et seq.). The Board, and its predecessor, the Commission, have been operating for twenty-five years. Being easily accessible the Board receives hundreds of submissions each year. In general, writing a letter to the Board suffices to start its enquiries and to obtain its verdicts. The courts are free to use or ignore the verdicts of the Board. However, the HR has held that these verdicts are of special value in subsequent legal proceedings. Courts therefore have to explain when they do not follow such verdicts. Therefore, in practice most of the discrimination cases are settled without any further litigation after the Board has given its verdict. In the past most complaints concerned pay differentials m/f. Currently, most complaints are about age discrimination and discrimination of the disabled. The trade unions do not generally play a role in these complaints, although they may incidentally support a complaint or even lodge complaints themselves. Often trade union-friendly lawyers have been nominated as members of the Board. Provisions in collective agreements have sometimes been identified by the Board/Commission as causes of unjustified inequalities. This has put pressure on the social partners to revise the relevant provisions in subsequent wage rounds.

34. A. de Roo & R. Jagtenberg, *Settling Labour Disputes in Europe* 209–263 (1994).

Chapter 7. The Inspection Ministry of Social Affairs and Employment

§1. The Inspection SZW (Labour Inspectorate)

40. The application of the vast majority of Dutch labour law is not controlled by the public authorities. The common means of securing compliance with this part of labour law is through civil lawsuits. Only the compliance with the provisions of the Health and Safety at Work Act, the WTA, the Minimum Wages Act, the Allocation of Employees by Intermediaries Act – *Wet allocatie arbeidskrachten door intermediaires* (AEIA) – and the Foreign Labour Act is controlled by a public agency. Since 1891 this has been the Labour Inspectorate.[35] Actually it is called Inspection Ministry of Social Affairs and Employment (SZW), which is part of the SZW.[36] This institution was formed in 2012 by a merger of the Labour Inspectorate with two inspectorates in the field of social security.

In the areas of working times, health and safety at work and illegal immigrant work the Inspection SZW traditionally not only has the power to enquire, but also to issue an order for observation (Article 4:1(5) WTA) and even an order to bring the operations to a halt (Article 8:2 WTA). The Inspection SZW can bring out reports that can be used in criminal law proceedings. In the field of the extended collective agreements, the Inspectorate SZW has got some additional powers to investigate (*see* paragraph 333).

41. In the 1960s and 1970s enforcement of labour law in the Netherlands stood at a rather mediocre level. It was not politically correct to put much emphasis on this aspect. Only a few labour laws were sanctioned by criminal law, labour inspectors preferred to give warnings and advice instead of reporting violations, and the public prosecutor was not very keen in starting cases in this field. Since the 1980s the impact of enforcement on Dutch labour law has been gradually stepped up. A first step has been the addition of administrative sanctions to the existing criminal law sanctions. It means that already the Inspection SZW can impose fines and only if the fined person objects the case will be dealt with by the court. The administrative fines are also much higher than the fines in the criminal courts used to be. A second development was the extension of this public law control to other fields of labour law, notably to the Minimum Wages and Minimum Holidays with Pay Act (*see* paragraph 139) and the AEIA (*see* paragraphs 254 et seq.). Recent years have seen a further expansion of the powers and tasks of the Inspection SZW, notably by virtue of the Act to implement the EU Enforcement Directive (*see* paragraph 190). The actual government desires another expansion of the tasks of the SZW Inspectorate to the area of anti-discrimination laws (*see* paragraph 91) and work with dangerous substances.

---

35. *See* J.v. Drongelen, *De ontwikkeling van de Arbeidsinspectie in een veranderende wetgeving*, Maastricht, 1991; on pp. 357–363 one finds an English-language description and discussion of the development of the Labour Inspectorate between 1891 and 1991.

36. *See* Info InspectieSZW (Dutch Labour Inspection) http://www.inspectieszw.nl/english/work_by_foreign_nationals/.

42. The main problem still is the staffing of the Inspection SZW. The main Dutch Trade union federation, FNV, frequently calls for more inspectors to enforce the law regulations more strictly. Even the works council of the Inspection SZW at a certain moment showed worries about the understaffing of the Inspection SZW and its overt politicized governance, which it considered as violations of the ILO standards on labour inspectorates. The ratio of labour inspectors on the working population used to be about 1 inspector to 20,000 workers. In fact this number had remained rather constant over many decades but it has deteriorated during the last decade. To prevent the many legal abuses which still exist on the Dutch labour market, the former government decided that additional inspectors, eventually rising to 35, would be temporarily appointed by the Inspection SZW. The actual government has increased the financial means of the Inspectorate with EUR 50 million so that the staff of the Inspectorate can increase with 400 to 2200 persons.

The actual government invested a further EUR 1 million in the Inspection SZW to better fight discrimination on the labour market. Some observers think that to allow to perform their increased tasks properly, the number of inspectors would have to be doubled.

43. In another attempt to cope with all the inspecting work to be done by this limited staff the management of the Inspection SZW has decided to exclude 'the traditionally well-behaving enterprises' from its random inspections and to concentrate these inspections on the most 'vulnerable' segments of the labour market. Nevertheless the remaining firms can – statistically – expect a visit once in ten years, unless some serious work accident has happened or specific serious complaints have been made. The number of inspections has decreased since 2010 until, actually, 1,000 a year. In 2009 a national complaints point was opened, where everybody can lodge complaints about unsafe and unhealthy working conditions as well as about violation of the laws on minimum wages, working time legislation and illegal migrant work. The address is: Postbus 820, 3500 AV, Utrecht, tel. 0800-2700000, www.inspectieszw.nl.

The enforcement of Dutch labour law was further stepped up by a measure of the legislator in 2013 to raise the maximum fines. They were brought from EUR 3,000 to 4,500 per violation. So, for instance, in 2016, EUR 1.3 million fines were send to temporary agency firms. Also extended was the kind of sanctions that the SZW Inspectorate may impose. The 2013 Act also inserted in the various Acts that are controlled by the Inspection SZW the provision that this Inspection shall publish its decisions to fine an employer for offences or to stop his activities or to clear him after a finished enquiry. This in order to promote the observance of these Acts and to inform about the performance of the Inspection. Also, the competence has been given to the Inspection SZW to share its information with the organizations of employers and employees and their own monitoring bodies (*see* paragraph 44).

§2. Other Means of Enforcement

44. In a number of sectors of the Dutch economy the social partners themselves have instituted monitoring bodies charged with reporting violations of employment rules (*see* paragraph 332).

For a number of years there has been some debate about introducing contract compliance as a tool to enforce labour law, but this was seldom put into practice.

Another tool, like naming and shaming, is increasingly used in Dutch labour law. We saw it already in the toolbox of the Inspectorate SZW (*see* paragraph 43), and we shall encounter it as the main sanction in the application of the Merger Code (*see* paragraph 361) and in some aspects of the laws on executive pay (*see* paragraph 288).

Part I. The Individual Employment Relationship and Labour Market Regulation

Chapter 1. Definitions and Concepts

§1. The Contract of Employment

45. In the old days of the Republic of the United Provinces (before 1795) there was an ample law on domestic servants, which varied from place to place and was only written down in a piecemeal fashion. Likewise clauses relating to the employment of journeymen, contained in numerous guild regulations, varied from guild to guild and from place to place. Little is known of the legal character of employment relationships in handicraft, draperies and shops.

After the French Revolution and the subsequent French occupation of the Netherlands (1795–1813) the paramount legal rules were henceforward given by the French Codes, notably the French CC, which had entered in force during the French occupation and which were kept on the Dutch statute book after the liberation from the French (1813–1815). These French Codes established an almost unrestricted freedom to contract and implicitly also a freedom to conclude contracts of employment.

The French CC contained only two articles on the contract of employment:

- an article banning contracts of employment concluded for lifetime;
- an article containing the procedural rule that the master was believed on his word in matters of the payment of wages and the termination of the contract.

The guild regulations, which bore some similarity with the relationship of serfdom, were definitively abolished in 1818. And although the municipal authorities until 1853 preserved the power to issue employment regulations, they in fact since 1809 no longer made use of this power.

The very brief representation of the *locatio conductio operarum* in the French CC did not meet with objections when it was maintained in Dutch law after the French withdrew in 1813. However, in 1820 proposals were published to replace the French CC with a new Dutch Code that heavily borrowed from ancient Dutch law. These proposals included an elaborate regulation of the contract of employment after the ancient Dutch master and servants law. However, these proposals came to nothing.

In 1838, the French CC was replaced by the Dutch CC, which was largely a translation of the French CC. On the issue of the contract of employment, the 1838 Dutch CC repeated the already mentioned two articles of the French CC, to which only one further article was added: a rule on the rupture of the contract of employment, which was more favourable to the master than to the servant. This rule was a relic of the ancient Dutch master and servant law.

Whereas in France and Belgium throughout the nineteenth century it was beyond doubt that the concise regulation of the contract of employment in the CC governed all employment relationships, in the Netherlands in the course of time the courts decided that these provisions were only applicable to the more humble kinds of labour. It was without doubt that the contracts of domestic servants and agricultural workers were governed by the few specific *Code Civil* rules on the contract of employment. However, their contracts were also regulated by the ancient laws on domestic servants, which in fact prevailed during the nineteenth century, and had legal relevance by way of 'custom'. Contracts of employment not being 'humble kinds of labour', were considered as 'innominate contracts', which meant that they were only subject to the general principles of the CC.

46. The industrial worker was a rare phenomenon during the first half of the nineteenth century in the Netherlands, and it was only after the French-German War (1870–1871) that industrialization in the country accelerated, leading to a sharp increase in harsh social conditions for the workers. This forced the government in 1891 to introduce a comprehensive Bill on the regulation of the terms of the contract of employment, which was heavily inspired by examples taken from the labour law in other Western European nations. After lengthy parliamentary debates this bill was finally adopted in 1907 and entered into force in 1909.

Since then the Dutch CC has contained an entire chapter with more than 150 sections to regulate various terms of the contract of employment. In 1997 these provisions were all in a modernized version inserted in the new Dutch CC.

In Chapter 10 of Book 7 of this Code there are now to be found rules about:

- the capacity of minors to enter into contracts of employment (Article 7:612 CC);
- the protection of the payment of wages (Article 7:616–633 CC);
- holidays with pay (Article 7:634–645 CC);
- equal treatment (Article 7:646–649 CC);
- non-competition clauses (Article 7:653 CC);
- the information of the worker about the terms of his contract (Article 7:655 CC);
- testimonials (Article 7:656 CC);
- civil responsibility for the health and safety of the worker (Article 7:658 CC);
- civil responsibility for errors made by employees (Article 7:661 CC);
- the contract of employment and transfer of undertakings (Article 7:662–666 CC);
- the law on dismissals (Article 7:667–686 CC);
- special provisions concerning commercial representatives contracts (Articles 687–689 CC);
- special provisions concerning secondment contracts (Article 7:690–691 CC);
- special provisions concerning seamen (Article 7:693–745 CC).

47. As the provisions of the CC on the contract of employment are only applicable if the contract is coined as a contract of employment, the definition of the contract of employment under civil law is very important.[37] Moreover in the law of social security and in tax law the courts tend to apply comparable, but not exactly the same, criterions for the qualification of a labour relationship as is done in labour law.[38]

The Dutch CC in Article 7:610 CC states that *een arbeidsovereenkomst* (a contract of employment) is a contract whereby one party, *de werknemer* (the employee), undertakes during a given period to perform work in the service of the other party, *de werkgever* (the employer), for remuneration.

Some still existing old Dutch labour laws do not refer to *werknemer* (employee), but to the older notion of *arbeider* (worker). As Dutch labour law does not differentiate between these terms, throughout this book, the terms 'worker' and 'employee' will be used as equivalents.

48. The legal definition of the contract of employment contains a number of elements which are interesting to reflect on.

The element 'work' is obvious and seldom raises legal questions. Even 'sleeping' occasionally may be considered as working![39] The most interesting question is in training relationships. Do they contain this element of 'work'? (*see* further paragraphs 71–72).

The second element of the legal definition is 'remuneration'. The word is taken in the very wide sense described in paragraphs 126 et seq. Not all working relationships are based on the classic *do-ut-des* pattern. The work of a housewife/houseman normally is not (but *see* paragraph 75). Also, the work of volunteers is not considered as a contract of employment because of this element, but also here some reservations must be made (*see* paragraph 84). Moreover the engagement of volunteers may charge the engaging organization as well as the volunteer with some obligations similar to those of the employer and employee under a contract of employment, for instance in the field of health and safety (*see* paragraph 158).

The same goes for certain labour relationships in which the worker is performing work without remuneration but with maintenance of a social security benefit. Work entirely compensated by tips of customers is not considered to be performed on a contract of employment.[40]

The third element of the legal definition of the contract of employment is 'during a given period' but this element has no great importance. In the Netherlands even very small jobs, covering only a few hours or days, may be classified as contracts of employment.

---

37. *See* G.J.J. Heerma van Voss, *The Concept of 'Employee': The Position in The Netherlands*, in *Restatement of Labour Law in Europe* Vol. I, 477–503 (B. Waas & G.J.J. Heerma van Voss ed., Oxford-Portland: Hart Publishing, 2017); R. Knegt (ed.), *The Employment Contract as an Exclusionary Device* (2008).
38. *See* D.V.E.M. van der Wiel-Rammeloo, *De dienstbetrekking in drievoud*, Kluwer, Deventer, 2008; on pp. 395–406 may be found an English-language description and discussion of the concept of contract of employment in labour law, tax law and social security law in the Netherlands.
39. Dutch Supreme Court, 15 Mar. 1991, NJ 1991, 417 and 418.
40. Dutch Supreme Court, 8 Oct. 1993, JAR 1993/245.

There is a fourth constitutive element for the contract of employment, which is not contained in Article 7:610 CC and that is the necessity for the employee to perform the work himself. He may not arrange to be replaced by a third party except with the consent of the employer (Article 7:659 CC, *see* paragraph 80). This element brought the HR to refuse in some cases to consider the work of newspaper boys as contracts of employment (*see* paragraph 58).[41] It also explains why legal persons cannot be party on the employee-side of the contract of employment. This element of 'personnel execution', however, is controversial as it is often merely used to circumvent the application of labour law and social security law.

49. Finally there is the most contentious element: 'in the service of the other party', a terminology which is often captured in the word *gezagsverhouding* (relationship based on authority), or the English equivalent: 'subordination'. This element traditionally served to distinguish the contract of employment from other agreements for the performance of labour.

This criterion has been elaborated by the Dutch courts through an abundant case law. According to a string of decisions the notion 'in subordination to' stands for the authority of the employer to unilaterally issue binding rules concerning the way in which the work has to be done or the organization of the enterprise (*see* paragraph 81). This 'control test' is the main legal tool used to distinguish a contract of employment from other contracts in which a promise to work is exchanged in return for some kind of compensation, such as the contract to render services involving an independent contractor (*opdracht*, contract for services, regulated in Articles 7:400 et seq. CC).

However, this legal tool increasingly appears defective. The scope of the employer's right to control may vary from case to case. Some workers are undoubtedly subject to detailed instructions as to the execution of their tasks. On the other hand, in the case of many highly skilled/specialized workers the employer's right to control is mostly restricted to the organizational aspects of the enterprise as a whole. A medical specialist serving in a hospital may, for instance, have to arrange his holidays to fit into the scheme set-up by the managing director of the hospital, but for the rest of the time he will be left entirely free to choose how to do his own particular job. Is he an employee or self-employed? On the other hand, some principals may give very detailed instructions to the independent contractor as regards the execution of the work.

Broadly speaking, the 'control test' is no longer seen as the unique or preponderant test distinguishing the contract of employment from other agreements for the performance of labour. The courts' assessment as regards the nature of the labour contract must be a balance of various factors which are relevant for the nature of the subordination.[42] Courts should not base their assessment on only one criterion.[43]

---

41. Dutch Supreme Court, 13 Dec. 1957, NJ 1958/35.
42. Dutch Supreme Court, 11 Feb. 2011, JAR 2011/75; Dutch Supreme Court, 17 Nov. 1978, NJ 1979, 140 and Dutch Supreme Court, 5 Nov. 1982, NJ 1983, 231.
43. Dutch Supreme Court, 8 May 1998, JAR 1998/168.

In fact the courts assess the status of a work relationship case-by-case on the basis of a checklist of indicators such as:

- whether the principal can give directives and the extent to which the worker is bound to them;
- the freedom of the worker to determine whether to work or not;
- the measure of liberty the worker has in the organization of his work and the fixation of his working hours;
- who bears the entrepreneurial risks?
- who provides and finances the raw materials and the equipment in the business?
- to what extent the worker is performing other activities besides the one concerned;
- whether during illness, holidays, etc. the remuneration is continued;
- whether the work was more or less incidental, etc.

However, much depends on the weight that is given to a particular factor.

Judging whether a contract can be classified as a contract of employment, the courts should take into consideration all the circumstances of the case, seen in a mutual connection. Not only the rights and obligations that the parties had in mind when concluding the contract but also the way in which the parties have implemented and executed their legal relationship should be taken into account. In addition not one single criterion should be decisive, but all the various legal consequences which the parties have attached to their relationship must be considered in mutual connection.[44]

The judicial decision whether or not to classify a contract as a contract of employment has always been very casuistic because the courts do not like to base their findings on appearances, but rather on facts. The courts will not automatically accept the qualification that parties themselves give to the contract. They will take into account both the intention of the parties and the way in which they have in fact executed their contractual relationship. In the valuation of the intent of the parties the courts must take into account the social rank of the worker. There is a lot of debate in scholarly writing about these guidelines of the HR and its application. The actual government intends to better explain the legal definition of 'subordination' as it must be perceived in tax laws. Moreover a State Commission is at work to advise the government on this and related items. It will certainly pay attention to the status of those who are engaged in the so-called platform economy (*see* further paragraph 69).

50. Sometimes one may be confronted with mixed types of contract, for instance the *leer-arbeidsovereenkomst* (contract of training and employment, *see* paragraph 71) or the *huur-arbeidsovereenkomst* (contract for rent and employment). For those situations, the CC provides that if a contract satisfies both the definitions of the contract of employment and of any other specific sort of contract regulated by the law, both the CC provisions on the contract of employment and the provisions on the

44. Dutch Supreme Court, 14 Nov. 1997, ECLI:NL:HR:1997:ZC2495 (Groen/Schoevers); Dutch Supreme Court, 9 Oct. 2015, ECLI:NL:HR:2015:3019 (Logidex).

other contract are jointly applicable. In case of conflict, the CC provisions on the contract of employment prevail (Article 7:610(2) CC).

51. The uncertainty as to whether a contract is to be regarded as a contract of employment appeared to be especially detrimental to workers in atypical employment relationships, such as freelancers (*see* paragraph 68) and labour-on-call workers (*see* paragraph 65). For this reason in 1999 two new provisions were inserted in the Dutch CC.

In the first one (Article 7:610a CC), it is provided that any person who for the benefit of another person performs work for remuneration by such other person for three consecutive months, weekly or for not less than twenty hours per month is presumed to perform such work pursuant to a contract of employment (Article 7:610(a) CC).

This legal presumption does not overturn the classical dogma concerning the contract of employment. It only reverses the burden of proof. In relevant cases it is the imputed employer who has to convince the court that the contract is not a contract of employment.

For the second one (Article 7:610b CC) *see* paragraph 65. These new provisions were the fruit of the drive for more protection from labour law for flexible workers (*see* paragraph 18).

As for both entrepreneurs and real independently working persons it is often a nuisance not to know beforehand whether a person is a real independently working person, the tax authorities in 2002 had created a document Declaration on the status of independent contractor – *Verklaring arbeidsrelatie* (VAR) which on request was delivered to persons who genuinely were certified as performing work as independents. However, this VAR system had become a source of abuse as the tax authorities did not have the manpower to scrutinize sufficiently *ex ante* the VAR requests and to verify them *ex post.* The VAR had become a glib formula for employers to escape the rules of labour law and social security law by contracting bogus-independent workers. So the VAR system was abolished in 2016 and replaced by the Act on the deregulation of the qualification of the employment relationship (*Wet DBA*). This Act brought a new complicated system, which immediately aroused fierce criticism and was put on ice within half a year after it was launched.[45] The actual government intends to replace the Act with a new system of certifications in 2020.[46] Meanwhile the DBA-rules are only applied to bluntly malevolent cases.

§2. Different Categories of Workers

52. The provisions of the CC on contracts of employment are applicable to all employees in the Netherlands, irrespective of income, function or the sector of industry where they work. They cover blue-collar workers as well as white-collar workers; according to the CC both groups are employees. And what goes for the

45. *See* Parliamentary Papers 34036, nos 40 and 61.
46. *See* Parliamentary Papers 31311, no. 212. Letter of the Minister of Labour Law to the Tweede Kamer of the Parliament, of 24 Jun. 2019 (no. 2019-0000089400).

CC goes for most other Dutch labour laws as well. However, in recent years the legislator has started to introduce some differentiations in labour law. The first is that labour law provisions sometimes make a distinction between workers employed in small firms as opposed to other workers.

The second is that there is sometimes a distinction made between workers employed after having reached the pensionable age of the AOW as opposed to other workers.[47] Actually the AOW-pensionable age is 66 + 4 months. It was planned that this pensionable age would further rise during these years step by step, but the legislator has delayed these adaptations in 2019.[48] The AOW-pensionable age shall remain 66 + 4 months in 2020, rise to 66 + 7 months in 2022, 66 + 10 months in 2023, 67 in 2024.

The workers that reach or have already reached the AOW-pensionable age in a number of cases have less protection than the workers in general (*see* notably paragraphs 80, 85, 119, 151, 152, 197–199, 216, 219, 225 and 230).

53. For seamen, commercial agents, temporary agency workers and managing directors deviating provisions may apply (*see* following paragraphs). Moreover, some provisions of the CC allow waivers by way of the individual contract of employment or by collective agreement (*see* paragraph 34), which are often used to create special regimes for certain groups, like professional football players.

I. Public Employment

54. According to the traditional idea that the relationship between the government and its servants is a special one, special rules have of old governed labour relationships in public employment. The civil servants were exempted from the common labour law. Most staff in the service of the national government, the provinces, the municipalities and the water authorities has acquired the special status of civil servants, subject to the *Ambtenarenwet* (Civil Service Act). Their labour relationship is not a contractual relationship; they have an appointment which is a unilateral act of the government. For some civil servants – judges, the military, the police, public education – there are special acts regulating their employment. Actually there are about 600,000 persons (8% of the workforce) covered by the general legal system on civil servants.

However, for a number of years the opinion has been growing that most aspects of the employment relationship no longer require an exceptional position for civil servants. An increasing number of common labour laws have successively been made applicable to civil servants as well: the rules on working times and health and safety, statutory social security, industrial democracy, equal treatment, etc. are covering the civil service as well. This process, called normalization, is now almost

47. Act of 30 Sep. 2015, Stb. 2015, 376; Parliamentary Papers 34073.
48. Act of 3 Jul. 2019, Stb. 2019, 246.

completed. Parliament adopted an Act, to bring the public service under the application of the rules on the contract of employment.[49] The Act will put this in force by 1 January 2020. Only the military and the judiciary are exempted from this transition.

II. Education

55. The above-mentioned Act will also bring the civil servants working in public education under the rules of the contract of employment. For employees working in private education (primary, secondary and higher education) this has already been the situation for many years.

III. Seamen

56. In the past the merchant marine used to be an important business in the Netherlands. Seamen already had their special rules on the contract of employment in the seventeenth century. In 1838, when, along with the French CC, the French Commercial Code was replaced by a Dutch Code, that Dutch Commercial Code in more than fifty articles gave an extensive regulation of the contracts of employment in the merchant marine. These articles were revised in 1931. In 2013 these provisions were revised again, *inter alia* to implement the 2006 ILO Maritime Convention, and they were transferred to Book 7 of the Dutch CC (Articles 693–745). These provisions must be seen as a *lex specialis* to the general regime of the CC. So the general regime of the CC on contracts of employment is also applicable to seamen as long as they are not set aside by the provisions of Article 7:693–745 CC.[50] Other important provisions for seamen are laid down in the Sea Ship Crews Act.

IV. Commercial Agents and Commercial Representatives

57. Contracts between firms and their commercial *agents* are regulated in Articles 7:426 et seq. of the Dutch CC. Such contracts are not considered as contracts of employment. However, the contracts of firms with their commercial *representatives* are branded contracts of employment if their remuneration partly of wholly consists of commission. Nevertheless, a number of the statutory provisions for the contracts between firms and their commercial agents are mandatorily applicable to the contracts with commercial representatives; other provisions are applicable unless they are waived in writing or are less favourable than the contractual terms of the commercial representatives (*see* Article 7:687–689 CC).

49. Act of 9 Mar. 2017, Stb. 2017, 123; Parliamentary Papers 32550.
50. G.W. van der Voet, *Maritime Labour Law*, in *Het 'natte arbeidsrecht* 43–82 (G.W. van der Voet ed., Den Haag, 2018).

V. Company Directors

58. Quite remarkably contracts between companies and their managerial directors under Dutch law have a dual character. The relationship is governed by a number of provisions on company law in the Dutch CC. However, the relationship is also considered as a contract of employment and thus in principle subject to common labour law, but on some issues special provisions apply (*see*, for instance, paragraphs 201, 205, 214 and 230). Since 2013 the newly concluded labour relationships with directors of a company quoted on the Amsterdam Stock Exchange are no longer qualified as a contract of employment but as a contract for services (Article 2:132(3) CC).

High-level professionals sometimes for fiscal reasons have their own limited company and in this formula they serve other companies. Sometimes the management of an enterprise is entrusted to such a legal person ('management agreement'), but due to the criterion of personal execution (*see* paragraph 48) this cannot be considered as a contract of employment.[51] It is a contract for services.

VI. Domestic Workers

59. In the Netherlands the labour law situation of domestic workers in private households is quite weak. Estimations are running to 150,000 persons working about 3 million hours in about 900,000 private households. Because of the wide coverage of the Dutch minimum wage law (*see* paragraph 139) they should be paid at least the minimum wage (about EUR 10 an hour, *see* paragraphs 139 et seq.) and are also entitled to the minimum holiday allowance (*see* paragraph 143), but what about the other labour laws?

A small minority of the workers in private households are working in the service of a specialized employer and may have a normal contract of employment on which all Dutch labour laws and social security laws are applicable. The same goes for another group of workers who have a private person as their employer and are working in his private household at least four days a week. If workers are employed in private households on less than four days a week then, in case of illness, they are only entitled to 70% of the wage during a maximum of six weeks (*see* paragraph 151) and for their dismissal no permit is needed (*see* paragraphs 203 and 214). However, often these domestic workers are directly engaged by the heads of the households on unclear contractual terms. Their employers are not obliged to give them spontaneously a written statement with the particulars of their job. They must only give such a statement if the worker so requests (*see* paragraph 74). The reality is that in such cases almost no written statements are given or requested. Therefore it is difficult for such workers to stand up for their rights. Certainly if they are 'sans

51. Dutch Supreme Court, 28 Jun. 1996, NJ 1996, 711.

papier' or illegally because of other reasons (taxation, social security).[52] Several EU countries have measures in force which give the domestic workers automatic access to social security, coverage by collective agreements or tax subsidies. Nothing of the kind exists in the Netherlands. By way of a Regulation on private households (*Regeling Dienstverlening aan huis*) the government has merely exempted the employers of the domestic workers from social burdens hoping to promote the legal employment of the domestic workers. No special rules have been issued to ensure them a suitable protection. As this situation is clearly in contradiction with ILO Convention 189 concerning decent work for domestic workers, the Dutch government decided not to ratify this Convention.[53]

60. A very remarkable group are thousands of nurses working in home care, organized by professional organizations (so-called *Alpha hulpen*). Their contracts are such that they are supposed to be in the service not of these organizations, but of the clients. Being a kind of domestic workers (*see* paragraph 59) their position is as weak as that of domestic workers. Some courts have disregarded this construction and recognize the relationship between the professional home care organization and the *Alphahulp* as a full-fledged contract of employment.

Of course not all nurses working in home care are in this legal situation. Many have normal contracts of employment with professional organizations, others are working as fully independent workers.

§3. Atypical Work

61. In the actual Dutch labour market one discerns all kind of labour relationships which are different from the traditional full-time open-ended contract of employment. Although the majority of the Dutch workers still perform their duties under a full-time contract of employment for an indefinite period, the number of other kinds of contracts of employment is steadily growing (*see* paragraph 9). One should think of part-time contracts of employment, contracts of employment for a definite period, on-call labour, temporary agency work, homework/telework, platform work and the growing numbers of self-employed.[54]

Such kinds of individual contracts of labour enjoy much popularity for various reasons. Several workers prefer them to the classical full-time open-ended contract of employment because they do not want to engage themselves for an entire working week, because they like to hop from one employer to another or because they want to have more independence in their work. Many employers prefer them

52. *See* A. Eleveld & F. van Hooren, *The Governmentalisation of the Trade Unions and the Potential of Union Based Resistance. The Case of Undocumented Migrant Domestic Workers in the Netherlands Making Rights Claims*, 27(5) Soc. Leg. Stud. 596–615.
53. Parliamentary Papers 29544, nos 507, 585 and 652 and 29427, nos 100 and 107.
54. *See* G.J.J. Heerma van Voss, *Atypical Employment Relationships: The Position in The Netherlands*, in *Restatement of Labour Law in Europe*, Vol. II (B. Waas & G.J.J. Heerma van Voss eds, Oxford-Portland: Hart Publishing, forthcoming); R. Knegt (ed.), *The Employment Contract as an Exclusionary Device* (2008).

because under these kinds of contracts they may escape several inflexible norms of the common labour and social security law.

62. It certainly is not possible to escape all labour and social security law by concluding such atypical contracts. In the course of the years the scope of a number of labour laws has been extended explicitly to workers who perform work under the direction of another, even if the contract is not formally a 'contract of employment'. Such an extension has appeared, for instance, in the law on equal treatment of fixed-term and open-ended contracts (*see* paragraph 100). In other laws, such as the Work and Care Act (*see* paragraph 125), the scope of (parts of) the law is extended with a long list of workers assimilated as employees, such as musicians.

Another technique used is that in the Act on Minimum Wages and Minimum Holiday Allowances ((AMW), *see* paragraph 139), which is also applicable to workers performing work on a contract for services (*opdracht*) unless this contract is entered into in the conduct of a profession or business. Moreover, the Minister may by decree extend the scope of this Act to other kinds of contracts which may be socially assimilated with the contracts which the Act is already covering (Article 2 AMW). The scope of the statutory provision on the information of employees about their employment conditions (*see* paragraph 74) is extended to any contract other than a contract of employment under which one party, being a natural person, undertakes to perform work for the other party for remuneration unless this contract is entered into in the conduct of a profession or business (Article 7:655(6) CC).

A third technique is the extension of the scope of the concept of employer beyond that of the party to contracts of employment. The employer's obligations under the Foreign Workers Act, the Health and Safety at Work Act, the Equal Treatment m/f Act, etc. are extended to all persons that are working under his authority.

All these concepts have made their appearance out of a concern of Parliament to extend the protection of at least some aspects of labour law to persons who are working on legal formulae, which are not in all aspects embraced by the notion of 'contract of employment' but who are seen as in need of an equivalent protection.

Moreover, as a result of the 'flexicurity philosophy' (*see* paragraph 18) the Flexibility and Security Act of 1999 (*see* paragraph 298) has substantially enhanced the position of workers, working under atypical labour relationships. Reform Acts of 2015 and 2020[55] have this trend further strengthened on some counts and corrected on other counts.

I. Part-Time Work

63. The most usual kind of atypical labour relationship in the Netherlands is part-time work. It can hardly be called an atypical contract as actually about 50% of Dutch workers are working on part-time contracts, twice as much as the average in the EU. All kind of labour relationships can be accomplished in part-time, but many part-time relationships are contracts of employment in the legal technical sense of

55. Act of 29 May 2019, Stb. 2019, 219.

the word. The contents of such contracts must, by law, be equal with full-time contracts (Article 7:648 CC) except in cases in which unequal treatment is objectively justified. Obviously this equality may be a proportional equality (*see* paragraph 100). Part-time work is further promoted by the Flexible Working Act – *Wet Flexible Werken* (FWA) (*see* paragraph 119).

II. Contracts of Employment for a Definite Period (Fixed-Term Contracts)

64. In the case of a contract of employment for a definite period the duration of the contract is limited.[56] The parties concerned may restrict this period either by including a fixed term (for instance, 'one year'), or by binding the end of the contract to a certain event (such as the completion of a particular job or the recovery of an employee who is absent due to illness).[57] The case law of the HR requires that the duration of this 'event' should be independent of the will of the employer.[58]

In order to implement an EU directive, Dutch law provides for equal treatment of workers on fixed-term and open-ended contracts, except in cases in which unequal treatment is objectively justified (Article 7:649 CC, *see* paragraph 100). The HR already once prohibited unequal remuneration based on a distinction between the permanent and temporary staff.[59] Moreover the employer must notify an employee who is under a contract of employment for a specific period in good time and in clear terms of any vacancy for employment under a contract for an indefinite period (Article 7:657 CC). Temporary agency workers are not covered by these rules (*see* paragraph 66).

Dutch statutory law does not require an objective reason for the conclusion of fixed-term contracts. Nor does it put a ceiling on the duration of a fixed-term contract. Some collective agreements contain such limitations. However, Dutch law provides that a contract of employment for a period in excess of five years or for the duration of life of a particular person may be terminated by the employee after five years, subject to a period of notice of six months (Article 7:684 CC).

On the termination of a fixed-term contract and its continuation *see* paragraphs 229 et seq.

III. Labour on Call

65. Recent decades have seen a substantial increase in casual work (labour on call). Many workers have contracts of employment that do not specify an exact number of working hours. The workers are summoned when work is available.

56. *See* S.S.M. Peters & A.G. Veldman, *Fixed-Term Employment Contracts: The Netherlands*, in *Fixed-Term Employment Contracts: A Comparative Study* 339–364 (R. Blanpain & C. Grant eds, Brugge, 2009).
57. *See* D.J.B. de Wolff, *De arbeidsovereenkomst voor bepaalde tijd*, Deventer, 1999; on pp. 395–400 may be found an English-language description and discussion of the legal rules in the Netherlands on fixed-term contracts of employment.
58. Dutch Supreme Court, 8 Jan. 1952, NJ 1952, 243.
59. Dutch Supreme Court, 8 Apr. 1994, NJ 1994, 704 (*Agfa*).

There are many varieties of casual work contracts and consequently also the legal situation of those workers differs. There are contracts which stipulate both a minimum and a maximum number of hours a week that the worker is prepared to/may be requested to work. Other labour-on-call contract leaves this element entirely open. Sometimes in such contracts both parties formally exclude the obligations either to offer or to accept work, sometimes it is stipulated that the employer shall offer work and the employee shall accept it. Some labour-on-call contracts regulate the conditions under which the employee will be engaged each time that he is factually summoned, while in periods between two summons there is no labour relation existing; other labour-on-call contracts are concluded as a continuous contractual relationship, under which however only the hours factually worked will be remunerated, etc.

Case law of the HR had established that contracts on call may be considered as contracts of employment but rejected the idea that the employer was under a general obligation to provide work. However, the HR recognized that employees with a non-specified number of working hours/periods in principle have the right to be effectively given work if part of the deal was that the employee is obliged to perform work and if the employee can prove, that there is work for him.[60]

The last element of course may be very difficult to prove. Therefore a factual dismissal of on-call workers is often easy when an employer simply stops summoning up the worker. So the legal position of labour-on-call workers was very weak. The Flexibility and Security Act of 1999 (*see* paragraph 193) has enhanced this legal position by a number of measures:

(a) the presumption provision (Article 7:610a CC, *see* paragraph 51);
(b) provisions on fixed-term contracts: if workers employed on on-call contracts are given further employment after the fourth call to work or beyond three years where contract is considered to be an open-ended contract (Article 7:667–668(a) CC, *see* paragraph 230);
(c) the provision stipulating that where a contract of employment has lasted for at least three months, the contracted work in any month is presumed to amount to the average working period over the three preceding months (Article 7:610b CC). This provision applies in cases in which no precise working time has been agreed or fulfilled. It is not applied if the employer can prove that the reality was different;
(d) finally, the provision which establishes a minimum rate of pay for on-call workers. Where a period of less than fifteen hours of work per week has been agreed and the times on which the work must be performed have not been fixed, or, if the contract is a call agreement, the employee shall be entitled to the remuneration to which he would have been entitled if he had performed work for three hours for every period of less than three hours in which he performed work (Article 7:628a(1) CC).

60. Dutch Supreme Court, 25 Jan. 1980, NJ 1980, 264 (Possemis-Hoogenboom); Dutch Supreme Court, 27 Jun. 1958, NJ 1958, 457.

These provisions have not only been invented in order to protect the employees, but also to discourage employers from making use of this kind of flexi-work. Nevertheless this kind of flexi-work has hardly diminished since 1999 – a clear proof that these provisions do not work well. In the Social Agreement of April 2013 (*see* paragraph 195) it has been laid down that the so-called zero-hour contracts may no longer be concluded in the hospitals and nursing homes, while social partners in other sectors may decide the same.

In 2020 the rights of on-call workers will be enforced as a result of the Act on Labour Market in Balance, 2019.[61] The Act now contains a definition of call employment agreements: these are contracts in which (a) the extent of the work has not been laid down as a number of hours per unit of time of a maximum of one month or a maximum of one year while the employee's right to pay is spread evenly over that unit of time, or (b) the employee is not entitled to the wage determined in terms of time if he has not performed the agreed labour (Article 7:628a(8) CC). Additional rules may be issued by Royal Decree (Article 7:628a(9) CC).[62]

For the calculation of the various periods in these rules, several employment contracts with the same employer that succeed each other at intervals of no more than six months are compounded. That same with successive employment contracts between an employee and various employers, who, irrespective of whether there is an insight into the capacity and suitability of the employee, must reasonably be deemed to be each other's successor in respect of the work performed.

In addition to the above-mentioned, already existing rules, it is now also provided that in call agreements:

(1) the employer cannot oblige the employee to respond to the call to perform work, if he has not informed the employee, in writing or electronically, at least four days in advance of the times when work must be done (Article 7:628a(2) CC). If the employer partially or fully withdraws the call to do work within four days before the start of the work or changes the times, the employee is entitled to the wage he would be entitled to if he would have performed the work in accordance with the call. The call to perform work is to be withdrawn or changed in writing or electronically (Article 7:628a(3) CC). The period of four days mentioned in these provisions may be shortened by collective agreement but not to less than twenty-four hours (Article 7:628a(4) CC).

(2) the employer must – in writing or electronically – always make an offer for a fixed amount of work within a month after the call employment contract has lasted twelve months. This offer must be at least equal to the average volume of work in that preceding twelve-month period. The period for accepting this offer is at least one month. For the calculation of the twelve-month period, employment contracts that have succeeded each other at intervals of no more than six months are added together (Article 7:628a(5)(6) CC). The same applies to successive employment contracts between an employee and various employers, who, irrespective of whether there is insight into the capacity and

61. Act of 29 May 2019, Stb. 2019, 219.

62. *See* Royal Decree of 19 Jun. 2019, Stb. 2019, 233.

suitability of the employee, must reasonably be deemed to be each other's successor in respect of the work performed (Article 7:628a(7)CC). During the period in which the employer has not complied with this offer-obligation, the employee is entitled to wages over the relevant amount of work (Article 7:628a(8) CC).

By collective labour agreement, it can be stipulated that the preceding provisions do not apply to positions in seasonal work (Article 7:628a(11) CC).

IV. Temporary Agency Workers

66. Temporary agency work appeared in the Netherlands in the 1960s and was quite successful. In temporary agency work there is a triangular employment relationship. Formally the temporary employment agency pays the wages and administers the taxes and social security contributions of the worker, who is temporarily placed at the disposal of a third firm. This firm pays a fee to the agency (out of which the agency pays the wages, taxes and social security contribution) and exercises factual authority over the worker. The relationship between the temporary agency firm and the user firm is that of a contract for services.

Various rules were bent to give it a proper and legal basis. The present rules to regulate temporary work agencies were introduced by the AEIA 1998 (*see* paragraphs 255 et seq.) and the Flexibility and Security Act of 1999 (*see* paragraph 193).

For many years the Dutch law was not entirely clear as regards the nature of the contractual relationship of the workers with the agency and with the factual employer. Since 1999 the law provides for a solution as far as the much-debated legal position of the temporary agency worker is concerned. The Dutch CC expressly stipulates that the worker's relationship with the temporary work agency (*uitzendovereenkomst*, in English sometimes called 'secondment contract') is a genuine contract of employment (Article 7:690 CC). This articles defines a secondment contract as 'a contract of employment whereby, within the framework of the conduct of a profession or business of the employer, the employee is placed by the employer at the disposal of a third party in order to perform work under the supervision and direction of the latter by virtue of a contract for services granted by the latter to the employer.' Consequently all statutory rules on the contract of employment are applicable to these contracts, with the exception of a few special rules in the area of dismissals (*see* paragraph 232), on situations in which no work has been performed (*see* paragraph 147) and on equal treatment of workers with fixed-term and open-ended contracts (*see* paragraph 100). Since 1998 the AEIA (Article 8, *see* paragraph 255) required for temporary agency workers at least equal treatment with the workers of the user firm in the same or equivalent functions as regards remuneration and a few working conditions. However, it allowed deviations from this rule in collective agreements, which was widely used. Since 2012 more elements of working conditions have been added to this equality principle. However, research has shown that agency 'temps' in reality were still earning 13%–27% less than their equivalents in the service of the user firm.

The relationship between the temporary agency worker and the user firm is a relationship sui generis, explicitly not being a contract of employment.[63] However, this relationship too may have some labour law consequences for the user firm and the temporary agency workers (*see* paragraph 158) and in the area of the works councils (*see* paragraph 380). Moreover, as regards the WTA (*see* paragraphs 110 et seq.) and the Health and Safety at Work Act (*see* paragraphs 159 et seq.), the user firm is considered as the employer of the temporary agency worker. The HR has rejected the possibility that a secondment contract can tacitly turn into a contract of employment with the user firm.[64]

For the dismissal of temporary agency workers *see* paragraph 232; for the remuneration and other aspects of the conditions of employment of temporary workers paragraph 256; for the civil responsibility for work accidents of temporary agency workers *see* paragraph 158.

67. A special form of temporary agency work is *payrolling.* In this formula employees are – like in secondment contracts – factual engaged by the real employer, but formally on a contract of employment with a payrolling-enterprise which performs all administrative and legal employers' duties. The main difference with the temporary agency firm is in the business model of those payroll firms: they are not actively operating on the labour market to hire out the temporary workers wherever they can. It is mostly the factual employer who looks for the worker he wants to engage, but he chooses the payrolling firm as an intermediary as he does not want a formal contract of employment with the worker. This may be for a variety of reasons, for example to escape the nuisance of a wage administration, and/or to escape a series of cumbersome obligations, such as protracted dismissal protection and unemployment payments. Even public and semi-public employers are making use of payroll enterprises because of the instability of their financial resources. The number of workers working in this formula increased from ca. 150,000 in 2009 to ca. 300,000 in 2018. Some scholars advocated that payroll firms would be excluded from the exceptions in common labour law (Article 7:690 CC) created for temporary work agencies because the payroll firms do not have an allocative function on the labour market. However the HR rejected this opinion.[65] And as from 2020 the AEIA requires the same working conditions for workers of a payroll enterprise and the workers of the user firm in the same or equivalent functions, save the arrangements on occupational pensions, which should not be 'the same' but 'adequate' (Article 8a AEIA, *see also* paragraph 256).

63. Dutch Supreme Court, 27 Nov. 1992, NJ 1993/293; Dutch Supreme Court, 25 Oct. 1996, JAR 1996/236.
64. Dutch Supreme Court, 4 Apr. 2002, JAR 2002/100.
65. Dutch Supreme Court, 4 Nov. 2016, NJ 2017, 370 (Care 4 Care). *See* Parliamentary Papers 29544, no. 761.

V. Free Professions, Freelance Work and Solo-Independent Workers

68. In the Netherlands there is a growing army of free professionals and freelance workers, in Dutch called: ZZP-ers (*zelfstandigen zonder personeel,* independent persons working without the help of employees). Their number rose from 600,000 in 1996 (8%) to ca. 1.1 million in 2018 (= 12% of the workforce) (*see* paragraph 9) so that the Netherlands is now also in this field leading in the EU. Traditionally free professions were dominant among doctors, architects, lawyers, etc. Freelance workers were also widespread in culture, media and education, but now they are also quite numerous in construction, gardening, etc. For several years (2012–2016), the bad employment situation in the Netherlands was a reason for the increase in solo-independent workers. However, actually the recession is over. Nevertheless the increase of this type of workers has not stopped. Many workers in sectors with a high shortage of personnel and in sectors where the wage systems are highly regulated adopt the status of solo-independent workers because in that status they can earn more money or have more pleasant working conditions than as an employee, for instance in the care sector. Freelancers who offer their services via websites ask in average ca. EUR 46 an hour. These instances show that not all switches from employee work to solo-independent work are leading to precarious situations for those persons. However, there are also numerous situations in which people hire themselves out as a solo-independent worker, although they would have preferred to be engaged as an employee but could not find such a job. Especially the persons in this category – which in the Netherlands is estimated at ca. 10% of the solo-independent workers – find themselves in a precarious situation. They earn less than the minimum wage, even if this is the main source of income for them. Many of them only stay on the labour market, thanks to a considerable tax concession for independent working persons.

To a certain extent, employers are deliberately contributing to this segment of independent workers as they sometimes stop offering jobs under employee status and instead offer the same jobs to workers under the solo-independent status. Many observers think that those are then in fact bogus-independent workers.

Workers on freelance contracts or solo-independent workers are normally assumed to work on a ‘contract for services’, which is specially regulated in Articles 7:400 et seq. Dutch CC (*see* paragraph 49). Of course the contractor enjoys much more freedom than the employee, but the flipside is that the contractor is much less protected than the employee. Contractors are not entitled to unemployment benefits, disability benefits, continuation of payment during the first two years of illness and not to paid holidays. They are not covered against the risks of accidents at work (*see* paragraph 158), they have no occupational pension, etc. Only one-fifth of the solo-independents is voluntarily insured against these risks.

However, in some cases, freelancers may now benefit from the above-mentioned presumption provision in the Dutch CC (*see* paragraph 51) which could result in the conclusion that the labour relationship must be seen as a contract of employment. They also may benefit from the statutory clauses extending the scope of specific labour laws outside the domain of the strict contract of employment (*see* paragraph

62). It is an item of political and scholarly[66] debate in the Netherlands whether the broad gap between the protection of contractors and the protection of employees is justified or should be narrowed. The State Commission actually at work (*see* paragraph 49) is supposed to advise the government on this item.

To prevent legal abuses by the use of bogus-independent workers, the former government has promoted an Act on the Sham Constructions,[67] the main priorities of which were to tackle sham self-employment, prevent the avoidance of payment of the minimum wage and social insurance contributions and enforce collective labour agreements. In that context, additional inspectors, eventually rising to thirty-five, have been temporarily appointed by the Inspection SZW (*see* paragraph 41).

Nevertheless, time and again new cases are emerging in which notably the trade unions are claiming that workers are in fact working under a contract of employment while employers claim that it is a contract for services, for instance in the parcel delivery services.

An increasing number of international organizations (OECD, EU Commission) has urged the Dutch government to stop the growth of the segment of sole independent workers. They consider this increase an undermining of the Social Structures of the Netherlands. The actual government of the Netherlands is about to propose a legal construction under which solo-independent workers will be entitled to at least a minimum tariff of EUR 16 an hour. Seeing the Court of Justice of the EU (CJEU) criticism on this kind of rules,[68] this may not be an easy enterprise.

69. A new special category is the *platform workers*. This category of workers is steadily increasing among delivery catering services, taxi services, cleaning services, etc. In this formula, those who need a service demand this on a digital platform; those prepared to offer the service accept it and perform it. The platform itself sees its function as a broker, but via digital technics (such as algorithms) it in fact may exert a certain control over the performers of the services. Does this create a contract of employment between the platform and the performer of the service with all the concomitant rights and obligations or are these performers of services independent workers? There are now some contradictory judgments of lower courts on the question of whether the performers of these services are to be considered as employees or as independent workers.[69] The government intends to act with the above-mentioned EUR 16 minimum tariff.

Another atypical group of workers are the *franchisees*, who in recent years in the Netherlands sometimes have come in open conflict with their franchisors. There is already a Dutch Franchise Code and the government is considering an improvement of their actual legal position.[70]

66. In G.C. Boot, *Arbeidsrechtelijke Bescherming*, 2005, may be found an English-language summary of this discussion.
67. Act of 4 Jun. 2015, Stb. 2015, 233, Parliamentary Papers 34108.
68. *See* CJEU 4 Jul. 2019, C-377/17 (*Commission v. Germany*).
69. *See* the Court of Amsterdam 23 Jul. 2018, JAR 2018/189 and the Court of Amsterdam, 15 Jan. 2019, both cases on Deliveroo runners; Parliamentary Papers 29544, no. 877; *see* N. Zekic, *Contradictory Court Rulings on the Status of Deliveroo Workers in the Netherlands*, 17 Comp. Lab. L. & Policy J. (2019).
70. Parliamentary Papers 31311, 206.

VI. Home-Based Work

70. At present, under Dutch law, there is no special protection for home-based workers. It is true that in 1933 a statute concerning home-based work (*Huisarbeidswet*) was adopted by Parliament. This statute rooted in the ILO attack on sweated labour (*see* ILO Convention 26) and aimed at protecting workers from attempts to save labour costs by decentralized factory production. This statute has never been properly applied and is not able to cope with new developments, in which the sewing machine and the loom have been replaced by the personal computer and visual display unit, otherwise known as telework. Actually the Netherlands has the highest percentage of full-time teleworkers in the EU: 13.7%. Beside this another 10% is performing telework on a partial basis. The new trend in the US to diminish telework is not yet noticeable in the Netherlands.

According to Dutch case law the mere fact that the work is performed outside the employers' premises does not exclude the exercise of authority by the employer, but it does not assume such authority either.[71] This, of course, brings a lot of uncertainty for home-based workers as to their rights under labour law as well as under social security law. The legal assumption of the existence of a contract of employment, since 1999 (*see* paragraph 51), may have improved the security of the home-based workers. Home-based work was also explicitly brought under the Health and Safety at Work Act, albeit with exceptions (*see* paragraph 163).

The Agreement between the European social partners on telework in 2002 has been implemented in the Netherlands in 2003 by a recommendation of the Dutch social partners, united in the Foundation of Labour, to suggest the parties to the collective agreements to insert clauses in the collective agreements on this subject in line with the said European Agreement. And indeed, many collective agreements now contain such clauses.

In 2015, the legislator brought telework implicitly also under statutory protecting by including the concept of a change of the 'place of work' under the rules of the FWA (*see* paragraph 119).

VII. Apprentices

71. A contract of apprenticeship is one under which a master agrees to teach and instruct an apprentice in the workshop. Many detailed regulations used to be laid down in the *Wet op het leerlingwezen* (Apprenticeship Act), issued to guarantee the quality of the teaching. Since 1995 this item is regulated in the *Wet educatie en beroepsonderwijs* (Education and Vocational Training Act).[72]

One of the formulas of this Act concerns the possibility that the students follow during one part of the week courses at school and are working the other part of the week in a company. He/she concludes a triangular contract with the school and the employer, called *leer-arbeidsovereenkomst* (contract of training and employment).

71. Dutch Supreme Court, 17 Nov. 1978, NJ 1979, 140; Dutch Supreme Court, 5 Nov. 1982, NJ 1983, 231.
72. M.v. Velzen, *Learning on the Fly* (2004).

For the legal position of this type of persons in the first place the provision of Article 610(2) CC is important (*see* paragraph 50) – employment law has priority. But is there a contract of employment? According to the case law of the HR, there is no contract of employment if the work done in a training relationship is merely directed to the extension of the knowledge and the experience of a person.[73] If, however, the work contributes to the realization of purposes of the employer, this is work in the sense of Article 7:610 CC. This may be the case for PhD-bursary assistants at Dutch universities, who are often charged with teaching courses.[74] Thus, as far as such a student is engaged in 'productive work' during his training the contract is also a contract of employment (*see also* paragraph 48). In that case the apprentice is covered by all relevant labour laws. This means, among other things, that the employer has to pay the apprentice at least the (proportional) minimum wage (*see* paragraph 139). Even though this minimum wage is very low for youngsters, employers often prefer to conclude training contracts without a formal aspect of a contract of employment. In such cases the employer can confine himself to paying the apprentice a small sum of pocket money.

All in all the system of apprenticeship is in the Netherlands much more weakly developed than in for instance Germany (*see* paragraph 260).

72. From the aforementioned it follows that *trainees* are not generally entitled to any remuneration, but in some sectors they are so thanks to collective agreements or unilateral decisions of the employers (for instance, in law firms). If however the contract is to be seen as a mixed contract – the trainee performing economic valuable work – the contract may be considered as a mixed learn/employment contract (*see* paragraph 50) and at least the minimum wage is due for the working part of the contract.

73. For the *au pair* some specific rules have been fixed by the Dutch government: only light work up to a maximum thirty hours a week and EUR 340 monetary compensation, while the guest family pays the travel and boarding of the *au pair*. If the *au pair* performs more hours of work the contract is considered to be a genuine contract of employment and the guest family must behave accordingly, so, for instance, paying at least the statutory minimum wage (*see* paragraph 139).

§4. Requirements Necessary to Conclude a Valid Contract of Employment

I. Formal Requirements

74. Agreement of wills (consent) is an essential precondition for all contracts and thus also for the contract of employment. The validity of the consent must be judged according to the general civil law principles of offer and acceptance, error,

73. Dutch Supreme Court, 28 Jun. 1996, JAR 1996/153.
74. Dutch Supreme Court, 14 Apr. 2006, JAR 2006/119; Dutch Supreme Court, 9 Oct. 2015, ECLI:NL:HR:2015:3019.

threat, deceit and so on (Article 3:44 CC). If such an agreement of wills is absent the entire contract or parts of it may be null and void or subject to nullification. Rare are the cases in which the entire contract of employment may be null and void or subject to nullification. More often only specific clauses or specific acts may be considered null and void or subject to nullification. Being null and void has an absolute character in Dutch law. Being subject to nullification is a more relative concept. It means that within three years the employee must in or outside court invoke its nullification otherwise the stipulation/act is valid and the court will uphold it (Article 7:614 CC).

In theory the contract of employment may still be informal; it can be entered into by words or by conduct, either expressly or by implication. Only in the case of certain stipulations, such as the probationary period (*see* paragraph 221) and covenants of non-competition (*see* paragraph 166), a written form is required. Furthermore, deviation from some sections of the CC is only permitted by written agreement; from other sections derogation is only permitted by collective agreement, which is *per definitionem* in writing (*see* paragraph 307).

Due to an implementation of Directive 91/533/EC of the EU, the employer is obliged to provide the employee with a written statement containing at least certain particulars such as the names and addresses of both parties, date of commencement of employment, period of time of those services, the position of the employee or the nature of his work, the place where the work is performed, terms of notice, wages, working time, the applicable collective agreement and so on. It must also clarify whether the contract is a contract concluded for a fixed or an indefinite period, whether the contract is an on-call contract, a contract with a temporary agency firm or with a payroll firm.

All this information may be omitted to the extent that these particulars are already specified in a written contract or in an itemized payslip. If they are specified in an applicable collective labour agreement, it is sufficient merely to refer to that agreement.

The only exception to this rule concerns persons working (almost) exclusively in private households on fewer than four days a week. The employer must only give them the written statement at their request (Article 7:655 CC).

Instead of providing the worker with the aforementioned particulars in writing, the employer may provide them by electronic mail, provided the workers do agree with that and the transmission is made in such a way that the worker can save it and it remains accessible to him.

If the contract of employment is itself in writing, the employer must supply the employee with a signed copy and bear the costs of the document (Article 7:654 CC). In order to combat illegal employment the law provides that a worker must be able to show an identification card when present at his workplace. Employers must keep records of the type and number of these identification cards. It is now common practice for employers to keep a copy of the identification card of all their employees in their administration. Under the new Privacy Regulation (*see* paragraph 107) these habits must be revisited.

II. Legal Capacity

75. Before 1956 a married woman needed the consent of her husband to conclude a contract of employment. Since the repeal of this provision there have been no legal differences between the capacity of men and women, either married or unmarried, to enter into an employment relationship. Until 1997 a contract of employment concluded between spouses was void. This provision has been repealed as well.

Although the legal age of majority is 18 years, anyone who is 16 years of age or is married can conclude a legally binding contract of employment. Contracts with such minors are treated on the same footing as contracts with an adult: the employer has to pay the wages directly to the employee, and it is only he/she (and not the parents) who can (in accordance with the employer) change the content of the contract of employment or terminate it.

A minor under 16 years can also conclude a contract of employment provided he/she has the consent of his/her father, mother or legal guardian. When a contract of employment has lasted for four weeks without being disputed the position of this minor is equal to an adult in everything relating to the contract of employment. However, the minor under 16 years cannot enter an appearance at law – he must be represented in court by his father, mother or legal guardian, except when it has become apparent to the court that the statutory representative is not in a position to express an opinion (Article 7:612 CC).

§5. Restrictions on the Work of Children, Young Persons and Foreigners

I. Child Labour

76. The first Act against child labour was introduced in 1874. It prohibited children below 12 years of age from working. In the beginning its enforcement was rather poor, although the situation improved somewhat when the first labour inspectors started work in 1890. However, their number initially was restricted to only three. Since then much has changed. The enforcement of the statutory provisions has been improved, and the age at which a juvenile is allowed to start work has been raised considerably.

The protection of children and young persons at work is now laid down in the WTA of 1996 (WTA, *see* paragraphs 110 et seq.). The Act prohibits child labour under the age of 16 (Article 3:2 to Article 1:2(1) WTA), but it allows children from the age of 13 on to do certain jobs at certain times. This notably concerns 'light work of a non-industrial character' outside school attendance times (Article 3:2 WTA, specified in a Ministerial Decree of 27 March 2007)). Other exceptions can be allowed on the basis of a special permit granted by the Inspection SZW. Such exceptions may be granted in individual cases on certain grounds, such as furthering the interest of education or the arts (Article 3:3(1) WTA, specified in Ministerial Policy Rules of 26 March 2007).

The prohibition of child labour is directed to all responsible persons (Article 3:1 WTA), therefore not only the employer, but also parents, legal guardians, etc., and prohibits all kinds of activities 'in execution of a contract' (Article 1:2(2) WTA).

The prohibition of child labour is one of the few parts of Dutch labour law which is enforced by penal sanctions. Research has shown that these provisions are still too often disrespected in practice. There has been an enormous increase of juveniles working in small jobs in the Netherlands in recent years. Various convictions show that employers not only go to the limits of what the law allows but also are even exceeding those limits. Even one-third of those 12 years of age seem to have small jobs. Nevertheless the government in 2007 relaxed the rules which offer exceptions. Moreover, the penal sanction on the employment of children is so narrowly construed that it can only be applied to a formal employer of the child, not to, for instance, the organizers of an event.[75]

Every year there is the special concern about hundred thousands of children and young persons who are performing jobs during a part of their annual school holidays. Research has shown that the employers often do not stick to the various rules protecting this kind of labour.

In 2019, the Dutch Parliament adopted the Act on the Duty of Care as regards Child Labour[76] which imposes on all enterprises doing business in the Netherlands a duty of care to make sure that in the products and services they offer in the Netherlands no use of child labour has been made.

II. Young Persons

77. In addition there are certain statutory restrictions on the employment of juveniles (from 16 to 18 years of age). The WTA 1996 allows adolescent labour (16 and 17 years) only in the day-time and then only in accordance with regulations on (part-time) compulsory education (Article 4:4 WTA). The minimum and maximum rules on working hours a day, rest periods and pauses are somewhat more restricted for juveniles than for adults (Article 5:3, 5:4: 5:5 and 5:7 WTA, *see* paragraph 113), Also no on-call time can be required (Article 5:9(1) WTA). In the first year after reaching school-leaving age a juvenile is only allowed to work for three days a week. For the remaining two days he or she has to receive some kind of general education provided by special institutes. This school time is counted as working time so the ceiling on the maximum working hours for these youth is proportionally lower. This statutory regulation does not seem to be working very satisfactorily, as many of the pupils who are supposed to benefit from the scheme refuse to attend these classes. There seems to be no adequate sanction against this. It is also reported that many youngsters are working irregular working hours (notably evenings and weekends), combining work with their studies.

Finally no-competition clauses (*see* paragraph 167) cannot be agreed with young persons.

---

75. Council of State 24 Oct. 2018, ECLI:NL:RVS:2018:3492 (affaire Rieu).

76. Parliamentary Papers 34506 (*Wet zorgplicht kinderarbeid*).

III. Foreigners

78. Since 1968 citizens from other EU countries have free access to the Dutch labour market, based on EU law (now EU Regulation 492/2011). At each occasion of a new entrance of Member States this freedom was extended to the citizens of the new Member States, sometimes after a certain transition period. Also the citizens of the European Economic Area (EEA) countries, Norway, Iceland and Liechtenstein, have free access to the Dutch labour market.

Until the beginning of this century there were not many migrant workers from other EU countries and the EEA countries in the Netherlands: fewer than 50,000 of the 7.5 million Dutch workers were nationals from other EU countries and most of them were frontier workers (only 10,000 were residents). Apparently the Dutch level of welfare was not so much higher than welfare levels elsewhere in the EU as to attract other EU citizens to the Netherlands. In addition there are always the language barriers, the housing shortage and similar social problems.

However, in recent years, an increasing number of nationals of the new EU Member States in Central and Eastern Europe have come to the Netherlands to work, mostly in construction, agriculture, etc. There are now about 200,000 workers from the new EU Member States in the Netherlands. Initially this influx was welcomed by most political and economic forces as a boost to the Dutch economy. In recent years, however, even the Dutch government has become worried by a number of undesired 'social dumping' effects of this development (*see* paragraphs 190 et seq.).

In the course of the 1960s the booming economy of the Netherlands saw the influx of growing numbers of migrant workers from outside the EU, notably from Morocco and Turkey to fill the gaps on the Dutch labour market. In order to regulate this phenomenon in 1964 the *Wet arbeidsvergunningen vreemdelingen* (Act on Work Permits for Foreigners) was adopted. When unemployment rose in the 1970s a more stringent legislation, the *Wet arbeid buitenlandse werknemers* (Act on the Labour of Foreign workers) was launched. In the 1990s this legislation was replaced by the actual Foreigners Labour Act – *Wet arbeid vreemdelingen* (FLA). This Act has been a few times amended, for instance in 2013 in order to implement the EU Directive on illegal migration.

On the basis of this Act, employers need a work permit for engaging foreign workers from outside the EU. The exact legal construction is not relevant: both contracts of employment and other types of employment relationships are under the scope of the act. Both profit and non-profit work, both business and private households are subject to the Act (Article 1(b) FLA). The permit is issued by the UWV (*see* paragraph 251) and has to be requested by the employer for a specific job (Article 7 FLA). As a rule the employer only gets such a permit if he can show that no workers are available for the job from EU countries. Other essential criteria are that the employer must have noticed the vacancy to the UWV at least five weeks before the request of the permit and must guarantee the payment of at least the going wage rate (Article 8 FLA). Work permits are granted for a maximum of one year (in some cases, such as Turkish citizens: three years) (Article 11 FLA). In practice 60% of the granted work permits are granted for six months. Most permits are granted for work in agriculture, services, culture and education. In some sectors which are very depended on third-country immigrants, for instance the Asian cooks, the Minister may fix quotas for a maximum number of third-country cooks that may be engaged without a work permit.[77] Until the beginning of this millennium most work permits were issued for migrants from outside the EU. Between 2004 and 2014 the main groups for which permits have been granted were nationals from eastern European states, which were already members of the EU but on which the EU rules on free movement of workers were not yet applicable.

Workers from outside the EU who have worked legally in the Netherlands for at least five years (Turkish citizens: three years) as well as persons admitted on humanitarian grounds are entitled to obtain a note on their residence permit that they no longer need a work permit.

An employer may obtain a permit for new arriving asylum seekers who have been at least half a year in the asylum procedure and are entitled to shelter facilities. The permit will be given for maximum twenty-four weeks within a totality of fifty-two weeks.

No work permit is required for citizens from outside the EU/EEA/Switzerland who work in the Netherlands within the framework of EU cross-border service provision, but the contractor must notify this to the UWV.

Some years ago a further exception has been introduced for the so-called knowledge migrants, persons from outside the EU who may make an important contribution to the Dutch economy or culture. Apart from some categories like PhD students, they should at least earn EUR 52,000 a year (EUR 38,000 if younger than 30 years). The Dutch Taxman is further stimulating the arrival of expats: during a maximum of eight years they enjoyed 30% reduction on their income tax. In 2019 this duration was reduced to five years.[78]

The Netherlands have only on a very minor point relaxed the rules on the admission of seasonal workers from outside the EU/EEA/Switzerland. It sticks to a very restrictive admission policy towards these workers, seen the ample offer of seasonal workers from the newest EU Member States.[79]

Initially the hiring of foreign workers without a work permit (if needed) was considered as a criminal offence, punished with a fine of at most EUR 5,000. In practice the average fine was about EUR 500 and not many cases were brought to the court. In 2007 the law was supplemented by the mechanism of administrative fines, which allowed a much easier punishment of employers. Actually many thousands of fines are imposed. The maximum administrative fines are now quite high: EUR 11,250 for a natural person and EUR 45,000 for a legal person (Article 19d FLA). The enforcement is in the hands of the Inspection SZW, but this inspectorate is understaffed (*see* paragraphs 41 and 42). So there are still a large number of illegally employed foreigners in the Netherlands. Estimations vary from 50,000 to 100,000, especially in agriculture, where 18% of the work is done by illegal workers.

In order to better control the work by immigrants, the employer is obliged to communicate to the SZW Inspectorate within forty-eight hours after a request copies of the identification papers of a migrant worker (Article 15a FLA).

77. *See* Parliamentary Papers 29544, no. 875.
78. Parliamentary Papers 35026.
79. Wet van 7 Jun. 2017, Stb. 2017, 282; Parliamentary Papers 34590.

Since 1998, the law has excluded illegal immigrants from most of the public social services, but illegally employed workers may invoke the protection of many labour laws. The employer must pay the illegally employed worker his remuneration. The act contains the legal assumption that such a worker has worked at least six months on the usual remuneration in the trade. It is up to the employer to prove a different reality (Article 23 FLA). The termination of the contract with an illegally employed worker is subject to all the normal rules of dismissal.

Chapter 2. Rights and Duties of the Parties to the Contract of Employment

79. In the Netherlands the correct payment of wages, a minimum level of remuneration, working times, paid holidays, health and safety at work and the termination of the contract are the elements of the contract of employment, that are regulated by statutory law in much detail. Many other elements of the contract of employment have been regulated as well, but often in a more superficial way. Consequently most legal questions in this field must be approached by general principles of law. In this chapter we shall pay attention to the general principles of the law, which are often used by the courts in the Netherlands to solve those questions: notions about the general duties of the employee and the employer, the non-discrimination/equal treatment principle, the bona fides principle and the fundamental rights.

§1. Duties of the Employee

I. Duty to Work

80. In the Netherlands there does not exist a direct duty of work on any person as the country is bound to the fundamental rights which guarantee that there shall be no slavery, forced labour, etc.

However, persons that are dependent of social security benefit may feel an indirect duty to work, as the social security rules are often requiring from them to accept 'suitable work' as a condition to receive social security benefits.[80] In the Netherlands this pressure is under control of the courts and mostly exercised with moderation (some people might say: with much laxity).

It follows from the definition of the contract of employment that the worker is obliged to perform the work agreed upon. He or she must perform the work himself. Only with the consent of the employer he or she may arrange to be replaced by a third party (Article 7:659(1) CC).

However, considering the fundamental right of workers on 'freedom of work' the legislator in 1979 provided that the duty to perform work may not be enforced by an action in court if application is made for a penalty forfeited on non-compliance or detention (Article 7:659(2) CC).

An employee who is prevented from performing the contracted work in connection with disability as a result of sickness must follow reasonable provisions given by the employer or an expert designated by the latter and cooperate with so-called reintegration measures; he must give his cooperation to the preparation, evaluation and adjustment of the reintegration action plan, and perform 'suitable work' (Article

80. A. Eleveld, *Labor Obligation, Justice and the Foundation of Social Security*, in *A Critical Perspective on the Reform of Dutch Social Security Law* 35–48 (A. Eleveld ed., Leiden University Press, 2012).

7:660a(1) CC). *See* for the flipside of this obligation in paragraph 85. This last-mentioned obligation (and its flipside) is not applicable to workers that have reached the AOW-pensionable age (Article 7:660a(2)).

II. Duty to Obey Lawful and Reasonable Orders

81. As has been mentioned above (*see* paragraphs 29 and 49), the notions of command and subordination are inherent in the concept of the contract of employment. Dutch statutory law explicitly lays down that the employee must observe the rules governing the performance of work and those designed to promote order in the undertaking of the employer issued to him – whether or not at the same time as issued to other employees – by or on behalf of the employer, provided these rules stay within the limits of generally binding provisions or of the contract (Article 7:660 CC).

In practice this duty – in other countries often indicated as the consequence of the right of management to give directives/the 'managerial prerogative' – regularly gives rise to uncertainty and conflicts as the employer and the worker often fail to see eye to eye about the reasonableness of a specific order. Conflicts may arise, for instance, when the worker is being ordered to perform a task which does not normally fall within the scope of his activities, or when he is ordered to work overtime (*see* paragraphs 117 et seq.), or to change the contents of a job. Sometimes these matters are explicitly regulated in the contract of employment or by a collective agreement, but even then there may be room for doubt about the interpretation of the provisions.

In fact, the exact contents of the function of the employee sometimes can be derived from the description in the contract of employment. In many sectors of the economy collective agreements have standardized the description of the functions, notably in relation to pay. This sometimes leads to some functional inflexibility in those sectors. In our days employers often like to have more *functional flexibility*, but it is not easy for employers to impose much functional flexibility on their workforce if this is opposed by the employees. Usually employees are reluctant to agree to abrupt changes in their conditions such as tasks, hours and the place of work. The present state of Dutch labour law easily underpins such resistance. According to a principle of Dutch labour law employers have only limited power to change unilaterally the contents of the contract of employment (*see* paragraph 173). Judges will on the basis of the bona fides (Article 7:611 CC) protect the worker who is unwilling to bow to the unreasonable pressure of the employer to consent to changes in the content of his/her function (*see* paragraph 102). This is more than mere legal theory. If in practice the employer tried to impose its will under the threatening alternative of a dismissal, it would find, as we will see in below (in Chapter 9 of Part I), that dismissal is not an easy option in open-ended contracts. This entire legal situation is one of the reasons why employers often prefer flexible types of employment relationships.

III. The Duty of Secrecy

82. In the private sector the worker is under an obligation not to disclose his employer's trade secrets or confidential information. This duty, which continues after the employment has ended, is backed by penal sanctions (Article 273 Criminal Code) and can, if violated, give rise to summary dismissal (Article 7:678(1)(i) CC) and also to a claim for damages by the employer. Sometimes collective agreements or company handbooks contain provisions in this field, sometimes enforced by fines. For the Civil Service, the Criminal Code (Article 272) and the Civil Service Act (Article 125a) contain specific rules in this area. The employer may also impose a duty to secrecy on the basis of his managerial prerogatives (*see* paragraph 81).

As long as the imposed duty of secret is reasonable the employee is bound to respect it, if only on the basis of the bona fides principle (Article 7:611 CC). Recently the Act on the protection of trade secrets[81] was adopted to implement EU Directive 2016/943/EU, which more precisely describes the protection of trade secrets that also the employee has to respect as well as the civil law consequences and procedures in case of violation. At the same time, this Act sums up a number of exceptions that employees may invoke, for instance because it infringes too much on his right to free expression (Article 11 Charter Fundamental Rights of the EU) and the so-called whistle-blower's protection (*see* paragraph 83) (Article 4).

83. In recent years the Netherlands like other countries has seen the phenomenon of the *whistle-blower*, an employee or a civil servant who believes, that in the general interest he must disclose some malpractices he has observed in his employment. To give some protection to these people the Civil Service Act since 2003 contains a regulation (Article 125a). In private business on this point there is a non-binding 'Declaration' by the Foundation of Labour, a provision in the Dutch Corporate Governance Code and there is a Support Point for whistle-blowers. In recent years increasing attention has been paid to all the tensions that may arise in this area, such as the tension between the obligation/right to secrecy and certain statutory reporting obligations of the employees, the uneasy position of the employees when controlling authorities are dealing with the employer, the tension between the whistle-blowers regulation and the protection of privacy and free speech. Courts mostly require that whistle-blowers first have announced abuses internally and, second, that the disclosure of confidential information must serve a substantial general public interest. Under specific circumstances this may be otherwise.[82] The Dutch Parliament has adopted a private member's bill, called the 'House of the Whistle-blowers' Act.[83] It obliges all employers (both private and public) with more than fifty employees to adopt an internal procedure to deal with whistle-blowers' complaints. Moreover it establishes that the National Ombudsman may receive a 'notification of a suspicion of a malpractice' made by an employee of a company, which is covered by the Act and will investigate the case provided certain requirements

81. Act of 17 Oct. 2018, Stb. 2018, 369.
82. Dutch Supreme Court, 26 Oct. 2012; JAR 2012/313.
83. Act of 22 Apr. 2016, Stb. 2016, 142; Parliamentary Papers 33258.

are fulfilled. Finally the Act gives the whistle-blower some protection against victimization by his or her employer. Up till now the Act is not functioning well and must be reviewed in the light of a recent EU Directive on this subject.

§2. Duties of the Employer

I. Duty to Pay Wages

84. The employer's duty to pay wages is an essential counterpart to the worker's duty to perform the work agreed upon. Without this duty there can be no contract of employment (*see also* paragraph 48). Thus a contract which obliges the worker to work for tips (from third parties) only, is not a contract of employment.[84] Also work performed voluntarily is not a contract of employment. Sometimes a certain compensation is paid to volunteers, for instance to cover travelling costs. As soon as such compensation substantially exceeds the real costs, parties risk that a court may classify the work as a contract of employment, with all concomitant rights and obligations.[85] The employer's duty to pay wages is extensively regulated by law (*see* paragraphs 126 et seq.).

II. A Right to Work, a Freedom of Work or a Duty to Provide Work?

85. It is a long tradition of the labour movement to claim a Right to Work, and in the liberal tradition there is the idea of a freedom of work or occupation. Such concepts are often included in international Charters or national Constitutions. In the Netherlands, the freedom of work and occupation is laid down in the Constitution (Article 19(3)), and we shall see that it has an impact on the regulation of some labour law issues as for instance the conventions of non-competition (*see* paragraph 166).

A Right to Work is not included in the Dutch Constitution – only the 'concern of the Dutch authorities to promote sufficient employment' (Article 19(1)), which supports the Labour Market Services and Policies of the State (*see* Part I, Chapter 10). Therefore Dutch courts will in general not honour claims of workers or trade unions against a specific employer, solely based on 'a right to work'. However, in incidental cases courts may conclude that an employer is under a 'duty to provide work'.

Normally employers will not be slow to offer their employees the chance to effectively perform the contracted work, if only because otherwise they run the risk to have to continue the payment of the wages even if no work is performed (*see* paragraph 130). However in specific circumstances employers could have reasons to withdraw the opportunity to work and to confine themselves to paying the agreed-upon remuneration: for instance, a contracted football player, who is only infrequently selected to play.

84. Dutch Supreme Court, 8 Oct. 1993, JAR 1993/245.
85. Dutch Supreme Court, 12 Oct. 2001, JAR 2001/2017.

According to the HR there is no general rule in Dutch labour law which obliges the employer to actually provide the worker with the contracted work. The Court pronounced that it depends from the nature of the employment relationship, the contracted work and the special circumstances of the case whether a claim of an employee to be effectively given the chance to perform the contracted work or other work can be adjudicated.[86]

Such adjudication then may be possible for instance in contracts where the duty to effectively provide work can be an essential part of the bargain, such as when the employer has guaranteed the worker the opportunity of acquiring fame (actors) or of maintaining or developing skills (football players), or if their remuneration is effectively partly or wholly dependent of the factual possibility to perform work. Employees may also have a right to be effectively given work if part of the deal was that the employee is obliged to perform work and if the employee can prove, that there is work for him.

In the case law of the lower courts one may observe the trend that the courts in principle do recognize the obligation on the employer to effectively provide the contracted work. They base this on Article 7:611 CC (the bona fides principle, *see* paragraph 102). The employer can only refuse the employee to effectively perform work if he has very serious reasons for that, such as the lack of work or (the fear for) misconduct of the employee.

In the practice of the courts (and notably in summary procedures) there is often a combination of the claim to provide work and to continue the payment of wages, notably in cases in which workers were laid off because of reorganization, or were suspended as a disciplinary measure (*see* paragraph 184), or in case a dismissed employee invokes an earlier agreement that he would be re-engaged on a later moment (*see* paragraph 208) or in case the employer does not allow him to continue working during the period of notice (*see* paragraph 217).

A special case is that of the duty to provide work to ill or partly disabled workers. In 2002 the legislators have inserted a very ample text in the Dutch CC.

The employer must ensure that an employee who is prevented from performing the contracted work by reason of unfitness due to sickness will be engaged in work in his business. If it is established that the contracted work can no longer be performed and no other suitable work is available in the business of the employer, the employer shall ensure during the period in which the employee is entitled to receive remuneration from him, that the employee will be engaged in work suitable for him in the business of another employer (Article 7:658a(1) CC).

The notion 'suitable work' in this respect means 'all work suited to the strength and abilities of the employee unless acceptance may not be required from him for reasons of a physical, psychical, mental or social nature' (Article 7:658a(3) CC).

This obligation, which is not applicable to workers that have reached the AOW-pensionable age, is further elaborated with various provisions for its practical application.

86. Dutch Supreme Court, 12 May 1989, NJ 1989, 801; Dutch Supreme Court, 26 Mar. 1965, NJ 1965, 163 and Dutch Supreme Court, 27 May 1983, NJ 1983, 758.

III. Duty to Provide Vocational Training

86. As from 2015 Dutch law has also saddled the employer with a duty to provide his employees with vocational training. Article 7:611a CC provides that the employer must enable the employee to follow training that is necessary for the execution of his job and, as far this can be reasonably expected from him, for the continuation of the contract of employment, if the function of the employee is deleted or if the employee is no longer able to fulfil it.

This provision is supported by the law on dismissals, which includes 'sufficient care of the employer for vocational training' as an important criterion for assessment of whether the employer has 'reasonable grounds' for a dismissal (*see* paragraph 197).

The employer, however, may deduct to some extent the costs of vocational training from the transition allowance (*see* paragraph 219) and obtain further reimbursement from various labour market instruments (*see* paragraphs 259 et seq.). About clauses on the restitution of training costs *see* paragraph 170.

§3. Equal Treatment and Non-discrimination

87. Following provisions in international law and building on the traditional tolerance and pluralism of the Dutch society, the Netherlands in recent years has seen a vast growth of anti-discrimination legislation, imposing on employers the obligation to treat their employees equally and without discrimination.[87]

Since 1983 Article 1 of the Dutch Constitution has proclaimed that all persons residing in the Netherlands must be treated equally in equal cases. Discrimination on the basis of religion, conviction, political opinion, race, sex or on any other ground is prohibited.

However, in Dutch constitutional law there is no supremacy of the Constitution over statutory law and there is no Constitutional Court, so in theory statutes which are not compatible with the Constitution, can nevertheless be in force. However, in a legal conflict between statutes and rules of international law, which are binding for the Netherlands, international rules may prevail (*see* paragraph 22). In this respect reference should be made to Article 26 of the International Covenant on Civil and Political Rights – a general anti-discrimination rule – which has been recognized by the Dutch courts as a supreme standard to which the courts are testing even the Acts of the Dutch Parliament. Courts are also prepared to give these standards 'horizontal effect' on the employment relationships by way of the bona fides rule of Article 7:611 CC (*see* paragraph 102). Nevertheless legislators have adopted a number of Acts of Parliament to clarify the impact of the non-discrimination principle on the Dutch labour market and to implement the non-discrimination Directives of the EU. The EU Directives on Equal Pay and Equal Treatment of men and women (now in the Sex Discrimination Directive, 2006), which forbid especially every kind of sex discrimination in employment are implemented by Article 7:646 CC and the Act on Equal Treatment of men and women (AETMW). In 2003 an Act

87. T. Loenen, *Non-discrimination Law: Comparative Perspectives* (1999).

on Equal Treatment based on Handicap and Chronic Illness (AETHCI) and an Act on Equal Treatment based on Age at Work (AETAW) were adopted by Parliament in order to implement Directive 2000/78/EC. Finally other legal provisions must ensure that employment offices and temporary work agencies are not involved in discrimination at the labour market (*see* paragraphs 251 et seq.).

Moreover, discrimination in office, occupation and trade based on race, religion, conviction, sex, sexual orientation and handicap[88] is prohibited under criminal law (Articles 137c, 137f, 137g and 429 *quater* Penal Code). This provision, however, is only applied in extreme cases of discrimination. Normally the fight against discrimination must be carried out on the basis of civil and administrative law statutes and procedures.

The General Act on Equal Treatment – *Algemene wet gelijke behandeling* of 1992 (GAET) prohibits unequal treatment irrespective of religion, political orientation, race, sex, nationality, sexual orientation or marital status, covering, among others, all aspects of behaviour on the labour market. According to the latter all clauses in contracts of employment contrary to this principle are void, a refusal to hire or a termination of employment on these grounds is illegal, etc. On the basis of this legislation discrimination can be attacked, not only by the persons affected by such discrimination, but also by interest groups.

88. In all this legislation the concept of equal treatment embraces both direct and indirect distinction as well as giving orders to discriminate.

There is direct distinction (discrimination) if a person is treated different than a person in a comparable situation has been, is or would be treated on the basis of religion, conscience, political conviction, race, sex, nationality, hetero- or homosexual orientation or civil status.

There is indirect distinction (discrimination) if an apparently neutral provision, criterion or action hits – in comparison with other persons – particularly persons with a specific religion, conscience, political conviction, race, sex, nationality, hetero- or homosexual orientation or civil status (*see* Article 1 sub *c* GAET). Indirect distinction, however, is allowed if it is objectively justified by a legitimate ambition and the means to reach that aim are suitable and necessary (Article 2 lid 1 GAET).[89]

The concept of discrimination in the GAET, the AETMW and Article 7:646 CC is covering harassment and (sexual) harassment under the word 'intimidation'. Intimidation means conduct relating to the religion, race, gender, etc. of a person which has as its object or consequence that the dignity of a person is impugned while creating a threatening, hostile, insulting, humiliating or offensive environment. Sexual intimidation means any form of oral, non-oral or physical conduct with a sexual connotation aiming at or resulting in the impugnation of the dignity of a person, in particular when a threatening, hostile, insulting, humiliating or offensive situation is created. The employer may not cause prejudice to an employee who rejects or passively submits to (sexual) intimidation (Article 7:646(5-9) CC).

88. But not discrimination based on age, *see* Parliamentary Papers 30950, no. 142.
89. Dutch Supreme Court, 25 Nov. 1988, NJ 1989, 730.

89. As far as labour law is concerned the various anti-discrimination acts provide that an employer may not discriminate on the prohibited grounds when offering and handling a vacancy, in the labour exchange, in entering into or terminating a contract of employment, in the appointment and discharge of civil servants, in fixing the terms and conditions of employment, in vocational training, in granting promotion and in health and safety matters (Article 5 GAET; Article 4 AETHCI; Article 3 AETAW). It is also prohibited to give orders for unequal treatment (Article 1(a) GAET) and harassment (Article 1a (GAET)).

If the Dutch legislation contains an elaborate regulation of a prohibition of discrimination, for instance on the grounds laid down in the GAET, then legal doctrine in the Netherlands assumes that no form of unequal treatment is allowed outside the exceptions explicitly mentioned in that regulation (so a closed system of exceptions). In other cases of discrimination courts will apply an open system of exceptions. If the ground for discrimination is not explicitly mentioned in the law (*see* paragraph 101), then courts will assume that unequal treatment is allowed if there is an objective justification for it.

The GAET is applicable not only to employment contracts but also to the free professions and the solo-independent workers (Article 6 GAET) and to the organizations of employers and employees (Article 6a GAET).

However, the GAET is not applicable to churches and their independent divisions and bodies as well as to other associations on spiritual basis and to employees in clerical professions (Article 3) and its provisions in the field of work and free professions are not applicable to:

- work relationships with a private character;
- requirements pertaining to the freedom of an organization offering private education or whose ethos is based on religion, belief or a political conviction, to make as regards individuals working for them, a difference of treatment based on religion, belief or political conviction, in sofar as these features, by reason of the nature of the specific occupational activities concerned or of the context in which they are carried out, constitute a genuine, legitimate and justified occupational requirement, having regard to the organization's ethos (Article 5(2)(a-c) GAET) – a recent amendment to narrow the so-called ethos-exception in the GAET;
- requirements in relation to the freedom of municipalities to make a distinction on the basis of religion or conviction as regards (extraordinary) civil servants of the Registrar's Office who make a distinction in performing his office, unless the distinction which he makes is based on the law (Article 5(2)(d) GAET) – a recent amendment to outlaw the refusal of (extraordinary) civil servants of the Registrar's Office to conclude same-sex marriages;
- differences of treatment based on characteristics related to religion, conviction, political opinion, race, sex, nationality, sexual orientation or civil status and such characteristic is because of the nature of the concerned specific professional activity or the context in which it is executed, an essential and determining professional requirement, provided the aim is legitimate and the requirement is proportional to that aim (Article 5(3) GAET);

- requirements pertaining to the political conviction that reasonably can be put in relation to the fulfilment of functions in the administration or advisory bodies (Article 5(4) GAET);
- requirements in relation to the political conviction that reasonably can be put concerning the fulfilment of confidential positions (Article 5(5) GAET).

The most problematic point is there when the fundamental right to equal treatment is clashing with other fundamental rights, for instance the fundamental rights to freedom of expression, to freedom of religion and freedom of education. Many lawyers hold that in this conflict the right to non-discrimination should always prevail (a mega fundamental right). Others hold that in such conflict both rights should be balanced. This is also the view of the HR (*see* paragraph 101).

90. In theory, contesting acts of discrimination could be hampered by the normal rules of civil procedure on the burden of proof. However, since 1988 in the Netherlands this normal rule has been quite flexible: the party who asserts must prove, unless the statute says otherwise or the court reverses the burden of proof on the basis of bona fides (Article 150 Code of Civil Procedure, *see* paragraph 37). In order to implement the relevant European Community (EC) Directives on equal treatment in all Dutch equal treatment acts the burden of proof is divided between the parties. Claimants have to establish facts from which it may be presumed that there has been discrimination; defendants must then prove that there has been no breach of the principle of discrimination (Article 10 GAET; Article 6a AETMW; Article 10 AETHCI and Article 12 AETAW).

Employers are fully responsible for the consequences of violations of the equal treatment principle, even if they have not committed a fault or – in cases of direct discrimination on the grounds mentioned in the GAET – if they had a justification.

If violations of the principle of non-discrimination have been established the court may order that damages should be paid, encompassing both the material and the immaterial damage. Clauses in contracts, rulebooks, etc. violating the Equal Treatment laws are absolutely void. Courts may annul certain actions and order that a more favourable rule should be applied instead of the less favourable one.

In case of a dismissal prohibited in any anti-discrimination rule or any other prohibition of unequal treatment or on account of the fact that the employee has invoked these provisions in a judicial proceeding or otherwise, the court, on the request of the employee, may annul the notice of termination by the employer, or, at the request of the employee, order the employer to pay a fair compensation for damages (Article 8 GAET, Article 1b(5) AETMW, Article 9 AETHCI, Article 11 AETAW and Article 7:681(1)(b) CC).

All these rules are completed by a prohibition of victimization: employers may not cause prejudice to employees on account of the fact that they have invoked, in judicial proceedings or otherwise the anti-discrimination laws or have given assistance in such a matter (Article 8a GAET; Article 7:646(14) CC).

In order to enable an effective fight against discrimination the legislators have provided for the establishment of the Human Rights Board (formerly called the Commission on Equal Treatment) (Articles 11–21 GAET). The Board may give judgments in all cases of discrimination, brought to it by victims or by interest groups and it may also itself hold enquiries and initiate court proceedings. Although the judgments of the Board do not have a legally binding character (*see* paragraph 39), statistics show that employers follow the judgments in 75% of the cases.

There are also several local points were complaints about discrimination can be reported. They too receive some hundreds of complaints each year. Also the public control on discrimination has been intensified. Discrimination is supposed to be included in the notion of 'psycho-social work burdens', which the employer should prevent or limit according to Article 3(2) of the Health and Safety at Work Act (*see* paragraph 161). So the Inspectorate SZW may control this. This Inspection is also involved in the cases in which the anti-discrimination rules are sanctioned under criminal law (*see* paragraph 87). In such cases a maximum fine of EUR 4,500 may be imposed. The capacity of the Inspection SZW for this task was strengthened in 2018 (*see* paragraphs 41–42). Finally it should be noted that also the works councils have the task to guard against discrimination (*see* paragraph 393).

91. Yet all this anti-discrimination legislation seems only helpful in combating formal discrimination. It lacks the ability to undo unequal treatment caused by the inherent backwardness on the labour market of certain groups of the population. For example, it appeared that long-term unemployment was especially severe among specific groups on the labour market such as disabled people, immigrants and parts of the female population. To combat the latter problem the instrument of *'affirmative action'* was much debated, but at the end of the day the measures taken in this field have never been as far-reaching as, for example, in the US. So, for instance, there is in the Netherlands no such a thing as 'contract compliance' (no government orders for companies that discriminate), although the government is considering this now. It is mostly by some soft forms of measures that the government is trying to stimulate the employment of the less favoured groups on the labour market. Some employers, notably in the field of the government and semi-public institution are committed to a policy of affirmative action, in the Netherlands called positive action or positive discrimination. It embraces measures to give priority to the employment of women and persons belonging to ethnic or cultural minorities, etc. Dutch law explicitly allows stipulations intended to put women or persons belonging to a specific cultural or ethnic minority into a privileged position in order to end or to reduce existing inequalities, provided they are reasonably proportionate to the intended object (Article 2(3) GAET). In 2005 the government decided that it is allowed that women and non-whites are notably invited to apply for a job, but that it is not allowed to apply a rigid positive distinction in vacancy procedures by totally excluding men or whites all together from the selection process. Only if candidates are equally fit for the job the employer may prefer a women or a non-white candidate.

On affirmative action based on ethnic background *see* paragraph 92; on affirmative action based on sex, *see* paragraph 94; on affirmative action in favour of handicapped persons *see* paragraph 248.

Successive governments have tabled their own policies to stamp out all remaining discrimination on the Dutch labour market. The actual government[90] intends to focus on the items of age discrimination, discrimination of migrant workers, narrowing the gender wage gap (*see* paragraph 144) as well as discrimination via temporary work agencies. Apart from numerous non-legislative actions, this government envisages amendments of the Health and Safety at Work Act (paragraph 163) to better engage the Inspection SZW to enforce the anti-discrimination rules.

I. Race/Ethnic Background/Nationality

92. Although the Netherlands has a long history of immigration, notably from persons of other European countries and from its former colonies in East Asia, until the 1960s it had an overwhelmingly white Dutch-speaking population. Only then started a large influx from immigrants of Morocco and Turkey who came to the Netherlands as 'guest workers'. The economic crisis in the mid-1970s impelled the Dutch government to restrict the entrance of migrant workers from non-EU countries (*see* paragraph 78). However, the 1970s, the 1980s and 1990s saw the entrance of large numbers of citizens of the former Dutch colonies in the Caribbean as well as of persons accepted on humanitarian grounds (asylum, family unification). So the number of persons belonging to ethnic minorities has risen quickly during the last decades until it is now about 12% of the Dutch population.

To overcome discrimination a special provision has been inserted in the Dutch Criminal Code, prohibiting race discrimination in office, occupation and enterprise (Article 429 *quater* Criminal Code). Besides this provision there is the prohibition of race discrimination in the GAET. This last prohibition allows only one small exception, viz. in cases in which the outer characteristics connected to the race of a person, must be decisive or required, provided the aim is legitimate and the requirement proportionate to the objective (Article 2 (GAET)).

Sometimes the question has risen as to whether the prohibition of race is also embracing distinctions based on nationality. The GAET provides indeed that unequal treatment based on nationality is forbidden. However it makes a general exception for unequal treatment because of general binding rules and international law and also in cases in which nationality must be decisive (Article 2(5)(b) GAET).

In the past Dutch social law was riddled with provisions excluding foreigners. This picture has been changed in recent decades. First of all because the Netherlands is part of the EU and under EU law many kinds of unequal treatment of nationals of other Member States are prohibited. In the second place because the government is concerned to have as much as possible the foreigners integrated in the Dutch society. Especially the high unemployment rate among immigrants is felt as a major problem.

Despite official disapproval of discrimination as regards race/ethnic origin, the first generation part of the migrant section of the Dutch population is still mainly confined to low paid and unpleasant jobs. Moreover, the rate of unemployment

90. Parliamentary Papers 29544, nos 748, 822, 834 and 849.

among migrants is constantly three times as high as that among ethnic Dutch. It is approved government policy to fight the substandard conditions of this section of the population as much as possible, as integration and participation of ethnic minorities in Dutch society is seen as the best way to fight racist sentiments. To this end in 1994 an Act to promote the participation of ethnic minorities on the labour market was adopted. Framed on a Canadian example it obliged employers to publish statistics on the share of workers from ethnic minority groups in their workforce and to take action in order to engage more workers from ethnic minorities. In 1998 this Act was replaced by a less stringent one, the Act on stimulating labour market participation of non-whites, which was revoked in 2004. What remained is a provision in the WCA, that the works council must promote the employment of minorities in the enterprise (*see* paragraph 393).

II. Sex Discrimination

93. Sex discrimination is forbidden under criminal law in the provision already mentioned (Article 429 *quater* Criminal Code). Moreover it is prohibited in the GAET as well as in the special AETMW and in Article 7:646 CC, all statutes that are also meant to implement the EU rules in this area.

Article 7:646 CC provides that an employer may not discriminate between men and women when entering into a contract of employment, providing training to an employee, fixing the terms and conditions of employment, granting promotion and giving notice of termination of the contract of employment. The AETMW extends the prohibition of unequal treatment m/f to the public civil service (Article 1(a) AETMW), to work done in another legal form than the contract of employment (Article 1(b) AETMW), to personnel recruitment (Article 3 AETMW), training (Article 4 AETMW) and the membership of trade unions, employers' associations and professional organizations (Article 4a AETMW). Moreover this act gives a more precise regulation of the equal pay m/w principle (Articles 7–12 AETMW, *see* paragraph 144) and applies the non-discrimination principle to the pension laws (Article 12a-b AETMW).

The AETMW prohibits both direct and indirect sex discrimination and qualifies unequal treatment based on pregnancy, confinement and motherhood as direct sex discrimination (Article 1(2)). However the law authorizes derogations from the equal treatment rule if it concerns stipulations relating to the protection of women, in particular in connection with pregnancy or motherhood (Article 7:646(3) CC). In fact, the Dutch legislators have abolished already several years ago most rules containing specific protection of women (such as a prohibition to work as stevedores in the ports and a prohibition to perform night work in various trades). This happened with the argument to ensure equal chances for women in the labour market. Nowadays only pregnant women and mothers during short periods after the confinement are protected by special provisions relating to their working hours (*see* paragraph 113) as well as a prohibition to dismiss (*see* paragraph 198).

The legislation on equal treatment for men and women forbids indirect discrimination as well, unless it can be justified on reasonable and objective grounds. This prohibition was often invoked to fight the unequal treatment of part-time workers, as they tended to be predominantly women. However, in 1996 a special provision (Article 7:648 CC) banned all unequal treatment of part-time workers unless objectively justified. In 2002 a new Article 7:649 CC did the same with respect to unequal treatment of workers on fixed-term contracts (*see* paragraph 100). A problem here is that young mothers still feel discriminated on the labour markets' fast-growing segment of the fixed-term contracts; they are often devoid of the prolongation of such contracts[91] (*see also* paragraph 230).

94. Moreover Dutch law explicitly allows stipulations intended to put female employees into a privileged position in order to end or reduce existing inequalities, provided they are reasonably proportionate to the intended object (Article 7:646(4) CC/Article 5(1) GAET). However, only in the public service and in subsidized organizations such as education and welfare work (about 15% of the Dutch labour market) a policy of priority of female employment is pursued, which sometimes goes as far as temporarily barring jobs for male applicants (for instance, at the Universities of Delft and Eindhoven).

In the Netherlands there is no quota legislation in favour of women on the labour market applicable, save for an Act of 2011 which mentions 30% as indicative ambition for women in top jobs (boards of directors and supervisory boards) to be reached in 2016 (Article 2:166 and 2:276 CC). By that time only the public sector had reached that target. In the private sector the figures stood at 15% women in supervisory boards and 11% women in the boards of directors. The Act is now prolonged until 2021.

Finally the concept of direct sex discrimination allows for four very strictly interpreted exceptions. There may be derogation from the prohibition of direct discrimination in such cases in which a distinction in the offering of a specific position may be made on the basis of a statutory provision and, to the extent that it concerns a public offering of the position, the basis for this distinction is explicitly made (Article 3(2) AETMW). There may be derogation from the prohibition of direct discrimination to the extent that it concerns the entry into the contract of employment and the provision of training in those cases where the different treatment is based on a characteristic connected with the gender and when such a characteristic, on the account of specific vocational activities or the context in which these are carried out, is an essential and decisive vocational condition, provided the object is legitimate and the conditions are proportionate to such object. However, this exception is only applicable to religious offices and activities mentioned in a governmental decree (Article 5(2-3) AETMW; Article 7:646(2) CC). There may be derogation from the prohibition of direct discrimination in matters of vocational training if this would conflict with the specific nature of an institution of special education, save for the examination and provided that there are comparable facilities for pupils of both sexes (Article 4(2) AETMW).

All these rules have highly contributed to the reduction of sex discrimination on the Dutch labour market. The Netherlands ranks number 1 on the list on Gender Equality 2014 of the UN; it ranks number 4 on the Gender Equality Index of the

91. Parliamentary Papers 29544, 30420, no 263 and 30950, no. 755.

European Institute for Gender Equality, although it ranks only 27 on the Global Gender Gap Index of the World Economic Forum.

III. Religion, Conviction and Political Opinion

95. Unequal treatment based on religion, conviction, and political opinions prohibited on the basis of the GAET and also the penal prohibition of discrimination covers the grounds of religion and conviction (Articles 137c, 137f and 429 *quater* Penal Code). Recent years have seen a rise in the number of cases in which the fundamental rights on freedom of and non- discrimination in matters of religion, conviction, political opinion as well as the right to privacy (*see* paragraph 106) had to be balanced against interests of employers on the non-expression of those attitudes at the workplace. For instance the claim of employees to wearing religious symbols during working time, the refusal of officials of municipalities to conclude same-sex marriages, etc. The last item has been outlawed by a recent amendment of the GAET (*see* paragraph 89). There is still an extra protection against dismissal which occurs for the simple reason that the employee has refused to perform his contracted work for grave reasons of conscience (*see* paragraph 198). In all these cases Dutch courts tend to scrupulously follow the case law of the European Court of Human Rights (*see* paragraph 107).

IV. Hetero- and Homosexual Orientation

96. The GAET also prohibits unequal treatment based on hetero- and homosexuality. In addition hetero- and homosexual orientation are covered by the prohibition of discrimination in criminal law (Articles 137c, 137f and 429 *quater* Penal Code). Today discrimination between hetero- and homosexual orientation has almost disappeared from the Dutch labour market. The most debated item left is the desire of some religious-based schools to refuse homosexual teachers. They invoke Article 5(2) GAET which has been deliberately inserted in the Act to accommodate this desire. However, the text of Article 5(2) GAET – being a political compromise – was ambiguous. It has been criticized by the European Commission. The text of this article has then been revised (*see* paragraph 89).[92]

V. Civil Status

97. Another form of discrimination prohibited in the GAET and other laws is equal treatment based on civil status. There are only a few cases on discrimination on civil status.[93] In one of them the HR prohibited unequal remuneration for the same work between married and unmarried persons.[94]

92. Act of 21 May 2015, Stb. 2015, 200; Parliamentary Papers no. 32476.
93. Dutch Supreme Court, 7 May 1993, JAR 1993/156.
94. Dutch Supreme Court, 30 Sep. 1994, JAR 1994/233.

VI. Handicapped Persons

98. In 2003 the AETHCI was adopted. The Act gives the same definitions of the concepts of distinction (discrimination), direct distinction (discrimination) and indirect (distinction) as the GAET, but it does not provide for definitions of the concepts of 'handicap' and 'chronic illness'. In this respect the case law of the CJEU may provide guidance as the AETHCI was meant to implement EU Directive 2000/78/EC.

The Act mentions three exceptions on the prohibition of direct discrimination. The first and the second are about cases that a distinction is necessary for the protection of health and safety or concern a regulation, norm or practice aimed at the creation or maintenance of specific facilities on behalf of the handicapped and the chronically ill person. The third one is that affirmative action (positive action/ positive discrimination) of handicapped and chronically ill persons is allowed provided it is in reasonable proportion to the intended object (Article 3 AETHCI). Even more: the Act provides that the prohibition of distinction also implies, that those addressed by this prohibition must make effective adaptations according to the needs, unless this would be for them a disproportionate onus (Article 2 AETHCI). Moreover the discrimination of handicapped and chronically ill persons has been made a criminal offence (Article 137c, 137f and Article 429 *quater* Penal Code).

Various other measures (*see* paragraphs 198 et seq.) have made it difficult for employers to fire handicapped and chronically ill employees, but once such employees have made redundant it is very difficult for them the find a new job. The works council must promote the employment of disabled persons in the enterprise (*see* paragraph 393).

On the protection of equal pay for handicapped workers *see* paragraph 145. On affirmative action in favour of handicapped persons *see* paragraph 248.

VII. Age

99. In 2003 the AETAW was adopted by Parliament, implementing EU Directive 2000/78/EC. However, the prohibition of age discrimination is not applicable:

- if the distinction is based on statutory labour market policies to enhance the labour market participation of distinctive age categories;
- if it concerns the termination of an employment relationship at reaching the age that entitles to the reception of pensions of the AOW or a higher age fixed by law or by mutual agreement;
- if it is objectively justified by a legitimate ambition and the means to reach that aim are suitable and necessary (Article 7 AETAW);
- on various aspects of the regulations regarding occupational pensions (Article 8 AETAW).

Especially the second and the third exception have given rise to quite a number of actual legal problems. The main problem is the automatic dismissal of people reaching the retirement age (*see* paragraph 231).

Another question is about specific measures favouring the continued employment of elderly workers, for instance extra paid holidays, a shorter working week and by liberating them from performing night work or shift work, etc. They appeared in the collective agreements in the Netherlands in the 1990s to relieve the burden of work on elderly workers, but have become suspect under the rules on age discrimination. Dutch case law does not completely prohibit such measures, but has put severe conditions to them. It is *inter alia* required that such measures must be part of a life-phase-conscious human resources policy. The courts are only prepared to allow these kinds of clauses if their necessity and proportionality are shown. As this is not easy this type of provision is now increasingly deleted from the collective agreements. More resistant are clauses on more convenient working schedules for older workers. The percentage of workers enjoying them even increased from 70% in 2006 to 73% in 2010.[95]

Further questions about the compatibility with the prohibition of age discrimination concern the increments according to age in wage scales and severance pay, the priority for the younger employees to be made redundant in collective dismissals (*see* paragraphs 224 et seq.), etc.

Age discrimination is still one of the most applied aspects of discrimination on the Dutch labour market. The actual government is committed to attack it more forcefully.[96]

VIII. Equal Treatment Full-Time/Part-Time, Fixed-Term/Open-Ended Contracts and Telework

100. Implementing EU rules the Dutch CC forbids the making of a distinction (discrimination) in the conditions of employment between employees on the basis of a difference in working period, in other words: discrimination of part-timers (Article 7:648 CC; *see also* paragraph 119). This article forbids employers to discriminate between employees on the basis of a difference in working hours in the conditions under which those employees enter, extend or terminate a contract, unless there is objective justification for such discrimination. Clauses that conflict with this ban are void. If the employer terminates the contract in contravention of the ban or terminates it because the employee has invoked this ban, the termination is subject to annulment. The same ban also applies to government employers (Article 125 Civil Servants Act).

Equally forbidden is different treatment on the ground of the temporary or non-temporary nature of the contract of employment (Article 7:649 CC). This concerns the differences between fixed-term and open-ended contracts. Research has shown that the realities in the Netherlands are different. Employees with fixed-term contracts earn 2%–7% less than those in open-ended contracts.

Also a different treatment of teleworkers is forbidden (*see* paragraph 70).

95. Antoine T.J.M. Jacobs, *Active Aging and Labour Law in the Netherlands*, in *Active Aging and Labour Law* 263–273 (F. Hendrickx ed., Intersentia: Antwerp, 2012).

96. Parliamentary Papers 30950 nos 140 and 142.

All three last-mentioned prohibitions, however, do not apply where there are objective reasons justifying such different treatment (*see* paragraph 88).

IX. Other Discrimination

101. Obviously other grounds of different treatment may occur. Traditionally employers operate many distinctions between their employees in matters of recruitment, remuneration, the contents of the jobs, granting promotion, etc. They may base such distinctions on the capacities, suitability experience, level of training, etc., but also by taking into account somebodies appearance, criminal or psychiatric record, etc. Are such differences in treatment equally prohibited unless they can be objectively justified?

Discrimination and unequal treatment based on other grounds than those mentioned under the subtitles I–VIII can be contested referring to Article 1 of the Dutch Constitution and/or Article 26 of the International Covenant on Civil and Political Rights which both are using a text, that makes the enumeration of grounds of discrimination open-ended. The Dutch courts may fetch these norms in the application of the law on contracts of employment by basing them on the bona fides principle (Article 7:611 CC, *see* paragraph 102). This purpose can also be served by anti-discrimination clauses in collective agreements which sometimes embrace more grounds than those enumerated in the subtitles I–VIII.

However, the HR is not inclined to do away with all types of unequal treatment. It has held that the general principle of equal treatment is not an overriding principle; other circumstances must be taken into account in balancing whether the employer acted contrary to Article 7:611 CC. Only when an agreed unequal pay is unacceptable judged to the tests of reasonableness and fairness, it must be adapted. This restraint by the courts is notably to be applied if unequal treatment is prescribed by a collective agreement with a trade union because in that case the principle of freedom of collective bargaining is at stake.[97]

§4. The Bona Fides Principle and the Fundamental Rights

102. One of the most interesting items of Dutch labour law is a general clause providing that the employer and the employee are obliged to act as a good employer and a good employee (Article 7:611 CC). The case law of the HR has established that this is a mere translation of the general principle of bona fides in contractual relationships, laid down in Article 6:2 and 6:248 Dutch CC.[98] In all Western nations similar general principles exist, but they normally have only a limited impact. They are predominantly used to perform *Einzelfallgerechtigkeit* (justice in very specific cases). However, in the Netherlands this principle is exploited to the full by lawyers.

97. Dutch Supreme Court, 30 Jan. 2004, ILLR Vol. 24, p. 215; JAR 2004/68 (*Parallel Entry/KLM*).
98. Dutch Supreme Court, 5 Mar. 1999, JAR 1999, 74; Dutch Supreme Court, 30 Jan. 2004, RvdW 2004, 26 and Dutch Supreme Court, 1 Jul. 1993, NJ 1993, 667; JAR 1993/195.

The idea of the 'good employer' and the 'good employee' are two sides of the same coin. When a worker in court is challenging the decision of his employer to send him to a different working place, his lawyer may argue that a good employer should refrain from doing so. On the other hand the council for the employer may argue that a good employee should not disobey such an order.

103. In case law this provision is often invoked as a basis for claims (or to resist claims!) which cannot be based on more specific rights and obligations laid down in the various labour law statutes. See, for instance:

- the issue of unilateral alteration of working conditions (*see* paragraph 173);
- the question of whether the worker is obliged to perform overtime (*see* paragraph 117) and the remuneration of overtime (*see* paragraph 130);
- the issue of disciplinary sanctions (other than dismissals, *see* paragraphs 182 et seq.);
- a right of the worker to be effectively provided with work by his or her employer (*see* paragraph 85);
- moonlighting (*see* paragraph 177).

Sometimes this Article 7:611 CC has been used by the courts to introduce innovations in labour law, which subsequently have been turned into statutory law, such as:

- the liability for damages by errors of the employee (*see* paragraph 175);
- a right of partially disabled workers on adapted working conditions or alternative work (*see* paragraphs 85 and 173);
- a right of employees to have their full-time contract on employment converted into a part-time job (*see* paragraph 119);
- a right to vocational training (*see* paragraph 86);
- the protection of trade secrets and the position of the whistle-blower (*see* paragraph 82/83/105).

However, time and again the courts make new case law innovations, which have not yet been turned into statutory law, such as, for instance:

- the recognition of the liability of the employer for health and safety of the workers outside the premises of the employer (*see* paragraph 158);
- a right to have gratuities not discontinued abruptly (*see* paragraph 129);
- the right to equal treatment on grounds not explicitly mentioned in statutes (*see* paragraph 101);
- the continuation of the payment of wages in case of situational illness (*see* paragraph 151);
- the validity of clauses on the restitution of continued wage payments during the time that the employee followed training (*see* paragraph 170).

The Dutch courts, in general, will be prudent in using the good employer/good employee principle to introduce innovations in Dutch labour law. However, they will use this power if they can base those innovations on important, although not yet binding, sources of labour law. In that way this general bona fides clause is being used by the judges to apply fundamental rights (such as the right on privacy protection, *see* paragraph 105)[99] or provisions of international treaties and its (quasi) case law (*see* paragraph 22) or cross-industry agreements of the Dutch social partners (*see* paragraphs 26 and 291) and to give civil law effect to public law standards in the field of health and safety, for example on sexual and psychological harassment (*see* paragraph 164).

The courts have been hesitant to use the bona fides principle of Article 7:611 CC in the field of wages, as there is the minimum wage legislation (*see* paragraph 137). The same in the field of the law on dismissals, because the general feeling is that the Dutch law on dismissals contains enough protection for workers and that there is no additional function for the bona fides principle in this part of the law. Nevertheless some Article 7:611 CC protection has been offered in the case of trial clauses (*see* paragraph 221) and other dismissal items (*see* paragraph 201).

104. This pro-employee exploitation of the bona fides clauses receives some counterweight in the case law of the HR, in which this court has emphasized the pro-employer consequences of this principle, most notably the obligation of partially disabled workers to accept an adaptation of working conditions[100] – these court rulings too were subsequently turned into statutory law (*see* paragraph 80). In the field of the law of civil servants, where a similar provision reigns (Article 125 *ter* Civil Service Act), this principle has been used by the courts to impose integrity (no financial conflicts of interest) and reticence as to moonlighting (*see* paragraph 177).

It is clear, that the extensive application of the bona fides clause has made Dutch labour law highly flexible and innovative, but also somewhat unpredictable. Therefore the role of this principle is one of the most debated issues among Dutch labour law scholars.

Although Dutch courts are competent to apply the good employer principle to the full, the HR has ruled that they must take into account the margin of appreciation that is due to the employer in view of the nature of his enterprise and its activities, to organize and arrange its operations.[101]

For this reason the courts prefer to limit their interventions to procedural tests. Did the employer hear both sides, make a careful balancing of the interests of the employee and give a motivation for his decision?[102] So the 'good employer' principle has notably been used to impose a more social and democratic way of decision-making on the employers. Some scholars have tried to develop this by outlining 'principles of behaviour for good employers', emphasizing the contract of employment as a mutual relationship. From both the employer and the employee it

99. O. Cherednychenko, *Fundamental Rights, Contract Law and the Protection of the Weaker Party* (2007).

100. Dutch Supreme Court, 26 Jun. 1998, JAR 1998/199 (*Lely/Taxi Hofman*); Dutch Supreme Court, 28 Apr. 2000, JAR 2000/120.

101. Dutch Supreme Court, 1 Jul. 1993, NJ 1993, 667, JAR 1993/195.

102. Dutch Supreme Court, 6 Apr. 1979, NJ 1979/492; Dutch Supreme Court, September 1980, NJ 1981/131 and Dutch Supreme Court, 13 Mar. 1981, NJ 1981/513.

may be expected that they take into account the justified expectations that each side may have from the other. Therefore the principle of the good employee is also used to encourage the employee to civilized behaviour, carefully respecting the interests of his employer, his colleagues and the clients of the company.

105. The use of the bona fides principle to make penetrate fundamental social rights in individual employment situations is very noticeable in the field of the law on the right to free speech in the employment relationship. The right to free speech has been recognized as a fundamental right in the Dutch Constitution (Article 7), in the European Convention on Human Rights (Article 10), in the UN Covenant on Civil and Political Rights (Article 19) and in the Charter of Fundamental Rights of the EU (Article 11). This right may be especially invoked by employees confronted with trade secrets (*see* paragraph 73) and those who have behaved as whistle-blowers (*see* paragraph 83).

106. Moreover, the use of the bona fides principle to make penetrate fundamental social rights in individual employment situations is noticeable in the field of the law on the freedom of religion and conscience in the employment relationship. The right to freedom of religion and conscience has been recognized as a fundamental right in the Dutch Constitution (Article 6), in the European Convention on Human Rights (Article 9), in the UN Covenant on Civil and Political Rights (Article 18). This right is often invoked by workers who want to wear religious symbols or who oppose performing certain tasks as being contrary to their beliefs (*see* paragraphs 95 and 198). But it was not strong enough to stop the legislator in denying municipal civil servants the right to invoke their religion or conscience contrary to anti-discrimination law (Article 5(2(d) GAET)) (*see* paragraph 89).

For other fundamental rights such as the right to work and the freedom of work *see* paragraph 85.

§5. Privacy in the Employment Relationship

107. The use of the bona fides principle to make penetrate fundamental social rights in individual employment situations is very noticeable in the field of the law on privacy. The right to privacy has been recognized as a fundamental social right in the Dutch Constitution (Article 10), in the European Convention on Human Rights (Article 8), in the UN Covenant on Civil and Political Rights (Article 17), in the EU Charter of Fundamental Rights (Article 8), etc. As there is not much specific statutory law in this field in the Netherlands, the courts are taken advantage of Article 7:611 CC to adjudicate cases about questions such as whether the employer is entitled to control his employees by way of computer systems[103] and open camera surveillance,[104] to subject them to alcohol and drugs-tests,[105] to private enquiries

103. Court of Appeal of ‘s-Hertogenbosch, 2 Jul. 1987, NJ 1987, 451.
104. Central Court of Appeal (Social Security), 10 Jul. 2008, TAR 2008/9, p. 537.
105. Dutch Supreme Court, 14 Sep. 2007, JAR 2007/250. Actually there are some doubts whether these tests can still be applied under the GDPR.

into their behaviour inside- or outside work, to enquire their private use of his Internet/email in work time, to visit the weblogs of his employees, to issue rules on the lifestyle of his employees in general and on cloth, hair-dress, tattoos, etc. in particular. In these last cases, employees are also often invoking the fundamental right on equal treatment (*see* paragraphs 87 et seq.) and respect of their personality as well as the right to freedom of religion and conscience (*see* paragraphs 95 and 107).

From this case law it can be inferred that Dutch employers must be careful with interference with the privacy of their employees. This does not mean that the employee's right on privacy vis-à-vis the employer is absolute. It will always be balanced against the serious interests of the employer and the public, such as security, business secrets and the image of the firm. In all those questions in the Netherlands, a very important factor is whether the employer has informed the works council about these infringements on the privacy of the workers and whether the works council (or the court) has given its endorsement to it. Indeed, up until now Parliament has preferred a decentralized canalization of the phenomenon of privacy: under the WCA company arrangements in the area of privacy have been made subject to the consent of the works council (*see* paragraph 391).

Only in a few items has Parliament taken the lead by issuing specific rules. There has been an Act on the Protection of Personal Data, implementing EU Directive 95/46, which ensured the privacy of the personal files of the workers in the Human Resources Management (HRM) departments. The employer needed the unequivocal consent of the worker for the handling of his personal data. This Act was revoked in 2018 to give way to the General Data Protection Regulation – *Algemene Verordening Gegevensbescherming* (GDPR) of the EU. This regulation is applicable to any structured set of personnel data which are accessible to third persons. Obviously the employment relationship provides a basis for data processing notably in the area of Human Relations Management, where recruitment and selection and the payroll administration are done. Moreover everywhere the employer exercises his right of authority and control when directing the enterprise and planning the work, where health and safety rules are implemented, contracts of employment are renewed or terminated, etc. All this is certainly a legitimate basis for data processing, but the links with the legitimate purpose must be able to be identified and shown to be necessary and proportionate (Articles 5 and 6 GDPR). All persons that work on and for the enterprise whose data are processed there have the right to a fair and transparent data processing; they have the right to access to their personal data and to have them rectified if needed (Article 8). However, if disputed, these rights can be balanced against other fundamental rights in accordance with the principle of proportionality (preamble no. 4 GDPR).

In the Netherlands, the GDPR is implemented by the Act on the Implementation of the GDPR.[106] It has created and charged the *Autoriteit Persoonsgegevens* with the tasks to enforce the GDPR and to advise the government and inform the public on the implementation of these rules.

106. Act of 16 May 2018, Stb. 2018, 144.

In addition there is a prohibition in Criminal Law on secret camera surveillance (Articles 139f and 441b Criminal Code), while the Medical Examinations Act restricts the possibility of employers to require medical examinations from their employees (*see* paragraph 108).

§6. Duties During the Process of Application for Jobs

108. From the aforementioned it may be inferred that in the Netherlands the duties of employers and employees do not start with the entering into a contract of employment. They start already in the phase in which employers announce their vacancies and workers are applying for the job. What then are the duties and obligations of the parties in this phase? As statutory law is hardly dealing with this matter, the guiding principles must be found in the rules about the rights and obligations of negotiating parties on contracts in general. The HR has ruled that in this phase of negotiation the parties must determine their behaviour not only by their own interests but also taking into account the justified interest of the other party.[107] Another rule of thumb is that the more the negotiations on the conclusion of a contract have progressed the less free the parties are to renounce of the conclusion of a contract without becoming liable to damages. In assessing this, a relevant factor may be whether the worker has already been tempted to give up another position. Still, judges will be very reluctant to intervene with the basic freedom of the parties to conclude or to refrain from concluding a contract of employment. A rupture of the negotiations must be truly 'unacceptable' to hold the breaking party liable. Court procedures can be brought on the basis of a tort (Article 6:162 CC) if no contract has been concluded, or on the basis of Article 6:74 CC, if the worker alleges that in fact a contract has been concluded on the basis of vitiated consent.[108] Dutch courts are not very eager to invoke the nullity of the contract based on the notions of error and coercion. As such court procedures are very rare in the Netherlands it is not completely clear what remedies are possible. Presumably damages, but the amount of the damages is not easy to indicate. An order to effectively engage a worker is improbable.[109] In the law of the civil servants courts would only test marginally the decision not to engage a person.[110] Has the contract of employment effectively been concluded and one of the parties still wants to withdraw, this can only be done by termination the contract according to the normal rules of terminating contracts of employment (*see* paragraphs 197 et seq.). If it appears after the conclusion of a contract of employment that during the negotiations the other party has shown reprehensible behaviour, for instance concealing facts that are relevant for the function, then this may give rise to a termination of the contract following the normal rules of termination contracts of employment. During the process of negotiating a contract of employment the employer may only put questions to the applicant which are relevant for the job. If the questions are relevant the applicant must answer them

107. Dutch Supreme Court, 12 Aug. 2005, NJ 2005, 467.
108. Dutch Supreme Court, 23 Nov. 1979, NJ 1980, 228.
109. Dutch Supreme Court, 25 Jan. 1985, NJ 1985, 559.
110. Central Court of Appeal, 8 Mar. 2001, TAR 2001/159.

according to the truth. If the questions are not relevant to the job the worker may lie or leave the question unanswered. This means, for instance, that the worker may stay tacit about health problems which are not relevant for the job. He must, however, spontaneously mention those illnesses of which he knows or should have known that they make him unfit for the job he applied too.[111] And he surely is not allowed to provide false information about it (Article 7:629(3)(a) CC). To openly or covertly ask the worker about pregnancy or 'family plans' is normally not allowed, considering the principle of equal treatment of men and women (*see* paragraph 93). More generally speaking an application procedure should intervene as least as possible with the fundamental right of privacy (*see* paragraph 105). This applies for instance on practices like employment screening. The possibility of employers using the Internet to obtain information about applicants is now also emerging as a problem. One may say that this is not allowed, but how to prevent it?

The Medical Examinations Act provides that within the framework of a selection procedure submission to a medical examination is only allowed if specific requirements to the health condition of a worker are indispensable. The Act gives detailed provisions on the various aspects of the medical examination and the rights of the examinee.

Attempts to further determine the duties of the employers during selection procedures have not led to more statutory provisions. They have, however, incited the social partners at all-industry level, united in the *Stichting van de Arbeid*, to issue Recommendations to the social partners in sectors and companies to lay down the rights and duties of the employers during the selection process in the collective agreements. In various collective agreements this is followed, often by referring to or quoting the norms which are contained in the Selection Code, drawn up by the Dutch Association of HRM. The employer who offers a job often can choose between several applicants. He is bound to select the person most competent seeing training, experience, etc. This is fully acceptable as long as the employer omits bias against certain categories as women, disabled persons, foreigners, etc. otherwise he will violate the strict rules on equal treatment (*see* paragraphs 87 et seq.). Some people advocate anonymous applications to avoid discriminatory behaviour.

§7. Duties at the End of the Contract of Employment

109. Article 7:656 CC stipulates that the employer is obliged to issue the employee, at his request, with a testimonial at the end of the contract of employment.

This testimonial has to contain a description of the job performed and the length of the employment relationship. It must also contain – but only if the worker asks for it explicitly – a statement on the way he or she has performed his duties, how the contract was ended and the reasons for terminating the contract if the employer has terminated the contract. If the employee has terminated the contract, and, as a result, has to pay a compensation to the employer, the employer is entitled to mention this in the testimonial.

111. Court of Appeal of Arnhem, 9 Nov. 2004, JAR 2005/81.

The employer is liable for damages if he does not issue a testimonial or its content is incorrect.

Moreover the employer must issue a declaration mentioning the number of paid holidays that the employee has not taken up (Article 7:641(2), CC (*see* paragraphs 120 et seq.)). About further duties of the employee at the end of the contract of employment *see* paragraphs 166 et seq. on covenants of non-competition.

Chapter 3. Working Time

§1. Limitation of Working Time

I. Statutory Regulation

110. Statutory rules on working hours are laid down in the WTA of 1996 (as amended in 2007), which replaced the Factories Act of 1919. That Act had been the fruit of the social turmoil in Europe by the end of World War I and was the realization of the ambitions of the worker movement for the eight-hour working day and a 45-hour working week. After a few years, when the revolutionary waves had calmed down, this was changed into a maximum of 8.5 hours a day and 48 hours a week in a working week of 5.5 days. This legislation also prohibited night work and shift work by women in factories. The prohibition of night work was repealed in two stages in 1986 and 1989, and this was one of the aspects which showed that the Act of 1919 was no longer in line with modern concepts. New legislation was also desired to reconcile employer calls for greater flexibility, with demands from trade unions and other groups for measures to ensure a better work-life balance for employees.

The advice of the Dutch SER of 1993 called for a more varied pattern of working hours, shorter working hours combined with extended business hours in response to the changing economic environment. At the level of the EU a Directive on the Organization of Working Time was launched in 1994.

111. All these developments prompted the Dutch lawmakers to review their 1919 legislation. Subsequently the new WTA was adopted in 1996. It implemented the EU Directive on the Organization of Working Time and gave way to the need for greater flexibility, both in terms of allowing companies to tailor working time to their own individual needs, and in terms of increasing company operating time, including work at nights and weekends. Greater flexibility would also, it was argued, help create employment.

The 1996 legislation maintained the idea of statutory regulation of certain maxima and minima as regards working day, working week, daily rest, weekly rest, overtime, etc. However, less emphasis was laid on the maximum per day than on the maximum per week/month/quarter. The latter had been reduced as compared to the Act of 1919 whereas the former has been prolonged. Until 1996 workers were allowed to work 8.5 hours a day; since that time they could be required to work 9 hours a day. To this 2 hours a day of overtime could be added as this could be required by the employer without authorization, which would bring the maximum including overtime to 11 hours a day, 54 hours a week, but all this should not exceed an average of 45 hours in a quarter of a year.

Another element of flexibility in the 1996-legislation was that it provided both a basic set of norms – the 'standard regulation' – that applied if no derogations were agreed upon, and an ultimate set of limits – the 'consultation regulation'. This consultation regulation required a collective agreement or other form of collective bargaining process with employees' representatives. Under this last formula one must think primarily of written agreements with the works council (*see* paragraph 391), but some other forms could be used as well. Any deviation from the norms contained in the standard regulation should not, however, exceed the ultimate limits laid down in the statute. If it was necessary to go beyond this ultimate limit the Labour Inspectorate could give special permits. For example, the maximum working day (overtime included), laid down in the WTA, was eleven hours. Yet, in a 'consultation regulation' parties could push this level up to maximum twelve hours. If a further extension was desired this was only possible on the basis of a permit from the Labour Inspectorate.

After a number of years, there was much disgruntlement among employers and economists about the 1996-legislation. In 2004 the Minister and the majority of Parliament were inclined to retrench the provisions of the WTA by reducing the various levels of protection to the minimum standards required by the EU Directive. This was strongly opposed by the trade unions which feared that the reduced protection would cause more stress and work accidents. However, in 2005 in the Social and Economic Council they forged a compromise with the employers laying the new level of protection somewhat halfway the EU minima and the level of the 1996-legislation. This was then followed in the Amendment Act of 2007, which had the purpose to bring additional flexibility in the statutory rules in order to promote the competitiveness of Dutch enterprises.

112. In its current text the Working Times Act contains a ceiling on the number of working hours a day: the maximum is laid at twelve hours a day and sixty hours a week. The average working time should not exceed fifty-five hours in a four weeks reference period and forty-eight hours in a sixteen weeks reference period (Article 5:7 WTA), but this is subject to deviations by way of a 'collective regulation' (Table 13).

Table 13 Statutory Maximum Working Hours per Day and per Week

	Daily	*Weekly*
France	10	35
Germany	8	48
The Netherlands	12	48
UK	13	48

In addition it is provided that there should be an uninterrupted daily period of rest of at least eleven hours within a consecutive period of twenty-four hours. Once a week this daily rest period may be shortened to eight hours if the work requires so (Article 5:3(2) WTA).

The Act requires a weekly uninterrupted period of rest of either at least 36 hours in a consecutive period of 7 × 24 hours or at least 72 hours in a consecutive period of 14 × 24 hours (Article 5:5 WTA). Moreover the Act now entitles the worker to a pause of 30 minutes as soon as he has worked 5.5 hours and a pause of 45 minutes as soon as he has worked 10 hours (Article 5:4 WTA). However, these pauses may be shortened by way of a 'collective regulation'.

The WTA has lifted many old restrictions on work during the evening, the night and the early morning hours. The employer is free to require from his workers the performance of night work (work between 12.00 pm and 6.00 am), unless it appears from a medical examination that night work is causing health problems to the employee, but this restriction only applies 'as far as this reasonably can be required from the employer' (Article 4:9 WTA). A night shift may not last longer than ten hours. For workers frequently performing night shifts the average working week in a reference period of sixteen weeks should not exceed forty hours. Also the daily rest period is longer (at least fourteen hours) after the performance of a night shift, which stops after 2.00 am. Finally the Act offers a restriction on the number of night shifts performed consecutively or within a certain period (Article 5:8 WTA), but it refrains from ordering compensation in time or salary for the performance of night work as ILO Convention no. 171 requires, which is one of the main reasons for the Netherlands not to ratify this Convention. From some of the rules on night work it can be deviated by way of a 'collective regulation'. For specific situations the employer may request the Minister of Social Affairs to grant a permit (Article 5:14 WTA). It is questionable whether these rules are sufficient to limit the negative effect that night work may have on the health of the workers. Actually ca. 15% of the workers in the Netherlands are sometimes or frequently performing night work.

Sunday working was subject to a general prohibition under the regime of the 1919 Act (except in sectors where it is unavoidable, such as healthcare and public transport). Under the WTA, especially since an Amendment Act of 2004, things are regulated a bit more nuanced. In principle it is now stated that the employer must organize the work such that the employee does not need to perform work on Sunday unless this is needed by the nature of the work and agreed with the employee. If the nature of the work so requires and the worker has agreed to that (mostly by entering the job), he cannot refuse to work on Sunday. This is the case in a limited number of sectors, such as public transport. In all other sectors derogation of the prohibition of Sunday is possible if business reasons necessitate so and consent is obtained from the works council or, in its absence, from the workers concerned. Nevertheless the employee must also personally give his consent. In these sectors the employee has the right to refuse to work on Sunday for whatever reason (church, sport, etc.) and he is protected by a prohibition to dismiss him because of a refusal (*see* paragraph 198). Moreover, even if the worker can be required to work on Sunday, the employer must free him from Sunday work on at least thirteen Sundays a year, but this condition may be waived by a 'collective regulation' (Article 5:6 WTA). These provisions must be applied *mutatis mutandis* to another day than Sunday for workers who because of religious or conscience reason celebrate the weekly day of rest on another day and have requested so to the employer in writing (Article 5:1 WTA).

Finally the WTA regulates the so-called on-call time (*bereikbaarheidsdiensten, aanwezigheidsdiensten, wachtdiensten* or *consignatie*) – a heated subject because of the case law of the CJEU in the cases of *Simap, Jaeger* and the like. The WTA defines on-call time as the period between two successive periods of work or during rest periods, in which the employee is only obliged to be within easy reach in order to perform the convened work on call in unforeseen circumstances (Article 1:7g

WTA). The Act then contains a number of limitations on the right of the employer to require on-call time of its employees (Article 5:9 WTA), but is silent about the remuneration of on-call time.

113. By way of a general provision the WTA urges the employer to develop his policy with regard to working time in connection with his policy on health and safety. More specifically, since the Amendment Act of 2004, it is provided that employers are obliged, in determining working hours and patterns, to consider the personal circumstances of workers, such as child care and other family and social responsibilities (Article 4:1 and 4:1a WTA). After having fixed a clear policy on working time and working patterns the employer should duly communicate them to the employees concerned (Article 4:2 WTA). These are pious statements but if the interests of the worker cannot be reconciled with those of the employer, in practice the employer will prevail.

The WTA does not contain any differentiation in norms between men and women. Only a few specific rules for pregnant workers and young mothers have been maintained.[112] During the entire period of the pregnancy and six months after the delivery the employer must organize the work of women in such a way that the specific circumstances of the women are taken into account. This means *inter alia* more pauses, stable working patterns, a stronger limitation on working hours, no obligation to perform night work, etc. (Article 4:5 and 4:7 WTA). The employer is not allowed to have any work performed at all by women during twenty-eight days before the presumable date of delivery and within forty-two days thereafter (Article 4:6 WTA). During the first nine months after delivery the woman must be enabled to nurse the child without loss of pay (Article 4:8 WTA).

(For the special rules on working times for children and young persons, *see* paragraphs 76–77).

114. The WTA is applicable to the territory of the Netherlands and its continental shelf as well as on workers in air, rail, road and sea transport working for Dutch employers (Article 2:8 WTA). It covers nearly all sectors of economic activities in the Netherlands. It is also applicable to the civil service. Many sectors such as, for instance, the police and ambulance drivers are complaining that they are unable to comply with the WTA rules because of financial constraints or shortage of specialized staff.

All sorts of employment relationships are covered by the Act as long as work is done 'under authority' (Article 1:1(2) WTA). So, for instance, also trainees are covered. Only independent persons are excluded, safe for some categories indicated in a decree, such as road haulage, which also covers the independent drivers (Article 2:7 WTA). In temporary agency work the responsibility for applying the WTA rules rests on the hiring company (Article 1:1(a)(2) WTA).

The Act is not applicable in case of a catastrophe (Article 2:2 WTA), on students' work at school (Article 2:3 WTA) and on certain activities of the military (Article

112. *See* M. Monster, *Bescherming van moederschap*, Nijmegen, 1995; on pp. 357–363 one finds an English-language description and discussion of the employment and social security laws concerning pregnancy and maternity in Dutch law.

2:4) and the police (Article 2:5 WTA). The Act authorizes the government to make further exceptions (Articles 2:1 and 5:12 WTA), which for instance have been made for road transport (Article 5:12(2) WTA). Here the Dutch rules had to be brought in line with the EU rules that put a maximum of forty-eight hours on the weekly working time. Many Dutch transport workers used to work considerably longer and with that earned a fair wage.

Besides all this, specific rules are applicable for shops, inland shipping and the merchant marine.

115. Further details and exceptions of the working hours rules are laid down in the Working Time Order (*Arbeidstijdenbesluit*) which specifies, *inter alia*, that most working hours regulations do not apply to employees with a salary exceeding about EUR 55,000 a year if these employees do not perform night work and dangerous work.

As had been said before the employer may in a number of cases deviate from the mandatory rules of the WTA if this is based on a 'collective regulation', concluded with either the trade union, the works council or the employee representative body – *personeelsvertegenwoordiging* (ERB) (Article 1:3 to Article 1:6 WTA) (*see* paragraph 371). However, a regulation with the trade unions prevails (Article 1:4(2) WTA).

In this respect it must be borne in mind that the WCA had given the works councils powers to control the fixation of working hours schedules (*see* paragraph 391). This stimulated a culture of discussing the pattern of working hours between employers and works councils, at least in the larger enterprises.

In most other cases the Inspection SZW retains the monitoring role and is responsible for acting if it judges that the rules in the WTA have been breached (Article 8 WTA). The WTA provides for fines for companies violating the Act (Article 11:3 WTA). Until 2004 those fines could only be imposed by a criminal proceeding, and the public prosecutors have not been keen to engage in such proceedings. Since 2004 the WTA enables the imposition of fines via administrative law proceedings, which are more easily brought (Article 10:1 WTA). Criminal proceedings are now reserved for repeated violations of the Act or for violation of an order of the Inspection SZW to halt the activities. The Act does not contain any explicit action for the individual worker to enforce his rights under the WTA, but courts may enforce them in actions based on the bona fides requirement in the individual contract of employment (*see* paragraph 102). For instance, the HR once held that an order of an employer to perform work contrary to the provisions of the WTA is not a reasonable order and may be disregarded.[113]

Also trade unions and works councils are now involved in monitoring and controlling the working time rules in practice. Under the 1919 legislation the government had full control over many aspects of working time, either directly or through the Labour Inspectorate. Deviations from the statutory working time limits had to be authorized by the Labour Inspectorate, which was also solely responsible for

113. Dutch Supreme Court, 27 Jan. 1995, JAR 1995/50.

enforcing the law. Since the WTA 1996 the trade unions and the works councils are supposed to take over a substantial part of this authorization, monitoring and enforcement function.

The Dutch trade unions are complaining that too much structural overtime is worked in the Netherlands. And indeed, an evaluating study in 2002 found that 10% of employees were exceeding the WTA norms on working hours. In two-fifths of the cases this was because their employer was not respecting the WTA. With the relaxation of the WTA in 2007 this presumably has changed. The application of the WTA is nowadays complicated by the fact that several workers have two contracts of employment at the same time (*see* paragraph 177) or are combining the work in a contract of employment with the performance of freelance work.

II. Working Hours in Collective Agreements

116. The ambition of the WTA is only to give maximum and minimum norms in order to protect the well-being of the workers and to enable them to combine work and family/care responsibilities. However – and this is notably different from the law in France – in the Netherlands the effective working hours (also in relation with pay) are not regulated by statute, but by collective agreements, covering some 80% of all workers. Collective agreements normally lay down a considerably lower 'standard' working time as a means of calculating the standard wage.

Since the 1960s collective agreements have made a forty-hour working week and a free weekend normal practice for the vast majority of Dutch workers. Since 1979 the unions have tried to reduce the weekly working hours even further. The unions saw their claims for a reduction in working time as a major weapon in the fight against rising unemployment. Cutting down on working hours, so they argued, would result in work for more people.

At the end of 1982 employers and trade unions in the *Stichting van de Arbeid* (Foundation of Labour) concluded a central agreement on forms of work-sharing, mainly through the reduction of working hours – *Arbeidsduurverkorting* (ADV) (the Wassenaar Agreement). The 1982 general reduction in working time by 5% from forty hours to thirty-eight hours per week was in most sectors of the economy compensated for by the abolition of the automatic wage indexation. Moreover, working time reductions were combined with increased flexibility in working hours, facilitating work at irregular hours and variable working time. Flexibility has been the major quid pro quo required and obtained by employers for working time reduction without equivalent wage reduction.

In the 1990s a further reduction of the standard working time to thirty-six hours a week was realized in a number of sectors of the economy. So the average standard working week in the Netherlands went down from about forty hours in 1980 to about thirty-seven hours in 2003. Sometimes the working time reduction had the aim of absorbing decreasing employment, as in the case of the banking sector. In other cases the strategy was more offensive, aimed at increasing jobs and strengthening the competitive position.

In many collective agreements this shortening of the working week has been realized in exchange for flexibility as far as the effective determination of working hours is concerned. A number of collective agreements provide for an average working time, allowing the employer, while maintaining full pay, to vary the working week according to business needs. An example is a collective agreement, which fixes the average working week at thirty-six hours, but allows variations between thirty and forty hours and requires work during the evenings, in the weekends, etc. without this being remunerated with extra pay. In recent years the reference period for the calculation of working hours has sometimes been extended to a yearly basis. However, the employer cannot unilaterally fix such working hours patterns. Most of the times he needs the consent of the works council (*see* paragraph 391) or of the individual employee (*see* paragraph 173). Sometimes this raises problems which easily may divide the staff. For many workers greater flexibility may not be a problem, but for other workers (notably those with substantial family/care responsibilities) it may be hard to accept (*see* Table 14).

Table 14 Yearly Hours Worked per Worker in Average in 2015

US	1790
Germany	1371
The Netherlands	1419

117. The reasonable working conditions and the individualism of workers in Western Europe make them averse to working excessive additional hours for their employers' business, except in jobs and trades where 'workaholics' dominate, e.g., doctors and truck drivers. This is also the case in the Netherlands, where the average annual hours actually worked by employees (1,419 hours) is considerably lower than the EU average. This because of the extremely high number of part-time workers in the Netherlands (*see* paragraph 8). The number of hours actually worked by Dutch full-timers (1,740 hours) equals the EU average.

In 2003 Dutch employers started campaigning for a lengthening of the working week, but only a few collective agreements have changed the standard normal working hours. What is slowly changing, however, is the extra remuneration for work on non-standard working times (Saturdays, Sundays and evenings). In a number of collective agreements this extra remuneration has been reduced. The actual situation is that the average normal standard for the working week of full-time workers in collective agreements is still 37.5 hours, while working an average 2 hours a week overtime has become usual.

118. Overtime under civil law – meaning, working in excess of the standard working week laid down in the contract of employment or in the collective agreement (where it is actually on an average 37.5 hours) – is perfectly allowed under statutory law as long as this overtime does not exceed the limits under public law (*see* paragraph 112). The worker cannot be required to perform overtime if the overtime would exceed the limits of public regulations and no permission for such overtime has been granted. As long as this situation does not arise, the question of whether the worker can be required to perform overtime depends on various circumstances, such as:

- What is said on this issue in the individual contract of employment or in the collective agreement?
- What are the customs and practices?
- Has the worker a reasonable ground to refuse to perform overtime and has the employer a reasonable ground to impose the overtime?

This last check is again the application of the bona fides criterion (*see* paragraph 102). On the remuneration of overtime *see* paragraph 130 (*see* Table 15).

Table 15 Usual Standard Working Week and the Average of Overtime Usually Worked – A Comparison

	Standard Working Week	*Average Overtime*
UK	37.5	+ 3
Germany	37.7	+2.8
The Netherlands	37.5	+ 2
France	35.6	+2.4

§2. Part-Time Work and the Adaptation of Working Time and Working Place

119. In the Netherlands some 50% of the labour force is working on a part-time basis (*see* paragraph 8). For many years the government has actively promoted part-time work through subsidies and information. However, discriminatory provisions concerning part-time workers in the Minimum Wage and Minimum Holidays Allowances Act and in the WCA were only repealed as late as 1993 and 1998 respectively. In November 1996, the principle of equal treatment of part-time and full-time workers was introduced in labour law (*see* paragraph 100). The law states that neither the employer nor the parties in a collective labour agreement may treat employees unequally with regard to the conditions under which the employment contract is started, prolonged or ended solely on the grounds of a difference in the number of working hours, unless such treatment is objectively justified (Article 7:648 CC). This law also applies to small part-time jobs and 'on-call' workers. It should also serve to make part-time employment more attractive to male employees. Over the past years coverage by social security of part-time and other atypical forms of work have improved considerably as well.

In a number of collective agreements employees have the choice to work longer or shorter working weeks. As the coverage of a collective agreement is not universal and not all collective agreements contain a right to work part-time, in 2000 a law was passed, the Working Hours Adjustment Act (*Wet Aanpassing*

Arbeidsduur),[114] in 2015 renamed FWA.[115] The Act gives employees the right to have their hours increased or decreased at their request or their working hours schedules rearranged, provided that there are no serious objections on the grounds of company interests (Article 2(5) FWA). Such reasons could, in the case of a requested reduction of working time, include serious problems to find replacements for the vacant hours, in the field of safety or of technical scheduling (Article 2(9) FWA). In case of a requested increase of working time, acceptable reasons for refusal could include serious problems of financial or organizational nature, the lack of available work or because the fixed seize of staff or the insufficiency of the personnel budgets (Article 2(10) FWA). And in the case of a requested change in working hours schedules such reasons include serious problems in the field of safety or of technical, financial or organizational scheduling problems (Article 2(11) FWA). Moreover the employer may deviate from the wishes of the employee as regards the working hours scheduling if his interests in this respect are thus, that they, according to the criteria of reasonableness and fairness, may outweigh those of the employee (Article 2(7) FWA).

The worker may also request a change of the place of work (for instance, to do telework) but the employer does not need a preponderant reason to refuse it. He must only discuss it with the worker if refusing the request (Article 2(6) FWA).

To qualify for the right to have their working hours or working place adjusted, employees must have at least half a year of service with the company (Article 2(1) FWA) and apply in writing at least two months in advance (Article 2(3) FWA). An employee may lodge a request in this respect only once every year (Article 2(3) FWA). Employees are not obliged to substantiate their requests with valid reasons for seeking a change in their working time, but employers must, after having talked with the employee, provide written arguments as to why he has not honoured the request (Article 2(8) and 2(14) FWA). If the employer has not taken a decision in respect of the request within one month prior to the intended time of commencement of the adjustment, the working hours or working place shall be adjusted in accordance with the employees' request (Article 2(12) FWA).

The peremptory provisions of this legislation apply only to companies employing more than ten workers. However, the small enterprises must adopt a proper system for the adaptation of working time or working place (Article 2(16) FWA).

From the rules of the FWA, except those on the reduction of working time, it may be deviated *in peius* by collective agreement or, if no collective agreement is applicable, in written accordance with the works council or the ERB (Article 2(15) FWA).

Moreover the Act provides that the employee cannot terminate the employment relationship for the mere reason that the employee has requested a change in his working hours or working place (Article 3 FWA). Finally the provisions of the Act with regard to changes in working hours are not applicable to employees that have reached the AOW-pensionable age (Article 1a FWA).

---

114. *See* A.T.J.M. Jacobs & M. Schmidt, *The Right to Part-Time Work: The Netherlands and Germany Compared*, 17 Intl. J. Comp. Lab. L. Indus. Rel. 371–384 (2001).
115. Act of 25 Nov. 2015, Stb. 2015, 464.

Since 2000 the Act has only had a limited impact on the amount of part-time work in the Netherlands, which was already at a high level (*see* paragraph 8). The persistent unwillingness of most men to take up part-time jobs has been identified as a major obstacle to the further growth of part-time working. Here the gender gap remains wide. Only 18.8% of Dutch men were employed on a part-time basis in 2008 compared with 75.2% of women. According to the government, the reasons for the disparity are prejudicial attitudes in the workplace against part-time work, especially in manufacturing industry. Many men fear that switching to part-time work would threaten their career development and be viewed negatively by colleagues and management.

§3. Holidays (Vacation)

120. Provisions for a minimum paid holiday (vacation) were inserted in the Dutch CC in 1966, now Article 7:634–642 CC. They have been improved and technically changed in the course of the years, among others to bring them in conformity with the EC Directive on the Organisation of Working Time and especially with the judgments of the CJEU on this issues. They are also to a large extent in conformity with ILO Convention no. 135 on this subject, but not for 100% and this is the reason why the Netherlands has not ratified this ILO Convention.

Since the 1980s the statutory minimum period of paid holidays in the Netherlands is set at four weeks a year after a full year of service. The reality in the Netherlands is that most workers are enjoying a substantially longer period of holidays, often as much as five or six weeks a year. Sometimes additional entitlements to paid holidays were granted to elderly workers, but in recent years such rights tend to disappear because of the principle of non-discrimination as concerns age (*see* paragraph 99). Actually employees in the Netherlands have an average of 25.3 days' paid holiday a year.

Moreover the employees may be entitled to some additional days of paid leave by way of scheduled days off (for instance, the day between a Sunday and a bank holiday when a resumption of business is more expensive than a standstill). During the 1980s and the 1990s several collective agreements became to include entitlements to such so-called ADV days. These days were introduced as a realization of the idea, that in periods of high unemployment this phenomenon should be countered *inter alia* by prolonging the holidays of the workers. However the employers wanted to have the legal right to fix those days on the less productive days of the business cycle and to get rid of them as soon as the unemployment problems were over. Consequently they were not termed as proper holidays and the courts have not subjected them to all rules on the statutory minimum paid holidays.

These various developments show that in Dutch law one must differentiate between (a) the basic four weeks of the statutory minimum to which the rules of Article 7:634–642 Dutch CC are fully applicable, (b) the supplementary paid holidays on which these rules are also applicable, but on some points these rules allow deviations for the holidays that are exceeding the statutory minimum, and (c) the so-called scheduled days off and ADV days, which are subject to the rules of the collective agreement, the individual contract of employment, custom and practice and the general rules of labour law. Finally there are the bank holidays (official feasts).

121. In legal technical terms the Dutch CC does not mention a statutory minimum period of paid holidays of four weeks a year after a full year of service. The statute gives an employee the right to paid holidays amounting to 'at least four times the agreed period of work per week' (Article 7:634 CC). This means that in the case of a five-day working week a worker, after one year of service, is indeed entitled to a holiday of at least twenty days. However, as in the Netherlands so many employees nowadays are not working on a stable five-day working week, but are working part-time or on infrequent schedules, the legislators have preferred to express the statutory minimum requirement of paid holidays not in terms of days but in terms of 'the agreed period of work per week'. This makes it easier to calculate the entitlement to paid holidays for workers in the various atypical employment relationships.

A further characteristic of this system is that Dutch law does not require a minimum period of service to accumulate this entitlement. Obviously, if the contract of employment has not lasted one full year, the entitlement to paid holidays is proportionally shorter than the four weeks yearly, but the worker is nevertheless accumulating rights to paid holidays. Thus, already a teenager, who during his school holidays is working in a supermarket four weeks of five days with four hours has acquired an entitlement to $4/52 \times (4 \times 4 \times 5 \times 60 \text{ minutes}) = 369 \text{ minutes} = 6$ hours and 9 minutes paid holiday!

In principle the entitlement to hours/days of paid holidays are accumulated only over the days on which the worker is entitled to wages. However, a worker will also accumulate holiday rights over types of days, mentioned in the statute, on which he is not receiving wages (Article 7:635 CC). Since a reform of the law in 2011 this accumulation is also over the full period during which the worker could not work because of illness (Article 7:635(4) CC). Periods during which the worker enjoys pregnancy and maternity leave or paternity leave cannot be counted as paid holidays (Article 7:635(2) CC and Article 3:4 Work and Care Act), but it may be agreed in writing, that other days during which the worker enjoys short-time leave as mentioned in Article 6:4 Work and Care Act may be counted as holidays, as far as they exceed the statutory minimum (Article 7:637 CC).

The worker retains the right to his normal remuneration during his holidays (Article 7:639 CC). He may not, during the term of his contract of employment, waive his entitlement to holiday in exchange for compensation. However, as far as this entitlement to a holiday exceeds the statutory minimum, there may be derogation from this prohibition by written agreement (Article 7:640 CC). Only at the end of the contract of employment the employee who is still entitled to statutory minimum holidays has the right to a payment in cash to an amount of the remuneration over a period corresponding to the entitlement. An employer is obliged to issue an employee with a declaration showing the period over which the employee is still entitled to holiday at the end of the contract of employment. If the employee enters into a new contract of employment, he is entitled as regards the new employer to unpaid holiday equal in length to his existing holiday entitlement as shown in this declaration, but from this rule again, there may be derogation, provided the employee remains entitled to not less than the statutory minimum (Article 7:641 CC). However, the problem here is of another nature. Can the employer at the end of the employment contract oblige the employee to take up the remaining holidays in order to avoid a monetary compensation? And can he set off those days against the period of notice?

The right of action for the granting of holiday is prescribed some period from the last day of the calendar year in which the entitlement arose. The original period of two years was prolonged in 2001 to five years in order to enable the worker to save up holidays for a longer period of time out (for instance, for parental leave or a sabbatical), but it was reduced considerably in 2011 to compensate employers for the new rule which provides for the accumulation of holiday entitlements during the full period of illness. The current prescription period for the minimum number of holidays with pay is now half a year from the last day of the calendar year in which the entitlement arose, unless the worker could not reasonably have taken up these holidays. In a written agreement between employer and employee it may be derogated *in melius* from this rule (Article 7:640a CC).

122. Each year an employer must give the employee an opportunity to take up the minimum statutory holidays. The employer shall determine the time when the holiday will begin or end in accordance with the wishes of the employee, where no important reasons prevent this. Where an employer has not notified the employee in writing of important reasons within two weeks after the employee made his wishes known in writing, the holidays shall be determined in accordance with the latter's wishes. From this rule there may be derogation by written agreement, by collective agreement or by a scheme made by a competent authority or by law. Anyway the holiday shall be determined in such a manner that the employee, if required, need not perform any work, to the extent his entitlement suffices thereto, for two successive weeks or for two one-week periods. In some sectors of the Dutch economy, notably in primary education and in construction, a fixed summer holiday period is indeed habitual. If no collective agreement is applicable to this item, the works council has the right to co-determination when the employer introduces or changes a company holiday scheme (paragraph 391). After having determined the holidays period the employer may only change that after consultation with the employee if he has important reasons to do so and if he indemnifies the employee for any loss the latter incurs as a result of the changes in the holiday period (Article 7:638 CC).

An actual problem is that sometimes employees feel so much pressure to finalize their work that they do not dare to take up all or part of their yearly holiday.

The HR has ruled that the employer cannot reject a timely and motivated request of the worker to take up a holiday for the celebration of a religious feast or for urgent family circumstances, unless it would seriously disrupt his business.[116] The worker, however, may not assume the consent of the employer with his wish to take up a holiday if the employer has not reacted on his request. A worker who has taken a holiday that had been refused by his employer may eventually be dismissed.

116. Dutch Supreme Court, 30 Mar. 1984, NJ 1985, 350.

In as far as the worker wants to have more holiday rights than have been granted by the law or the collective agreement, this in principle is only possible on a non-paid basis and if the employer agrees to it. Some collective agreements may contain more favourable rules for the worker and in addition there is now a proliferating trend to statutory leave regulations (*see* paragraph 125).

The statutory rules on paid holidays are only applicable to those working on a genuine contract of employment and, as from 2020 also to civil servants, who, until then enjoy already comparable rules inserted in the Statute on Civil Service. Genuine independent workers cannot claim the statutory rights on holidays with pay, and this fact explains why, for solving the question of whether a contract is a genuine contract of employment, courts often take into account what had been convened or practised on the item of holidays (*see* paragraph 49); bogus-independent workers may successfully claim paid holidays even after the prescription period.

123. The AMW (Article 15) obliges all employers to pay their employees a yearly holiday allowance equal to at least 8% of the yearly wage (to a maximum of three times the yearly minimum wage = ca. EUR 61,000 yearly wage).

Also this Act has a minimum character, but there are not many collective agreements or individual agreements offering a more generous holiday allowance, apart from the three times maximum limit.

124. In the Netherlands there does not exist a statute on official bank holidays, but there is an old agreement between the social partners at cross-sector level summing up the generally respected bank holidays such as Christmas, Boxing Day, New Year's Day, Easter Monday, the King's Birthday (27 April), Ascension Day and Whit Monday, which should as far as possible be respected and the wages should be continued. Liberation Day (5 May) is only an official holiday once every five years. Carnival, Good Friday and the 1st of May are not official bank holidays. Other feast days with continuation of wage payment may however exist in some regions on the basis of collective agreement or customs and practice. With only seven official bank holidays a year the Netherlands has the fewest of this kind of holiday of all Member States of the EU (*see* Table 16).

Table 16 Number of Official Feast Days

Germany	13	UK	9
France	11	The Netherlands	7

§4. Leave Regulations

125. Since 1907 the CC has contained a provision on a short paid leave for exceptional situations. In the last decades this provision has developed into a rich bunch of statutory rules on leave for a variety of reasons, paid as well as unpaid. Many of them are created to implement EU rules or to follow foreign examples. To a large extent they reflect the ambition of the legislator to create the conditions for a better work-life balance. In 2001 most of these rules were consolidated in an overall Work and Care Act. In 2014[117] and 2018[118] they were modernized. In all cases this concerns minimum rules, which are often improved by collective agreements.

All employees have a right to paid *leave for calamities, etc.* during a short and reasonable, but not further specified amount of time for:

- unforeseen circumstances that require an immediate interruption of work;
- very special personal reasons, such as the confinement of his wife or partner, or the death and funeral in a narrow circle of family members of the employee;
- the right to vote in elections;
- unremunerated legal duties, which cannot be discharged in the employee's spare time;
- the necessary care on the first day of illness of a partner, a child or another narrow relative of the employee;
- urgent visits of an employee, his/her partner, child or narrow relative to a hospital or medical doctor that cannot take place outside working time (Article 4:1 Work and Care Act).

However, should the occasion arise the employee may agree to a deduction of this leave from his paid holiday entitlements that are exceeding the legal minimum (mentioned under paragraph 150) (Article 4:6 Work and Care Act).

Female employees are entitled to sixteen weeks of *pregnancy and maternity leave* – a low number if one compares it with many other EU Member States. The woman must provide a certification from her doctor or obstetrician, stating the likely date of the delivery. The pregnancy leave must start between four and six weeks before the presumed date of delivery (according to the choice of the employee). The pregnancy and maternity leave is prolonged with four weeks in case more than one child is expected. After the birth of the child the mother is entitled to the remaining ten–twelve weeks. In the case of premature births, time will be added to the period after the birth of the child to make up to the full the entitlement, while if the birth is late, the women is still entitled to full ten–twelve weeks of leave after the birth (Article 3:1 Work and Care Act). The pregnancy and maternity leave is remunerated with 100% of the wage of the employee out of social security funds (Article 3:13 Work and Care Act). The self-employed are entitled to maternity benefits over a sixteen weeks period at a sort of minimum wage level (Article 3:18–3:25 Work and Care Act).

If the mother dies during or shortly after the delivery the remaining rights on maternity leave are transferred to her partner (Article 3:1a Work and Care Act).

The partner of the employee is entitled to one week paid *birth leave* (Article 4:2 Work and Care Act). As from 1 July 2020 this partner may take up five weeks of additional leave which is remunerated with 70% of the wage of the employee out of social security funds, to be taken up within the first six month after the birth of the child (Article 4a–4c Work and Care Act).

117. Act of 17 Dec. 2014, Stb. 2014, 565; Parliamentary Papers 32855.
118. Act of 14 Nov. 2018, Stb. 2018, 451; Parliamentary Papers 34967.

Both adoptive parents and foster-parents are entitled to six weeks of *adoption leave* remunerated with 100% of the wage out of social security funds (Article 3:2 and 3:13 Work and Care Act).

All employees are entitled to twenty-six weeks unpaid *parental leave*, provided the child is under the age of 8 years (Article 6 Work and Care Act). The employer may modify the request for parental leave because of serious objections on the grounds of company interests but not as regards the first three days of parental leave immediately taking up after the birth leave (Article 6:5 Work and Care Act). In a number of sectors parental leave is fully or partly paid by the employer. The state supports continued payment of wages by tax facilities (EUR 650 a month in case of full-time parental leave). Yearly about 75,000 parents make use of this facility. After having taken up the period of parental leave the employee may ask the employer an adaptation of his working time patterns for a certain period and of course also for an adaptation of his working hours (Article 2 FWA) (*see* paragraph 119).

All employees are entitled to yearly two times the agreed weekly working time paid *short-term nursing leave* in order to take care of ill family members (Article 5:2 Work and Care Act). Payment should be 70% of the regular pay, but at least the statutory minimum wage and at most of a maximum of about EUR 45,000 yearly (Article 5:1 and 5:6 Work and Care Act).

All employees are entitled to yearly six times the agreed weekly working time unpaid *long-term nursing leave* to take care for the terminally ill partner, child or parent of the employee (Article 5:9–5:10 Work and Care Act).

There existed between 2002 and 2012 regulations with respect to career breaks which could have been taken up for whatever reason and were facilitated by taxes and employers contributions (life course arrangement, *levensloop*).[119] They have been repealed recently.

Finally, the Dutch CC contains a stipulation on unpaid *political leave* for employees who are members of political institutions such as Parliament and municipal councils (Article 7:643 CC).

All the aforementioned statutory forms of leave are intended as a minimum. More generous provision is often made by the social partners via collective agreements. In some cases collective agreements can also derogate *in peius* from the abovementioned arrangements on parental leave (*see* Article 6:8 Work and Care Act). In the cases of nursing leave (both short-term and long-term) derogations are also possible by a written agreement between the employer and the works council if there is no collective agreement about this item applicable (Articles 1:5, 4:7 and 5:16 Work and Care Act). Another recent statute eliminated obstacles in social security legislation in taking up unpaid leave. Some employers have started to codify all the rules on holidays and leave arrangements in a rule book, which may contain the conditions and the procedures to effectuate them.

119. A. Eleveld, *A Critical Perspective on the Reform of Dutch Social Security Law* (2012).

Chapter 4. Remuneration (Wages/Pay/Salary)

§1. General Observations

126. As mentioned above (paragraph 84), the employer's promise to pay remuneration (wage/salary) to the worker in exchange for the worker's promise to perform work is an essential element in the contract of employment. Remuneration, in other words, is the counter-performance of the employer to which the contract of employment entitles the worker.

The Dutch CC devotes a number of sections to the employer's duty to pay wages and the way it has to be executed.[120] It contains provisions regarding the payment in kind or in currency (*see* paragraph 131), provides for a chain liability for wage payment (*see* paragraph 132), obliges the employer to pay wages at the specified time (*see* paragraph 133) and provides for the issue of an itemized payslip, the protection of the employee against the so-called truck system and against deductions, seizure and transfer of payment of the wage (*see* paragraphs 134/135). Also provided for is the right to a guaranteed payment of the wage in certain situations in which the work is not performed (*see* paragraphs 147 et seq.). Some of the more important sections will be outlined below.

It should be noted that there is no uniform definition of remuneration/wage/salary in Dutch law. These words have different meanings in labour law, social security law, tax law, etc. and even within the field of labour law itself. Compensation paid for overtime, for example, is regarded as remuneration by the CC but only in a limited way comes within the definition of remuneration provided in the AMW (*see* paragraph 139). The holiday allowance[121] and bonuses[122] are frequently but not always considered to be 'wage/remuneration'. Pensions are not regarded as 'wages' for most regulations, save for the equal treatment rules. Tips are not 'wages' in the sense of most provisions of the Dutch CC, but it may be included in the concept of 'wages' in the AMW. Money paid by the employer for expenses incurred, such as telephone costs and travelling expenses, is not regarded as remuneration as long as it is merely a compensation and not a hidden wage.[123] In that case the surplus will be regarded as wages. All these examples may demonstrate that in Dutch labour law there is no simple and uniform definition of 'wage/remuneration'.

However, the HR has once given a definition of wages, which is applicable for a number of provisions in the CC Chapter on the contract of employment: 'wages are the compensation due by the employer to the employee in relation to the agreed work'.[124]

120. *See* J.M.v. Slooten, *Arbeid en loon*, Deventer, 1999; on pp. 413–422 may be found an English-language description and discussion of the obligation to pay wages and the obligation to work in the Dutch law on employment contracts.
121. Dutch Supreme Court, 5 Jun. 1998, JAR 1998/137.
122. Dutch Supreme Court, 22 Sep. 1999, NJ 1999/737.
123. Dutch Supreme Court, 3 Jun. 1982, NJ 1982, 206.
124. Dutch Supreme Court, 18 Dec. 1953, NJ 1954, 242.

§2. MANNER OF PAYMENT

I. Calculation of Payment

127. Wages can be calculated on a time basis (per hour, per day or per month), on a performance basis (for instance, according to the weight or measure of the material produced), or on some other basis. There are practically no statutory provisions regulating the mode of calculation; in general the choice is left to the parties and collective bargaining.

128. Flexible forms of remuneration are now seen by many an economist as an alternative to the fixed methods of remuneration and classic generalized pay rises. They make labour costs more flexible and may reduce the number of dismissals in a slump. In the Netherlands opinions differ on this issue, both on the employers' and on the trade union side (*see also* paragraph 297). Many employers are in favour of performance-related pay. Others are sceptic about such methods of payment, because of related high administrative costs, difficulties in measuring performance, etc. Until recently Dutch unions opposed individual pay arrangements but agreed on collective flexible pay schemes. So collective bonuses have been agreed with Shell and collective profit–sharing with DSM and Tata Steel NL, but the introduction of performance-related pay for individual workers was opposed by the unions at Philips and Akzo Nobel. In IT variable pay already is very widespread, notably among higher personnel. It used to be the same in the banking and insurance sectors, but here steps backwards are noticeable as a lesson learned from the banking crisis (2008–2009, *see* paragraph 288). On average in the Netherlands the volume of variable income actually paid out as a percentage of the total amount of salaries is less than 10%.

For low-level staff the variable income depends in practice seldom on the operating results. For middle-level staff the variable income is mostly linked to individual and departmental objectives; it is only for a minority of them that an actual relationship has been established between the development of the operating results and the variable income. For the senior management in the majority of the companies, a certain relationship between operating results and variable income is usual.

Profit-sharing arrangements are widespread in the Netherlands (*see* paragraph 405). A recent study put the Netherlands in the second place in the EU as regards the incidence of profit-sharing schemes (27%). Such schemes are not governed by legislation, which leads to a wide diversity in the type of schemes in existence. Provisions on these schemes can only be found in a small number of collective agreements (only about 12%). Therefore most employers are entirely free whether or not to negotiate with the unions such a scheme.

The law only provides that if all or part of the remuneration has been made dependent on any data that must be obtained from the books, records or other data carriers of the employer, the employee has the right to require the employer to produce such documentary evidence as he needs in order to establish such data (Article 7:619 CC).

129. Gratuities, such as the payment of a thirteenth month at the end of the year, a leased car, etc., can give rise to problems. If the employer is obliged to pay the extra it is considered to be remuneration, but if he is free to grant it or refuse it, it is not. However, the difficulty lies in determining whether a worker is entitled to a gratuity. This problem becomes acute when the question arises as to whether the employer can discontinue such payments after having them granted during a certain period. The answer has to be found in the interpretation of the contract in question. Also custom and practice may be important (*see* paragraph 32). Ultimately the courts will apply the bona fides principle (*see* paragraph 102). On that basis one may conclude from case law of the lower courts that the employer who has spontaneously granted gratuities for a number of years cannot abruptly discontinue such payments without a compelling reason. At the most he can dismantle them gradually or buy them off. Recently the HR has established[125] that the question of whether a course of action followed by the employer towards the employee during a certain period of time leads to a (supplementary) employment condition that applies between the parties cannot be answered in a general sense. It depends on the meaning that the parties have assigned (and in the circumstances reasonably could assign) to each other's conduct (and related statements). In this context significant viewpoints are (i) the content of the relevant course of action, (ii) the nature of the employment contract and the position that the employer and the employee take towards each other, (iii) the length of the period during which the employer has followed the relevant course of action, (iv) what the employer and the employee have declared (or precisely have not declared) to each other in connection with this course of action, (v) the nature of the advantages and disadvantages for the employer and the employee resulting from the relevant course of action and (vi) the nature and extent of the circle of employees towards whom the relevant course of action has been followed.

130. Overtime normally is remunerated; it often is even extra remunerated. The worker not only gets paid for the overtime hours but also is even paid extra for these hours, for example 150% of the hourly wage. However, this (additional) remuneration is not required by Dutch statutory law. Statutes are completely silent on this issue. The (additional) remuneration is habitually fixed by collective agreements, by agreements with the work's council or in the individual contract of employment. Or it can be deducted from custom and practice and the bona fides principle. In most of the higher–paid functions, overtime habitually is not additionally remunerated as it is considered to be included in the normal wage.

According to case law of the lower courts, it is normally not considered to be unequal treatment to pay overtime rates only when full-time working hours are exceeded. However, the individual parties as well as the social partners may agree to award overtime pay as soon as work is performed above the number of contractual agreed hours. Dutch courts will be inspired by verdicts of the CJEU on this matter.

125. Dutch Supreme Court, 22 Jun. 2018, ECLI:NL:HR:2018:976.

II. Payment in Currency or in Kind

131. Wages can be paid in currency or in kind. There are statutory restrictions on payment in kind. The law says that the adopted form of remuneration may not be other than (a) money; (b) things suitable for the personal use of the employee and the members of his household, with the exception of alcoholic drinks and other stimulants that are harmful to health and only if this form of remuneration is customary or desirable owing to the nature of the undertaking of the employer; (c) the use of a dwelling and the lighting and heating thereof; (d) services, facilities and work to be performed by or for the account of the employer, including training, board and lodging; (e) securities, accounts receivable, other claims and documentary evidence thereof and vouchers. The matters, services and facilities, referred to under (b), (c) and (d) may not be attributed a value in excess of their real value (Article 7:617 CC).

The CC obliges the remuneration to be paid in the Dutch legal tender or by giro transfer (Article 7:620(1) CC). The Dutch legal tender, since 1 January 2002, is the euro. As the number of workers with a bank account has increased rapidly during recent years, the use of this transfer system to pay wages and salaries has become a normal procedure. Legislation acknowledged this, and since 1992 the CC clearly mentions payment through bank or post office giro account as a legally acceptable way of payment in this respect (Article 6:114 CC). The legislator went even one step further and requires payment by giro or bank account of the part of the wage equal to the minimum wage (except for domestic workers, *see* paragraph 59).

The statute further provides that remuneration fixed in money may be paid in foreign currency if this has been agreed (Article 7:620(2) CC). Components of remuneration fixed otherwise than in money shall be paid in accordance with what has been agreed or, if nothing has been agreed in this respect, in accordance with usage (Article 7:620(3) CC).

A payment of the remuneration fixed in money which does not take place pursuant to Article 6:114 CC shall, at the discretion of the employer, be made either at the place where the work is generally performed or at the office of the employer if this is situated in the same municipality as that in which the majority of the employees reside or at home of the employee (Article 7:622 CC).

Payment of remuneration contrary to Article 7:617 or 7:620 CC does not constitute a discharge. The employee retains the right to claim the proper remuneration, without being obliged to return that which has been received when the payment not constituting a discharge was made (Article 7:621 CC).

132. In 2016 a set of provisions has been inserted in the Dutch CC in order to better guarantee the payment of wages in a subcontracting chain. If work is performed in the service of an employer in the execution of one or more contracts concluded between a principal and a contractor, then every principal is liable for the payment of the wage which the formal employer is due to the employee. Sure, first there should have been a lawsuit against the formal employer or the next lower principal/party. Only if such a lawsuit has been made and failed, a lawsuit against the next higher principal/party is possible. Moreover principals are not liable if they have undertaken due diligence obligations. This rule of subcontracting liability does not apply to natural persons not acting in exercising a profession or business (Article 7:616b CC). The chain liability applies to work performed in the Netherlands irrespective of the applicable law on the contract of employment (Article 7:616c CC). Self-evidently the principal/party who has effectively paid the wage has redress against the formal or next principal/party that owed the wage (Article 7:616d CC).

III. Periods of Payment

133. An employer is obliged to pay the employee his remuneration at the specified time (Article 7:616 CC). The employer must pay the remuneration fixed in money per unit of time on each occasion after the end of the period in respect of which the remuneration must be calculated pursuant to the contract, provided that the period for payment is not shorter than one week and not longer than one month. However, the period after which the remuneration must be paid may – within certain limits – be extended by written agreement (Article 7:623 CC).

In the past the wages of a large number of employees in the Netherlands were paid in weekly payments. Nowadays most of them have been converted into monthly or four weekly salaries.

If the remuneration is dependent on the results of the work to be performed, the employer shall observe the payment instalments which apply to the remuneration fixed per unit of time for comparable work, if not agreed otherwise. If the amount or remuneration cannot yet be determined on the payday, the employer must pay an advance for which the statute gives some minimum rules. If the remuneration is dependent on any data that must be obtained from the books, records or other data carriers of the employer, the employer must make payment whenever the amount of that remuneration can be determined, provided that payment is made at least once a year (Article 7:624 CC).

In this connection it should be mentioned that a worker who is not paid at the appropriate moment is entitled to an increase for the delay if this non-payment can be attributed to the employer. This increase shall be 5% per day for the fourth to the eighth working days, inclusive, and 1% for each subsequent working day, provided that the increase shall never exceed half of what is owed. Moreover, the court may limit the increase to such amount as it deems fair in the circumstances (Article 7:625 CC). The HR has judged that the judges shall be reticent in exercising this power of mitigation and motivate it if they use it.[126] It has further established that the circumstance that a worker has done nothing to earn an alternative income is an appropriate reason for the court to exercise this power of limitation.[127]

An employer who is temporarily unable to pay the remuneration, to the extent that this is fixed in a form other than money, in circumstances where this inability is not of the employee's doing, shall owe such compensation as is fixed by contract or, in absence of such a contract, by the court in accordance with what is customary or fair (Article 7:630 CC).

126. Dutch Supreme Court, 30 Oct. 1998, JAR 1999/11.
127. Dutch Supreme Court, 21 Dec. 2007, JAR 2008/16.

In cases about the delayed payment of wages the employee may also claim the statutory interest (Article 6:119 CC) besides the increase of Article 7:625 CC.[128] The court cannot mitigate this statutory interest.[129]

Claims about the payment of wages become barred by lapse of time after five years (Article 3:308 CC). Only in exceptional cases this five-year period, during which wages can be claimed, can be prolonged[130] or abbreviated earlier.[131] Apart from exceptions the employer may reclaim the erratic payment of an oversized wage amount.

The employer must pay the surviving dependants of the deceased employee a benefit equal to the remuneration to which the employee was last entitled by law, over the period from the day following the death up to and including one month following the day on which the death occurred (Article 7:674 CC).

§3. Prohibition of Truck System, Deductions, Seizure and Transfer: The Itemized Payslip

134. The so-called truck system is banned by a provision declaring null and void stipulations whereby the employee gives an undertaking to the employer to spend the remuneration received or his income or a part thereof in a given way or to buy his necessities at a given place or from a given person (Article 7:631(2) CC).

If the employee has entered into a contract with the employer or a third party as the result of such a stipulation, he has the right to claim from his employer what he has paid on this account. If he has entered into the contract with the employer, he is also entitled to nullify the contract (Article 7:631(6) CC).

Also a nullity is a stipulation whereby the employer obtains the right to withhold any amount from the remuneration on the payday, without prejudice to the right of the employee to give the employer a written authority to make payments in his name from the remuneration to be paid. This competence of the employee does not apply to the part of the remuneration that equals the minimum wage with the exception of the obligation in Article 13(2) AMW. This authorization may be revoked at any time (Article 7:631(1) CC).

The statute on the employment contracts mentions a number of social funds on which the two preceding paragraphs do not apply, such as pension funds and pension insurances (Article 7:631(3) CC). In other places in the law this is extended to deductions in accordance with tax laws, social security laws, etc.

135. Dutch law further provides that the employer is restricted in setting off his debts in respect of the remuneration to be paid to an employee. The limitations are on the subjects and on total amount.

128. Dutch Supreme Court, 5 Jan. 1979, NJ 1979, 207; Dutch Supreme Court, 28 Jan. 1994, NJ 1994, 20 and Dutch Supreme Court, 24 Jun. 1994, JAR 1994/154.
129. Dutch Supreme Court, 30 Oct. 1998, JAR 1999/11.
130. Dutch Supreme Court, November 2002, JAR 2002/278.
131. Dutch Supreme Court, 8 Dec. 1989, NJ 1990, 474.

Except at the end of the contract of employment, the employer may set off his debt only against the following debts of the employee: (a) the damages owed by the employee to the employer; (b) the fines owed by the employee to the employer, however, within certain limits (*see* next phrase); (c) the advances on the remuneration made by the employer in cash to the employee, provided that there is written evidence thereof; (d) the amount of any excess remuneration paid; (e) the rent of a number of items which have been hired out by the employer to the employee by written contract (Article 7:632(1) CC).

Moreover the employer may not apply a set-off against such part of the remuneration as equals the minimum wage, unless an earlier written agreement with the employee concerning the advances on the remuneration (*see* Article 475(c)–475(f) Dutch Code on Civil Procedure).[132] Concerning the fines owed by the employee to the employer (*see* paragraph 183) the maximum set-off is 1/10 of the amount of the fines and not more than left untouched the minimum wage (Article 7:632(2) CC).

The same amount of remuneration, which is immune for seizure by garnishment, applies to a transfer, pledge or any other act as a result of which the employee grants any right to his remuneration to third parties (Article 7:633 CC).

136. The employer is obliged to provide the employee with an itemized payslip at each time of payment of the wages. It must mention the amount of the remuneration, the specific amounts of which it is comprised and the specific amounts withheld from the remuneration.

The payslip must also mention the amount of the remuneration to which a person of the age of the employee is entitled by or pursuant to the AMW in the period over which the remuneration is calculated, unless no change has occurred in any of these amounts since the previous payment. Moreover mention must be made of the name of the employer and the employee, the period over which the wage has been calculated, whether there is an employment contract for an indefinite period of time that has been entered into in writing and whether there is a call agreement.

The payslip may be provided by electronic way, provided the employee has explicitly given his consent to it (Article 7:626 CC). The employer must be ready to show the payslip to the Inspectorate SZW (Article 18(b)(2) AMW).

§4. The Amount of the Wage

137. The CC has hardly any impact on the determination of the amount of the wages. It protects the effective payment of the agreed wage, but it does not lay down rules as to the amount of the wage to be paid. Only if no remuneration has been fixed does the law provide that the employee shall be entitled to the remuneration which was customary at the time of the conclusion of the contract for work of the agreed kind or, in the absence of such a criterion, remuneration that is regarded as fair in the circumstances of the case (Article 7:618 CC).

So there is no general applicable legal concept of 'fair wages' in Dutch labour law, but there is a concept of minimum wages, which must be applied universally

132. Dispositions modernized by the Act of 8 Mar. 2017, Stb. 2017, 110.

(*see* paragraph 139). In addition there is the legislation on equal pay for men and women (*see* paragraph 144). Other statutory provisions have extended the concept to equal pay on other grounds such as between part-time and full-time workers (*see* paragraph 100).

Finally there is the general clause of bona fides in employment contracts (Article 7:611 Dutch CC, *see* paragraph 102), which may be invoked in each employment dispute to attack wages which are not 'reasonable'. Because of the aforementioned pieces of legislation and the extensive coverage of collective agreements, the courts have not been active to term a wage 'unreasonable', but in extreme cases they might do so.

138. Until World War II the determination of the amount of the wage was entirely left to the parties. After this war the Netherlands had for more than thirty-five years a state-directed wage policy, the terms of which were scrupulously laid down in government orders. In the 1980s state-controlled wage policy was abolished (*see* paragraphs 281 et seq.) and ever since the determination of wages has been left to free bargaining between employers and employees. The only remaining statutory interference with the amount of wages is now in the area of the minimum wage (*see* paragraph 139 et seq.), equal pay (*see* paragraph 144) and on executive pay in the (semi-) public sector (*see* paragraph 288).

As circa 80% of the Dutch employees are covered by legally binding collective agreements, the wages for these employees are to be taken from collective agreements. As collective agreements most of the time only lay down minima, the real wage may of course be higher. In some enterprises, the real level of wages may be as high as 125 to 150% of the wage level laid down in the sectoral collective agreements in the private sector.

Statistics show that the wages earned in the Netherlands are much in line with those in some neighbouring Member States of the EU but substantially higher than those in other Member States (Table 17).

Table 17 The Average Net Monthly Wage in 2017 (EUR)

Germany	2,431	UK	2,235
The Netherlands	2,152	Italy	2,390
France	2,225	Spain	1,806

§5. The Minimum Wage

139. In the Netherlands there is no statutory maximum wage level, apart from a 2013 law on executive pay in the public and semi-public sector (*see* paragraph 288). There are, however, minimum wage levels laid down by the AMW of 1968.

This Act fixes the minimum wage in the Netherlands actually (1 January 2020) at EUR 165,360 gross a month for a standard working week employment relationship. This applies to all employees in all sectors of economic life without any exception or differentiation. This minimum wage used to apply to all workers as from the age of 23. However in 2017 the legislator[133] lowered this age in two steps: as from 1 July 2017 it became 22, and as from 1 July 2019 it became 21. Youngsters are entitled to a minimum youth wage which is a percentage of the full minimum wage, varying from 30% at 15 years to 80% at 20 years. No minimum wage is provided for juvenile labour in the ages of 13 and 14.[134]

Employees are entitled to the minimum wage if they are employed at 'the normal working time'. Part-timers are entitled to a proportional minimum wage (Article 12 AMW). A little problem here is the fact that 'the normal working time' is not statutory standardized in the Netherlands. It varies somewhere between thirty-six and forty hours a week, depending on the sector of the economy (*see* paragraphs 117 et seq.). Therefore it is not possible to give a general applicable hourly minimum wage,[135] but on average it is about EUR 10 an hour. Employees working more than the agreed normal working time can claim on the basis of this Act a proportionally higher minimum wage (Articles 12 and 13a AMW).

In 2017 the legislator amended again the AMW[136] to ascertain that the Act is applicable not only to persons working on a contract of employment *strictu senso* but also to persons working on a contract for services, unless they perform such work within the framework of their profession or business. The Act is thus expressly applicable to bogus-independent workers in order to avoid the circumvention of the Act but not to genuinely self-employed persons (i.e., those recognized by the tax authorities as such) (*see* paragraph 51). Moreover the Minister may by decree extend the scope of this Act to other kind of contracts which may be socially assimilated with the contracts which the Act is already covering (Article 2 AMW).

If the employee is performing his work outside the Netherlands, the AMW is in principle only applicable to persons living in the Netherlands whose employer is established in the Netherlands (Article 4).[137] It is certainly applicable to foreigners working in the Netherlands (*see* paragraphs 188 and 190 et seq.).

The statutory minimum wage is also applicable to persons working after having reached the AOW-pensionable age.

140. The statutory minimum wage is automatically linked to the development of the general level of wages. The procedure for adopting the minimum wage is very simple and depoliticized. Every six months the Dutch Public Office of Statistics works out the average level of wage rises in the collective agreements of Dutch workers, and the Minister subsequently adjusts the minimum wage with the same percentage by Royal Decree. There is never any political debate on this point. No Minister would dare to tamper with this procedure. Only if the economy has run into big trouble may government and Parliament, after an open debate, adopt exceptional legislation to skip automatic adaptation of minimum wages for a year or so.

133. Act of 25 Jan. 2017, Stb. 2017, 24; Parliamentary Papers 34573.
134. This was approved by the Dutch Supreme Court, 11 Nov. 2006, JAR 2006/306; ILLR Vol. 27, p. 21.
135. Actually there is a private members bill in Parliament to change this.
136. Act of 29 Mar. 2017, Stb. 2017, 290.
137. Dutch Supreme Court, 30 May 1980, NJ 1980, 634.

This was done several times between 1983 and 1995. As a result, the level (measured in terms of purchasing power) of the statutory minimum wage has been effectively reduced if one compares its current level with that of the 1970s (corrected for inflation).

The Dutch statutory minimum wage is very much functioning as a 'red line' for all low incomes in the Netherlands because all minimum social security benefits and the social assistance are linked to the statutory minimum wage (*see* paragraph 10). In principle every two-adults household is entitled to minimum benefits at the level of one net minimum wage, be it by way of old-age pension, survivors' benefit, sickness pay, unemployment benefit, disability benefit and so on. Nobody is obliged – in order to receive such payments – to accept or perform work below the level of the statutory minimum wage.

141. Any stipulation in contravention of the AMW is a nullity (Article 19 AMW). It is automatically replaced by the statutory minimum wage. In principle, the employee must himself go to court to enforce payment of the statutory minimum wage, though if the statutory minimum wage is asserted in the collective agreement (which is often the case) then the trade unions can also in their own right take the employer to the court (*see* paragraph 332). On the payslip – which is obligatory under statutory law (*see* paragraph 136) – the employer must state the relevant statutory minimum pay so that the employee can easily compare it with the salary received.

Until the beginning of this century there was no public enforcement of the minimum wage legislation. Lawmakers had deliberately avoided attaching criminal sanctions to this law. Enforcement was left to the workers themselves or their representatives in the civil courts. It was only provided that the Labour Inspectorate shall regularly control the payment of the minimum wages. When violations were observed both workers and employers would be informed. No wonder the minimum wage legislation was often violated[138] although in 2003 the Labour Inspectorate revealed that at that time violations were down to about 1% of the cases in which the minimum wage should have been paid. In subsequent years, however, the extension of the EU with many nations in Central and Eastern Europe caused a huge influx of workers from these countries at the Dutch labour market (*see* paragraph 78), who often did not obtain the Dutch minimum wage. In order to stop these violations since 2007 a number of measures have been taken. The AMW is now enforced by a system of administrative fines (Article 18b–18q). Since 2011 the Inspection SZW has regularly monitored payment of the statutory minimum wage if it suspects violations. It may seize the wage administration of the employer and impose fines. It may even give an order to halt the operations of the company. Moreover since 2010 the payment of the minimum wage is further guaranteed by chain responsibility provisions (*see* paragraph 132). Nevertheless the violations of the AMW in respect of foreign workers have risen during the recent economic crisis (2012–2015) which have led to the earlier mentioned adaptations of the AMW concerning the scope of that Act.

---

138. Parliamentary Papers TK 2004-2005 92800 XV no. 60.

In the Netherlands a statutory minimum wage has coexisted with an extensive system of collective bargaining for almost half a century. Its function has been to prevent the small part of the Dutch economy in which no collective agreements exist to undermine wages in the rest of the economy, and so it has ensured that all working people in the Netherlands have a decent (minimum) share in prosperity.

The existence of a statutory minimum wage may weaken the pressure on workers to unionize. One might ask whether the low unionization rate in the Netherlands – around 20% (*see* paragraph 272) – has something to do with the existence of a statutory minimum wage and the generous practice of *erga omnes* extension of collective agreements (*see* paragraph 324).

Obviously, the statutory minimum wage has an indirect effect on higher wages as it effectively (not formally) forces employers to increase all wages above the minimum wage by at least the same percentage as the rise in the minimum wage. However, the rise in the minimum wage is the retroactive expression of average pay rises, so the minimum wage cannot be blamed as the cause of this chain of events.

142. The Dutch minimum wage is very close to the amount of the minimum wage in the neighbouring countries. However, expressed in a percentage of the national average wage it is one of the lowest in the EU (Table 18).

Table 18 Minimum Wages in Western Europe and the USA

	Bruto Minimum Wage Per Hour in Euro (2017)	*Minimum Wage as Percentage of Average Wage (2017)*
Luxembourg	12	42.7%
The Netherlands	10	39.3%
France	10	49.9%
Belgium (based on nat. coll. agreement).	9.50	39.8%
Germany	9	42.5%
UK	9	44.3%
US	7.25	

In the Netherlands ca. 6% of the workers are earning not more than the minimum wage, notably workers in the pubs, hotel and restaurants, in the retail, in cleaning, in agriculture, in domestic employment and in temporary agency work.

The Dutch minimum wage of ca. EUR 1,650 a month is considered well above the 'living wage', which for the Netherlands is estimated at EUR 1,040 a month for a single person (*see* paragraph 10). Notably during the 1960s and 1970s there was a strong drive for 'social justice' and 'solidarity pay'. Upgrading the minimum wage was an aim of most political parties. Some political parties even wanted a maximum wage to be fixed at a level no higher than four or five times the minimum wage! When during the 1980s a recession hit the Netherlands and the standard of living fell, Dutch politicians tried frantically not to touch the lower-income sections of the population. The Netherlands remained one of the countries in which differences in income levels were the smallest[139] (*see* paragraph 10). By the end of the 1980s and the 1990s economic prosperity returned to the Netherlands and differences in income levels grew substantially. However, this occurred, not so much as a result of lowering the incomes of the low paid as by allowing the incomes of the middle class and above to rise more substantially. The described policy of moderate wage increases was pursued to stabilize standard (collectively agreed) pay levels (not to lower pay levels), and it left room for all sorts of extra pay rises, which were agreed individually.

Pleas of economists to lower the statutory minimum wage have been unsuccessful, although the repeated cancellation of the automatic linkage to the rise of wages in the period 1983–1995 has in effect reduced the level of the minimum wage.

At the beginning of the 1990s it was discovered that the effective minimum wage in collective agreements was often 10% to 30% above the statutory minimum wage because in collective agreements the lowest wage scales (just above the minimum wage) were removed or not used. Economists blamed this as one of the reasons for much of the long-term unemployment in the Netherlands, although the economy was booming again. This incited the Dutch government to press the social partners to engage workers at the statutory minimum wage level by threatening to refuse to extend collective agreements to outsiders if they did not reintroduce into their collective agreement the lowest wage scales or scales just above the statutory minimum wage (*see* paragraph 326).

Thus, the minimum wage from time to time is seen as one of the causes why unemployment is often persistent among the low-skilled workers. It may be too high for employers to offer certain jobs. As, however, lowering the minimum wage is a taboo in the Netherlands, the alternative may be to subsidize employers in paying minimum wages. For this reason in the past Dutch governments have applied various forms to subsidise the payment of minimum wages, such as reductions in taxes and social security contributions for workers paid at or near the minimum wage level.

The actual form is as of 1 January 2017 laid down in a Decree called the Low Income Advantage – *Lage Inkomens Voordeel* (LIV). It contains a subsidy of at most EUR 1,000–2,000 a year for employers concerning each worker that they employ at a wage of not more than 125% of the minimum wage (*see also* paragraph 244). The effects of this new subsidy are not known yet, but the subsidy is contested in left-wing circles, who see it as a subsidy to the profits of companies and as a disincentive for employers to increase the wages (as they then lose the subsidy). The FNV would rather see an increase of the minimum wage to EUR 14 an hour. The LIV costs the Treasury EUR 500 million a year and benefits some 100,000 employers with some 400,000 employees (4% of the Dutch labour market).

Moreover there is a special wage subsidy to compensate employers for the recent lowering of the age for the adult minimum wage (Article 3.3–3.4 WAA, *see* paragraph 139).

---

139. *See* reports from IFO, the German Institute for Economic Research.

143. Besides creating a minimum wage Article 15 of the AMW also creates a right to a minimum holidays allowance at the level of 8% of the normal wage up to a maximum of three times the minimum wage. Of course, more than these three times may be agreed, but it cannot be claimed on the basis of this Act (*see also* paragraph 123).

§6. Equal Pay for Men and Women and for the Disabled

144. The principle of equal pay for equal work by men and women is laid down in Article 7:646 CC and in the AETMW (Articles 7–12). In order to establish whether there is true equal pay one has to compare the wage of the employee with the wage that is earned by an employee of the other sex, performing the same work or work with the same or almost the same value in that enterprise (Article 7 AETMW). The Act emphasizes especially that job rating systems must be subservient to this principle (Article 8 AETMW). Indirect pay discrimination is equally prohibited,[140] unless there is an objective justification for it, for instance a difference in seniority. Especially for women it is important that the unequal payment for part-time workers has been prohibited by Article 7:648 CC (*see* paragraph 100), as it is still mostly women doing their jobs part-time (*see* paragraph 8). Also unequal pay based only on the fact that a person is married or the 'breadwinner' is forbidden.

A worker can sue his or her employer if he or she thinks that this principle has not been respected. Before going to court, the worker may put the problem before a commission of experts, the Human Rights Board (*see* paragraph 39). This board then makes a recommendation on the problem in writing, if necessary after an investigation.

Any stipulation in contravention of the Equal Pay principle is null and void. Claims about the unequal payment of wages become barred by lapse of time after five years (Article 3:308 CC).

Equal pay for men and women is now generally accepted, but this does not prevent large differences persisting. The gender pay gap in the Netherlands is slowly diminishing from about 20% in 2008 to circa 16% in 2019 but is still one of the largest in the EU. According to research between 5% and 7% can be attributed to direct unequal pay. Other differences are due to hidden discrimination, for instance in job classification systems. However, these inequalities are also due to lower seniority, lower education and the availability of women on the labour market, which results in an average lower pay for women than for men. Those factors cannot easily be stamped out, although governmental policies are trying to close the gender pay gap. Interesting: recent research has established that 19% of the women in the Netherlands are now earning per hour more than their male partners, notably in the age group 25–30.

---

140. Dutch Supreme Court, 24 Apr. 1992, NJ 1992, 689 (*KLM/Bouma*).

In order to further reduce the wage gap m/f Parliament is now discussing a private members bill which will strengthen the existing equal pay m/f rules *inter alia* by the introduction of a certification system for companies that fully comply with the equal pay norms.[141]

145. Employees with a handicap or with a chronic illness are in principle entitled to the same customary wage as healthy employees for equal work or work of equal value on the basis of the Act on Equal Treatment on the basis of handicap or chronic illnesses (AETHCI, *see* paragraph 98). A lower wage is null and void. If the work performance of the handicapped worker is substantially lower than that of healthy employees, the disablement benefits authorities shall not declare that worker 100% disabled but, e.g., 50% disabled; this person shall keep 50% of his disablement benefit, while the employer must pay the worker 50% of his normal wage. A worker with less than 30% disability does not obtain a disability benefit. The employer must pay such a worker the full wage according to statute and collective agreement, but he may qualify for a subsidy (*see* paragraph 244). For young-disabled workers the system is somewhat different.

§7. Remuneration and Work

146. Remuneration is given in exchange for work performed. Traditionally no remuneration was owed for the period during which an employee has not performed the contracted work (Article 7:627 CC). However, in the course of time an increasing number of derogations of this 'no work, no pay' principle has been made. Obviously, a worker is entitled to a continuation of the payment of his or her wages during holidays (*see* paragraphs 120 et seq.) and during a number of arrangements of paid leave (*see* paragraph 125). Other categories of exceptions will be outlined below.

I. The Entitlement to Remuneration if No Work Is Performed

147. Another important exception to the basic rule of 'no work, no pay' is Article 7:628(1) CC stating that the employer must pay the agreed remuneration fixed per unit of time if the employee has not wholly or partly performed the contracted work, unless the wholly or partly non-performance of the contracted work is due to a cause which, reasonably, should be for the account of the employee. Because this is a somewhat vague rule, the question arises as to which causes should be for the account of the employee and which for the account of the employer? On this question there is a variety of case law. From this one can infer that a lack of commercial orders or stagnation in the supply of material generally must be considered as for the account of the employer.[142] The same applies to governmental

141. Parliamentary Papers 35157.
142. Dutch Supreme Court, 21 Dec. 2001, JAR 2002/19.

prohibitions which the employer himself has provoked[143] and calamities against which the employer, reasonably, could have insured himself. In those kinds of risks the employer can only very seldom invoke force majeure to be liberated from his obligation to pay the workers.[144] As to other causes of the non-performance of the work by the employee, such as traffic problems, it is less certain whether they are for the account of the employer.

Because of the high risks that they run to continue payment of the wages, employers may be tempted to exclude these risks explicitly in the contract of employment. However the legislator has restricted that possibility. Only during the first six months of the contract of employment there may be a derogation from the basic rule of Article 7:628(1) CC to the detriment of the employee, and this only by written contract (Article 7:628(5) CC). By collective agreement this period of six months may be extended for functions in which the work has an incidental character and no fixed extent (Article 7:628(7) CC). It may be possible to agree that paid non-worked hours are later compensated by non-paid overtime hours, but this may require the consent of the parties to the collective agreement, the works council and/or the individual employees. Moreover, the Minister on a proposal of the Foundation of Labour may provide that on certain sectors or subsectors these derogations are not applicable (Article 7:628(8) CC). In addition the Minister may – possibly under conditions – provide that the basic rule of Article 7:628(1) CC wholly or partly does not apply if the non-performance of the contracted work is due to exceptional circumstances. This provision will be used to continue the existing ministerial regulations which provide for a system of short-time working as described in paragraph 149. In the temporary agency business the derogation *in peius* of the basic rule of Article 7:628(1) CC is possible via written contract for the first six months during which the agency worker has worked (Article 7:691(7) CC). Further derogations during at most 1.5 years are possible based on a collective agreement (Article 7:691(8) CC).

148. Article 7:628 CC is widely used in Dutch labour law by lawyers to base on it claims for the continuation of the payment or remuneration in cases:

- of a dismissal, which is challenged by the employee (*see* paragraphs 197 et seq.);
- of casual work contracts, when the employer is not using the preparedness to work of an employee (*see* paragraph 65);
- of the suspension of an employee without the continuation of the payment of remuneration (*see* paragraph 184);
- of partial disability to work when the employer refrains from offering suitable alternative work to the employee (*see* paragraph 85);
- of a strike, when the employer stops the payment of wages for non-striking workers (*see* paragraph 352); and
- in cases that the worker stays at home because the labour relation is allegedly disturbed by the employer (*see* paragraph 151).[145]

143. Dutch Supreme Court, 27 Mar. 1981, NJ 1981, 492.
144. Dutch Supreme Court, 23 Jan. 1925, NJ 1925, 381.
145. Dutch Supreme Court, 27 Jun. 2008, JAR 2008/188 (*Mak/SGBO*).

For the chances of those claims *see* the paragraphs referred to. At any rate there is the general condition for those claims to be successful viz. that the employee has been truly ready and able to perform the contracted work.[146] This readiness should have been there during the entire period over which the continuation of remuneration was claimed[147] and must have been clearly communicated to the employer. If this has not been done the court may reject or mitigate the claim on the basis of reasonableness and fairness.[148]

II. Short-Time Working

149. Working may become impossible because of abnormal events, such as war or floods or epidemics and it would be a shame if such causes would bring the employers to lay off valuable workers that they would bitterly need at a later moment. To cope with this problem in the Netherlands just like in other nations, some mechanism has been developed, which is called *werktijdverkorting* (short-time work).[149] This scheme (the so-called Calamities Regulation of 2004) offers the possibility that, if a slackness in business affairs over a prolonged period is considered as temporary, employers may keep their workers on the payroll with a temporarily reduced wage burden, while the unemployment office grants the workers unemployment benefits.

It requires a permit of the Ministry of SZW which is granted on the basis of ministerial policy rules.[150] According to these rules a short-time working permit is only granted when the reduction in the weekly working time of the employees concerned is at least 20%. The reduction must have lasted at least two weeks, so the enterprise has to pay the wages for the first weeks before a temporary stop is seen as an abnormal risk. Moreover it is required that the extraordinary circumstances which are the cause for the reduction in activity cannot, reasonably, be considered to be part of the normal operational risks. Short-time working may take various forms. Which form will be chosen depends on the enterprise applying for short-time. This can be, for instance, working two days in one week and three days in the other. Working zero hours will be allowed in the case of, e.g., fire. In principle short-time working authorization is only granted for a six-week period at most. Extension to a maximum of three such periods is possible.

If the Ministry has given its permit the social security authorities will pay unemployment benefits to the workers according to the Unemployment Benefits Act (UBA), as this Act does not require a formal end of the contract of employment before the granting of unemployment benefits is possible. Unemployment benefits can be granted if the worker cannot actually work and the employer is not obliged

146. Dutch Supreme Court, 18 Jan. 1991, NJ 1991, 273; Dutch Supreme Court, 2 Oct. 1992, JAR 1992/101; Dutch Supreme Court, 3 Mar. 1995, JAR 1995/79 and Dutch Supreme Court, 17 Oct. 1997, NJ 1998, 130.
147. Dutch Supreme Court, 1 Feb. 1952, NJ 1953, 366.
148. Dutch Supreme Court, 1 Jul. 1993, NJ 1993, 666.
149. *See* W.A. Zondag *Werktijdverkorting* (PhD Erasmus Universiteit Rotterdam), 2001; on pp. 621–629 one finds an English-language summary of the developments in Dutch labour law in this field.
150. Policy Regulations of 8 Oct. 2004, Stcrt. 2004, 199.

to continue the payment of wages. As the unemployment benefit for most workers will be less than 100% of their normal wages, usually – as part of the deal – the employer will supplement the unemployment benefits up to the amount of the net wage. Sometimes the trade unions are involved in the negotiations about all these arrangements.

Workers on short-time are not obliged to register with the public employment services and to actively apply for another job, because it is the very intention of the short-time work arrangements to keep workers for re-employment in their own business. For the government it is convenient that workers on this scheme do not count as unemployed!

Although avoiding dismissals in periods of temporary slackness in business is a recognized purpose of the Dutch labour market rules, it must be observed that the Dutch regulation concerning short-time work is very strict. Normally Dutch governments are not keen to use this instrument in situations of economic problems of firms due to merely economic causes. Short-term permits for a reduction of activities caused by cyclical and structural economic reasons are considered as subsidies to loss-makers and to hamper necessary restructuring and are therefore refused. Dutch governments want to reserve this instrument for situations of economic problems caused by non-economic reasons, such as an epidemic, high water and an explosion. As a consequence of the relative strictness, the use of short-time work in the Netherlands is low: in 1990–1993 0.2% of the labour force was affected, compared with 1.0% in Germany. One of the last times this instrument was used was in 2001 during the mad cow disease crisis in agriculture, which forced many persons in this sector temporarily out of work.

150. However, during the financial crisis of 2008–2010, the Dutch government temporarily abandoned this restrictive policy and launched a specific short-time working scheme, enabling firms hit by this financial crisis to reduce the number of working hours of their staff by maximum 50% for a maximum of nine months. During this period the employees received unemployment benefits for the hours that they were not working. The scheme was accompanied by training agreements between the unions and the employer to enable the workers to receive training during the inactive period. This temporary regulation, which was abolished in 2011, has been very effective in keeping Dutch business going in this period. About 70,000 employees have benefited from this scheme.

III. Absence due to Sickness

151. The CC (Article 7:629) stipulates that employers must continue to pay the salary of ill employees during the first two years of sickness: at least 70% of the salary up to about EUR 50,000 a year, but at least to the full statutory minimum wage during the first year of illness. In reality – often based on collective agreements – most Dutch employers in case of illness pay their employees 100% of the wage during the first year of illness. During this period of two years the employee may not be dismissed (*see* paragraphs 198–199).

For employees performing (almost) exclusively domestic personal services for his/her employer on fewer than four days a week and for workers that have reached the AOW-pensionable age, this right is limited to a period of six weeks (Article 7:629(2) CC).

Several categories of workers are completely exempted from this regime – for them the old Sickness Act, a true social security act, secures a sickness benefit at the same level. This concerns notably (a) workers on a fixed-term contract who are still ill, after their contract of employment has expired; (b) on-call workers; (c) temporary agency workers; (d) workers with a recent illness past, who have been given a new employment; (e) pregnant women and young mothers, etc.

Finally, there are a number of cases in which the employee is deprived of the right at sickness pay (Article 7:629(3) CC). In fact three exceptions are made.

The first exception is if the sickness has been due to the own intent of the employee or for the time during which the actions of the employee have impeded or delayed his recovery. These concepts are very narrow construed in the case law of the courts as far as the minimum requirements for this statutory right are concerned. The 'intent' must have been directed towards causing the disablement.[151] For supra-statutory aspects (notably the usual 100% continuation of the wage instead of the statutory 70%), the courts accept more ample exceptions as criteria. So, for instance, participation in an unhealthy or dangerous sport is not accepted by the courts as a reason to deprive the worker of the right to continue the payment of 70% of the wage, but this criterion may be used to deny the employee the supplement to a 100% wage compensation.

Sometimes an employee alleges to be ill as he is not psychically able to come to his work because of a disturbed relationship with the employer or the colleagues. The courts are not accepting this as a ground for the continuation of wage payment under Article 7:629 CC, but it may be that continuation of payment of wages in these cases can be based on the bona fides article (*see* paragraph 102).

The second exception is made for the time during which the employee, although able to do so, does not without good reason perform suitable work or refuses to cooperate with measures to enable him to perform such work. The notion 'suitable work' in this respect means 'all work fit for the forces and faculties of the employee, save if acceptance of this work, cannot be requested from the employee for physical, psychological or social reasons' (Article 7:658a(3) CC). This exception does not cover workers that have reached the AOW-pensionable age.

The final exception is made for the time during which the employee refuses to cooperate in the creation of an action programme for his return to work (*see* paragraphs 80 and 199).

152. Moreover, the employer has the right to suspend the payment of the remuneration during a period in which the employee fails to comply with such reasonable rules as the employer has given in writing regarding the provision of the information which the employer needs in order to determine the entitlement to the remuneration (Article 7:629(6) CC).

151. Dutch Supreme Court, 14 Mar. 2008, JAR 2008/110.

All these rules may easily lead to a conflict between employer and employee. Such conflicts can only be solved by a verdict of the courts. The legislator has taken a few steps to facilitate employees the access to the court. So the costs of these procedures are to be borne by the employer (Article 7:629a(6) CC). However, the courts will only receive claims under Article 7:629 CC if the claim is accompanied by a certificate of an expert appointed by the UWV concerning the inability of the employee to perform the contracted or other fitting work (Article 629a(1) CC).[152] So, in reality, the UWV physician is the real arbiter in these cases, as normally both the employer and the employee will avoid a court case after the UWV physician has given his judgment.

Apart from all these obligations in the field of the continuation of the remuneration and the duty to provide the disabled employee with suitable work (*see* paragraph 86), there is a number of bureaucratic obligations on the employer such as the obligation to draw up an action plan for the reintegration of the employee (Article 7:660a CC). The period of two years continuation of the payment of wages shall be extended when the employer is negligent in executing this obligation as well as a number of other obligations in the Disability Benefits Legislation (Article 7:629(11) CC). This provision is not applicable to workers that have reached the AOW-pensionable age.

In order to stimulate the responsibility of the employee for his health, the lawmakers have given not only the parties to the contract of employment but also the parties to the collective agreement the liberty to agree upon no wage at all for the first two days of illness (Article 7:629(9) CC), but this possibility is seldom used.

All these rather draconian rules replaced former arrangements under which public sickness funds used to grant sickness benefits as from the first day of illness. This new arrangement was imposed on the Dutch employers by Parliament in 1996 and 2003 to counter the unacceptably high level of sick leave and disability benefits in the Netherlands, which had reached some 9% in the 1990s.[153] It was hoped that these rules would stimulate employers to pay more attention to illness prevention and stimulate employees to be more careful in taking sick leave. Since the 1990s sick leave has indeed dropped to – currently – circa 4% on average (*see* further paragraph 165).

Dutch employers have often insured themselves with private insurance companies against this risk, but not all of them have done so. This insurance is often considered too costly by small employers. Other employers sometimes calculate that it may be cheaper to bear the risk themselves, which may be true for large companies, but small companies can be ruined if they have to continue wage payment over such long periods. A small consolation may be that the lawmakers have laid down some special rules on the basis of which the employer may have recourse against persons that may have been responsible for the illness/accidents of his employees (Article 6:107a CC).

152. Dutch Supreme Court, 14 Sep. 2018, ECLI:NL:HR:2018:1673.

153. *See* B. Hoogendijk, *De loondoorbetalingsverplichting gedurende het eerste ziektejaar*, Arnhem, 1999; on pp. 307–313 are found an English-language description and discussion of the legal position of the sick employee during the first year of illness.

The Dutch trade unions are very dissatisfied about the high pressure that employers actually are putting on ill workers to resume their work. They distrust the impartiality of the company doctors in the P&P. The European Committee on Social Rights which supervises the ESC has given a negative verdict over the Dutch rules in this field, and the Dutch legislator has recently strengthened the independence of the company doctors (*see* paragraph 163). Another debated aspect is the privacy protection of the employees in this arrangement.[154]

Employers and notably the small ones have continued to pressure for a less burdensome legislation in this field and notably for a shortening of the two-year period of continuous wage payment to ill workers. The government until recently resisted this pressure, but the actual government has concluded in December 2018 an agreement with the employers' associations to create a sort of subsidy for the small employers, confronted with this risk.[155]

§8. Rights to Remuneration in the Case of Employer's Insolvency

153. In the Netherlands pay claims relating to work performed after the bankruptcy judgment (or after the start of a procedure of judicial leave to defer payments of debts) are classed as debts *of* the estate (Articles 40 and 239(3) Bankruptcy Act (BA)), which must be discharged preferentially. They rank first, apart from the payment of debenture holders and mortgagees (secured creditors). Case law has defined that this concept of pay also includes pay during the notice period, travelling costs, holiday bonuses, the employee's part of the contributions to a pension fund, other funding contributions payable and the entitlement to payment for unused days of annual holiday of an employee dismissed by the receiver after bankruptcy. This high priority for pay claims relating to work performed after the bankruptcy is always the main reason why the curator (receiver) uses to dismiss immediately all or most of the staff, which according to Dutch law he can do easily (*see* paragraph 228).

Employees' pay claims relating to work performed prior to the bankruptcy judgment are classed as debts *against* the bankrupt's estate. Pay claims for the current and previous year and claims deriving from the termination of the contract of employment (which was already agreed before the date of bankruptcy, even if the dismissal was realized after the date of the bankruptcy judgment) have priority over other debts against the bankrupt's estate. But they have to give way to the debenture holders and mortgagees, the post-bankruptcy claims, the bankruptcy costs (such as the receivers' fee) and the claims of the tax authorities and social security (Article 3:278 and 3:288(e) CC). In reality this means that in 97% of the cases such pre-bankruptcy claims of the worker cannot be recovered whatever the legal preferences are. So this workers' preference is often worthless.

154. *See* I. van der Helm, *The Privacy Protection of the Sick Employee: The Dutch Case from a Comparative Perspective*, 15(3) Eur. J. Soc. Sec. 273–296 (2013).
155. Parliamentary Papers 35074, J pp. 5–6; 29544, no. 873.

154. More important, therefore, is a special title in the UBA, Articles 61–68, which, in the case of the employer's insolvency, gives a worker right to recover some of his wage claims from the *Algemeen Werkloosheidsfonds* (General Unemployment Fund), which is jointly financed by contributions of employers and the state.

This facility dates back to the 1960s when in the context of a wave of bankruptcies it became evident that the traditional protection provided under bankruptcy law had become fully insufficient. This new concept was intended to ensure that employees in a bankruptcy situation were more certain of recovering a greater proportion of their claims, with less delay, than there would be on the basis of bankruptcy law. This new concept was adopted for the whole of the EC in Directive 80/987/EEC (now Directive 2008/94/EC), relating to the protection of employees in the event of their employer's insolvency and found a following even at world level, viz. in the ILO's Convention of 1992 on the subject.

The claims deemed eligible for guaranteed payment are those relating to:

(a) pay for a maximum of thirteen weeks immediately preceding the date of termination of the employment relationship. 'Pay' is traditionally understood to include broadly everything actually owed by the employer to the employee by virtue of the contract of employment, such as a thirteenth-month pay (pro rata), compensation for removal costs, essential use of credit cards, compensation for the loss of a company car, necessary legal costs and so forth;
(b) pay for the notice period, limited to the period of notice specified in Article 40(1) BA, so to a maximum of six weeks' pay;
(c) holiday pay and holiday bonuses for one year preceding the date of termination of the employment relationship.

As from 2016 there is a cap on these payments at of about EUR 76,000 yearly wage.

The financing of pension liabilities is covered to a limited extent. However, the payment of the transition allowance (*see* paragraph 219) is not provided for in dismissal cases in situations of bankruptcy or judicial leave to defer payments.

This scheme is only applicable in cases of bankruptcy of the employer and in other cases in which an employer is unable to pay. However, the courts do not consider the legal procedure of judicial leave to defer payments of debts (*surséance van betaling*) as a situation in which the UWV should take over the payment of the wage debts as in this legal situation the employees can still cash in on their wage claims. In such cases the salary and the benefit premiums relating to the employment contract are debts of the estate as from the commencement of the judicial leave (Article 239(3) BA).

There is a provision against the abuse of this scheme (Article 63(3) lid 3 UBA) and the subrogation of the UWV of the claim of the employee is provided for (Article 66 UBA).

§9. Remuneration of Public Servants

155. As opposed to the private sector the remuneration of civil servants until 2020 has been entirely based on statutory law (Article 125 Civil Service Act). The concrete rules were laid down in regulations of the state and the various public corporations (municipalities, etc.). Those regulations were unilaterally fixed by the authorities, but in reality not without negotiations with the trade unions (*see* paragraph 299). As of 1 January 2020 the statutory rules on the remuneration of public servants – a few exceptions apart – are the same as for workers in the private industry (*see* paragraph 54). So also the remuneration of the public servants will henceforward be regulated by collective agreements.

Since many years the remuneration of civil servants uses to be in average as good as in the private industry. For low-level employees they might have been somewhat better, but for high-ranking employees they were less favourable (*see also* paragraph 288). Consequently the wage differences among civil servants are less than in the private sector.

Chapter 5. Health and Safety

§1. Duty to Provide Safe and Healthy Working Conditions on the Premises

156. During the industrialization of the nineteenth-century workers were increasingly confronted with industrial injuries. Some employers established company funds to give relief to workers who had suffered an accident at work and a few progressive employers concluded private insurance for their workers against the consequences of those injuries. Most employers, however, did not bother about such situations and a 1886 state enquiry into the conditions in industry brought to light cases of poignant misery among workers who had met with an industrial accident. They were thrown on private charity or on the charge of the parish. Although the old Dutch CC in principle opened the possibility of holding the employer responsible for damages as a result of tort or negligence, in reality this right to compensation could hardly be exercised. Finally in 1907 the new provisions on the employment contract in the Dutch CC brought a clear obligation on the employer to protect his workers in the workplace. Article 7:658 CC obliges the employer to make such provisions for the organization and maintenance of the places in which and the implements and tools with which he has the work performed and to take such measures and issue such directives for the performance of the work as may reasonably be deemed necessary to prevent the employee from suffering damage in the course of his work. An employer shall be liable to an employee for any loss which the employee suffers in the course of his work, unless he performed this obligation or that loss was to a large extent the result of intent or deliberate recklessness on the part of the employee.

Yet, like in most other Western countries, this employers' liability has since the beginning of last century to a very large extent been neutralized under social security legislation, which organized a special social security scheme for accidents at work. So the liability of Article 7:658 CC was largely a dead letter. However, in 1967 the Dutch social security legislation was reorganized. The special social security scheme for accidents at work was merged with the general schemes on sickness pay, disability benefits, pensions for old-age persons and survivors and healthcare costs. Within the framework of this reorganization the liability based on Article 7:658 CC was revived, although the Dutch social security statutes continue to limit the possibilities for recovery on the employer by the social security institutions to cases of 'intentional damage' or 'consistent recklessness' on the side of the employer, which is seldom the case.

157. In the first years after 1967 the liability, based on Article 7:658 CC, was seldom invoked as Dutch social security law continued to cover the damages from accidents by providing healthcare, sickness and disability benefits to the victims as well as pensions for their survivors. It was only in cases where those social security benefits did not make up for all the expenses connected with accidents at work that the employers could be held liable under Article 7:658 CC.

Since the 1980s, however, actions against employers based on Article 7:658 CC have become much more numerous. There are two main reasons for this. First, social security benefits have been gradually mitigated so that now more often than in the past the costs of work accidents are exceeding the benefits from social security. Second, because ever more people are not satisfied with the benefits given by social security and believe that in cases of work accidents they are entitled to more compensation. The courts were prepared to grant compensatory damages on top of the social security benefits in ever more cases.

158. At the same time experience has taught that the words of Article 7:658 CC and its context can be too narrow to deal satisfactory with these claims, for instance in case of a disease incurred in the past but which took long time before manifesting itself, such as illnesses caused by working with asbestos. So there have been various pressures to a further expansion of the employers' liability under Article 7:658 CC.

The first pressure was to change the liability under Article 7:658 CC from a fault liability to a risk liability. This pressure was only partly successful. Article 7:658 CC has remained a fault liability. The employer is not liable if it has not failed in any particular manner towards the employee.[156] However, the Dutch judiciary will not easily reach this conclusion. The HR holds the employer already liable if it has failed at any moment in his duty of care towards the employee by omitting to take – within reason – any necessary measures to prevent exposure of workers to health risks.[157] The courts are even not prepared to diminish the liability of the employer if the damage to the employee has wholly or partly been caused by the negligence of the employee. Only extreme cases of gross negligence of the workers may exonerate the employer.[158]

The second pressure was to reverse the burden of proof for Article 7:658 CC liability. In the 1980s and 1990s the courts had already gone down this road and Parliament in 1997 finished this process of reversing the burden of proof by statute. It is now the employer who has to prove that it has not failed in any particular manner in its duty of care to the employee.

The third pressure was and is to widen the scope of this liability. The statute links this employers' liability narrowly to the 'workplace'. And indeed the courts have traditionally refused to extend this liability to damages deriving from accidents outside the workplace, even though they may be linked in a certain way to the fulfilment of the contractual obligations of the employee. For instance, the postman distributing letters out in some neighbourhood. In recent years the courts on more occasions have brought accidents on public roads under the coverage of Article 7:658 CC,[159] although in those cases the duty of care of the employer may be more limited.[160] Moreover, the courts in these cases have pointed to the possibility that

156. Dutch Supreme Court, 5 Nov. 2004, JAR 2004/278.
157. Dutch Supreme Court, 15 Oct. 1982, NJ 1984, 21.
158. Dutch Supreme Court, 20 Sep. 1996, NJ 1997, 198.
159. Dutch Supreme Court, 12 Dec. 2008, JAR 2009/15.
160. Dutch Supreme Court, 11 Nov. 2011, JAR 2011/316; Dutch Supreme Court, 30 Mar. 2012, NJ 2012, 687.

the employer may be obliged to conclude an insurance for his employees against accidents, not on the basis of Article 7:658 CC but on the basis of Article 7:611 CC (*see* paragraph 102).[161]

The fourth pressure has been to widen the employers' liability under Article 7:658 CC to illnesses that only become manifest many years after the work has been done, such as mesothelioma caused by contact with asbestos or Chroom 6, which *inter alia* required from the court's deviations from the strict rules on prescription.[162]

The fifth pressure has been to widen the employers' liability under Article 7:658 CC to merely psychological illnesses, such as burn-out, which has led some courts to resort to proportional liabilities.[163]

The sixth pressure has been to extend the scope of this liability *ratione personae*, now that an increasing part of the Dutch labour market is filled by workers, who are not working on a formal contract of employment (*see* paragraph 68). It has been extended by the courts to volunteers[164] and in some cases also to independent subcontracting persons of the employer.[165] One of the main-bottle-necks is the so-called platform workers (*see* paragraph 69), but there are more sources of anxiety. The government is actually searching for a solution. Temporary agency workers who under Dutch law do have a formal contract of employment may hold both the temporary agency and the user firm liable for work accidents (Article 7:658(4) CC).

Every responsible employer in the Netherlands nowadays is aware of the risks of liability from Article 7:658 CC and has insured himself against those risks. The insurance companies, however, will increase the insurance premiums if the courts or Parliament is substantially increasing the liability of the employers under this article. As such premiums must be paid by employers, the employers are reluctant to see their liability broadened. Nevertheless the Netherlands in recent years has seen an increased emphasis on employers' liability for safe and healthy working conditions under civil law.[166]

One of the problematic aspects of the Dutch approach, however, is that the fights about including new developments in this area in the existing case law are often taking many years, which can be very dejecting for the victims. So there is also pressure now on the government to set up intermediate arrangements to overcome the liability problems in a more victim-friendly way, but this seems difficult to realize.[167]

161. Dutch Supreme Court, 1 Feb. 2008, JAR 2008/56; Dutch Supreme Court, 12 Dec. 2008, JAR 2009/15 and Dutch Supreme Court, 11 Nov. 2011, NJ 2011, 597.
162. Dutch Supreme Court, 24 Mar. 2017, JAR 2017/72.
163. Dutch Supreme Court, 7 Jun. 2013, ECLI:NL:HR:2013:BZ1721.
164. Dutch Supreme Court, 15 Dec. 2017, ECLI:NL:HR:2017:3142.
165. Dutch Supreme Court, 23 Mar. 2012, JAR 2012/110; ILLR Vol. 32, p. 151.
166. *See* B. Barentsen, *Arbeidsongeschiktheid, aansprakelijkheid, bescherming en compensatie*, Leiden, 2003; on pp. 257–263 may be found an English-language description of the history of the legislation on employers' liability, workers compensation and disability benefits in the Netherlands. *See also* M. Vegter, *Vergoeding van psychisch letsel door de werkgever*, The Hague, 2005; on pp. 697–715 may be found an English-language description and discussion of the question under what circumstances an employee who has become mentally ill as a result of his work may obtain compensation from his employer. *See also* A.T.J.M. Jacobs contribution to E.H. Yates & J.F. Burton Jr., *International Examinations of Medical-Legal Aspects of Work Injuries*.
167. Parliamentary Papers 25883, nos 277 and 295.

§2. Health and Safety Regulations under Public Law

159. Public law rules on health and safety emerged by the end of the nineteenth century. They were both general enactments, such as the Safety Act (*Veiligheidswet* 1895), and specific statutes (such as the White Phosphor Matches Act, 1901; the Caisson Act, 1905; the Mining Regulation, 1906; the Stonemasons' Act, 1911; and the Stevedore's Act, 1914). The *Veiligheidswet* 1934 replaced the *Veiligheidswet* 1895 and served to rule this field of the law until 1980, several times updated to keep pace with the technological developments. In the 1970s it was felt that a more comprehensive overhaul of the existing legislation was needed. These were the days of the concept of *Humanisierung der Arbeit* (humanization of work), which required that work should not only be safe and healthy but also contribute to the well-being and joy of living of the workers. The radical changes of the laws on health and safety in Norway and Great Britain served as model for the Dutch to revise their legislation in 1980. The *Veiligheidswet* 1934 was replaced in 1980 by the HSA. This Act was no longer only aimed to prevent work accidents and occupational diseases. Its wider ambition was reflected by adding the notion of well-being to the purposes of the Act. Moreover the realization of these purposes was no longer seen as a primary responsibility for the state. Safety, health and well-being were now regarded to be the prime responsibility of employers and employees together. Employers should not limit themselves to respect the legal provisions but conduct a positive and active policy of well-being. The employees were given the possibility to participate in the decision-making in this field. As all this would require a major transposition – 30 decrees and 1,200 provisions would be needed – it was the intention to bring the new legislation in force over a period of eight years.[168]

Unfortunately the Act was born exactly at a moment on which the long expansion of the welfare state in the Netherlands had ground to a halt and the country had to face protracted years of economic slump and unemployment (*see* paragraph 17). This led the government to start a process of deregulation and the HSA became one of its first targets. The Act was criticized because of its overdose of legislative detail. This was only slightly diminished by an Amendment Act of 1987 which repealed some of the most pious vows of the Act. Later the government introduced a much-deregulated edition of the existing legislation, which became the HSA 1998. However, this new legislation was also quickly considered by many people as being too much a demonstration of the desire to regulate and a fresh attempt was made to deregulate. Out of an ambition to stop all superfluous regulation and to improve the competitiveness of Dutch industry many people wanted the HSA to be stripped of most of its provisions that went further than ILO and EU rules in this field require. After much debate a consensus could be reached between trade unions and employers in the Social-Economic Council which was then taken over by the government and resulted in a major Amendment Act in 2007. That is the legislation in force in the present day albeit with some further minor amendments since then.

168. *See* A.J.C.M. Geers, *Recht en humanisering van de arbeid*, Deventer, 1988; on pp. 369–375 may be found an English-language description and discussion of the development of the Dutch law on health and safety at work to a comprehensive law on humanization of the working place.

160. Despite all this deregulation the Health and Safety at Work Act continues to be not only aimed at health and safety at work but also more generally at human working conditions and the welfare of the workforce. In recent years this legislation even received new missions, such as combating sexual harassment and psychological harassment ('mobbing') (Article 4 HSA) and contributing to the prevention of sick leave and incapacity for work, which were considered too high in the Netherlands (*see* paragraph 151). In the Dutch Health and Safety at Work Act health, safety and well-being are considered to be a common responsibility of all concerned: employer, employees, company doctors, safety experts, government agencies, etc. In the recent amendments to this legislation one notices a tendency to shift the care for good working conditions further to the joint responsibility of employers and employees and to restrict government involvement to the formulation of general rules and specific rules for the prevention of serious risks. The objective of most of the actual health and safety rules is to set out what should be achieved and to lay less emphasis on how it should be achieved. Businesses thus have greater freedom to coordinate their working conditions and policies with their own possibilities and needs. The government intends to make more use of certification, a process in which the social partners and others are supposed to draw up standards and procedures relating to parts of the production processes in the various branches of industry.

It is not easy to measure the success of the Dutch legislation on health and safety at work. Judged by the number of mortal accidents the situation in the Netherlands is not unsatisfactory. The death toll of work accidents has decreased from a yearly 100 in average in the 1990s to a yearly 50 in average in the period 2005–2011 and a yearly 40 in average in the period 2012–2016. Actually in the Netherlands the chance to become a victim of a deadly work accident is 0.8 on 100,000 workers – an all-European law. However it also has been established that at least half of the Dutch working population is still confronted with health risks, caused by working. There are still many victims of work with unhealthy agents like asbestos, Chroom-6 and the like. The Netherlands has more occupational cancer deaths than the EU average. Each year 3,000 persons die because they have been exposed at work to dangerous substances. Also work stress, bullying at the workplace and bad nutrition in workplace canteens are now seen as health risks. In 2013 almost 50% of the cases of illness had a psychosocial character. In 1998 this was 30%. In 2017 and 2018, a total of 16% to 17% of the active population suffered from burn-out problems.

161. The Health and Safety at Work Act is a framework Act. The statute itself contains various general principles and obligations, most of them directed to the employer, some to the employees and the employee representatives.

The Act lays the general obligation on the employer to have a specific health and safety policy, based on a number of principles to be taken into account in the organization of work (Article 3 HSA):

- to ensure that the work is not detrimental to the safety and health of the worker;
- to eradicate, as much as possible, the risk for safety and health at its sources and otherwise to take collective and individual measures to protect the workers and to put individual means at their disposal;

- to adapt to the workers as much as possible the configuration of jobs, work methods and work devices;
- to avoid or limit as much as possible monotonous and tempo related work;
- to offer the workers escape routes and damage limitation in case of danger;
- to prevent or limit psychosocial work burdens (stress, mobbing, aggressing, intimidation, sexual harassment, discrimination).

All this the employer must do taking into account the state of science and the professional service. The text of the Act reads that several of the aforementioned obligations must be fulfilled 'unless this reasonably cannot be expected from the employer'. This phrase gives the enforcing authorities the possibility to balance these obligations against organizational, technical and economic arguments.

The HSA further obliges the employer to:

- adapt the jobs of employees with structural, functional limitations (Article 4 HSA);
- draw up a list of the risks involved in the work processes and a work plan how to reduce those risks and to define who will undertake that task and when; an evaluation must be made on an annual basis which – together with a new risk list – will then serve as the point of departure for the next cycle in the process of improving working conditions (Article 5 HSA);
- prevent grave accidents with dangerous substances (Article 6 HSA);
- inform and educate the workers on all health and safety aspects of their tasks (Article 8 HSA);
- notify to the Inspectorate SZW about all work accidents and occupational diseases (Article 9 HSA);
- prevent danger for third persons (Article 10 HSA);
- allow workers to submit themselves to a periodical medical examination (Article 18 HSA).

The employer is under the obligation to actively take care (Article 3(4) HSA); he should not wait until the Inspection SZW has given him warnings.

If several employers are present on one and the same location they are obliged to cooperate for the fulfilment of the health and safety obligations (Article 19 HSA).

As the Act is based on the philosophy that employer and employee must cooperate in the execution of health and safety policies at the level of the enterprise, the legislator has imposed on the employer a number of specific obligations to this end, such as to engage employees to discuss health and safety matters with the employer on a regular basis, both in work progress discussions and in discussions with the works council (Article 12 HSA, *see* paragraph 394). Consequently the Act confers a number of rights to the works council, for instance that the works council must be informed on the risk list and give its consent to it. The works council often has delegated these powers to a special health and safety committee.

162. Moreover the government stimulates labour and management at sector level to conclude covenants on health and safety in order to diminish the special risks for health and safety which occur in that sector. The social partners may also draw up codes of practice on health and safety (*Arbo-catalogus*), which are not binding to the employers, but will be used by the Inspection SZW in its enforcement policy. These *Arbo-catalogi* have been issued in most sectors of Dutch business.

The legislator has imposed on *the employee* the general obligation to assume the necessary prudency and diligence and – as far as possible – to the take care for his own safety and that of other persons (Article 11 HSA). All this in conformity with his level of training and the instructions given to him by his employer. This means *inter alia* that he must use the protective devices in the right way, leave safety devices in good order, participate in health and safety education, notify safety risks, etc. At the same time the Act recognizes the right of the worker to interrupt his work or to refuse to proceed with his work in case of imminent serious danger (Article 29 HSA). Such a refusal cannot be punished by dismissal or a less serious punishment provided the worker has timely informed his employer of the situation if this was possible.

In addition to the more general regulations there were a large number of implementing orders containing meticulous rules on various aspects of health and safety at work. These orders were in 1996 consolidated in one single Health and Safety at Work Order (*Arbeidsomstandighedenbesluit*), now based on Article 16 HSA. In addition there are the Health and Safety at Work Regulation (*Arboregeling*) and the Health and Safety Policy Rules (*Arbobeleidsregels*), containing all sorts of detailed prescriptions. In the Health and Safety at Work Order a frequent use has been made of the technic of maximum norms of exposure and of workload.

By way of the Health and Safety at Work Act and the Health and Safety at Work Order the Netherlands had assumed that it had implemented the entire body of EU and ILO rules in this area. It is estimated that about 90% of the Dutch health and safety rules are now in fact implementations of EU and ILO norms. Some critical observers hold that the Dutch legislator in bringing Dutch law in line with international standards has at the same time deleted various provisions that were more favourable to the workers, contrary to the intentions of these international norms.

The HSA imposes the obligation on the employer to call in expert assistance in the implementation of his health and safety policies. He must appoint one or more of his employees as prevention assistants or – if not possible – to call in this assistance from outside the firm. The nomination of the prevention assistant, his position in the work organization and his tasks must have the consent of the works council (Article 13 HSA). He/she must be involved in the drawing up of the risk list (*see* paragraph 161) and the advising of the works council in health and safety matters and for this reason he/she must have the necessary expertise, experience, equipment and time allotted for this work. Small enterprises (maximum twenty-five employees) do not need the appointment of such prevention assistants if the employer has the expertise, experience and equipment to perform these tasks himself (Article 13(10) HSA). Moreover the employer must appoint one or more of his employees as rescue workers, who must be able – in case of accidents or emergencies – to perform first medical aid, fire-fighting and the organization of evacuation (Article 15 HSA).

163. Some specific tasks in the field of health and safety must be entrusted to specialists, such as a medical doctor or other certified experts. This concerns medical examinations and periodical medical check-ups of the staff, the reintegration of ill and partially disabled employees and the completing of the definite text of the risk list. The first company doctor in the Netherlands was engaged in 1912. The obligation to create a company medical service was only laid on large companies and so, still in 1994, 60% of the workers were not surveyed by a company medical doctor. In that year Parliament decided to make it obligatory for every employer to be affiliated to a so-called *Arbodienst* (P&P service) – a professional service, not only comprising company doctors, but also other professionals who can carry out activities related to the protection and prevention of occupational risks for the enterprise. At the same time these services were given a crucial role in establishing the illness and the reintegration of ill workers (*see* paragraphs 135 and 165). Existing P&P services expanded their field of activities to other clients, and thousands of new services sprang up as these regulations required employers to affiliate to external commercial P&P services. However, the Netherlands was condemned by the CJEU for this arrangement. The Court found that EU law (Article 7(3) of Directive 89/391/EEC) gave priority to internal services. Only if such services cannot be organized for lack of competent personnel in the undertaking may the employer enlist competent external services or persons.[169] So the Dutch law was amended to give the priority to internal services (Article 14 and 14a HSA). This has led to a new expansion of the company-bound P&P services and to a reduction of the external ones.

Nevertheless some critical observers held that the Dutch legislator had gone somewhat too far in reducing the involvement of the state in this field.[170] In a recent Amendment Act[171] the independent position of the company doctor and other certified prevention specialists was strengthened and the access of the workers to them was better guaranteed (Article 14 HSA). These persons got the task to report the occurrence of occupational illnesses (Article 9(3) HSA). To improve the professional quality of the P&P services the Act now contains a number of requirements. Also the sanctions of the HSA have been strengthened by this Amendment Act.

The Dutch Health and Safety at Work Act has a very broad scope of application. It applies to all work done both in private business and in the public sector. All employers must apply the health and safety regulations and measures to all workers, irrespective of their legal status (Article 1 HSA), thus also to trainees, students of educational institutions, leased staff (the employees hired from temporary work agencies), illegal immigrants, and all other type of work done under their authority (Article 2 HSA). In practice there are problems with the health and safety of temporary agency workers. They have 70% more chance to be a victim of work accidents than the core-workers.

169. ECJ 22 May 2003, C441/01 (*Commission v. The Netherlands*).
170. A. Jaspers & F. Pennings, *Occupational Health and Safety in The Netherlands*, in *Health and Safety at Work: European and Comparative Perspective* 329–374 (E. Ales ed., Deventer: Wolters/Kluwer Law and Business, 2013).
171. Act of 25 Jan. 2017, Stb. 2017, 22; Parliamentary Papers 34375.

The Minister has the power to grant exceptions and permits to deviate from the HSA rules (Article 30 HSA), but he also may give extensions to the coverage of the health and safety rules (Article 1(2a)(2) HSA). This last power he has used as regards home-based work, volunteers and independent working persons. Home-based work is covered by the HSA if it is done by non-independent workers, although they are exempted from the application of a number of HSA provisions. Independent home-based workers in principle are not covered by the HSA, but some of the HSA rules have been made applicable to them. Volunteers in general are not covered, but employers who are working with volunteers need to apply to them the HSA provisions relating to the most serious risks. The same applies to independent persons working on the premises of the employer.

The Inspection SZW (*see* paragraphs 40 et seq.) plays a key role in the enforcement of the Health and Safety at Work Act and is responsible for acting if it judges that the health and safety rules have been violated. Only in the transport sector the Inspectorate of the Ministry of Transport is in charge. The Inspection SZW visits companies on its own initiative, after notification of serious accidents, or after complaints of trade unions, works councils, etc. Enforcement of health and safety of youth working during their holidays, pregnant employees, small part-time workers, etc. is receiving special attention of the Inspection SZW.

This inspection may lead to official requirements to certain employers to take specific measures to fulfil the obligations of the Act. The Inspection SZW may even give an order to halt certain activities if it contains serious risks for persons. The Inspection SZW may also make a warrant if it has observed serious violations of the Act, entailing or threatening danger for life and serious damage to the health of workers, which may lead to criminal proceedings. Usually this is only done if work accidents have caused the death or very serious injuries of persons. In such procedures both employer and employees may be accused of 'death by fault/negligence'. It almost never happens that a convicted employer or employee is condemned to imprisonment, but light or heavy fines will be imposed. Until 2004 those fines could only be imposed by a criminal proceeding and the public prosecutors have not been keen to engage in such proceedings. Since 2004 the HSA enables the Inspection SZW to impose fines via administrative law proceedings, which are more easily brought (Article 33 HSA). Such fines can go up to a maximum of EUR 34,000. Some critical observers believe that the Inspection SZW is too understaffed and not working efficiently enough to adequately perform its enforcement functions in this area, but the government is working to remedy this (*see* paragraph 41). At the same time it was revealed by a research report of the Inspection SZW that only one-third of the visited 1,300 enterprises were observing the rules on the prevention assistants, rescue workers, contact with the P&P service and risk evaluation.

164. The works council may enforce its co-determination rights in health and safety matters through the procedures laid down in the Works Council Act (*see* paragraph 394). Individual workers cannot enforce the HSA rules, but may bring actions against the employer based on Article 7:658 Dutch CC or on the bona fides requirement in the individual contract of employment (*see* paragraphs 102/156–158). This is particularly interesting in the case of statutory rules, such as in the Health and Safety at Work Act, which do lack provisions for the enforcement by employees.

Suppose the worker is obliged to do work on screens in a working environment which is contrary to the provisions in the relevant Health and Safety at Work Order. He may claim damages from the employer arguing that a good employer would have ensured a workplace according to the requirements of the Health and Safety at Work Order.

Besides all these 'sticks' to promote the preventions of health and safety dangers at work, there is also the 'carrot': since 1975 the government has applied various subsidy schemes to help companies to alleviate the burden of heavy work of their employees by investing in better work methods. The actual one has only minor subsidy to offer.[172]

Finally it should be recalled that besides the HSA several other statutes of a more general nature continue to exist, which are relevant for the safety, health and well-being at the workplace, such as statutes which contain requirements for certain engines and dangerous substances. Moreover there is the Tobacco Act, which contains the obligation to provide employees smoke-free places of work.

§3. Number of Persons Benefiting from Sickness and Disability Schemes

165. One of the main social topics preoccupying Dutch governments over the recent decades has been the rising rate of short-term sickness and long-term disability. The Netherlands was plagued by a large sickness absence and a huge number of persons claiming disability benefits. In the 1990s more than 1 million persons or 15% of the active working population of the Netherlands were receiving benefits under these schemes. Rates of absence from work had reached such high proportions of the workforce that there was genuine concern that this was affecting the competitiveness of Dutch business. Notwithstanding much research the reasons for this phenomenon could not unequivocally be established. Some linked it to the rather generous benefits schemes and the lax way in which they have been applied. Other commentators, particularly the trade unions, believed that trends such as work intensification were its root cause. The Dutch government and Parliament have grappled with this problem most intensively in recent years, on the one hand by privatizing the sickness benefits scheme (*see* paragraph 151) and by narrowing access to the disability benefits scheme and making its benefits less favourable, while, on the other hand, promoting the access of partially ill or handicapped persons to the labour market and hindering their dismissal (*see* paragraphs 199 and 248).[173]

Parliament has taken a number of measures to stimulate workers to depend less on these benefits and to stimulate employers to implement preventive policies and to retain or to hire partly disabled people. By the privatization of the sickness scheme (*see* paragraphs 151 et seq.) and by introducing financial incentives for employers in the disability scheme employers are directly confronted with the cost

172. Subsidieregeling eerlijk, gezond en veilig werk, Staatscourant 2019, 31367.
173. S. Devetzi & S. Stendahl, *Too Sick to Work? Social Security Reforms in Europe for Persons with Reduced Earning Capacity* (2011).

and benefits of their action. They can no longer shift the costs of their behaviour on to a collective pool. This should encourage employers to reduce risks by improving working conditions and by cutting extra-statutory benefits. Yet a drawback of the reform is the increased risk selection in recruitment, which weakens the position of certain groups such as older workers and disabled persons. Employers are increasingly using probationary periods, temporary agencies workers and fixed-term contracts to monitor an employee's health and are pressing for a priority access to medical treatment for their workers. In order to avoid adverse selection at the expense of the labour market position of vulnerable groups, the government introduced new laws against age discrimination and discrimination of disabled people (*see* paragraphs 98 and 99) and against the abuse of medical examinations as well as providing financial support to employers to cover additional costs associated with taking on employees with weak health (*see* paragraph 248).

On the basis of legislation in 2002 the employer is obliged to provide suitable work for the partially ill worker and to draw up a reintegration programme (Article 7:658a CC; *see* paragraph 85). If it fails to make these efforts it may be punished by the social security authorities, which may oblige it to continue the payment of wages to the ill worker for another year (*see* paragraphs 151 et seq.). The (partially) ill worker is obliged to cooperate with rehabilitation attempts and to perform other suitable work (Article 7:660a CC, *see* paragraph 80). If not, the ill worker loses his or her entitlement to sick pay (*see* paragraphs 151 et seq.) and protection against dismissal (*see* paragraph 199). These provisions are not applicable to workers after the retirement age of the AOW (66+4 month).

The new laws require an intensive and often bureaucratic cooperation between the employer and his *arbodienst* (P&P service, *see* paragraph 163).

Almost twenty years later the results of this policy are remarkable. Absence because of illness was down from 9% in the 1990s to around 4% in 2018 (*see* paragraph 152). In 2012 there were 818,000 workers on disability benefits instead of 1,000,000 in 2002. This is in sharp contrast with several other industrialized countries where the number of employees on disability benefit schemes was rising. The Netherlands is now at the forefront of experience with measures to keep as much as possible partially ill and disabled workers on the labour market. Yet it only has to find sufficient jobs for them (*see* paragraph 248).

Chapter 6. Covenants of Non-competition

166. Although it is not explicitly prohibited by any statutory provision, it is generally accepted that workers (unless they have obtained their employer's consent) are not allowed to compete with their employer during the employment relationship; sometimes, contracts of employment contain an express clause to this effect. When the contract of employment has been terminated, however, the worker in principle regains his or her freedom, and generally speaking, may compete with his or her previous employer – either as an independent contractor or in the service of a competitor of his previous employer – within the limits set by the law of torts (no unfair competition is allowed).

167. Nevertheless, after the contract of employment is ended, often workers are hindered from finding new work by a non-competition clause in their former contract of employment. Such clauses are restraining the employee in its liberty to take up a new employment after the termination of the employment relationship (*see* paragraph 85).

Non-competition clauses are in principle allowed under Dutch law,[174] but Article 7:653 CC requires, on pain of nullity, that non-competition clauses have been convened in writing between an employer and an adult employee in a contract for an indefinite time. It can also be convened in a fixed-term contract if the employer has motivated in writing that it is necessary for weighty interests of the business or service. In addition, it is stated that the employer cannot invoke the non-competition clause if the termination or non-continuation of the contract of employment is due to serious reproachable acts or omissions to act of the employer.

The restrictions in the statute are quite minimal as compared to those in other countries, although they have been enhanced somewhat in 2015. Still, there are no limitations on the duration or the territorial and occupational scope of these clauses mentioned in the statute. In theory they may last ten years and extend to all of Europe even in the contract of employment of a common supermarket cashier!

Instead of giving more restrictions the Dutch legislators have given wide powers to the courts to further limit the force of non-competition clauses. The court may wholly set aside a non-competition clause in a fixed-term contract clause if it considers the clause not necessary because of weighty interests of the business or service. It may also wholly or partially set aside a non-competition clause if it considers that – in respect to the protectable interests of the employer – the employee is unfairly disadvantaged.

If, in the covenant of non-competition, parties have agreed that a penalty must be paid in case of competition, the court may mitigate such a penalty on the basis of Article 6:94 CC. Finally, if a non-competition clause restrains to a considerable extent an employee from working otherwise than in the service of the employer, the court may order the employer to pay a compensation to the employee for the duration of the restraint. The court fixes the amount of the compensation to be paid

174. *See* F.B.J. Grapperhaus, *Werknemersconcurrentie*, Deventer, 1995; on pp. 389–409 may be found an English-language description and discussion of the rules in Dutch labour law in the field of competition of former employees vis-à-vis their former employers.

regarding the circumstances of the case. However, such a compensation is not due if the termination or non-continuation of the contract of employment is due to serious reproachable acts or omissions to act of the employee.

What the CC tries to do here, of course, is to reconcile two conflicting principles: the principle of the worker's free choice of employment, on the one hand, and the principle of the freedom of contract (i.e., the validity of the non-competition clause freely entered into), on the other. Of course the court would not condone unreasonable clauses and use its ample powers for intervention. This may be after lengthy procedures, which would be especially harmful to workers who want to know where they stand as quickly as possible, the more so, as the question of the (degree of) validity of a non-competition clause often arises when the worker has an opportunity to get a new job, a situation which usually calls for a quick decision on his part. In such cases, however, the employee may ask the court for an injunction by which the court may order the employer to refrain from using the non-competition clause until the end of the normal court proceedings. As all this will require judicial steps to be taken by the employee, the reality is that a non-competition clause, notwithstanding the legal restrictions, often binds a worker more tightly to his employer than would have been necessary taken into account the existing case law.

168. All the more so, because the existing case law is not very clear, although some trends can be discerned. One of these trends is that possibly a new non-competition clause must be concluded if changes in the employment relationship have occurred which are so radical that the non-competition clause has become considerably more onerous than before. This rule, however, does not mean that the non-competition clause loses its validity completely and requires a new agreement in writing under all circumstances. It only does so in as far as the aggregate circumstances of radical changes in the employment relationship make this loss of validity necessary in order to – on the one hand – protect the employee against a non-well-considered conclusion of a clause of non-competition, and – on the other hand – to protect the interest of the employer in this clause of non-competition.[175]

A further trend in the case law is that in cases of a transfer of the undertaking (*see* paragraph 178) the new employer may use the existing non-competition clauses.[176] This does however not apply in cases of a tacit transfer of a worker from one company to another within the same group. In those cases the existing competition clause is no longer valid.[177]

In bankruptcy cases the curator in principle may require the dismissed workers to stick to non-competition clauses, but this occasionally may be different.[178]

It also appears that the courts only very seldom use their power to impose a compensation on the employer.

Finally it should be recalled that the employer, who failed to conclude a non-competition clause, is not totally powerless towards unfair competition by his

175. Dutch Supreme Court, 5 Jan. 2007, JAR 2007/37 and JAR 2007/38; ILLR 2008, Vol. 27, p. 125.
176. Dutch Supreme Court, 23 Oct. 1987, NJ 1988, 235.
177. Dutch Supreme Court, 31 Mar. 1978, NJ 1978, 325; Dutch Supreme Court, 23 Oct. 1987, NJ 1988, 234 and 235; Dutch Supreme Court, 20 Apr. 1990, NJ 1990, 729 and Dutch Supreme Court, 24 Apr. 1992, JAR 1992/23.
178. Court of Appeal of 's-Hertogenbosch, 23 January 2007, JOR 2007/58.

former employee. As was said at the beginning of this paragraph, he may act against him and/or against the new employer in a tort procedure, but it is clear that this situation has several disadvantages compared to the situation in which there exists a non-competition clause.

169. Somewhat similar to the non-competition clauses are the so-called relationship clauses. These are clauses in which the employee is prohibited after the termination of the contract of employment, to approach clients of the former employer. Article 7:653 CC is applicable to such clauses.[179]

In the same vein it should be pointed out that employers have occasionally agreed not to take on each other's employees without the permission of the other employer. It goes without saying that these so-called gentlemen's agreements can also very effectively restrict the worker's free choice of employment, but against such informal practices there are no effective legal sanctions.

170. In some contracts of employment the employees are obliged to repay the employer partly or fully the costs of training if the contract is ended within a certain lapse of time. Such a clause, like competition clauses, can have the effect of limiting the worker in his freedom to choose another job. For that reason the HR has formulated a number of criteria to which such clauses must obey[180] if the employer wants to invoke them. The obligation to restitute (a) should decrease accordingly as the employment contract endures, (b) is limited by mandatory law (e.g., the minimum wage) and (c) may be limited/absent in some cases of dismissal.

179. Dutch Supreme Court, 5 Jan. 2007, JAR 2007/37.
180. Dutch Supreme Court, 10 Jul. 1983, 10, NJ 1983/796.

Chapter 7. Inventions by Employees and Copyright

171. According to the Patents Act of 1995 the employer is entitled to patents on inventions produced by his employees in the course of their employment if the nature of the employment relationship implies that the employee uses his specific knowledge for such kind of inventions (Article 12 Patents Act). If the employer obtains a patent on that basis, however, the worker inventor is entitled to be named as the inventor (Article 14 Patents Act). Apart from this moral satisfaction, the worker is also entitled to 'reasonable compensation' for a patented invention, unless such compensation is supposed to be covered by his wages (Article 12(6) Patents Act). Case law of the HR has given this last phrase of the law a very broad interpretation.[181] Employers may easily state that the wage of the worker covers a compensation for the invention, and it is very difficult for the employee to demonstrate the contrary. Moreover the statute does not give any clarification about the amount of the compensation.

172. If the work of the employee consists of the production of a work of literature, art or science, produced in the course of the employment relationship, the copyright belongs to the employer, except where the parties have agreed to the contrary (Article 7 Copyright Act).

181. Dutch Supreme Court, 1 Mar. 2002, JAR 2002/66; ILLR 2003, Vol 22, p. 223.

Chapter 8. Miscellaneous

§1. Changing the Terms and Conditions of the Contract of Employment

173. Obviously, in employment relationships working conditions tend to change the longer the employment lasts, both on primary and secondary items. Modern business strategies are requiring from both employers and employees much flexibility as regards the organization of work, the use of materials, equipment and technologies, etc. Therefore the promotion of intern mobility and flexibility is considered as a primary goal for human resources development. This may serve not only the interests of the employer but also of the employee. His/her private life situation may also require adaptations in the terms and conditions of employment. Thus modern human resources policies in Dutch firms are experimenting with new concepts, such as amalgamated contracts (*fusiecontracten*), which leave the worker large sovereignty on the organization of his working times, only requiring certain agreed results. Sometimes elderly workers are switched to a less demanding level of productivity (demotion). Mergers and takeovers often make changes in the terms and conditions of employment desirable or unavoidable.

Dutch labour law is only step by step being adapted to cope with these new requirements. The rules on the changes in the conditions of mergers and takeovers have been substantially evolved during recent decades (*see* paragraph 178). Statutory law now contains several criteria for the adaptation of terms and conditions of employment in cases in which the worker has partially fallen ill or disabled for a substantial period (*see* paragraph 85/165). A statute of 2000, amended in 2015, has laid down rules for situations in which the worker desires a change in the number and scheduling of working hours and in the working place (teleworking) (FWA, *see* paragraph 119).

Other situations must be judged according to the general principles of labour law. From them it may be concluded that the employer can unilaterally adapt working conditions as far as the organization of the work is concerned, as this is a characteristic of the contract of employment. However, the employer is limited in this power by statutory law, the individual and collective contract, the powers of the works council, customs and practices (Article 7:660 CC, *see* paragraph 81) and also by the fundamental rights of the worker (*see* paragraphs 106 et seq.).

As regards the more crucial terms and conditions of the contract of employment – notably the duration of the contract, wage, place and amount of work, working time schedules and other essentials of the job – those general principles imply that changes in it can only be brought about by mutual consent between the employer and the employee. They may formalize such consent by amending the existing contract of employment or by concluding a new contract of employment. Formally the law requires from the employer to lay down such changes in a written document (Article 7:655(3) CC, *see* paragraph 74), but practice teaches that in many cases parties do not live up to this obligation and simply go on working with each other on new terms and conditions. The HR has ruled that the employer may only rely on the consent of an employee with a change of his working conditions which imply a deterioration for him if the employee has been given clearness about the impact of the change and on the basis of declarations and behaviour of the employee it may be assumed that the employee has deliberately agreed with that change.[182]

For a number of years, there has been a long debate among Dutch scholars about the question of how far the employer may go in imposing unilaterally changes in the essential terms and conditions of employment.

There is a strong protection in Dutch labour law against this possibility, because of the strong rules on the binding force of mandatory statutory law and collective agreements and because of the powers of works councils. However, these sources are only protecting the minimum conditions of employment and therefore cannot protect terms and conditions which are more favourable for the worker nor those aspects of an employment relationship which are not precisely defined such as, often, the contents of a job.

Sometimes an employer already at the start of the employment relationship has inserted in the contract of employment a written provision pursuant to which he is empowered to alter a working condition set out in the contract of employment. However, Dutch labour law provides that he may only invoke such a provision if he has such an important interest in the alteration that, according to standards of reasonableness and fairness, the interest of the employee which would be harmed by the alteration must be overridden (Article 7:613 CC).

For all other cases of modification of the contract of employment some scholars referred to the general law on contracts which allows a unilateral change of a contract if reasonableness and fairness so require (Article 6:248 CC) or in cases of 'unforeseen changes of circumstances' (Article 6:258 CC), but the HR had already narrowed the interpretation of these concepts to situations in which it would be in all reasonableness and fairness unacceptable to require the observance of a contractual obligation.[183]

Most courts found the solution for this problem in referring to the bona fides article in Dutch labour law, Article 7:611 CC (*see* paragraph 102). May a 'good employer' demand a specific alteration from his employee and may a 'good employee' reject such an alteration? The HR has ruled, that an employee is only justified to refuse proposals of the employer to change his conditions of employment if the acceptance of such proposals cannot in all fairness be required from the employee. According to the HR the application of this criterion should not one-sidedly put the accent on what may be expected from the employee. The courts must also check whether the changes of circumstances is such as to have moved the employer, acting in bona fides, to propose changes in the conditions of employment and whether these changes are reasonable.[184] In any case the courts will require that proper procedures have been followed, such as sufficient dialogue and negotiations with the employee. Later the HR ruled that the standard of its 2008 judgment is also applicable to post active workers.[185]

182. Dutch Supreme Court, 12 Feb. 2010, ECLI:NL:HR:2010:BK3570; HR 23 Nov. 2018, ECLI:NL:HR:2018:2168 (Bogra).
183. Dutch Supreme Court, 19 Nov. 1993, NJ 1994, 680.
184. Dutch Supreme Court, 11 Jul. 2008, JAR 2008/204; ILLR Vol. 28, p. 291.
185. Dutch Supreme Court, 26 Jun. 2015, ECLI:NL:HR:2015:1743.

174. Finally the relationship of this problem with the law on disciplinary measures (*see* paragraphs 182 et seq.) and dismissals should not be ignored. Employers may try to extort the consensus or at least the acquiescence of the employee concerning the proposed alterations in the terms and conditions of employment by open or concealed threats to discipline or dismiss the worker if he does not cooperate. In this respect it should be mentioned that the Dutch labour law is not very rich in requiring employers to offer grievances procedures (*see* paragraph 39), but is quite strong in its dismissal protection (*see* paragraph 192 et seq.). In cases of dismissals or resignation, originating in a refusal of the worker to consent with proposed alterations, the courts will apply the above-described tests to establish whether the termination is justified.

§2. The Principle of *Respondeat Superior*

175. If an employee, in the performance of the contract, causes damage to the employer or a third party, the question arises as to whether he is liable for such damages. Generally speaking the principle of *respondeat superior* applies here. Article 7:661 CC reads that an employee who, in the performance of the contract causes damages to the employer or to a third party to whom the employer is oblige– to compensate such damage shall not be liable to the employer for this unless the damage was a result of his intent or deliberate recklessness.

This last-mentioned exception will not easily apply, because the case law of the HR has given a very narrow interpretation of the concepts of 'intent or deliberate recklessness' (similar with these concepts under Article 7:658 CC, *see* paragraph 158). The worker is only liable for the damage if he has actually realized how reckless he was, which is hard to prove!

However, two more exceptions on this basic rule are made:

- the responsibility may be different because of the circumstances of the case and having regard, among other things, to the nature of the contract; in the case law of the HR this exception has been applied to the responsibility for the traffic fines, directed to the employer for the behaviour of his workers in road traffic in the course of their employment. Only in special cases the employer bears the liability for them;[186]
- there may be derogation of the basic rule to the detriment of the employee provided this has been laid down by written contract and only to the extent that the employee is insured for this risk.

176. If a worker, in the performance of his task, has caused damage to a third party, the worker is liable to the third party if his act is considered to be a tort under the CC (Article 6:162) (i.e., in defiance of the written or unwritten rules of law). Moreover, it is provided that the employer too may be liable for damages to a third party caused by acts of his subordinate personnel (Article 6:170 CC). For this liability of the employer the courts will require that the functional relationship between

186. Dutch Supreme Court, 13 Jun. 2008, JAR 2008/185; ILLR Vol. 28, p. 401.

the damage and the work can be established. This question has recently acquired significance in cases about sexual abuses of persons in the context of their employment relationship.

So there is joint liability. The third party may claim damages from the employer, the worker or from both, but payment by one of the debtors will release the other from his debt. In practice third parties prefer to sue the employer, as its financial strength will normally be greater than the worker's. In this situation the employer who has paid for the damage may only seek recourse against a worker if the damage was a result of the employee's intent or deliberate recklessness. If a third party claimed and collected damages directly from the worker, then the worker would be entitled to recourse on the employer unless the damages were intentionally or deliberately recklessly inflicted by him.

All this is on the same standards and with the same exceptions as laid down in Article 7:661 CC (*see* paragraph 175).

If the worker by his own mistakes has harmed his own health then the responsibility is according to Article 7:658 CC (*see* paragraphs 156 et seq.). If he has damaged his own properties (for instance, driven his own car total loss while doing work for his employer) then he may be entitled to recourse on the employer unless the damages were intentionally or deliberately recklessly inflicted or the two other exceptions mentioned in paragraph 168 are applicable. The employer is not according to Article 7:661 CC responsible for damages which occurred in private situations on objects such as a car or a laptop provided by the employer which the employee was allowed to use in private situations. However such responsibility for the employer may eventually stem from Article 7:611 CC (bona fides).[187]

A final reservation must be made in respect of the employees who are charged with managerial responsibilities. In certain cases they can be personally liable for damages to third persons and for illegal actions, under both civil and criminal laws.

§3. Moonlighting

177. Moonlighting is on the increase in the Netherlands. In 2005 only 5.5% of the active population worked in that formula, in 2017 it was 7.5% (or 600,000 persons).

Dutch law is not very clear when it comes to the question of moonlighting – an employee who fulfils simultaneously two or more jobs. The Working Times Act (*see* paragraphs 110 et seq.) put clear ceilings on the maximum of the working hours which employees may perform in a certain day, week, months, etc. The combined working times of the employee in his various jobs should not surpass these ceilings. Moreover the employer may be critical of additional jobs of his employee, because they may be such a burden on the employee that he is not executing his primary employment well, or because in his second job he is causing competition with the employer of his primary job (*see* paragraph 170) or because the second job is damaging the honour and reputation of the employer of his primary job.

187. Dutch Supreme Court, 11 juli 2011, ECLI:NL:HR:2014:1629.

Sometimes the individual contract of employment or the collective agreement contains a prohibition or a limitation of moonlighting. For instance in the collective agreement for the construction industry there was for many years a prohibition for the workers to perform building activities in their free time. However, most of the time there are no absolute prohibitions but rules requiring that the employee must ask the consent of the employer for performing another job or a summary of the grounds on which the employer can prohibit the performance of another job. Dutch statutory labour law is silent on this matter, safe for civil servants' law, which prohibits moonlighting if it is detrimental to the good performance of the civil servant in his job (Article 61 ARAR). Employees and civil servants, who are performing work with more than one employer, are required to provide, spontaneously and timely, each of these employers with all the information about their work which is necessary for the application of the working time rules (Article 5:15(6) WTA).

It is certain that a worker who is only performing for his employer a part-time job cannot easily be prevented by this employer from taking on other activities, as employees sometimes simply must supplement their salary with another job in order to survive. But even if a worker performs a full-time job it will be difficult for the employer of the full-time worker to prevent his worker to take on a second job. If these practices or clauses are challenged in court the court will balance the interest of the employee against the interest of the employer. In this balancing act the court uses the bona fides principle of Article 7:611 (*see* paragraph 102) in order to apply constitutional law aspects (the fundamental right of freedom to work). From the scarce case law we can conclude that the courts will not allow another job which is competing with the business of the primary employer. In other cases they are less restrictive.

§4. Transfer of an Enterprise; Job Security

178. Before 1981 there were no statutory provisions in force in the Netherlands on the issue of employees' rights in the event of a business transfer. In order to implement European Directive 77/187 of 14 February 1977 on the harmonization of workers' rights in case of transfer of undertakings specific provisions were inserted in the CC (Article 7:662–7:666 CC). They should protect the acquired rights of the workers in the case of a transfer of (parts of) an enterprise.[188]

In conformity with the EU Directive (and its subsequent amendments), it is laid down in Article 7:663 CC that as a result of the transfer of an undertaking the rights and obligations arising for the employer concerning the persons who at that time are working in that undertaking under a contract of employment between him and an employee working there, shall be transferred to the transferee by operation of law. For a year after the transfer, however, the employer shall remain jointly and severally liable together with the transferee for the performance of the obligations under the contract of employment which arose before that date.

188. *See* R.M Beltzer, *Overgang van de onderneming*, Deventer, 2000; on pp. 381–387 one finds an English-language description and discussion of the implementation in Dutch law of Directives 77/187/EC and 98/50/EC on workers' rights in the case of transfer of undertakings.

So the new employer, the transferee, in principle must continue to apply the conditions of employment in force at the moment of the transfer, even if this were conditions typical for the transferor. According to the HR also a non-competition clause (*see* paragraphs 166 et seq.) is transferred by operation of law to the transferee.[189]

Of course the new employer may try to change those conditions but he must do this within the limits set out in paragraphs 173 et seq.[190]

A special provision is made for the rights of workers relating to occupational pension schemes and savings schemes (Article 7:664 CC), which provides that the rights and obligations of the employer arising from a pension commitment in some specific situations are not applicable in case of a transfer.

Dutch law clarifies – in accordance with EU law – that 'transfer' means the transfer arising from a contract, merger or division of an economic unit which keeps its identity. 'Economic unit' means a complex of organized means established for the pursuit of an activity whether or not this constitutes its principal activity. An establishment or part of an undertaking or establishment shall be regarded as an undertaking (Article 7:662(2) CC). The HR has ruled that Article 7:662–666 CC is applicable to all those who are protected under labour law, even the director of the undertaking, but only those workers can claim the protection of these articles who were effectively employed in the transferred undertaking.[191]

The crucial problem here is, whether an economic unit has kept 'its identity'. On this point there is already a flood of case law of the Court of Justice EU, which is closely followed by the Dutch courts.[192] This case law, for instance, has taught that the notion 'contract' in the definition of transfer must be so amply understood that these provisions are also applicable if subsidies are transferred from one institution to another. Also the outsourcing of certain activities, such as cleaning, may be covered, but it depends on the circumstances whether a later change of the contract partner is to be considered as 'transfer'.[193] Only in a few sectors of the economy (for instance, in public transport) a statute or a collective agreement is requiring the incoming contractor to take over all the personnel of the outgoing contractor. It is currently an item of political and scholarly debate and research in the Netherlands whether the protection of workers in subcontracting processes should be enforced,[194] for instance by way of extending the notion of joint liability.[195]

189. Dutch Supreme Court, 23 Oct. 1987, NJ 1988/235.

190. *See* S. Jellinghaus, *Harmonisatie van arbeidsvoorwaarden in het bijzonder na een fusie of overname*, Deventer, 2003; on pp. 335–347 one finds an English-language description and discussion of the existing practices and legal possibilities under Dutch law to establish a harmonization of employment conditions in companies which were part of a merger or an acquisition.

191. Dutch Supreme Court, 11 Feb. 2005, JAR 2005/67.

192. *See* Dutch Supreme Court, 24 May 2019, ECLI:NL:HR:2019:792.

193. R. Beltzer, *The Transfer of Undertakings and the Importance of Taking over Personnel – A Vicious Circle*, Intl. J. Comp. Lab. L. Indus. Rel. (2007), http://dare.uva.nl/document/224144.

194. *See* L. van den Berg & S.S.M. Peters, *Study on the Protection of Workers' Rights in Subcontracting Processes – The Netherlands, Core Report and Survey Report,* published in Yves Jorens, Saskia Peters & Mijke Houwerzijl, *Study on the Protection of Workers' Rights in Subcontracting Processes in the European Union: Final Study* (p. 192) (research commissioned by the European Commission), June 2012, http://ec.europa.eu/social/keyDocuments.jsp?advSearchKey=subcontracting+&mode=advancedSubmit&langId=en&search=Search).

Posted workers are transferred if the posted workers agency is transferred, not if the user company is transferred. Posted workers inside a group of undertakings are transferred if the undertaking where they actually were employed is transferred.[196]

However, often companies are transferred from one owner to another by the acquisition of shares. According to legal opinion in the Netherlands such transfers are not covered by Article 7:662–666 CC as there is no formal change in the legal identity of the employer, although here the Merger Code and the WCA may apply, imposing information and consultation (*see* paragraphs 362 et seq. and paragraph 386). However, only a soon as the legal person, mentioned as 'employer' on the contracts of employment, is changed the Article 7:662–666 CC must be applied.

179. The employer must inform the employees of a projected transfer, either directly (Article 7:665a CC) or via the trade unions (*see* paragraph 361) or via the works council or the 'ERB' (*see* paragraph 386). The direct information must be done to his own employees involved in the transfer of undertaking in good time. It must embrace the intended decision for the transfer, the intended date of the transfer, the reason of the transfer, the legal, economic and social consequences of the transfer for the employees and the measures considered with regard to the employees. The HR[197] has ruled that the employer is obliged to inform his workers clearly about the various options in case of a transfer.

The law also stipulates that the employer may not give notice of termination of a contract of employment of an employee who works in his undertaking on account of a transfer (Article 7:670(8) CC). Transferred workers can, of course, be dismissed for reasons of technical, economic or organizational nature. However, the new owner can only do this within the limits of the stringent Dutch law on dismissals (*see* Part I, Chapter 9). Workers being taken over by a new employer continue to enjoy their full seniority with regard to the length of the period of notice and the severance pay, which the new employer will have to respect in case of dismissal.

Article 7:662–666 CC is not applicable if only one or more seagoing vessels are transferred. These articles, however, do apply if a seagoing vessel is part of the transfer of an enterprise, if the transferee is within the territorial scope of the EU and the transferred enterprise remained under that scope (Article 7:666a CC).

Already since 2002 these provisions have been made applicable to employees, who perform work in an undertaking maintained by the state, province, municipality, water control corporation or any other body under public law (Article 662(1) CC). They thus also govern privatization operations.

180. The transfer by operation of law is not dependent on the consent of the employee, but he is also not obliged to enter the service of the transferee. A refusal to be transferred may be inspired by the fear of disadvantages. For this situation,

195. M.S. Houwerzijl & S.S.M. Peters, *Liability in Subcontracting Processes in the European Construction Sector – Netherlands* (research commissioned by the European Foundation for the Improvement of Living and Working Conditions (Eurofound)), January 2009, http://www.eurofound.europa.eu/publications/htmlfiles/ef08877.htm.

196. Court of Justice EU, 21 Oct. 2010, no. C-242/09 (*Albron*).

197. Dutch Supreme Court, 20 Oct. 2007, JAR 2007/285; Dutch Supreme Court, 26 Jun. 2009, JAR 2009/183.

since the Dismissal Reform Act of 2015, it is provided that – in view of the application of Article 7:673 CC (the transition allowance, *see* paragraph 218) – the contract of employment shall be deemed to have been set aside or discontinued for a reason which is for the account of the employer, if the transfer of an undertaking results in a substantial alteration of the conditions of employment to the detriment of the employee and for this reason the contract of employment is terminated by or on the request of the employee or the contract of employment for a fixed period, after having been terminated by the operation of the law, has not been continued on the initiative of the employee (Article 7:665 CC).

181. The applicability of these provisions to transfers effectuated in the context of bankruptcy proceedings became the subject of heated debate in the Netherlands in the 1980s. Various courts submitted references for a preliminary ruling on the matter to the European Court of Justice. In reply the Court ruled in 1985 that Directive 77/187 does not apply to a bankruptcy-related transfer. Shortly afterwards the HR followed suit by ruling that the articles on business transfers in the CC do not apply to the transfer of an undertaking if the employer has been adjudicated bankrupt and the undertaking forms part of the bankrupt estate. And this is now also codified in the present Article 7:666 CC. Consequently, the transferee acquiring an enterprise in a bankruptcy context is free, under Dutch law, to choose whether to have employees transferred to his employment, and if so which employees. He is also under no obligation to continue to offer those employees who are transferred to his employment the same rights and obligations as those which they had with respect to their former employer. In short, in a bankruptcy-related transfer the transferee has complete freedom. This legal situation can be abused by employers who deliberately have their firm declared bankrupt and subsequently have a downsized enterprise emerge from the bankruptcy. Although abuses may be attacked under Article 17a and/or 13a BA (*see* paragraphs 228 et seq.), this happens seldom. In conformity with case law of the European Court of Justice Article 7:662–668 CC do apply in case of reorganization procedures under Dutch law, which functions as a kind of 'pre-bankruptcy' state, the so-called *surséance van betaling* (judicial leave to suspend payment of debts). Recently Dutch lawyers developed a new form of bankruptcy proceedings in which a court-appointed prospective insolvency administrator investigates the possibilities for continuation of the activities of an insolvent undertaking by a third party and prepares for acts which must be carried out shortly after the court declaration of insolvency to enable such continuation (a 'pre-pack'). However the CJEU has ruled that also in this procedure the EU rules on transfer of the enterprise are applicable.[198]

§5. Disciplinary Sanctions

182. Employers who are dissatisfied with the performance of their employees may consider a large variety of disciplinary sanctions towards their employees: warnings and rebukes, imposing fines, sending homeworkers with pay, placing

198. CJEU 22 Jun. 2017, C-126/16 (Smallsteps).

workers on non-pay, suspending certain perquisites, denying a promotion or gratifications facilities, transferring the worker to another function or another department, demoting or taking away certain powers. All this with or without its mentioning in the personal file of the worker. The ultimate sanction then is dismissal which will be dealt with in paragraphs 192 et seq. Of all the other possible sanctions Dutch statutory law only mentions 'fines' explicitly.

183. The concept of a 'fine' is not defined in Dutch labour law, nor does the statute give any procedural requirement. It only is provided that the employer may only impose a fine for the infringement of one of the rules set out in the contract of employment if the contract of employment indicates the rules the infringement of which will be subject to a fine and the amount of such fine. A contract of employment in which a fine is stipulated must be entered into in writing and shall state precisely the use to which the fine will be put. Fines may never be used, directly or indirectly, for the personal advantage of the employer himself or of those to whom the employer has given the power to impose a fine on employees. Each fine stipulated in a contract shall be fixed at a specified amount and expressed in the currency in which the remuneration is fixed in money. The fines imposed on an employee in any week may not together exceed his remuneration fixed in money for half a day. No individual fine may exceed this amount. Each stipulation contrary to all this is null and void, although there may be derogation from the last-mentioned three conditions by written agreement, but only in respect of employees whose remuneration fixed in money exceeds the applicable minimum wage. The court shall always have the power to fix the fine at a smaller amount if it considers the amount imposed excessive (Article 7:650 CC or Article 6:91(4) CC). The possibility of imposing a fine is without prejudice to the right to compensation under the law. However, an employer may not both impose a fine and claim compensation in respect of the same fact (Article 7:651 CC). He may deduct fines owed by the employee from his wage, provided that written proof has been submitted by the employer showing the amount of each fine and the time at which and the reason for which it is imposed and stating the relevant provision of the contract entered into in writing that has been infringed (Article 7:632(1)(b) CC) and only within the limits of Article 7:632(2) CC (*see* paragraph 135).

184. About half the collective agreements in the Netherlands are mentioning the suspension as a possible sanction. Moreover, there are a number of court decisions on 'suspension' as a sanction, making a differentiation between suspension with pay or suspension without pay. Suspension without pay risks to be attacked by the employee on the basis of Article 7:628 CC (*see* paragraph 148), which says that the employee retains the right to remuneration if he has not performed the contracted work due to a cause which, reasonably, should be for the account of the employer. So the employer must be able to convince a court that in this case the non-performance is, reasonably, not for his account. From the case law of the HR[199] it has become clear that courts shall not easily reach this conclusion and will at any

199. Dutch Supreme Court, 21 Mar. 2003, JAR 2003/91 (*Van der Gulik/Vissers*).

rate require that the sanction of suspension without pay has been laid down in writing either in the contract of employment or the collective agreement.

Suspension with continuation of payment risks to be attacked by the employee on the basis of Article 7:611 CC (*see* paragraph 102), the bona fides principle (*see* paragraph 103). On that basis he may in court claim a 'right to work' (*see* paragraph 80/85). Courts will only allow this sanction if there was sufficient reason for this sanction in the behaviour of the employee.

185. This last kind of reasoning is applied by the courts in all other kinds of sanctions that the employer may impose (*see* paragraph 182). At the end of the day the courts will consider any sanction short of dismissal on the bona fides principle. They do so even if the other sanctions can be based on the text of the contract of employment, a collective agreement or a company handbook or simply on the management prerogative (*see* paragraph 81). In court cases the judges will often require that a proper procedure has been followed, whether lesser sanctions (for instance, warnings) have been given earlier in comparable cases, whether the sanction is proportional, etc.

186. Also the employee has a certain number of sanctions available in case the employer is not living up to his obligations. The most forceful sanctions are in the collective field; in court together with colleagues and or trade unions/works councils (*see* paragraphs 35 et seq.), through collective conflict (*see* paragraphs 334 et seq.) and the tools of workers' involvement (*see* paragraphs 356 et seq.). As an individual the employee may take the employer to court with or without assistance of a trade union. For example if he feels that he is not duly paid, denied an advancement, etc. However these type of sanctions are not easy effectuated as they cost money. The main disadvantage, however, is in the fact that taking your employer to court may seriously disturb the employment relationship. If the employee for whatever reason can afford to lose his job he can resign possibly even summarily[200] or ask the court to rescind the employment contract (*see* paragraphs 211 et seq.). In the last case he may even ask for a compensation/severance pay. For instance in case he/she was victim of sexual harassment or has been squeezed out.[201]

187. Finally there is the sanction of a refusal to perform. The employee may decide to not perform all or certain aspects of his task because he considers that his employer is not observing his obligations, while at the same time claiming continuation of payment and protection against victimization/dismissal. Statutory law in the Netherlands has recognized this sanction explicitly in a few cases: in case of immediately threatening danger for his safety and health (*see* paragraph 162) and if he does not wish to perform work on Sundays (*see* paragraph 112). In the past the employee could also refuse to perform the contractual work because of grave reasons of conscience (ex-Article 7:681(1)(e) CC), but this protection has been weakened (Article 7:669(3)(f) CC, *see* paragraph 197). Moreover it is likely, that courts will also in other cases, not specifically mentioned in the statutes, recognize the

200. Dutch Supreme Court, 17 Mar. 2000, JAR 2000/102.
201. Dutch Supreme Court, 26 Jan. 1990, NJ 499.

right of the worker to refuse to perform all or part of his obligations, taking into account the customs of the industry and the bona fides principle (*see* paragraph 102). The courts will in any case require that the disregard of his obligations by the employer is so serious that it justifies a refusal to perform by the employee[202] and that, if possible, the employee has warned the employer in advance.[203] One may derive that from numerous dismissal cases in which the courts had to judge dismissals on the grounds of not performing the ordered tasks. In all these cases one notices the court balancing the interest of the employer in a correct fulfilment of his tasks by the employee against the interest of the employee in a proper fulfilment by the employer of his obligations and respect for the interests of the employee.[204]

§6. Conflicts of Law

188. In the past the Dutch courts – not much different from those in other European countries – developed conflict rules for cross-border employment contracts which were primarily oriented towards the individual and left room for the autonomy of the parties. The choice of the parties as to the law applicable was respected with an exception only for mandatory domestic laws. When the contracting parties had not exercised their autonomy, 'connecting factors' were used to establish the law applicable. These factors were the habitual place of work, the actual place of work, the place of business of the undertaking, the place where the contract was concluded and the origin and nationality of the parties.[205] This line of case law has been confirmed by the Convention on the Law applicable to Contractual Obligations of 1980 (the 'Rome Convention'), which since it came into effect in 1991, has to a certain extent unified private international law in the field of employment contracts within the EU. This norm was replaced by Regulation no. 593/2008 of 17 June 2008 on the Law Applicable to Contractual Obligations.

The first rule is that if the parties to the contract of employment have themselves chosen the applicable law, this choice is upheld. However, this rule cannot have the result of depriving the employee of the protection afforded to him by provisions that cannot be derogated from by an agreement under the law that would have been applicable if the parties had not made a choice of the applicable law (see hereunder) (*see* Article 8(1) EU Regulation 595/2008).

The second rule is that if the parties have not themselves chosen the applicable law, the contract shall be governed by the law of the country in which or, failing that, from which the employee habitually carries out his work in performance of the contract. The country where the work is habitually carried out shall not be deemed

202. Dutch Supreme Court, 29 Sep. 2006, JAR 2006/263.
203. Dutch Supreme Court, 12 Jan. 1990, 475.
204. Dutch Supreme Court, 24 Jun. 1966, NJ 1966, 457.
205. *See* M.V. Polak, *Arbeidsverhoudingen in het internationale privaatrecht*, Deventer, 1988; on pp. 159–170 one finds an English and a French language description and discussion of the rules on contracts of employment in Dutch international private law; A.A.H. van Hoek, *Internationale mobiliteit van werknemers*, The Hague 2000; on pp. 553–580 may be found an English-language description and discussion of the rules on contracts of employment and collective agreements in Dutch international private law.

to have changed if the employee is temporarily employed in another country. If such a country cannot be determined (e.g., because the worker works in different countries), then the contract shall be governed by the law of the country where the place of business through which the employee was engaged is situated. Nevertheless, the law of another country shall apply where it appears from the circumstances as a whole that the contract is more closely connected with that other country (Article 8(2-4) EU Regulation 593/2008).

Nothing shall restrict the application of the overriding mandatory provisions of the law of the forum and under special conditions also the overriding mandatory provisions of the law of the country where the obligations arising out of the contract have to be or have been performed. Overriding mandatory provisions are provisions the respect for which is regarded as crucial by a country for safeguarding its public interests such as its political, social or economic organization, to such an extent that they are applicable to any situation falling within their scope, irrespective of the law otherwise applicable to the contract (Article 9 EU Regulation 593/2008).

The application of a provision of the law of any country specified by this Regulation may be refused only is such application is manifestly incompatible with public policy (*ordre public* of the forum) (Article 21 EU Regulation).

Although these are all EU rules and so only applicable to contracts in which citizens of EU countries are involved, Dutch courts will apply them nowadays on all cross-border employment relationships.

189. Initially the CJEU did not have any jurisdiction over the Rome Convention, so these questions had to be solved exclusively by national courts. Actually the CJEU is competent to interpret the Regulation. However up till now there has not been much case law, neither of the CJEU nor of Dutch courts to clarify these points with regard to the Dutch legislation.

Important legal questions for labour law have been:

(a) When is a clause an 'overriding mandatory provision', and when is it a 'provision which cannot be derogated from by agreement'? The Regulation does not provide for clear definitions but its recitals suggest that the first concept must be construed more restrictively than the second.
(b) What is the law applicable to employees posted abroad for a more or less short-time?

A very interesting question that has come up has been the question of whether the Dutch system of *ex ante* dismissal permits (*see* paragraph 202) is applicable to international employment contracts. The HR has held that a dismissal permit is obliged if there is a sufficient connection with the Dutch labour market in a way that the social-economic relations in the Netherlands were concerned. If the work has been performed in the Netherlands and the employer was situated in the Netherlands such a connection is sufficiently satisfied.[206]

206. Dutch Supreme Court, 24 Feb. 2012; ILLL Vol. 32, p. 3.

190. Taking the various uncertain points together the problem of social dumping has come to the surface. Social dumping may result from, on the one hand, free movement of capital, services and labour on the European market, and on the other hand, the incomplete process of EU harmonization of the national systems of labour law and social security. Notably in Germany and France, in the 1980s and 1990s, labour markets were to some extent disturbed by the import of cheap labour from low-wage countries by temporary work agencies.

In the Netherlands the conflict of law rules have in the past had a devastating impact on the employment of Dutch workers in international road transport, which used to be a substantial part of the Dutch labour market. Dutch transport firms opened up subsidiaries in Central and East European Member States and had their international transport business done by lorry drivers from these Member States on substantially lower working conditions. The case law of the CJEU on the question of what law is applicable to such drivers[207] requires a very detailed examination of numerous practical aspects of the case which is apt for completely different assessments and therefore not easy to establish.[208]

As regards the impact of cheap labour by temporary work agencies[209] the EU launched the so-called Posting Workers Directive (Directive 96/71 EC), designed to help advance the legal certainty of posted individuals. This directive was initially implemented in Dutch law by the Cross-Border Work (Terms and Conditions of Employment) Act of 1999.[210] In order to implement EU Directive 2014/67/EU on the Enforcement of the Posted Workers Directive this 1999 Act was replaced by the EU Posted Workers (Terms and Conditions of Employment) Act – *Wet arbeidsvoorwaarden gedetacheerde werknemers in de Europese Unie* (EUPWA) of 2016.[211] This EUPWA sums up a number of provisions contained in the Dutch CC on employment contracts as mandatorily applicable to contracts of employment of workers, normally working in another EU Member State, who are temporarily posted to the Netherlands under contracts governed by foreign law (Article 2 EUPWA). This summary only embraces provisions on which there could be legal doubt as to whether they are mandatory, such as several wage payment rules (*see* paragraphs 132 and 136), the written statement (*see* paragraph 74), the civil responsibility of the employer for health and safety (*see* paragraphs 156 et seq.), minimum holidays with pay (*see* paragraph 120), equal treatment of men and women (*see* paragraph 93) and of part-time and full-time work (*see* paragraph 100) and the prohibition of dismissal of pregnant workers (*see* paragraph 198). Many other parts of labour law, such as the AMW, the WTA, the Health and Safety Act and so on, which

207. Cases CJEU 15 Mar. 2011, C-29/10 (Koelzsch) and CJEU 12 Sep. 2013, C-64/12 (Schlecker).

208. *See* Dutch Supreme Court, 23 Nov. 2018, ECLI:NL:HR:2018:2165; Dutch Supreme Court, 23 Nov. 2018, ECLI:NL:HR:2018:2174.

209. *See* W.M. Been & P.T. De Beer, Case study report, *The Regulation of Employment Conditions of Labour Migrants in the Temporary Work Agencies Sector: The Cases of the Netherlands and the UK* (2018). J.H. Even, *Striking the Right Balance with Regard to Posted Workers*, in *Balanceren met detacheren* 69–135 (J.H. Even ed., Den Haag: Boom, 2018).

210. M.S. Houwerzijl, *The Dutch Understanding of Posting of Workers in the Context of Free Services Provision and Enlargement: A Neutral Approach?*, in *Cross-Border Services, Posting of Workers, and Multilevel Governance* (Stein Evju ed., Institutt for Privatretts Skriftserie 193/2013: Oslo, Privatrettsfondet, 2013).

211. Act of 1 Jun. 2016, Stb. 2016, 219; Parliamentary Papers 34408.

are beyond doubt of a mandatory nature, are not mentioned in this EUPWA, but they will surely be applied to this category of workers. But what about the Dutch law on dismissals in general? It is not at all clear whether this important part of labour law is applicable to this category of workers. Perhaps this may be clarified by a new Act, which the Netherlands like all EU Member States has to adopt to implement the most recent EU Directive in this field, Directive 2018/957/EU.

This EUPWA has also resulted in an amendment of the Act on the Extension of the Terms of a Collective Agreements (Article 2(6)) (*see* paragraph 324) which now provides that the employment contracts of posted workers of EU Member States are equally subject to the extended collective agreements as regards their provisions on working times, paid holidays, minimum wage, health and safety at work, protective measures concerning the work of children, adolescents and pregnant women, anti-discrimination conditions as well as the rules on temporary agency work (Article 2(6) AEIA).

191. Besides the item of the law applicable there is the item of the competent court in employment law matters. As far as international contracts of employment are concerned this issue too is now regulated for the Netherlands by EU law, initially the European Jurisdiction and Execution Convention, in 2002 replaced by the Jurisdiction and Execution Regulation (EC/44/2001), as from 2015 replaced by EU Regulation 1215/2012. On the basis of these regulations employees may sue their employer in Dutch courts in all cases on contracts of employment if the work is habitually done in the Netherlands. These courts are also competent with respect to a certain number of items in cases on contracts of employment, in which the work is only temporarily done in the Netherlands.

The employer may bring proceedings only in the courts of the state in which the employee is domiciled. This last provision has the somewhat cumbersome result that the frequent cases in which employers are requesting the court to rescind/dissolve the contract of employment (*see* paragraph 211) the cases concerning workers domiciled in Belgium, Germany, etc. should be brought before courts in these countries, which are not familiar with these procedures.

Chapter 9. The Termination of the Contract of Employment

§1. The Development of the Dutch Law on Dismissals

192. Employers may wish to dismiss individual employees either for economic reasons or for reasons relating to the employee's person. These latter reasons may include unsuitability for the job, poor performance or inappropriate conduct. The enactments on the termination of the contract of employment have to reconcile different and often conflicting basic values. The protection of the worker has to be reconciled with the necessary power of the employer to terminate the contract of employment if the situation warrants it. During the last century the emphasis placed on these different values has shifted.

Until 1940 the law on dismissals in the Netherlands was very liberal. The employer's prerogative of dismissal was virtually absolute. According to the CC it could dismiss at will. A reasonable cause for dismissal was not required; no reason for the dismissal had to be given. The CC did not much more than laying down short minimal periods of notice to be mandatory in all cases of dismissal except for cases of summary dismissal, a probation period or a termination of fixed-term contracts.

During the World War II the German occupier prohibited any dismissal without an administrative permit and this system was upheld after the liberation in the Extraordinary Decree on Labour Relations 1945 (*Buitengewoon Besluit Arbeidsverhoudingen*) which has been maintained in force until 2015!

According to the Extraordinary Decree on Labour Relations 1945 an employer could only terminate an open-ended contract of employment if he had the prior permission of the Director of the Regional Employment Office. Later this authority was called Central Organization for Work and Income – *Centrale Organisatie voor Werk en Inkomen* (CWI) and finally this authority was called the UWV (*see* paragraphs 39, 205 and 252). This office had to give permission to the employer in order for the dismissal to go ahead.

Originally this *ex ante* control on dismissals was primarily intended as a provision to regulate the labour market in the post-war reconstruction period. In that period it was used, for instance, to prevent workers in essential industries (such as the building and food industry) from moving too easily to less essential services. At that time requests for permission to terminate the contract originated from workers rather than from employers, and they were often refused with a call on the needs of the labour market. In later years, however, the 1945 Decree increasingly lost its labour market regulating function. The requirement for workers to obtain a dismissal permit was already almost a dead letter for many years and was formally abolished in 1999. However, for employers this requirement has been maintained. Today it mainly serves as a protection of workers against unreasonable dismissal. It is assumed that the mere existence of an *ex ante* control on dismissals would restrain employers from dismissing workers or in any case stimulate them to think twice before effectuating a dismissal.

In 2015 the Extraordinary Decree on Labour Relations 1945 was abolished, but the requirement of employers to obtain a dismissal permit has been maintained. It is now based on a number of provisions, partly included in the CC, partly laid down in a Ministerial Decree.

Moreover in the years 1945–1980 the CC was amended to make its provisions on dismissals less liberal, by prolongation of the period of notice, judicial control of unfair dismissal, the introduction of the possibility of compensatory awards, severance pay and even statutory designation of specific causes, which cannot provoke a dismissal and of specific situations in which a dismissal is not allowed.

In the 1980s the Dutch system of employment protection came under sharp attack from many economists. The existing procedure, which requires dismissals to be approved beforehand by a third party, was widely criticized as opaque, time-consuming and confusing. It was claimed that by inhibiting an easy discharge of workers the cost of dismissing workers is much higher in the Netherlands than in other countries. It was submitted that these high dismissal costs have a detrimental impact on total labour demand and are conducive to an unequal distribution of job opportunities among the labour force.

Many labour lawyers, however, claimed that high dismissal costs are the case in most European states and not just the Netherlands. Moreover, the emphasis on employment protection is consciously made by the Western European legislators, the main argument being that strong dismissal protection improves the status of the worker. Dignity is connected to a person's work and dismissal protection enables workers to stand up for their rights. So there is a powerful humanitarian argument for strong employment protection, even if that is detrimental to the flexibility of the labour market.

It is against the background of this debate that the Dutch have asked themselves whether the law on dismissals had to be reformed and in what direction. As the government was hesitating in what way to adapt the system business itself found the holes in the system to change it, notably by an increasing use of the procedure of termination by judicial rescission (*see* paragraph 211) and so-called flexible labour contracts – casual workers (on on-call contracts), fixed-term contracts, workers hired through temporary work agencies, freelance contracts and contracts with quasi self-employed workers. In 2000 it was estimated that about 15% of the Dutch labour market was filled with these types of workers (*see* paragraph 9). Initially the use of flexible labour contracts was strongly opposed by the trade union movement, but when they realized that the rise of this type of work was unstoppable, the trade unions switched to a policy of improvement rather than of eradication of flexible contracts.[212]

193. The political debate on the reform of the law on dismissal jumped from one proposal to another. Based on an advice of the Social-Economic Council (1994), the Kok administration (1994–2002) finally decided not to abolish the system of administrative dismissal permits but to allow some procedural reforms which would smooth the discharge of workers and the use of flexible workers, and, at the same time, enhance the legal position of flexible workers. The government invited the social partners to conclude an agreement on more flexibility in the labour market. In April 1996 the main confederations of employers and trade unions, gathering in the bipartite *Stichting van de Arbeid* (Foundation of Labour) reached an agreement on increased flexibility combined with strengthening the position of employees on

212. T. van Peijpe, *Employment Protection under Strain* (*Sweden, Denmark, The Netherlands*) (1998).

fixed-term contracts and temporary agency workers. The *Stichting van de Arbeid* acknowledged the need for more flexible labour relations but sought to avoid the segregation between core permanent workers and peripheral temporary workers. It recommended the government to modernize labour law by combining the aims of flexibility and security (*see* paragraph 17).

Following this compromise Parliament adopted the Flexibility and Security Act 1999. Its main feature was that the legislator upheld the traditional dominant characteristic: the necessity of an *ex ante* approval by the administration or the court of every unilateral termination of open-ended contracts of employment. However, to please the employers the possibilities to get around this system by concluding flexible contracts had been grossly enlarged. In return the trade unions obtained some substantial improvement of the employment rights of these workers on flexible contracts.

In the meantime the courts had started to standardize the severance pay for dismissed workers at (roughly) one or two monthly wages for each year of service. Trade unions and individual employees followed this example in most of the collective or individual agreements about a termination of employment.

All these adaptations have so much complicated the Dutch law on dismissals and flexible workers that it has become a legal minefield and therefore a lawyers' paradise. This made dismissals more costly for employers than they had been ever before.

194. In 2001 a State Commission under the chairmanship of the late Dutch labour law professor, Max Rood, advocated a more radical reform of the Dutch dismissals system. Subsequently the Dutch government asked the social partners to make their views known, but they could not agree on a new overhaul of the Dutch law on dismissals and advised the government (July 2003) to keep the Dutch law on dismissals and flexible workers unchanged.

The government and Parliament were prepared to do so but desired at least one modification: a limitation to the severance pay. However, also this ambition evaporated after great protest manifestations of the trade unions. The only change in the law on dismissals that could be brought about, was a modification of the last-in-first-out rule in economic dismissals, 2006 (*see* paragraph 225). Moreover in 2006 as well, there was a change in the law on unemployment benefits which had a considerable impact on the law of dismissals. The strict criteria for the involuntary character of a termination of employment were substantially relieved so that since then it became much easier for the parties to separate (often based on a contract of termination with an agreed severance pay) without risking to lose the entitlement to an unemployment benefit (*see* paragraph 201).

After neither the social partners (within the framework of the Social-Economic Council) nor the coalition-parties in the fresh centre-left government could agree on an wholesale overhaul of the law on dismissals and unemployment, another report was requested of a high-level expert group, chaired by Mr Bakker (November 2007). However its report, advising indeed major changes in the existing arrangements, was unacceptable to the trade union movement. Together with the employers they convened with the government (September 2008) to keep the Dutch law on dismissals and flexible workers unchanged, apart from one aspect: a cap on the severance pay: a maximum of one yearly wage for those earning more than EUR 75,000 a year. Also this idea came to nothing, save for the directors of (semi-)state institutions (*see* paragraph 288).

For the private sector of the economy it has been the courts that effectuated a noticeable change in the law on dismissals (Autumn 2008): the standardized severance pay was reduced by about 30%.

When it became clear that the banking crisis was going to affect the Dutch economy, the government in 2009 introduced two temporary changes in the law on dismissals: a prolongation of the authorized chain of fix-term contracts for employees under 27 years (*see* paragraph 229) and some additional adaptation of the rules on collective redundancies (*see* paragraphs 224 et seq.).

In 2010 the new right-wing coalition government embarked on the old approach to not ambition a large scale review on the law on dismissals, although the Minister of Labour did some proposals on specific items, which were never implemented. After the fall of this government (spring 2012) an interim-government attempted a large scale change but this again was a still-born project.

195. The subsequent government was equally ambitious when it took office (autumn 2012), but trade unions and employers have been quick to stop it. In the Social Agreement, April 2013, the social partners agreed on just a small reform: (a) maintenance of the two classic roads of *ex ante* dismissal control in a more transparent shape (*see* paragraph 202); (b) replacement of the courts-invented severance pay by a cheaper and more universal 'transition allowance' (*see* paragraph 218); (c) some detailed changes to reduce the abuse of flexible contracts. On the basis of this Social Agreement the government introduced an Amendment Act (called the Work and Security Act) which made it onto the Dutch statute book by July 2014. Most of its provisions entered into force on 1 July 2015, and the rest in 2016.

Many observers of the 2015 Reform Act assessed that its provisions have gone a bit too far in 'making fixed contracts more fixed, and flex contracts more flex', and so the actual government, which came in power in 2017, is committed to bring the legislation more 'in balance'. To this end in 2019 an Amendment Act was adopted by Parliament called 'Labour Market in Balance'[213] which will enter into force by 1 January 2020. It enlarges the reasonable grounds for a dismissal (*see* paragraph 197), brings some modification in the transition allowance (*see* paragraphs 218 et seq.), widens the possibility to conclude a chain of fixed-term contracts (*see* paragraph 230) and improves the rights of employees on call (*see* paragraph 65) and of so-called payrolling firms (*see* paragraph 67). In earlier and following pages of this monograph the Dutch law is described as it will be when the Labour Market in Balance Act has fully entered into force.[214]

---

213. Act of 29 May 2019, Stb. 2019, 219.

214. *See also* G. Heerma van Voss, *Dismissal Protection – The Position in the Netherlands*, in *Restatement of Labour Law in Europe*, Vol. III (B. Waas & G.J.J. Heerma van Voss ed., Oxford-Portland: Hart Publishing, forthcoming).

§2. Dismissal Practices in the Netherlands

196. In the Netherlands there is a high degree of juridification in dismissal practices. There are very few examples of dismissals which are regulated by the tools of (threat of) industrial conflict such as strikes, sit-ins and boycotts (*see* paragraphs 334/339 et seq.). The trade unions and the employers' associations play a major role in the shaping of the law of dismissals – in fact the reforms of the law on dismissals of 1999 and 2015 were both based on agreements between the cross-sector social partners (*see* paragraphs 193 et seq.). However they play only a minor one in the application of that law, save for the law on collective dismissals. It may strike Americans that anti-discrimination law is not very important in dismissal protection in the Netherlands. The reason is that in the Netherlands the idea that a dismissal must be founded 'on reasonable grounds' is the dominant criterion (*see* paragraph 197), and discriminatory dismissals are already filtered out in the *ex ante* dismissal controls.

However, most employers try to avoid compulsory redundancies as far as possible. They prefer to reduce the size of the workforce through a recruitment freeze, overtime reduction, natural attrition, internal replacement and outplacement, severance pay contracts, VUT, or emission to the disability and unemployment benefit schemes. And since the middle of the 1980s employers have increasingly made use of flexible labour contracts, as this enables them to smoothly reduce the workforce if economic reasons require it by not renewing fixed-term contracts and abandoning the use of other flexible labour such as temporary workers, subcontracting, labour-on-call, freelance contracts and so on. These measures are commonly called 'natural personnel turnover' and they are always preferred above 'forced dismissals'. The dark side of this policy is that in times of slack business the workers on flexible contracts are the first to lose their jobs – a fact that became very apparent in the Netherlands in the economic downturn after 9/11 2001 and during the banking crisis in the autumn of 2008. Nevertheless the claim of 'no forced dismissals' is popular among the unions and in public opinion and therefore in various sectors of the Dutch economy the employers have developed the mechanisms to prevent a dismissal/redundancy that can damage the image of the company or can too easily be contested before the UWV (Employees' Social Security Administration, *see* paragraph 39) or in court. This, for a long time, has given the impression that in many sectors redundancies could not occur and that a kind of a lifelong employment was secured. Nowadays no sector of the Dutch economy will claim that it guarantees lifelong employment or can guarantee that workforce reductions will always avoid forced dismissals. Only in a few cases employers are prepared to guarantee at maximum for a short period (two or three years) that they will avoid compulsory redundancies (*see* paragraph 302). In most sectors of the economy, such as agriculture, small engineering firms, construction, retail trade, road transport and catering, employers have never guaranteed lifelong employment. Dismissals on economic grounds have always occurred in these areas and were always authorized if they could be sufficiently justified.

In some countries employers may try to avoid dismissals in situations of slack business by simply sending homeworkers without pay. In the Netherlands this is in general not possible considering the law on continuation of wage payment. Only in exceptional cases this method may be applied (*see* paragraphs 147 et seq.).

§3. The 'Reasonable Grounds' for Dismissal by the Employer

197. Since the reform of the Dutch law on Dismissals, 2015, the section of the CC on termination of the open-ended employment contract opens by putting in the foreground a 'semi-closed system' of valid reasons for the employer to terminate an open-ended contract of employment.

A 'reasonable ground' may be (Article 7:669(3) CC):

(a) the disappearance of the job as a result of the termination of the activities of the enterprise or as a result of the necessary (seen over a future period of at least twenty-six weeks) disappearance of jobs due to measures of efficient entrepreneurship required by economic reasons;
(b) the unfitness of the employee, after two years of illness or infirmity, to fulfil the contracted work and provided it may be assumed that within twenty-six weeks – for persons who have reached the AOW-pensionable age: six weeks (*see* paragraph 52) – no recovery will take place and that within this period no work in adapted form can be performed;
(c) the frequent inability to perform the contracted work as a result of illness and infirmity with unacceptable consequences for the business, provided this is not a sequel of insufficient care of the employer for the health and safety of the employee and it may be assumed that no recovery will take place within twenty-six weeks – for persons who have reached the AOW-pensionable age: six weeks – and within this period no work in adapted form can be performed;
(d) the unfitness of the employee to perform the contracted work otherwise than as a result of illness or infirmity, provided the employer has timely informed the employee of this and has allowed him sufficiently to improve his functioning and the unfitness is not the result of insufficient care of the employer for training or the health and safety of the employee;[215]
(e) culpable acting or omitting to act by the employee, such that it cannot reasonably be required from the employer to continue the contract of employment;
(f) the refusal of the employee to perform the contracted work because of grave reasons of conscience, provided it may be assumed that the contracted work cannot be performed in adapted form;
(g) a disturbed working relationship,[216] such that it cannot reasonably be required from the employer to continue the contract of employment;
(h) other than the aforementioned reasons which are such that it cannot be reasonably required from the employer to continue the contract of employment;

215. Dutch Supreme Court, 14 Jun. 2019, ECLI:NL:HR:2019:933.
216. Dutch Supreme Court, 16 Feb. 2018, ECLI:NL:HR:2018:220.

(i) a combination of circumstances mentioned in two or more of the grounds sub c–h which is such that it cannot be reasonably required from the employer to continue the contract of employment.

Moreover, if not otherwise convened, the employer may terminate the contract of employment on the day after which the employee has reached the pensionable age of the AOW or – when a different pensionable age is applicable to him – having reached that age (Article 7:669(4) CC).

The employer may only terminate a contract of employment if one of the aforementioned 'reasonable ground' is applicable and replacement of the employee in a suitable function within a reasonable time whether or not with help of training is not possible or reasonable.[217]

'Replacement' is in any case not reasonable if the employee has acted or omitted to act in a culpable way. Replacement is not required if the employee serves in a religious function (Article 7:669(1)(2) CC).

The Minister of Social Affairs and Employment may issue more detailed regulations in respect of a 'reasonable ground' for dismissal, the 'replacement' and the 'reasonable time' mentioned in the basic rule of Article 7:669(1) CC. He did so in the important so-called Dismissal Regulation, *Ontslagregeling* (DR),[218] notably concerning the dismissal on economic grounds. In this regulation he made distinctions according to categories of employees and gave rules on the order of the disappearance of jobs, mentioned above, from which however it may be derogated by commissions established by collective agreement (*see* paragraph 225).

§4. Prohibited Dismissals: Special Protection for Certain Categories of Workers

198. Quite comparable with the law in many other countries, in the Netherlands an employer is prohibited from terminating a contract of employment in a number of statutorily indicated circumstances (Article 7:670(1-10) CC).

By virtue of these bans the employer may not terminate the contract of employment, on pain of the dismissal being ruled null and void:

(1) during the first two years – for persons who have reached the AOW-pensionable age: 6 weeks – in which an employee is unfit to perform his work on account of sickness, except for the situations mentioned in paragraph 199;
(2) during pregnancy, during the period in which the employee is entitled to confinement leave and, after resumption of work, during the six-week period immediately following such period of disability to perform work caused by the confinement or the preceding pregnancy and which immediately follows such confinement leave, as well as during the period in which the partner of a deceased mother had taken over the confinement leave (*see* paragraph 125);
(3) during military service or alternative compulsory service;

217. Dutch Supreme Court, 18 Jan. 2019, ECLI:NL:HR:2019:64.
218. Official Gazette (Staatscourant) 2015, 12685, pp. 15–16; adapted in Staatscourant 2016, 34013.

(4) during membership of a works council[219] or its standing committee, an ad hoc (preparatory) committee of a works council, a European Works Council, an ERB and other bodies of workers' involvement in the enterprise;
(5) because of membership of and participation in the activities on behalf of a trade union, unless such activities are performed in the working time of the employee without the employer's consent;
(6) because of the attendance at meetings of political bodies of which the employee is a member;
(7) because the employee exercises his right to parental leave or other types of leave (*see* paragraph 125);
(8) because of the transfer of the enterprise (*see* paragraph 179);
(9) on account of the fact that the employee does not consent to work on Sundays because of business reasons as referred to in the WTA (*see* paragraph 112);
(10) of an employee who is included on a list of candidates for a works council or an ERB, or who, less than two years previously, was a member of a works council, an ERB, a committee of such bodies, a European Works Council, a special negotiation group, a preparatory committee, etc., or who performs work as expert employee under the Health and Safety at Work Act (*see* paragraph 163) or as official performing data protection work according to the General Privacy Regulation (*see* paragraph 107).

Only the third of the above-mentioned prohibited dismissals can be waived by way of a collective agreement (Article 7:670(14) CC).

On several of these prohibited dismissals there are exceptions in the Act (Article 7:670a). For instance the prohibited dismissals under (1)-(4) and (10) are not applicable:

(a) if the employee has in writing given his consent with the termination (Article 7:670a(2)(a)); however, during fourteen days after the date of the consent the employee may, without reason, revoke it by way of a written declaration to the employer (Article 7:670a(5)(6) CC, *see* paragraph 201);
(b) during the probationary period (*see* paragraph 221);
(c) in case of a summary dismissal (*see* paragraph 222);
(d) in case of termination of (part of) the business (safe for employees on pregnancy and maternity leave);
(e) in case of termination because of reaching the AOW-pensionable age, provided the termination has nothing to do with the circumstances protected by the said prohibitions of dismissal (*see* paragraph 197).

199. The most remarkable Dutch rule in this field is the provision that the employer is prohibited from terminating a contract of employment during a period of two years in which an employee is unfit to perform his work on account of sickness (Article 7:670(1) CC). However this strong protection of sick workers was modified. It does not apply:

219. Dutch Supreme Court, 8 Apr. 2016, ECLI:NL:HR:2016:604.

- if the sickness has started after the UWV/sector committee has received an application of the employer for a dismissal permit (Article 7:670(1)(b) CC, *see* paragraphs 204 et seq.) or after the court has received the request for a judicial rescission (Article 7:671b(7) CC, *see* paragraphs 211 et seq.);
- if a worker without good reasons and after having been warned by the employer, refuses to cooperate with his reintegration or is not prepared to perform other suitable work (Article 7:670a(1) CC *see* paragraph 80);
- to workers beyond the pensionable age (for them the prohibition to terminate in case of illness is only six weeks).

200. In case of a dismissal prohibited in Article 7:670 CC or any other comparable statutory prohibition to dismiss – see notably those on discrimination (*see* paragraph 90) – the court, on the request of the employee, may nullify the notice of termination by the employer, or, order the employer liable to pay a fair compensation for the damages (Article 7:681(1)(a)(b)(c) CC). The employer must invoke these dismissal prohibitions within two months otherwise the dismissal is valid (Article 7:686(4)(a) CC).

§5. Termination by Mutual Consent

201. The contract of employment is concluded by mutual consent and it can be terminated in the same way. The habit to conclude a written termination agreement has been greatly extended in the Netherlands since in 2006 the requirement that the termination had to be 'involuntary' in order not to put to risk the unemployment benefit, had been modified. The social security authorities may assume that a termination by mutual consent leads to 'involuntary unemployment' (that entitles to an unemployment benefit) if (a) the initiative of the termination has been at the employer's side, (b) it should not have had the character of a summary dismissal (*see* paragraph 222) and (c) the applicable period of notice (*see* paragraph 216) has been respected.

Already since many years the courts have protected the employees against spontaneous or unconscious acts of the employee to resign or a reckless consent to a proposal of the employer to terminate the contract of employment. The HR has uphold such an act or consent only if there has been a clear and unequivocal declaration of the employee to this end.[220] Eventually the employer must enquire if the act or consent is serious. All this is derived from the classic doctrine of 'vitiated consent'.[221]

Since the 2015 Reform the CC now contains special provisions on this subject, respectively dealing with the case that a formal contract of termination is concluded, and the case that the employee has simply given his consent to the intention of the employer to terminate the contract of employment. In both cases the law now requires that the consent should be in writing. And for both cases the law provides that the employee may revoke its consent within two weeks. This period is three

220. Dutch Supreme Court, 8 Apr. 1994, JAR 1994/95; Dutch Supreme Court, 25 Mar. 1994, JAR 1994/92.
221. Dutch Supreme Court, 5 Feb. 1999, NJ 1999, 652.

weeks if these rules are not mentioned in the contact of termination nor were communicated by the employer to the employee. These two last rules are not applicable if the parties within six months after the aforementioned termination are again terminating a contract of employment. Moreover these rules on revocation are not applicable to managing directors (Article 7:670b CC and Article 7:671(1-6) CC).

§6. Methods of Unilaterally Terminating Employment

202. The Dutch system of dismissal protection is unique in Europe. The Netherlands is the only country in the EU with a comprehensive system of *ex ante* control of dismissals. Any employer, before dismissing a worker, who works on an open-ended contract of employment needs to have either the permission of the UWV or the sector committee (Article 7:671 CC) or the rescission of the contract by the court.

The employer has to ask the permission of the UWV or the sector committee if the termination of the contract of employment is motivated by economic reasons. If the termination is for reason of the unfitness of the employee after two years of illness of the employee he must ask the permission of the UWV. If the termination is for other reasons, notably due to the other capacities or the behaviour of the employee, the employer must obtain a rescission of the contract by the court (*see* paragraphs 211 et seq.).

There are some exceptions on this requirement (*see* paragraph 203), but there are no thresholds in the applicability of this system of *ex ante* control as regards the employment record of the worker or the size of the enterprise.

203. No permit UWV or rescission of the court is needed during a probationary period and in cases of termination by mutual consent, summary dismissal and the termination by operation of the law (e.g., fixed-term contracts).

Moreover the employer does not need a permit UWV or a rescission of the court for a few categories of persons (Article 7:671 CC), such as domestic workers (if they work less than four days a week (almost) exclusively in the household of a natural person), persons reaching the AOW-pensionable age, directors of a legal person, employees in a clerical profession, employees in private education (but only if the reason for termination is in acting or omitting to act of the employee which is incompatible with the religious or ideological basis of the school and the dismissal has been permitted by an independent commission satisfying the criteria of Article 7:671(1) CC (*see* paragraph 204)).

See paragraph 214 for the remaining dismissal protection for these employees.

204. Save for cases in which no UWV permit is required (*see* paragraph 203) any unilateral termination of an open-ended contract of employment without either the consent of the UWV/sector committee or the rescission of the court, may on the request of the employee, be nullified, or, the court may, at the request of the employee, order the employer liable to pay a fair compensation for damages (Article 7:681(1)(a) CC). The employee must invoke this nullity within two months; otherwise the dismissal is valid (Article 7:686a CC).

A void dismissal implies that the employer has to continue to pay wages to the worker provided the worker has shown his willingness to continue working. Because of the lengthy proceedings involved, wage claims taking two years or even longer are no exception. The courts may reduce such a claim for uninterrupted wage payment if, in the given circumstances, such an award would have unacceptable consequences, provided it is set at not less than the wage over the statutory period of notice nor less than the wage for three months (whichever is the highest) (Article 7:680a CC). The courts have freely made use of this opportunity to mitigate but have been admonished by the HR to apply this competence with reticence.[222] Among the circumstances taken into account by the courts as a reason to reduce a wage claim are the short duration of the contract of employment, the fact that the dismissal was at least partly caused by the conduct of the employee or the poor financial position of the employer.

§7. Dismissal with a Permit of the UWV

205. If an employer intends to terminate an open-ended contract of employment for economic reasons or because of the protracted illness of the employee, he must apply in writing for a permit by the *Uitvoeringsinstituut Werknemersverzekeringen* (*UWV*, Employees' social security administration) (*see* paragraphs 251 et seq.)[223] (Article 7:671a(1) CC).

The UWV shall assess whether or not to give the permit for termination because of economic reasons by tests based on the wording of Article 7:669 CC:

- The disappearance of the job must be a result of the termination of the activities of (part of) the enterprise;
- The disappearance of the job must be a result of the necessary (seen over a future period of at least twenty-six weeks) disappearance of jobs due to measures of efficient entrepreneurship required by economic reasons;

  The replacement of the employee in a suitable function within a reasonable time whether or not with help of training is not possible or reasonable.

206. The UWV will not give its permit if it is requested in order to replace workers by cheaper workers! In addition the UWV shall refuse the permit if the employer has not beforehand terminated the employment relationship with persons working of the same jobs as the cancelled jobs – in the following order (*see* Article 11 DR) – (1) who have reached the AOW-pensionable age, (2) who worked on on-call contracts, (3) who worked on fixed-time contracts and (4) who worked as temporary agency workers (Article 7:671a(5) CC).

The Minister has given further directives about the discharge of these powers by the UWV in the already mentioned DR (Articles 2–8).

222. Dutch Supreme Court, 13 Sep. 2002, NJ 2002/496; Dutch Supreme Court, 26 Mar. 2004, NJ 2004/322.
223. F.B.J. Grapperhaus, *The End of the Affair* (2006).

207. The UWV shall assess whether or not to give the permit for termination because of the protracted illness of the employee by tests based on the wording of Article 7:669(3)(b) CC:

- the employee must be unfit to fulfil the contracted work after two years of illness or infirmity, and
- it may be assumed that within 26 weeks – for persons who have reached the AOW-pensionable age: 6 weeks – no recovery will take place and
- that within this period no work in adapted form can be performed and;
- that the replacement of the employee in a suitable function within a reasonable time whether or not with help of training is not possible or reasonable.

208. The Minister shall give rules regarding the procedure for the granting of the dismissal permits by the UWV (Article 7:671a(8) CC). He did so in the so-called *Regeling UWV Ontslagprocedures* (dismissals permits procedures rules).[224]

The request for a dismissal permit to the UWV must be done on a template published on the UWV website and should contain all the relevant information, such as a clear justification of the dismissal. Within a few days the UWV sends the employee a copy of the request giving him fourteen days to respond in writing. Only exceptionally will there be an oral hearing of the parties and also only exceptionally a committee, made up of employers' and union representatives under the chairmanship of an UWV official, will be consulted. The decision on a request for a dismissal permit will be delivered in writing at the same time to both the employer and the employee (Article 7:671a(4) CC). If the dismissal is authorized, the employer has four weeks in which to make use of the permit and to dismiss the employee in writing, mentioning the reason for the dismissal (Article 7:671a(6) CC).

The UWV permit will normally contain the condition that the employer – not being a temporary work agency – is prohibited to hire within twenty-six weeks after a termination for economic reasons another employee for the same activities as those which the employee performed before notice of termination was given without having given the employee the opportunity to resume his former activities on the conditions usual at that company. If the employer violates this rule, the court, on the request of the employee, may nullify such a notice of termination, or, on the request of the employee, order the employer to pay a fair compensation to the employee (Article 7:681(1)(d) CC). The same applies *mutatis mutandis* in cases of a judicial rescission – in that case there is no nullification, but restoration per date of termination (Article 7:682(4) CC) (for a comparable provision for the temporary agency workers, *see* paragraph 232).

The Minister may issue regulations about what must be deemed to be 'employer' for the application of this work resumption condition, in what cases and under what conditions this condition does not apply and in what order successive employees must be enabled to resume their formal activities (Article 7:682a CC). The Minister has done so in Articles 18–33 of the DR.

224. Official Gazette (Staatscourant) 2015, 12688.

In the past the proceedings for obtaining a dismissal permit of the UWV were often criticized by lawyers, for instance in a research of the National Ombudsman, 2007 and they have incidentally given rise to judicial condemnations.

Although the UWV requires the necessary information about the financial position of the firm, it refrains from a thorough investigation of the underlying business reasoning. On the other hand it checks more in-depth, whether the termination of a specific employee was in accordance with the selection criteria in economic redundancies (*see* paragraphs 206 and 225). This is also done in case of an individual dismissal based on economic reasons.

The UWV shall not give a permit in case a dismissal prohibition (*see* paragraph 198) is applicable, but if it wrongly does so, the employer cannot legally use the permit. If it would be used the employee has the remedy, mentioned in paragraph 200.

The UWV issues the permits on average within six weeks after it has been requested. In the case of collective redundancies owing to economic circumstances, that are not contested by the unions or worker(s) concerned, the UWV may grant its permit after a shortened delay. The result of this should be that 60%–70% of requests can be decided within four weeks.

Over the years statistics showed that the dismissal permit is granted in 85%–90% of the cases in which it has been requested. In about 10% to 15% of the cases the employer's request is refused or withdrawn and the employment has been continued or ended because a mutual settlement has been reached. The refusal of a permit was often based on the fact that the employer did not submit sufficient facts or had failed to look for alternative employment for the worker.

209. An employer who sees his request for a dismissal permit refused may try later again if he has new arguments. However he also may turn to the cantonal judge of the subdistrict court to ask for a rescission of the contract of employment (*see* paragraph 211).

If on the other hand the employer has terminated the contract of employment with the permission of the UWV, the employee may turn to the cantonal judge to request a revision of the situation. If the cantonal judge finds the termination contrary to the 'reasonable ground' mentioned in Article 7:669(1)(a) CC (economic reasons), it may, on the request of the employee, order the employer to restore the contract of employment, or it may order the employer liable to pay a fair compensation if the restoration is not reasonably possible because of a circumstance concerning serious culpable acts or omissions to act by the employer (Article 7:682(1)(a)(b) CC). If the court finds the termination contrary to the 'reasonable ground' mentioned in Article 7:669(1)(b) CC (protracted illness), it may, on the request of the employee, order the employer to restore the contract of employment, or it may order the employer liable to pay a fair compensation if the termination because of the circumstances of this ground for termination is the result of serious culpable acts or omissions to act by the employer (Article 7:682(1)(a)(c) CC). If the court makes an order to restore the contract of employment, it will stipulate a time at which the contract of employment must be restored and make provisions regarding the legal consequences of the interruption of the contract of employment (Article 7:682(6) CC).

210. In 2015 the legislator has opened the possibility that the social partners at sectoral or company level may replace the authority of the UWV to issue dismissal permits based on economic reasons. The social partners may, by way of a collective agreement, appoint an impartial committee independent from the employer, to issue the dismissal permit in cases of dismissal for economic reasons (not because of the unfitness of the employee after two years of illness). The collective agreement must be concluded with trade unions which are active on behalf of their members in the enterprise and – including its predecessors – having the status of a legal person for at least two years (*see* paragraph 313). The collective agreement must contain rules on hearing of both sides, the confidential treatment of the submitted data, a reasonable time limit for reactions of the employer and the employee and a reasonable time limit for the decision. Also the Minister may issue rules on these commissions and their procedures (Article 7:671a(2)(3) CC). Both parties in such conflicts may appeal the decision of the committee to the cantonal judge according to the rules described in paragraph 209.

Up until now the social partners have only in rare cases made use of this alternative.

§8. Termination by Judicial Rescission

211. The second way to terminate a contract of employment in the Netherlands is the rescission or dissolution (German *Auflösung*) of the contract by the cantonal judge of the District Court.

Obviously, according to a general principle of contract law, courts can always rescind a contract if one of the parties has failed to live up to its obligations (breach of contract). This is confirmed for the contracts of employment in Article 7:686 CC. However, this method of termination is practically never used as far as contracts of employment are concerned, because the Dutch CC provides a special procedure for rescinding the contract of employment.

Since the 2015 Reform this special procedure for rescinding the contract of employment is laid down in Article 7:671b CC (rescission requested by the employer) and Article 7:671c CC (rescission requested by the employee).

Article 7:671b CC empowers the cantonal judge to rescind the contract of employment upon a request of the employer. This court may rescind the contract:

(a) on all reasonable grounds, apart from those for economic reasons or the protracted illness of the employee;
(b) also on the grounds of economic reasons or the protracted illness of the employee, if the UWV or the sector committee has refused a dismissal permit;
(c) idem in the case of a fixed-term contract of employment that cannot be terminated interim.

The court can only rescind the contract if at least one of the conditions for termination – the so-called reasonable grounds, described in Article 7:669 CC (*see* paragraph 197) – are fulfilled. The court may not rescind if there are statutory dismissal prohibitions (*see* paragraphs 198–200) applicable (Article 7:671b(2) CC) but in a number of cases the court may nevertheless rescind the contract, for instance if the request has no relation with the circumstances on which the prohibition is based (Article 7:671b(3-6) CC).

If the court rescinds an open-ended contract or a fixed-term contract that can be terminated interim, it determines the termination of the contract at the date the contract would have ended in case of the regular notification of the termination (in other words: at the end of the applicable period of notice). However, provided that the rescission is not caused by serious culpable acts or omissions to act on the side of the employer, this period is reduced with the time between the request for rescission and the rescission decision, provided the remaining notice period shall not be less than one month. The court may deviate from this rule and determine the termination of the contract at an earlier date if the rescission is caused by serious culpable acts or omissions to act on the side of the employee. The court may award the employee 'fair compensation' if the rescission is caused by serious culpable acts or omissions to act of the employer (Article. 7:671b(9) CC).[225] If the rescission is based on Article 7:669(3)(i) CC (the combination of reasonable grounds) the court may award the employee a compensation of at most half the transition allowance (*see* paragraph 218) (Article 7:671b(8) CC).

If the court rescinds a fixed-term contract that cannot be terminated interim, it determines the date of the termination of the contract. The court may award the employee a compensation of at most the amount of the wage over the remaining period that the contract should have lasted if terminated by operation of law. Besides this compensation the court may award a fair compensation if the rescission is caused by serious culpable acts or omissions to act on the part of the employer. If the rescission is caused by serious culpable acts or omissions to act on the side of the employee, the court may award the employer a compensation of at most the amount of the wage over the remaining period that the contract should have lasted if terminated by operation of law (Article. 7:671b(10) CC).

212. Article 7:671c CC empowers the cantonal judge to rescind the contract of employment on the request of the employee. The court may upon a request of the employee rescind the contract of employment on account of circumstances which are of such nature that the contract of employment should, in fairness, terminate immediately or after a short period.

If the court rescinds a contract for indefinite time or a fixed-term contract that can be terminated interim, it determines the date of termination of the contract and may award the employee a fair compensation if the rescission is caused by serious culpable acts or omissions to act of the employer.

If the court rescinds a fixed-term contract that cannot be terminated interim, it determines the date of the termination of the contract. The court may – if such appears fair in the light of the circumstances – award the employee a compensation of at most the amount of the wage over the remaining period that the contract should have lasted if terminated by operation of law. Besides the compensation the court may award a fair compensation if the rescission is caused by serious culpable acts

225. On the amount of this compensation *see* Dutch Supreme Court, 3 Jun. 2018, ECLI:NL:HR:2018:878 (Zinzia); Dutch Supreme Court, 30 Nov. 2018, ECLI:NL:HR:2018:2218.

or omissions to act on the side of the employer. If the rescission is caused by serious culpable acts or omissions to act on the side of the employee, the court may – if such appears fair in the light of the circumstances – award the employer a compensation of at most the amount of the wage over de remaining period that the contract should have lasted if terminated by operation of law. Moreover a higher compensation is possible for certain functions, indicated in a regulation of the Minister.

213. Al legal proceedings in dismissal cases in the District Court can be initiated with a petition and need no writ of summons (Article 7:686a(2)(3) CC). Most of the time they must be presented within two or three months after termination of the contract of employment (Article 686a(4) CC). The courts will start the proceedings not later than four weeks after the reception of such requests (Article 7:686a(5) CC). The decisions of the District Court in rescission cases are normally delivered within a delay of at most two months after the request. They cannot have a retrospective effect.[226]

Before rescinding the contract of employment the court shall notify the parties of its intention and allow the petitioner a period within which to withdraw its application. If the petitioner has done so the court shall only decide about the litigation costs (Article 7:686a(6)(7) CC).

In all these rescission procedures the normal rules of evidence of civil law are applicable.[227]

§9. Judicial Control *Ex Post*/Appeals

214. As already indicated (*see* paragraph 203) for a minority of employees there is no *ex ante* judicial control of the UWV/sector commission or the court available for ministers of a church, managerial directors, employees in the households of private persons, and certain employees in private education (Article 7:671(1) CC). The same applies to pensioners, whose contracts of employment were concluded before reaching the AOW-pensionable age (Article 7:671(4) CC). For these persons there is only a dismissal control *ex post.*

As regards the employees in private households and certain employees in private education the court may, at the request of the employee, order the employer to restore the contract of employment if it finds the termination contrary to the 'reasonable grounds' mentioned in Article 7:669(1) CC or order the employer liable to pay a fair compensation if the termination has been the result of serious culpable acting or omitting to act by the employer (Article 7:682(2) CC). If the court orders to restore the contract of employment, it will stipulate a time from which the contract of employment must be restored and make provisions regarding the legal consequences of the interruption of the contract of employment (Article 7:682(6) CC). As regards directors of legal persons or employees in clerical professions, the court

226. Dutch Supreme Court, 26 May 1966, NJ 1966, 345.
227. Dutch Supreme Court, 23 Dec. 2016, ECLI:NL:HR:2016:2998 (Mediant).

may, at the request of the employee, order the employer liable to pay a fair compensation if it finds the termination contrary to the 'reasonable grounds' mentioned in Article 7:669(1) CC or the result of serious culpable acting or omitting to act by the employer (Article 7:682(3) CC). Also to these four categories of employees the court may award a compensation of at most half the transition allowance CC (*see* paragraph 218) if the rescission is based on Article 7:669(3)(i) CC (the combination of reasonable grounds) (Article 7:682(7) CC).

215. All decisions of the District Court in dismissal cases are open to full appeal to the Court of Appeal and appeal in cassation at the HR (*see* paragraph 36). However, appeals and appeals in cassation against decisions of the court to rescind, taken at the request of the employee on the basis of Article 7:671c CC (*see* paragraph 212), are limited to the amount of the compensation (Article 7:683(2) CC). Appeals against the decisions of the District Court in dismissal cases do not suspend the execution of these decisions (Article 7:683(1) CC).

If the court in appeal concludes that the request of an employer to rescind has been wrongly sustained or that the request of an employee for nullification of a notice of termination or a restoration of the contract has been wrongly rejected, it may order the employer to restore the contract or to pay a fair compensation to the employee (Article 7:683(3) CC).[228] If the court orders to restore the contract of employment it stipulates a time at which the contract of employment must be restored and makes provisions regarding the legal consequences of the interruption of the contract of employment (Article 7:683(4) CC).[229]

If the court in appeal concludes that the request of the employer or the employee to rescind the contract of employment has been wrongly rejected, it determines the date at which the contract shall end and applies the Article 7:671b and 7:671c CC with respect to the ordering of a compensation (Article 7:683(5) CC).

If finally the court in appeal concludes that the request of an employee for nullification of a notice of termination or a restoration of the contract has been wrongly sustained, it determines the date at which the contract shall end (Article 7:683(6) CC).

§10. Periods of Notice

216. Notice of termination is required to terminate a contract of employment entered into for an indeterminate period (Article 7:667(6) CC; for the notice in fixed-term contracts, *see* paragraph 230).

When the UWV has granted its permission to dismiss (or if this permission is not required and the worker concerned is not covered by special statutory protection described in the preceding paragraphs), the employer may proceed to terminate the contract, but still has to take into account the contractual terms of notice as well as the statutory terms laid down by the CC.

228. Dutch Supreme Court, 8 Jun. 2018, ECLI:NL:HR:2018:857.
229. Dutch Supreme Court, 25 Jan. 2019, ECLI:NL:HR:2019:80.

For the *employer* the minimum statutory period of notice to be taken into account is after a period of service of:

- less than five years, one month;
- more than five years and less than ten years, two months;
- more than ten years and less than fifteen years, three months;
- more than fifteen years, four months (Article 7:672(2) CC).

Employees who have reached the AOW-pensionable age may be dismissed with a period of notice of one month (Article 7:672(3) CC).

From these statutory periods of notice may be deducted the time that the employer has awaited the decision on his complete request of the UWV permit, provided the remaining notice period shall not be less than one month (Article 7:672(6) CC).

A reduction of these statutory periods of notice is only permitted by collective agreement. An extension may be agreed by the parties to the contract of employment, provided it is in writing (Article 7:672(7) CC).

For the *employee* the minimum statutory period of notice to be taken into account is basically one month (Article 7:672(4– CC). On-call workers may dismiss with the minimum period of calling, set for the employer (*see* paragraph 65) (Article 7:672(5) CC).

From this period it may be derogated in writing. In the case of an extension, this period may not exceed six months, while then the period to be observed by the employer should not be less than twice that applicable for the employee (Article 7:672(8) CC). That last condition is not applicable if the deviation is made by collective agreement, but the period to be observed by the employer shall not be shorter than that for the employee (Article 7:672(9) CC).

For the calculation of the duration of the contract of employment, employment contracts of one and the same employee successively employed by different employers shall be deemed to constitute one continuous contract of employment if these employers must reasonably be considered to be one another's successor.[230] Also for the purpose of calculation of the period of service, employment contracts shall be deemed to constitute one continuous contract of employment upon restoration of the contract pursuant to Article 7:682 and 7:683 CC (Article 7:672(10) CC) (*see* paragraph 218).

Finally the period of notice for both the employer and the employee must be prolonged until the exit day (*aanzegdag*), which is by the end of a calendar month unless another day has been specified in respect thereof by written contract or in accordance with custom (Article 7:672(1) CC). This requirement does not apply to workers on call (Article 7:672(5) CC).

Abbreviated periods of notice apply in case of bankruptcy or judicial leave to suspend payments (BA, *see* paragraph 228).

217. The party that terminates the contract of employment at an earlier day than the legally applicable one owes the other party a compensation equal to the wage

230. Dutch Supreme Court, ECLI:NL:HR:2018:2222 (European Sport Service).

over the period that the contract should have lasted in case of a legal termination (Article 7:672(11) CC). The Court, however, may mitigate this compensation if this seems fair, regarding the circumstances, but the compensation cannot be less than the wage over the statutory period of notice, nor less than the wage for three months (whichever is the highest) (Article 7:672(12) CC).

During the period of notice the employees are obliged to fulfil their contractual obligations. However, sometimes employers do not allow them to enter the workplace, but they have at least to continue to pay them the wage. In order to ensure this, the worker should preferably by written statement confirm his preparedness to work (*see* paragraph 131). He also may, by way of an injunction, seek a court decision requiring the employer to let him work (*see* paragraphs 85 et seq.).

The term of notice is meant to give the worker time to look for a new job. However Dutch law does not order the employer to allow the employee take leave during the term of notice. A few collective agreements have filled this gap.

§11. The Transition Allowance

218. The employer owes the employee a transition allowance if the contract of employment is terminated by the employer, rescinded by the court on request of the employer or, after termination by law not has been continued on the initiative of the employer (Article 7:673(1)(a)).

The transition allowance is also due if the contract of employment because of serious culpable acts or omissions to act on the side of the employer, is terminated by the employee or is rescinded by the court on request of the employee or, after termination by operation of the law has not been continued on the initiative of the employee (Article 7:673(1)(b) CC).

The amount of the transition allowance is equal to 1/3 of the monthly wage for each calendar year that the contract of employment has lasted, and an equivalent proportion of it for a service period shorter than one year. The maximum of the transition allowance is EUR 81,000 or an amount equal to at most the wage of one year if that is higher than EUR 81,000. This amount will be indexed yearly with the average pay rise (Article 7:673(2)(3) CC). The Minister shall give rules for the application of the concept of 'wage' in this provision (Article 7:673(10) CC).[231]

For the calculation of the duration of the contract of employment are disregarded the weeks in which less than twelve hours work have been performed beneath the age of 18. Also for this calculation employment contracts between the same parties not interrupted during more than six months must be computed. Contracts of employment of one and the same employee successively employed by different employers shall be deemed to constitute one continuous contract of employment if these employers must reasonably be considered to be one another's successor with regard to the work performed, irrespective whether these employers had insight in

231. *See* Decree on the concept of wage for the compensation of the announcement term and the transition allowance, Stb. 2014, 538; further Regulation in Staatscourant 2014, 36823, amended in Staatscourant 2015, 34289; *see* Dutch Supreme Court 19 Apr. 2019, ECLI:NL:HR:2019, 632.

the qualities and suitability of the employee (Article 7:673(4) CC).[232] In the last-mentioned eventuality earlier payments of a transition allowance may be deducted (Article 7:673(5) CC). On conditions laid down in a Royal Decree[233] the transition allowance may be diminished with the costs of measures to prevent the unemployment of the employee or reduce its duration as well as with the costs for the promotion of the employability of the employee made during the contract of employment (Article 7:673(6) CC).

In case of a substantial and permanent reduction of the working hours laid down in the contract of employment, the employee is entitled to a proportional transition allowance.[234]

No limitation of the transition allowance is possible on the basis of reasonability.[235]

219. The transition allowance is not due if the contract of employment is terminated or not continued:

(a) before the employee has reached the age of 18 and the average amount of the performed work has not been more than twelve hours (Article 7:673 (7a) CC);
(b) in relation to or after reaching the pensionable age established by statute of contract – or if no other age is applicable – at the AOW-pensionable age (Article 7:673(7b) CC);
(c) as a result of serious culpable acts or omissions to act on the side of the employee (Article 7:673(7c)),[236] but the court may nevertheless award a full or a partial transition allowance if its denying would be unacceptable on reasonability grounds (Article 7:673(8) CC). This exception will normally mean that in cases of a justified summary dismissal (*see* paragraph 222) no transaction allowance is due, but in exception a transaction allowance may be due, viz. if no blame attaches to the employee.[237]

Until 1 January 2020 for employees over 50 years old with at least ten years of service the transition allowance is half the monthly wage for every half-year of service. This provision is not applicable to employers with less than twenty-five employees (Article 7:673a CC), although the Minister may exempt certain employers from this exception. Also until 2020 the Minister could meet the special needs of the small firms by excluding certain months from the duration of the contract of employment for the calculation of the transition allowance (Article 7: 673d CC).

Employers may invoke a regulation which offer them a compensation for this transition allowance out of social security funds in a small number of eventualities,

232. For this concept of the 'successive employership' *see* S. Palm, Opvolgend werkgeverschap, Boom, Den Haag, 2019; on pp. 205–208 there is an English-language summary.
233. Royal Decree 23 Apr. 2014, Stb. 2015, 171.
234. Dutch Supreme Court, 14 Sep. 2018, ECLI:NL:HR:2018:1617.
235. Dutch Supreme Court, 5 oktober 2018, ECLI:NL:HR:23018: 1845.
236. Dutch Supreme Court, 8 Feb. 2019, ECLI:NL:HR:2019:203 (*Woondroomzorg*).
237. Dutch Supreme Court, 30 Mar. 2018, ECLI:NL:HR:2018:484.

such as the termination of the contract of employment after two years of illness or disablement or the termination of the activities of a one-owner small business by the retirement, illness or disability or death of the employer (Article 7:673e CC).[238]

The transition allowance is not or no longer due if the employer has gone bankrupt or has judicial leave to suspend payments. Moreover the Minister may make specific arrangements if the payment of a transition allowance would have unacceptable consequences for a company (Article 7:673c CC).

It must be assumed that most of these statutory rules on the transition allowance are mandatory minimum provisions, even the statutory maximum of EUR 81,000 or an amount equal to at most the wage of one year. Parties to the contract of employment as well as parties to a collective agreement may agree on a transition allowance which is more favourable to the employee or is awarded to the employee in other cases than required by the statute.

Moreover in a collective agreement a derogation of these statutory rules in case of a dismissal on economic grounds is possible if an arrangement has been agreed with the purpose to limit unemployment and/or to offer a reasonable financial compensation. Such a collective agreement must fulfil the criteria mentioned in paragraph 313 (Article 673b CC).

§12. Death of the Employee or the Employer

220. A contract of employment ends automatically with the death of the worker (Article 7:674 CC, *see also* paragraph 116). The death of the employer, however, does not automatically terminate the contract. The employer's heirs are still bound, but the law includes some provisions which make it easier for them as well as for the employee to terminate a fixed-term contract (Article 7:675 CC).

§13. Dismissal During a Probationary Period (Trial Clauses)

221. If a contract of employment contains a probationary period (trial clause) each of the parties is entitled, until the expiry of such period, to give notice with immediate effect (Article 7:676 CC). During this period the ordinary rules governing dismissal do not apply (Article 7:669(7) CC); parties have only minimal rights as far as dismissal is concerned – no *ex ante* dismissal control, no application of a number of the prohibited forms of dismissal (those mentioned in sections 1–4 and 10 of Article 7:670 CC, *see* Article 7:670a(2) CC and paragraph 198) and no periods of notice. However, on the request of an employee the employer must give him/her a written statement of the reason of termination (Article 7:676 and Article 7:670a(2) CC) and in exceptional cases the employee may be protected against dismissal during the probation period on the basis of the bona fides principle (*see* paragraph 103).

Because of these severe consequences Parliament has narrowly limited the use of trial clauses, most recently in 2015 and 2019. Article 7:652 of the CC requires a trial

238. Already provided for the Act of 12 Jul. 2018, Stb. 2018, 234; Parliamentary Papers 34699.

clause to be in writing and equal for both parties. In a contract of employment for an indefinite period and in a contract for a fixed period longer than two years, trial clauses are allowed to a maximum duration of two months. No trial clause can be concluded in contracts with a maximum duration of six months. If the length of the contract of employment is for longer than six months and less than two years or the duration has not been set at a calendar date, a trial period is allowed to a maximum of one month. This last rule can be waived by way of a collective agreement.

All trial clauses contrary to these rules are void. Also void are trial clauses contained in a successive contract of employment with the same employer, unless that new contract requires clearly other abilities or responsibilities from the employee than the former contract. This is the same when the trial clause is contained in a successive contract of employment with a different employer who must reasonably be considered to be the other's successor with regard to the work performed.

The trial clause is narrowly construed by the courts. The nullity of *contra legem* trial clauses is absolute. They are not converted into a valid trial clause within the limits of the law, but are null and void *in toto*, which leaves a normal contract of employment to which the usual rules of dismissal apply.[239] It has also been ruled, that even no work has been performed during (parts of) the probationary period, e.g., because of the worker's sickness, the period cannot be extended.[240]

The maximum probationary period (two months) for new workers is relatively short in the Netherlands. It is claimed that this does not allow employers sufficient time to screen new workers in order to reduce subsequent 'firing-risks'. However, Dutch legislators have deliberately kept the probationary period short because of the weak status of the worker during this period. Employers who need a longer time period to screen new workers should use the fixed-term contract. That is the idea. And in fact the rules on a chain of fixed-term contracts (*see* paragraphs 229 et seq.) allow Dutch employers a period up to two years to test a worker!

§14. Summary Dismissal

222. A summary dismissal is the act by which an employer or an employee immediately and unilaterally puts an end to the contract of employment. Dutch law authorizes both sides of the contract of employment to terminate the contract immediately because of an urgent reason, that has been immediately communicated to the other side (Article 7:677(1) CC). Moreover the courts are insisting that the summary termination is immediately effectuated after the reason for it has appeared,[241] although in some cases a short delay is accepted.

239. Dutch Supreme Court, 8 Jul. 1987, No 1988, 232; however invoking the nullity in case of only a trivial transgression of the period may be contrary to reasonableness and fairness, *see* Dutch Supreme Court, 27 Oct. 1995, NJ 1996, 254.
240. Dutch Supreme Court, 9 Apr. 1954, NJ 1954, 446; Dutch Supreme Court, 23 Dec. 1983, NJ 1984, 332.
241. Dutch Supreme Court, 10 Aug. 1984, NJ 1985, 34; Dutch Supreme Court, 18 Jan. 2019, ECLI:NL:HR:2019:55.

Summary dismissal is possible if one of the parties has shown such misconduct that the other party cannot reasonably be required to allow the contract of employment to continue. Employers may dismiss individual employees summarily for a range of 'urgent reasons', such as the refusal to obey reasonable orders, cases in which the employee has deliberately misled the employer; theft or other conduct which leads to a breach of trust; drunken, reckless or insulting behaviour; a refusal to carry out set tasks; and gross neglect of duties. Under Dutch law, unlike the situation in Germany, employers may not summarily dismiss workers for economic reasons. Employees may leave their employer summarily on urgent reasons, such as serious delay in the payment of wages and sexual harassment. Several forms of serious misconduct are listed in the CC (Article 7:678–679), but the lists are not exhaustive nor are the mentioned examples per se to be recognized as sufficient reasons for any summary dismissal.

The case law of the HR has provided some guidance.[242] The court has, for instance, ruled, that all the circumstances of the case in connection which each other must be taken into account. In the first place this are the nature and the seriousness of the violation, the nature and the duration of the employment, the way in which the employee has performed his contractual obligations and the personal circumstances of the employee, such as his age, as well as the consequences of the summary dismissal for the employee.[243] Nevertheless, even if the employee had a faultless employment record, or the consequences of the dismissal are very serious, a summary dismissal may be justified.[244] Moreover the Court ruled that a summary dismissal may be justified even if the employee cannot be blamed, although this is an exceptional situation![245] And that a summary dismissal may be founded on a reason which already has occurred before the contract had started (for instance, lying during the application procedure).[246] However, decisive elements are left to the circumstances of the case and the lower courts are master of fact-finding in the case and weighing the arguments. So there can never be absolute certainty whether a summary dismissal is justified. To give only one example: frequent or prolonged absenteeism of the employee is a usual reason for summary dismissal. Nevertheless the HR once ruled that prolonged detention of an employee in itself is not a sufficient reason for a summary dismissal. Sufficient justification depends on all the circumstances of the case such as the relationship between the offence and the job and the question of whether the employer was harmed by the offence and the detention.[247]

In case of a justified summary dismissal by the employer most of the legal rules concerning dismissal, as described above, do not apply. No period of notice is

242. C. Loonstra & J. Quist. *The Dutch Supreme Court versus the Lower Courts: Summary Dismissal and the Catalogue of Viewpoints*, in *The Legitimacy of the Highest Courts' Ruling* 343–368 (N. Huls et al. ed., TMC Asser Press, The Hague, 2009).

243. Dutch Supreme Court, 21 Jan. 2000, JAR 2000/45.

244. Dutch Supreme Court, 26 Apr. 1996, NJ 1996, 489.

245. Dutch Supreme Court, 29 Sep. 2000, JAR 2000/223; Dutch Supreme Court, 3 Mar. 1989, NJ 1989/549. In such exceptional situations even a transition allowance (*see* paragraph 209) may be justified, *see* Dutch Supreme Court, 30 Mar. 2018, ECLI:NL:HR:2018:484.

246. Dutch Supreme Court, November 1954, NJ 1954, 782.

247. Dutch Supreme Court, 17 Dec. 2010, JAR 2011/19.

required, no transition allowance is due (apart from the above-mentioned exceptional situation), nor is the UWV permission to dismiss or the rescission of the court required (*see* Article 7:671(1)(c) CC). As regards the prohibitions to dismiss (paragraph 212), the nos (1)–(4) and (10) and comparable statutory prohibitions are not applicable in cases of summary dismissal – the others are applicable (Article 7:670a(2)(c) CC).

223. The employee that wrongly has terminated an open-ended contract of employment in a summary way is only acting against the provisions about the period of notice – for the consequences *see* paragraph 217.

The employer that wrongly has terminated in a summary way an open-ended contract of employment has not only violated the provisions about the period of notice – for the consequences *see* paragraph 217 – but has also violated the rules on the *ex ante* dismissal protection, for the consequences *see* paragraph 204.[248] To mitigate such consequences employers may follow a 'second defence line'. After having summarily dismissed a worker who may contest the validity of the dismissal, the employers may ask the court to rescind the contract of employment ex-Article 7:671(1)(a) (*see* paragraph 211) 'in so far as the contract will be deemed not to have ended on account of the summary dismissal'.[249] Should the court later decide against the employer as far the summary dismissal is concerned, the retrospective effect will be less severe as the contract of employment has ended properly in the meantime along the second defence line.

The party that wrongly in a summary way has terminated a fixed-term contract that cannot be terminated ad interim is due a compensation to the other party equal to the wage over the period that the contract should have ended by operation of law. However the court may mitigate this compensation if such appears fair in the light of the circumstances, but not to less than the amount of wage for three months. Moreover the employee may ask the court to quash the termination (Article 7:677(4) CC) or to award an additional compensation (Article 7:681 CC).

The party that with intent or fault has given the other party an urgent reason to terminate immediately the contract of employment is due a compensation to the other party if that party has used that competence. In an employment contract for indefinite time or a fixed-term contract that can be terminated interim, this compensation is equal to the wage over the time that the contract should have lasted in case of a regular termination; in case of a fixed-term contract that could not have been cancelled interim the compensation is equal to the wage over the period that the contract should have ended by operation of law (Article 7:677(2)(3) CC). However the court may mitigate these amounts but also increase them if such appears fair in the light of the circumstances, or for certain functions indicated in a regulation of the Minister (Article 7:677(5)(6) CC).

248. Dutch Supreme Court, 13 Jul. 2018, ECLI:NL:HR:2018:1209.
249. Dutch Supreme Court, 23 Dec. 2016, ECLI:NL:HR:2016:2998 (Mendiant).

§15. Collective Dismissals

224. For collective dismissals special rules apply *inter alia* to implement the EU Directive on collective dismissals. Under the Notification of Collective Dismissals Act (NCDA) (*Wet Melding Collectief Ontslag* of 1976, slightly amended in 2012 and 2014), any employer intending to terminate the employment contract of at least twenty workers in the same UWV district within the period of three months is required to give written notification of this to the UWV. For the calculation of the minimum of twenty employees those discharged with mutual consent and on the basis of a rescission of the court must be included. Excluded are dismissals on merely personal reasons, dismissals during the probationary period and contracts terminated by operation of the law.

The employer's notification among others must contain: the reasons for the intended collective dismissal and the number of workers normally employed and to be dismissed, sub-divided according to function, age and sex, the dates envisaged for the termination of the contracts, the criteria for the selection of the workers to be dismissed, the way of calculation of redundancy payments and the way it wants to terminate the employment contracts.

The employer must also send the UWV a copy of the notification of the trade unions and inform it about the involvement of the works council.

The employer cannot give earlier notice for termination than one month after the notification of the collective dismissal to the UWV and the trade unions, unless the trade unions have given a declaration that they have been consulted and can agree with the terminations. The UWV is not dealing with the request for dismissal permits before the employers have fulfilled all the obligations of notification and have declared in writing that he has consulted the trade unions and the works council. The UWV shall renounce of this waiting period when the employer makes plausible that this waiting period could jeopardize the employment situation of the enterprise as a whole (see about the obligation to inform and consult the trade unions on collective dismissals paragraph 360 and paragraph 386 for the involvement of the works council on the basis of the WCA).

At the request of the employee a termination of the contracts of employments can be annulled by the court if the employer has not fulfilled the obligations of the notification, not consulted trade unions and/or works council or has untimely terminated the contract. The court can also determine a compensation.

All in all, the NCDA is a sort of a stimulus for management to explore the possibilities of mitigating the consequences of the collective dismissal, prepare the ground for retraining or redeployment of the redundant labour force and to negotiate with the trade unions a so-called social plan (*see* paragraph 226).

In case of a collective dismissal the UWV will give the permit to dismiss according to the criteria mentioned in paragraphs 197, 204 and 206, including the obligation to replace. If there are vacations (coming up) in the company the employees under threat of a collective dismissal are the first to be eligible if those functions are suitable.[250]

---

250. Dutch Supreme Court, 13 Jul. 2018, ECLI:NL:HR:2018:2012.

225. For a collective dismissal as well as an individual dismissal aimed at reducing the workforce for business reasons (and not to completely close down a business) the question of the selection criteria regarding who is to be made redundant is of paramount importance. In such cases the employer must first terminate workers on temporary contracts and persons above the AOW-pensionable age and exclude from the dismissal the workers protected by a dismissal prohibition (*see* paragraph 198). For the remaining selection traditionally the last-in-first-out principle ('lifo' rule) used to be applied, but this left many firms with a workforce comprised of senior workers and harmed the interest of young workers and new entrants on the labour market. In 2006 the proportionality principle was given priority over the 'lifo' rule. The 2015 Reform has in principle confirmed these rules (now in Article 7:669(5) CC juncto Articles 11–16 DR). The basic idea is that employees should be made redundant in such a way that the age-situation of the firm remains unchanged (Article 11 DR). If there are workers to be made redundant in several categories of worker, the employer may first divide his workforce in categories of employees whose functions are interchangeable, indicating how many workers are to be made redundant in each category. Then he must divide each category into age groups (15–25, 25–35, 35–45, 45–55 and from 55 to the AOW-pensionable age). On each age group he must then apply the percentage of the intended reduction in order to find the number of those to be dismissed. He then may make redundant the number of employees per category according to the last-in-first-out rule.

Still the employer may exclude from this procedure at most 10% of the numbers of workers to be made redundant on the ground that they are functioning (or are going to function) 'above average'. This facility, however, is bound to severe requirements (Article 16 DR).

Finally, from all these rules it may be derogated by collective agreements and independent commissions mentioned in paragraph 210 (Article 7:669(6) CC).

The actual rules on the selection in redundancies for economic reasons are not to everyone's satisfaction. They are criticized for being too complicated and have contributed to an increase in dismissals of elderly workers. Moreover they have given rise to the question of whether this is a justifiable age discrimination (*see* paragraph 99), but for the moment they seem to survive this test. Sex or racial discrimination will certainly not be accepted in the rules about collective dismissals.

In the past those aged 55 years and older could be discharged with priority when they could benefit from attractive VUT schemes (*see* paragraph 247). Although this facility was repealed in 1994, managers still try to oust primarily senior workers on the basis of a termination by mutual consent (*see* paragraph 201).

Some employers have tried to circumvent the selection criteria in economic dismissals by closing down one or more entire departments or function groups, so that all employees concerned can be dismissed and then subsequently creating a new department or function group and taking on only the best of his former staff.

§16. Social Plan

226. In the Netherlands there are no statutory regulations on social plans.[251] For many workers a social plan is more or less a direct result of the collective agreements. If no collective agreement with rules on a social plan is applicable or if an adaptation of the framework of a social plan contained in a collective agreement is desired the social plan may be established on an ad hoc basis when the trimming of the labour force is imminent.

The social plan is most of the time negotiated with the unions, which are parties to the collective agreement of that sector or enterprise. Where such a collective agreement is absent the social plan may be negotiated with the works council of even with an assembly of workers of the enterprise. However the last two forms are regarded by labour lawyers and the courts with more or less suspicion as a fair equality of power may have been lacked. Therefore it is uncertain whether the court will attribute a binding force to such social plans. They may contain entitlements that are less favourable to a worker then would have been resulted from other sources of labour law. The problem of the binding force of social plans is anyway not completely solved under Dutch law. Social plans are considered as collective agreements if they comply with all the criteria for collective agreements (*see* paragraphs 307 et seq.). If not, then their binding force depends on the circumstances of the case.

As employers and trade unions are free to conclude a social plan, such plans show a great diversity. A major point of departure of almost every social plan is the promise, that forced dismissals and forced external replacement will be avoided as much as possible. Redundant employees will preferably be replaced internally. In most social plans it is stated that the enterprise will try to find a suitable function for the employees, taking into account personal situations, seniority, health and age. Usually the old salary is guaranteed or other equivalent working conditions are offered. Quite often in the social plan the employee has a right to (re)training or a compensation for the costs of accepting another position internally. In the case of reorganizations many social plans in the Netherlands state that the employees who accept a new lower-paid function in another enterprise will receive from their former employer a supplementary payment up to 100% of the former net salary. During the outplacement employees remain on the payroll of the enterprise. Also provisions related to the costs of outplacement and other provisions to assist the employee are often present. This policy is mainly applied in large (groups of) companies, but it is not widely used in the Netherlands. Most Dutch workers are reluctant to accept imposed geographic and professional mobility if these are not balanced by an increase in wages, status and/or job security.

Furthermore the social plan deals with the order of redundancies and the selection of the type of employees to be made redundant. The rank of redundancy or dismissal is, in most cases, based on age, number of years in service, pension and VUT rights and the form of contract (*see* paragraph 225).

---

251. *See* J. van der Hulst, *Het Sociaal Plan*, Deventer 2000; on pp. 353–360 may be found an English-language description and discussion of the practice in the Netherlands of establishing a so-called social plan in case of collective dismissals.

Almost without exception in social plans it is stated what measures and provisions apply for redundant employees with whom the contract must be broken. Procedures in case of dismissal (period of notice) are of importance here. Quite often social plans deal with all sorts of support for employees made redundant in finding another suitable job by means of retraining, secondments and placements for a specific period.

227. Until 2015 social plans used to contain provisions on redundancy payments for the employees that lose their jobs on account of the collective dismissal. Since the 2015 Reform Act statutory law requires also from the employer that effectuates a collective dismissal to pay the transition allowance (*see* paragraph 218). As the statute basically mentions minimum amounts for this transition allowance there is space for bargaining for higher amounts between the unions and the employer, which will take place in due regard of the financial position of the enterprise.

In almost all social plans the establishment of a joint advisory commission is provided for in order to accompany the process.

It may be concluded that the results of social plans to a large extent achieve their aim of limiting forced dismissals and easing financial consequences for the employees involved. The Minister of Social Affairs and Employment considers social plans a good instrument to smooth reorganizations and make them more gradual, with relatively few dismissals. To a certain extent the Ministry is involved in this negotiating process. In the very past often the possibilities of financial support by the government to ailing companies were considered. Against the backdrop of the EU rules on state aid to companies and the reluctance in Dutch financial circles to this approach, this possibility is nowadays available only in exceptional cases (*see* paragraph 238). Still alive is the possibility that the Ministry may come up with some kind of financial support for alternatives such as retraining (*see* paragraph 259). Also the alternative of short-time working will be researched (*see* paragraph 149), which may involve the social security authorities and the Inspection SZW.

§17. Dismissals in Case of Insolvency of the Employer

228. In the Netherlands an employer can be declared bankrupt by the District Court. The effect is that the employer can no longer handle his own affairs; that power will be vested in a receiver (*curator*) under the supervision of a judge, both of whom are appointed by the Court.

The bankruptcy judgment does not *ipso iure* signify the end of the current contracts of employment nor does it constitute grounds for summary dismissal. However, the *curator* (receiver) can terminate the contracts of employment and dismiss employees, if he has obtained permission from the supervising judge (Article 68(2) BA). In practice this permission is almost never refused because of the interests of the bankruptcy creditors. Pay owed as a post-bankruptcy liability or expense of the estate would be too large a burden on the estate if the receiver could not dismiss the employees (*see* paragraph 137). However, the receiver may decide to continue the contracts of employment with (some of) the employees, if he thinks that this is beneficial for the estate.

In bankruptcy situations[252] the *ex ante* dismissal controls of the UWV or the District Court are not applicable (Article 40(4) BA). The worker as well as the *curator* (receiver) can give notice according to the agreed or statutory applicable terms of notice, but it never needs to be more than six weeks (Article 40(1) BA). Even the rules on the exit day (*aanzegdag*) (*see* paragraph 216) cannot result in a further prolongation of the notice period in bankruptcy situations. As we have seen (in paragraph 224), in the Netherlands, a collective dismissal according to Dutch law normally cannot be effectuated until a period of one month has elapsed after notification of the UWV. However, this rule has been waived for collective dismissals in bankruptcy situations. In these situations the normal written notification to the UWV is only necessary at the latter's own explicit request. This seldom appears to happen in practice.

The specific prohibitions to dismiss (*see* paragraphs 198 et seq.), except the one that applies during maternity leave, do not preclude dismissal of the entire workforce by the receiver. However, the specific prohibitions to dismiss may have effect in case of selective dismissals by the receiver, certainly as far as the prohibitions deriving from anti-discrimination legislation are concerned.

In a bankruptcy situation the receiver does not have to pay the transition allowance and may immediately stop all transition allowance payments already due by the employer (*see* paragraph 218). Bankruptcy lawyers insist that the *curator* (receiver) should not spontaneously grant such a payment nor should he effectuate any redundancy payment promised under an individual or collective agreement or social plan, as this would be to the detriment of other claimants in the bankruptcy.

If the bankruptcy is later overturned by the court, all dismissals operated by the *curator* (receiver) must be made undone retroactively (Article 13a BA).

A first problematic point here is the insolvency of a plant which forms part of a group. Dutch courts are very reluctant 'to lift the corporate veil', holding the mother company responsible. A second problem is that of the 'resurrection' (*doorstart*) of the bankrupt company shortly after the bankruptcy, being bought as a going business by a new owner (but how related is the new owner with the old one?). In case of such a resurrection the new owner is considered not to be bound to pick up all the employees of the bankrupt firm and to continue the conditions of employment of those workers as he would have been in case of a transfer of the enterprise (*see* paragraphs 178–181). He can pick and choose who and what he wants!

Resurrection is actually a much-used practice as a cheap form of a collective dismissal (short terms of notice, no dismissal control, no transition allowance, no automatic transfer of the contracts of employment (*see* paragraphs 178 et seq.)). Until this day numerous Dutch workers have been confronted with such kind of bankruptcies which left them without their jobs and without any redundancy payment. All in all in the Netherlands the protection of workers in case of liquidation/bankruptcy/insolvency is weak. In theory trade unions have legal tools to better protect the workers in bankruptcy cases (appeals, seizure of stock, buildings, machinery, etc.), but they are not much used out of fear that they would further increase the harm to the workforce.

---

252. A.T.J.M. Jacobs (ed.), 'Employee Rights in Bankruptcy', *Bulletin of Comparative Labour Relations*, Deventer, 2002.

Most of the aforementioned derogations on the law of dismissals do only apply in the genuine bankruptcy procedure. In case of the procedure of *surséance van betaling* (judicial leave to suspend payments) the normal law of dismissals apply, safe as far as the periods of notice and the transition allowances are concerned. There is a cap of six months on the contractual and statutory periods of notice in case of the *surséance van betaling* (Article 239 BA). Also the payment of transition allowances may be discontinued.

However, the fact that most of the special rules on dismissals in cases of bankruptcy do not apply to the pre-bankruptcy procedures, has severely sharpened the differences between bankruptcy and the pre-bankruptcy procedure. It has made this latter procedure less attractive for reorganizing businesses.

The government in 2019 has opened a public consultation on a reform of the laws on dismissals in case of insolvency of the employer.

§18. Fixed-Term Contracts

229. Traditionally, fixed-term employment contracts (*see* paragraph 64) form an escape from the rigid Dutch law on dismissals. A contract of employment for a definite period ends automatically on the expiry of the period agreed upon or indicated by the law (Article 7:667 CC). For its termination by operation of law at the fixed moment no *ex ante* control is necessary (like it is necessary in the Netherlands for open-ended contracts). The prohibitions to dismiss (*see* paragraph 198) do not prevent the automatic expiry either. In a contract of employment for a definite period job security is implied during the contractual period, but after the end of that period the worker no longer enjoys much protection. In general the employee working on a fixed-term contract has no right on a continuation of the contract, although exceptionally a non-continuation can successfully be attacked in case of serious culpable acts or omissions to act on the side of the employer (*see* below) or as a kind of discrimination.

Notice of termination of a fixed-term contract on the expiry of the agreed period or indicated by the law is only necessary if this has been provided by written contract or the law. Notice of termination of a fixed-term contract before the end of its term may only be given if such a right has been agreed in writing to each of the parties (Article 7:667(1)(2)(3) CC). If such a clause is missing the employer cannot terminate the contract prematurely, but he can request the court to rescind the fix-term contract if it is for economic reasons or because of the illness of the employee. If the employee is dismissed prematurely in contravention to these rules he may ask the court to annul this dismissal or instead ask for a compensation. More about the rescission of fixed-term contacts in paragraphs 211–212. For summary termination of a fixed-term contract *see* paragraph 223.

If a contract of employment has been entered into for a period in excess of five years or for the duration of the life of a particular person, the employee shall nonetheless be entitled to terminate it from the date on which five years have passed since its commencement, subject to a period of notice of six months (Article 7:684 CC).

The Act also contains two provisions which must prevent that an open-ended contract is first converted into a fixed-term contract and then smoothly terminated by operation of the law without an *ex ante* control. If an open-ended contract of employment, terminated otherwise than by valid notice or by the court's setting it aside or by the receiver, has been succeeded by a fixed-term contract either immediately or by an interval of not more than six months, prior notice (and thus: *ex ante* control) shall be required for the termination of the succeeding contract of employment. The notice period shall be calculated from the date the open-ended contract of employment was entered into. However, this rule does not apply if the open-ended contract was terminated because of reaching the AOW-pensionable age. A continued contract is also deemed to exist where one and the same employee has successively been employed by different employers who must reasonably be considered to be one another's successor with regard to the work performed and irrespective of whether these employers had insight into the quality and suitability of the employee (Article 7:667(4)(5) CC).

230. Until far into the 1980s fixed-term contracts could not become an easy escape route from the rigid Dutch law on dismissals, as the old text of the law contained the rule that a prolonged fixed-term contract of employment was quasi-treated as a contract for an indefinite period: all normal dismissal protection rules would apply to such a continued fixed-term contract. After the courts had rejected[253] employer creativity to circumvent this rule (workers did the same job, alternately on a direct contract with the employer and on the basis of lease via a temporary work agency) employers pressed hard for a relaxation of the law on repeated fixed-term contracts. They won it as part of the deals under the Flexibility and Security Act 1999 (*see* paragraph 193). This Act opened the possibility to renew fixed-term contracts twice, provided that the total length of these contracts did not exceed three years. Only after either the third renewal (i.e., upon the fourth contract) or a renewal over the threshold of three years, was the fixed-term contract deemed to have been entered into for an indefinite term.

As a result of the 1999 Reform it has become a widespread practice that employers renounce of offering the worker an open-ended contract after the three contracts/ three years duration were over. Many were simply replacing the worker by another worker, newly hired on a fixed-term contract. A temporary Act of 2010 until 1 January 2012 even allowed a chain of four temporary contracts or a chain of at most four years for employees up to 27 years old in order to combat youth unemployment. Derogation of these provisions to the detriment of the employee was allowed by collective agreement. This possibility for derogation *in peius* by collective agreements was not limited and indeed, in many sectors of the Dutch economy such waivers have been agreed, often allowing chains of five to ten years!

These provisions were narrowed by the 2015 Reform Act but part of this reform will be revoked in 2020 (Labour Market in Balance Act). To further improve the position of employees working on fixed-term contracts it is provided that the employer must announce in writing the employee at least one month before the expiration date of the contract whether he wants to continue the contract after the

253. Dutch Supreme Court, 22 Nov. 1991, NJ 1992, 207.

expiration date and if so on what terms. This rule is not applicable to contracts for less than six months nor to contracts that do not expire on a given calendar date. If the employer has untimely or not at all fulfilled this announcement he is due damages for (a pro rata part of) one month salary. In case of bankruptcy or judicial leave to suspend payments this penalty stops. Finally: if the contract has in fact been continued this will be deemed to have been under the same conditions and for the same time but not for more than one year (Article 7:668 CC).

Subsequently it is provided that if the other conditions are fulfilled employees on fixed-term contracts are entitled to the so-called transition allowance (*see* paragraph 218) if their contract is not continued on the initiative of the employer (Article 7:673(1)(a)(3) CC). Moreover, if this discontinuation is caused by serious culpable acts or omissions to act of the employer, the court may eventually besides a transition allowance award a fair compensation (Article 7:673(9) CC).

Finally the rule that a chain of successive temporary contracts is automatically transformed into a permanent contract after a certain period has been completed is also revised. A renewed fix-term contract will become permanent after three years or two renewals, unless the chain of temporary contracts has been broken by an interval of six months or longer (was: three months or longer (Article 668(1) CC)). Moreover, the possibilities for the collective agreements to derogate from these rules are limited.

To be more precise: as from 2020 the rules on the chain of fixed-term contracts (Article 7:668a CC) read as follows:

> From the time when, between the same parties,
>
> (a) fixed term employment contracts have succeeded one another over a period of 36 months or more at intervals of at most 6 months, the last employment contract shall be deemed to have been entered for an indeterminate term as from that time;
> (b) more than three fixed term employment contracts have succeeded one another at intervals of not more than 6 months, the last employment contract shall be deemed to have been entered for an indeterminate term.

What has been written under (a) shall not apply to a contract of employment entered into for at most three months which is immediately consecutive to a contract of employment entered into for thirty-six months or more between the same parties.

The aforementioned applies, *mutatis mutandis*, to consecutive contracts of employment between an employee and different employers who must reasonably be considered each other's successor with regard to the work performed, irrespective whether these employers had insight in the quality and the suitability of the employee. However, from this rule it may be derogated *in peius* by collective agreement (Article 7:668a(2)(6) CC).

Further derogations *in peius* are possible by collective agreement:

– as regards the period of thirty-six months mentioned under (a) which may be prolonged to at most forty-eight months; and

– as regards the number of three mentioned under (b) which may be increased to six but only if the wider use of fixed-term contracts is necessary for specific functions or groups of functions by the intrinsic nature of the business (Article 7:668a(5) CC).

Also by way of a collective agreement the entire regime of chains of fixed-term contracts may be set aside for certain functions indicated by the Minister[254] as functions for which it is customary and necessary to be fulfilled by fixed-term contracts (not being secondment contracts) (Article 7:668a (8) CC). Equally by collective agreement derogations are possible for certain agreements with a dominant educational (training) content (Article 7:668(9) CC). Moreover professional soccer-players are exempted.

The chain-rules on fixed-term contracts are not applicable at all on apprentices and on employees under 18 years, with an average working week of at most twelve hours (Article 7:668a(11) CC).

By written agreement derogation of the provision under (a) is possible as regards members of the board of directors of companies (Article 7:668a(7) CC).

For persons who have reached the AOW-pensionable age the maximum period of the chain is widened to forty-eight months and the maximum number enlarged to six (Article 7:668a(12) CC). For seasonal workers (less than nine months) the interval period of six months may be shortened to three months by collective agreement (Article 7:668a(3) CC) or by ministerial regulation (Article 7:668a(14) CC). This entire Article does not apply to replacement teachers (Article 7:668a(15)CC).

§19. OTHER FORMS OF TERMINATION BY OPERATION OF LAW

231. Contracts of employment may contain clauses which bring about an automatic end to the contract if a certain event occurs.

The law declares null and void stipulations under which the contract of employment terminates by operation of the law on the marriage, the civil partnership, or the pregnancy or confinement of the employee (Article 7:667(7)(8) CC). And it explicitly allows a termination by operation of law in secondment contracts (*see* paragraph 232).

The Dutch courts have not completely ruled out other clauses in this field, but they have determined that the validity of clauses of termination by the operation of the law can be accepted only in exceptional cases. Such a clause cannot result in the termination of a contract of employment if it is reasonably incompatible with the system of dismissal protection. This must be considered from case to case, taking into account the nature, the content and the context of the clause.[255]

Finally, it is a tradition in Dutch labour law, that without any stipulation to the contrary, open-ended contracts of employment are deemed to end automatically

254. Ministerial Regulation 24 Jun. 2015, Staatscourant 30 Jun. 2015, no. 17977.
255. Dutch Supreme Court, 2 Nov. 2012, RvdW 2012/1372, JAR 2012/314 (HTM Personenvervoer NV/Mohabir).

when the worker reaches the AOW-pensionable age, which used to be 65 but is currently on the rise. Actually it is on 66 + 4 months (*see* paragraph 247). Sometimes the retirement at this age is explicitly laid down in the text of the individual contract of employment or the collective agreement. Research has revealed that at least 70% of Dutch workers are working under a collective agreement containing such clauses. In 2002 the HR has held that there is not yet a general feeling of non-acceptance of the reasonableness of 65 years for such a termination. Consequently the employee in these cases is not protected by the law on dismissals. In recent years this idea has increasingly be challenged by a minority of employees who want to stay in their jobs after reaching the retirement age. Between 2008 and 2012 there have been a number of cases of lower courts which did not accept the thesis of automatic termination of the contract of employment. Employers' associations strongly opposed this trend. Trade unionist and learned writers are divided on the subject. Often the necessity of more chances for youngsters on the labour market and the objective character of the automatic termination are put forward as justification of the automatic termination. Article 7(1)(b) of the AETAW allows – without requiring an objective justification – termination of the employment at the statutory retirement age (*see* above) or at a conventionally agreed higher age (*see* paragraph 99). Recently the HR has affirmed that this AOW-pensionable age may still be indicated in collective agreements as the automatic termination of the contract of employment.[256] By declaring so the HR has availed itself from the margin of appreciation which on this point the EU Member States have been accorded in the case law of the CJEU on this point.[257] This is different as regards clauses in collective agreements about automatic termination at a pensionable age lower than the AOW-pensionable age. Article 7(1)(c) AETAW has now forbidden such clauses unless there is an objective reason for it. In its KLM-judgment[258] the HR accepted the mandatory retirement age at 60 of KLM pilots, as it considered the objective reason sufficiently established in this case.

In the Reform Act of 2015 the idea of an automatic termination of open-ended contracts of employment upon reaching the statutory pensionable age has been matched by rule that such an employee may be dismissed without *ex ante* control (Article 7:671(1)(g) CC, *see* paragraph 205) and without entitlement to the transition allowance (Article 7:673(7)(b) CC, *see* paragraph 218).

§20. The Dismissal of Temporary Agency Workers

232. In the past the law on dismissal of temporary agency workers was not clear. Sometimes it was disputed whether temporary agency workers were employed on a genuine contract of employment. Often those workers were leased on fixed-term contracts, which would also remove them from the ordinary law on dismissals, etc. As part of the deals under the Flexibility and Security Act 1999 (paragraph 193) the law on the dismissals of temporary agency workers was clarified.

256. Dutch Supreme Court, 13 Jul. 2012, ECLI:NL:HR:2012:BW3367.
257. CJEU 21 Jul. 2011, C-159/10 (Fuchs and Köhler).
258. Dutch Supreme Court, 13 Jul. 2012, ECLI:NL:HR:2012:BW3367.

The contract of the temporary worker with the temporary work agency (the secondment contract) is now explicitly called a contract of employment (*see* paragraph 66), which means that in principle the normal law on dismissals is applicable to these contracts. However, at the same time Parliament established a number of exceptions to accommodate the temporary agency business.

First, the rule on the succession of fixed-term contracts (*see* paragraph 230) applies to a temporary agency worker only once the employee has performed work in a period of more than twenty-six weeks (Article 7:691(1) CC). However, by collective agreement this period may be enlarged to seventy-eight weeks (Article 7:691(8) CC). Moreover the rule of a maximum of thirty-six weeks and three times of the chain-regulation for fixed-term contracts (*see* paragraph 230) may by collective agreement be enlarged to forty-eight weeks and the number of renewals to six (Article 7:668a(5)(a) CC). The main collective agreements for the temporary agency workers (the Federation of Temporary Work Agencies (ABU) and the NBBU collective agreement) have used both rules with the result that the temporary work agencies can have their workers on temporary contracts for a maximum of 5.5 years (including the interval periods) and to a maximum six different contracts before a secondment contract shall be deemed to have entered for an indeterminate term!

Second: in a contract with a temporary agency worker it may be stipulated in writing that such contract shall end by operation of law on account of the fact that the placing of the employee by the employer at the disposal of a third party ends upon the request of such third party.

Moreover the employer is freed of the obligation to inform the employee about the future of his contract (*see* paragraph 230).

The main collective agreements for the temporary agency workers (the ABU collective agreement) explicitly provide for the immediate and automatic termination of the contract of a temporary agency worker in case of illness and disability in these twenty-six weeks.

If such a stipulation is included in a secondment contract the reverse of the medal is that also the employee may forthwith give notice of termination of that contract. All such stipulations are no longer in force if the employee has performed work for the employer in a period of more than twenty-six weeks. On expiry of this period also the right of the employee to give notice forthwith also lapses (Article 7:691(2)(3) CC).

For the calculation of the periods in these rules successive periods in which work is performed with intervals of less than six months shall also be taken into account. In the same vein periods in which the work is performed for different employers who, in respect of the work performed, must reasonably be considered to be each other's successors, shall also be taken into account (Article 7:691(4)(5) CC), but this last provision may be waived by a collective agreement (Article 7:691(8)(b) CC). Moreover these rules shall not apply to a secondment contract whereby the employer and the third party form part of the same group (= *Konzern*, *see* paragraph 374) (Article 7:691(6) CC).

In secondment contracts the important rule on the continuation of wage payment if no work has been performed (Article 7:628(1) CC, *see* paragraphs 149 et seq.) can be waived in a written agreement between the temporary agency and the employee for only a maximum duration of twenty-six weeks (Article 7:691(7) CC). By collective agreements, however, prolongation of the period of twenty-six weeks in the aforementioned provisions is possible until seventy-eight weeks (Article 7:691(8)(a) CC). This possibility of derogation far beyond the twenty-six weeks is a standing practice in the temporary agency business in the Netherlands.

Third: the protection against replacement hiring (*see* paragraph 208) is adapted to the temporary work business. If within twenty-six weeks after a termination of one of its employees for economic reasons a vacancy occurs for the same or comparable activities as those which this employee performed before notice of termination for economic reasons was given, the temporary employment agency must enable this former employee to apply for this vacancy and being proposed to the user company. If the agency fails to do so, the court, on the request of the employee, may nullify the earlier notice of termination, or, at the request of the agency, order him liable to pay a fair compensation (Article 7:681(1)(e) CC). The Minister may issue regulations on what must be deemed to be 'employer' for the application of this provision, in what cases and under what condition this provision does not apply and in what order of succession employees must be proposed to a user company (Article 7:682a CC).The same applies, *mutatis mutandis* in cases of a judicial rescission – in that case there is no nullification, but restoration per date of termination (Article 7:682(5) CC).

In the past temporary agency workers were not subject to the selection rules in the case of redundancies of workers because of slack business (*see* paragraph 225). Provided that at least 50% of the wages are paid in the temporary agency employment business a company could make the selection according to some special rules.

§21. The Termination of Freelance Contracts

233. Contracts for services (Dutch: *opdracht*) may be terminated at all times by the principal (Article 408(1) CC). They may be terminated by the contractor who has concluded the contract within the framework of his profession or business only if the agreement was concluded for an undetermined period and is not ending by fulfilment (Article 7:408(2) CC).

Contracts for services may be terminated by judicial rescission on the basis of Article 6:258. This may be because of breach of contract of the other party or because of *imprévision*.[259]

259. Dutch Supreme Court, 8 Nov. 1996, NJ 1997, 217.

Chapter 10. Labour Market Services and Policies

§1. Introduction

234. Article 19(1) of the Dutch Constitution reads: 'It shall be the concern of the Dutch authorities to promote the provision of sufficient employment.' In order to implement this honorary obligation there has been since the end of World War II a continuous employment policy. That policy is part of economic and monetary policies all directed at keeping the Dutch economy in good health.

§2. Macroeconomic Policies

235. In the first twenty-five years after World War II consecutive Dutch governments have successfully applied the various instruments of Keynesian economy to improve the employment situation which indeed reached the target of the full employment in the course of the 1960s. However, in that period the Netherlands became part of the EEC and with the intensification of this EEC the Dutch authorities have successively lost most of the instruments of Keynesian macroeconomic policies. They can no longer regulate import and exports with other countries, they have – since the EU Monetary union was created – lost control over the currency, they may no longer favourise Dutch products and services, control the influx of workers from EU countries, etc. They even have lost – since the Eurozone Stability Pact – much sovereignty on budget policies. Being only a small country the employment situation in the Netherlands is nowadays a reflection of the business cycle in the global economy and more especially of that in its main trading partners, Germany, the US and the UK.

The employment policies of the Dutch government are nowadays largely determined by the variations in the business cycle. In times of a slump the macroeconomic policy focuses on the resumption of economic growth as the most important instrument for a higher level of employment. This was the case in the Netherlands for the last time between 2009 and 2014. In such circumstances some governments abroad have taken various measures to promote consumer spending. In general, however, Dutch governments are reticent in taking measures to promote consumer spending because of the open character of the Dutch economy. Most additional consumer spending leaks to abroad. So the Dutch most of the time wait until other governments, such as Germany, France and Britain, take initiatives in this field and then the Dutch will join in with equivalent measures.

A much more classic instrument in times of a slump for Dutch governments is to promote wage restraint. However, the Dutch government lost much direct influence on workers' wages when it had to abandon its interventionist policies in this field in the 1980s and 1990s (*see* paragraphs 283 et seq.). Since then the governments can only hope to influence wage developments indirectly through consultation with the social partners and by taxation measures. The government may admonish labour and management to wage restraint. Being itself directly or indirectly the employer of 15% of the Dutch labour market it will take the lead in this policy of moderation, but it cannot impose it on the private sector. In addition the government does have a direct influence on the statutory minimum wage level and the level of social security benefits. As the trade unions in the Netherlands are very keen to maintain at minimum level a link between wage raises in the civil service and the market sector, and a complete linkage between minimum wage increases and increases in social security benefits to the movement in wages fixed by the collective agreements, the government uses this mechanism (partially laid down in Dutch laws) to put pressure on the social partners to moderate wage developments (*see* paragraphs 266 and 284).

236. Since 2015 the Dutch economy has dramatically improved. Unemployment is on historical depths, and it is clear that this situation does not require the stimulation of economic growth and consumer spending. In the actual situation on the Dutch labour market in which low unemployment has returned (*see* paragraph 7) wage restraint is slowly abandoned under the pressures of labour market shortages.

§3. Specific Labour Market Policies

237. In the last half-century in times of a slump economy successive Dutch governments have concretized their efforts to maintain/restore full employment by launching 'job programmes', often in agreement with the social partners. Most recently this was done in 2013. Most economists are critical on such ambitions. They argue that such plans are never very successful – the government should stimulate economic growth.

One of the key points of such job programmes was often the creation of public and semi-public work activities in order to diminish the number of idle persons. However, because of the budgetary discipline required by the EU, the possibilities in this area are small and when the economy improves this tool is also quickly stored away.

So what remains is policymaking at a more sustainable, business cycle independent level. Stimulating innovation as a guarantee for sufficient employment in the future, better education of the manpower, keeping the Netherlands attractive as a country for investment, etc. The current industrial policy focuses on macroeconomic policies, tax policies, technological innovation, infrastructure, etc. Research and development are promoted through fiscal measures.

Especially for the labour market the focus of the Dutch government is on increasing the level of participation, especially in segments of the labour market where the participation is still under the average; moreover on keeping in place institutions which serve a good functioning of the labour market, etc.

Increasing productivity gains can provide the means necessary for employment and social policy, but it is not easy to translate the gains in productivity into additional employment and improved labour force skills rather than higher incomes for those who already have a job.

Dutch authorities are always stressing the importance of innovation for the Dutch labour market. However, in this field the Dutch are not particularly well-performing. Although the government in the past has taken several measures to boost the intensity of private research and development, the Netherlands still is not in the top of the EU. Sweden, Switzerland, Finland and Germany spent 3% of GDP on research and development; in the Netherlands the figure is only a poor 1.4%.[260] The European Commission considers the Netherlands as the best innovation follower but not as a leader of innovation.[261]

In conformity with European employment guidelines the Dutch government sees education as a key foundation for labour participation. Government policies are directed towards a reduction of early school-leaving and fostering lifelong learning, towards investing in excellence and a better alignment between educational programmes and the labour market. Not only these are pious resolutions of all consecutive governments but also in this field the effects on the unemployment rate are slow.

§4. Delicate or Doubtful Instruments

238. In the past the government policy in periods of large unemployment involved methods such as large subsidies to firms in difficulties, an extension of recruitment subsidies and public works to combat unemployment and an expansion of the public sector. In the 1970s in the Netherlands many jobs were rescued by public intervention in order to save companies from bankruptcy or to help them in reconversion and corporate restructuring. Since the 1980s, however, this instrument is much less used, for economic reasons, while it costs a lot of money which is bad for budgetary discipline as well as for legal reasons, because the EU does only allow *State aid to national business* on a very limited scale. Socio-economic policy shifted from maintaining employment in ailing enterprises towards creating general conditions favourable to the development of production and (new) employment. However, when large companies run into trouble, governments do not completely stand aside. In very incidental cases, such as some years ago with Volvo-Nedcar, Daf, Fokker and De Schelde, the Dutch government has again given financial aid in one form or another. During the recent banking crises some EUR 30 billion was spent to save Dutch banks and insurance companies from bankruptcy. So the Netherlands governments are not always consequent in this respect. Moreover there have always been certain forms of indirect state aid, for instance by offering cheap gas to the horticulture greenhouses. A number of Dutch municipalities nowadays do the same when they come to the rescue of their loss-making local professional soccer clubs! However, such financial support can only be of a limited character because of the EU rules. Statistics show that in the Netherlands state support to enterprises amounts to 0.9% of the GDP, which is on the EU average.

The instrument of *short-time working* may be used to help ailing companies to survive, but normally the Netherlands government is not keen to use this instrument in situations of economic problems of firms merely due to economic causes. However, during the financial crisis 2008–2010 the Dutch government temporarily abandoned this restrictive policy (*see* paragraph 149).

---

260. Competitiveness and Innovation Monitor of the Erasmus University, Rotterdam, 2013.
261. *See* the Innovation Union Scoreboard 2013.

239. In the past the Dutch government has frequently combated unemployment by organizing and financing *public works* to be executed by jobless people. In times of economic upswing these jobs were deleted, but in times of recession they frequently returned in various formulae and under various titles. During the 1990s, the Dutch government has set up a number of schemes of subsidized jobs to assist the young unemployed and the long-term unemployed. These are so-called additional jobs in museums, schools (school wardens), etc. The number of those subsidized jobs reached a peak in 2002 with 89,000 jobs (= about 1% of the labour market). Later the government reduced the number of these jobs substantially but in 2008 they have risen again. Since 2008 municipalities could create jobs in order to help people who are far removed from the labour market to gain experience while retaining their social security benefits (participation jobs). However after 2010 the government again proceeded to drastically diminish this instrument, basing itself on research which has revealed that the persons in these subsidized, 'artificial' jobs do not, as it was hoped, find a regular job afterwards. The general conditions and the financing of persons employed in such jobs are nowadays regulated in the PW (Article 10a). However, as has been said, not many persons are employed under this scheme in the present (2019) labour market situation.

In recent years *public procurement* has emerged as a tool for labour market policies. Also this instrument was not easy to apply because of the EU rules on public procurement as well as the case law of the CJEU.[262] However, these rules have been widened in 2014 and[263] many authorities are nowadays requiring that the contracted work is performed as much as possible by workers on social security benefits.

240. Finally the *independent entrepreneurship*. The government is committed to promote independent entrepreneurship, notably as this seems prolific to the expansion of service sector employment in the Netherlands. The promotion is done by way of a variety of measures; however most of them, such as tax facilities, are outside the area of labour law. Traditionally statutory social security in the Netherlands is rather favourable for independent entrepreneurship as it contains several schemes that are covering the entire population. In other branches of social security self-employed persons have access to voluntary schemes. The government is committed to give these workers a real chance in public procurement procedures and to ensure them a uniform definition in all legislation. The government does not want to see labour law being undermined by bogus-independent entrepreneurship and is fighting that with various measures (*see* paragraph 68).

§5. Labour Market Reform

241. The Dutch government considers structural adjustments of the labour market as essential to allow the labour market to function better. Although the *labour market participation* is already high (*see* paragraph 7) the European authorities are

262. ECJ 3 Apr. 2008, C-346/06 (Rüffert).
263. Directives 2014/23/EU, 2014/24/EU and 2014/25/EU.

pressing the Netherlands to further increase it, *inter alia* by further reducing tax disincentives for second-income earners, fostering labour market transitions and addressing rigidities. The Dutch government, obediently, is steadily trying to increase labour participation, notably because of the rising dependency rate. The government is pursuing various avenues to increase labour participation among older people, the unemployed and secondary earners (usually women), people with a handicap and young people (*see* paragraphs 244 et seq.).

Another instrument of the Dutch labour market policies is *labour market reform* to reduce the burden of non-wage costs for the employer. The main focus in labour law is then on the law on job protection (Part I, Chapter 9). It should be noted that in the Netherlands job protection is high. Many employers, economists and right-wing politicians believe that strong job protection reduces labour market flows and productivity. According to them the Dutch government should not maintain or improve job security but stimulate employment security.[264] Improving employment security would mean: investing in broad employability, on-the-job learning and smooth transitions from work to work. The aim is to initiate the transition to other work in time even before a job has been terminated.[265] However all this is to a large extent rhetoric. Due to political reasons there has not been a radical reform of the Dutch job protection law since 1999. Only small adaptations were made. The former government in 2015 has even slightly strengthened the job protection in the Work and Security Act. The actual government is committed to partly undo this strengthening with the *Wet Arbeidsmarkt in balans* (Labour Market in Balance Act), already adopted by Parliament, which is due to enter into force in 2020 (*see* paragraph 195).

242. A next focus is on *the costs of social security*. In all countries it is clear that there is a tension between social security and the competitiveness of the national economy. If social security is at a high level, employers must pay its price, their products are expensive and this is harmful on an open international market. A deterioration of competitiveness easily causes unemployment, certainly in the Dutch economy which is very much dependent on export. The labour charges (taxes and contributions) are high in all the EU countries, but not the least in the Netherlands, where they amount to 34% of the wages costs.

A nation can support such high costs if the productivity is high. Some decades ago the Netherlands had a *labour productivity* which was one of the highest in Europe, but in recent years the growth in labour productivity has been somewhat lower than among the competitors of the Dutch and this has alarmed the economists and authorities. Also for this reason the Dutch government is promoting innovation, automatization, digitalization, robotization and lifelong training (*see* paragraphs 6 and 237).

264. *See* Green Paper on the modernizing of labour law to meet the challenges of the 21th century, European Commission, 2006, COM 2006/708; *see* H. Pruijt & P. Derogee, *Employability and Job Security, Friends or Foes? The Paradoxical Reception of Employment Security in the Netherlands*, 8(3) Socio-Econ. Rev. 437–460 (2010).

265. *See* N. Zekic, *Werkzekerheid en arbeidsrecht*, Tilburg, 2014; on pp. 325–337 one finds an English-language summary of the developments in Dutch labour law in this field.

243. Although there is the pressure by economists to make *reductions in social security charges* by reducing the level of social security benefits, this is not the official policy in the Netherlands. Most politicians try to avoid this as this is an explosive option. Thus all emphasis is placed on a reduction of the entitlement to social security benefits.[266] In the Netherlands there is evidence that a considerable proportion of those who enter non-employment benefit schemes (sickness, disability, lone parent and VUT benefits) have remaining work capacity. Consequently, reforms aiming to apply activation strategies: the 'mutual obligation' approach to them (albeit with appropriate modifications) is being increasingly applied. In addition, in the past few years, there have been substantial institutional reforms in unemployment insurance and disability insurance, in particular by making the programmes less generous. During this period, the Netherlands has experienced reducing inflow rates in these benefits programmes. However, the disability insurance programme is still very substantial (*see* paragraph 165). As regards the unemployment benefit scheme and the social assistance benefits schemes: these schemes have been trimmed ca. 2015, not by reducing the level of the benefits, but by reducing the length of the entitlement and by raising the criteria for entitlement. The legislator is also frequently making the existing range of sanctions more stringent and is stepping up the combat against fraud.

All this represents the approach of the 'stick'. The alternative is the approach of the 'carrot'. This approach is also present: part of the measure to pressure unemployed people to accept 'suitable' or 'current' work is a wage supplement scheme that guarantees that it will be financially advantageous for benefit recipients to accept lower-paid work. This 'carrot' alternative is also present in a number of taxation measures that the Dutch government has taken to entice employers to engage older and partially disabled workers (*see* paragraphs 244 et seq.) and to discourage older workers to leave the labour market before the pensionable age.

§6. Targeting Labour Market Policies to Special Categories

244. The Dutch government is constantly at work to target its social policy better as to help the truly needed. The Netherlands had historically lacked such a targeted, active, labour market policy. Dutch labour market policy was mainly characterized by the emphasis laid on general wage cost moderation (*see* paragraphs 235, 281 et seq.), the maintenance of a public employment service (*see* paragraph 251) and on income support measures (benefits for the unemployed) and less by dynamic measures to activate the unemployed.

Since the 1990s the government has actively encouraged cooperation between the social security authorities and the manpower services to help the unemployed find work. Existing programmes to help the long-term unemployed and young people

266. *See* P.S. Fluit, *Verzekeringen van solidariteit*, Deventer, 2001; on pp. 301–305 one finds an English-language description and discussion of the question to what extent have the restructuring measures implemented between 1980 and 2000 in the social insurance schemes on wages loss for employees altered the solidarity nature of these schemes.

finding work were combined. Also the municipal authorities became actively involved in providing individual, customized assistance (*see* paragraph 251).

Around 1990 many experts and politicians pleaded for a more active labour market policy, according to the Swedish model. And indeed, such a change in policies has been effectuated by the Dutch governments of the 1990s. Special job programmes were designed to further the participation of low-skilled workers, foreign nationals and young people. The participation of women was supported by a major extension of child day-care centres. The chances of all these groups on the labour market were also improved by means of a reduction of social security contributions for employers and by tax incentives for the employment of those in particular at or near the minimum wage level. There was a growing awareness of the need to invest in 'job-to-job' transitions, although it had to be recognized that employees who work at large companies benefitted the most from job-to-job arrangements.

These policy changes have been supported within the framework of the European Employment Strategies and its Guidelines. As early as 2002 the European Commission identified as main challenge for the Netherlands to increase the participation of disabled workers. Moreover, the link between labour supply and demand needed to be strengthened. There is also a need to prevent drop out from schools, with a particular focus on ethnic minorities.

The former government had decided to organize many of the targeted policies to special categories by way of sector plans, but in view of the decreasing unemployment this policy was discontinued under the actual government. Another trio of new acts of Parliament was the Act on the harmonization of the instruments to improve work participation of disabled persons (*Wet harmonisatie van instrumenten ter bevordering van arbeidsdeelname van arbeidsbeperkten*),[267] the Wages Allowances Act – *Wet tegemoetkomingen loondomein* (WAA), 2015[268] and the Act on streamlining wage cost subsidies (*Wet stroomlijning loonkostensubsidies*).[269] On the basis of Article 3.1.–3.2 WAA a new Decree has been issued, called LIV (*see* paragraph 141). It provides for EUR 1 subsidy for the employer for each paid working hour of his worker (who works at least twenty-four hours a week) and is earning between EUR 10 and 12.50 (which is: 100–125% of the Dutch Minimum Wage) to a maximum of EUR 2,000 a year. This wage subsidy is benefitting 400.000 workers (4% of the Dutch labour market) employed by ca. 100.000 enterprises and will cost the Treasury yearly EUR 500 million. This measure was and is contested. The largest trade union confederation in the Netherlands (FNV) holds that this measure incites employers to keep wages down and so is pushing out Dutch workers in favour of cheaper foreign workers.

245. The unemployment percentage among *unskilled workers* is roughly twice as high as the average unemployment percentage. In the past successive governments have taken various specific measures targeting this category in force. However, it is clear that many of the general measures (*see* paragraph 244) are foremost benefiting this category.

267. Act of 23 Dec. 2015, Stb. 2015, 547; Parliamentary Papers 34194.
268. Act of 23 Dec. 2015, Stb. 2015, 542; Parliamentary Papers 34304.
269. Act of 17 Nov. 2016, Stb. 2016, 444; Parliamentary Papers 34514.

There is still some support for innovative projects in the market sector to help *long-term unemployed* persons find work. Long-term unemployed persons for whom the municipal social service departments are basically unable to find paid employment, may perform unpaid activities and retain their benefit. This ensures that they do not become entirely alienated from the labour market or the requirements that the market imposes on them.[270]

246. In the Netherlands *youth unemployment* (age 15–25) went up from about 8% in 2008 to 16% in 2013. Actually (2019) youth unemployment is down to a less worrying 7%, but this is still almost two times the average unemployment rate. In the Netherlands the young people (15–24 years) who are not in either employment or education/training is actually 5% – the lowest figure in the EU.

Over the years there have been several kinds of measures in force to combat youth employment with subsidies to employers. Employers who engage youngsters earning the minimum wage may obtain a wage subsidy (Article 3.3–3.4 WAA). In 2010 it was decided to temporarily (only one year) allow employers to conclude four (and not three, as the law in general provides, *see* paragraph 230) fixed-term contracts with youngsters under 27 before it the contract was transformed in a contract for indefinite time. However this measure only lasted one year. A special 'Ambassador for Tackling Youth Unemployment' has been nominated to arrange a better cooperation between the municipalities, employers and the educational institutions to reduce youth employment. The government wants not only to tackle youth unemployment but also to prevent it by providing a high standard of education that meets the needs of the labour market. The government is therefore adopting measures to improve the match between education and the labour market. Another of the government's priorities is to reduce the number of early school-leavers since young people who leave education with a basic qualification are more active in the labour market and less often unemployed.

The former government has earmarked an additional EUR 50 million to provide a boost for regional efforts to tackle youth unemployment and has launched School Ex 2.0, a programme intended to encourage young people in secondary vocational education (MBO) to continue studying longer and to choose a course with greater relevance for the labour market. The additional funds will be used to encourage young people in the regions to follow an education and to help them in their search for work. In 2013 some municipalities started to award 'starters' bursaries' (*see* paragraph 259). As said above (*see* paragraph 244) the regional approach has also been supplemented by a sector campaign. The government has called on the social partners to consider the employment of young people in the sector plans that they draw up, for example by providing sufficient places for traineeships and work placements. Agreements will be made on this on the basis of the Technology Pact, concluded in 2013 (*see* paragraph 260).[271] The government is willing, under certain conditions, to provide co-financing for the sector plans.

---

270. A. Paz-Fuchs & A. Eleveld, *Workfare Revisited*, 45 Indus. L. J. 60–88 (2016).
271. Parliamentary Papers 32637.

247. During the last three decades the Netherlands has followed a zigzag course concerning *the elderly workers*. When unemployment rose sharply in the 1980s the policy was directed towards a smooth departure from the labour market of elderly workers so that the young generation could replace them. So, although there traditionally was the 'lifo'-rule in collective redundancies (*see* paragraph 225), a new rule was introduced that in cases of dismissal for economic reasons, under certain conditions, workers of 55 and older could be shed with priority if they could enter a VUT scheme (*see* paragraphs 197–198/225 et seq.). Consequently VUT schemes emerged. Together with other exit routes it effectuated that in 1995 only one out of four persons in the age category of 55–65 was working. The average age of withdrawing from the labour market had fallen to below 60 years (*see* paragraphs 5 and 7). Then the government veered round and started to promote the participation of older workers in the labour market. The preferential dismissal of older workers was ended and the best preferential treatment in collective redundancies weakened (*see* paragraphs 224 et seq.). In 2004 the Dutch government decided to stop the tax incentives for earlier retirement schemes and even started to tax those schemes, leading to a dramatic reduction of the schemes. In 2009, taking advantage of the worries about the banking crisis the government finally decided to rise the retirement age in the AOW. This trend was followed in the occupation pension schemes, were in a number of sectors and companies workers for long years have been subject to pensionable ages even younger than 65. In 2019 this trend was suddenly delayed (*see* paragraph 52): a Social agreement and a subsequent amendment of the statutory Old Age Pensions Act (AOW) delayed the rise of the AOW-pensionable age and opened new possibilities for sector VUT schemes!

Also since the 1990s the government has tried to increase the labour market participation of elderly workers by diminishing the labour costs of these workers and/ or in subsidizing their employment (*see* below) and by promoting the intensification of the vocational training and retraining of these workers (*see* paragraph 259). All these measures have contributed to increase the percentage of elderly people from 10% of the working population in 2003 to 20% in 2017.

Not only the policy of the government towards the elderly workers has changed, also that of the social partners, be it more slowly. The last decades of the past century had seen many measures in collective agreements to relieve the burden of work on elderly workers. This was done by measures offering elderly workers a shorter working week or more paid holidays, by liberating them from performing night work or shift work, etc. However, these types of measures are in fact increasing the labour costs of these workers and therefore not exactly conducive to incite employers to take on or to maintain older workers in its workforce. Moreover these measures have become suspect under the rules on age discrimination (*see* paragraph 99). So they are on the retreat now. More resistant are clauses on more convenient working schedules for older workers. The percentage of workers enjoying them even increased from 70% in 2006 to 73% in 2010.[272] Working time arrangements/ adjustments in order to allow older workers to stay on the job are facilitated by the Flexible Work Act, 2015 (*see* paragraph 119).

272. Antoine T.J.M. Jacobs, *Active Aging and Labour Law in the Netherland*, in *Active Aging and Labour Law* 263–273 (F. Hendrickx ed., Antwerp: Intersentia, 2012).

One of the tools to keep more elderly workers in the labour market is to promote demotion. The percentage of the workers covered by clauses in collective agreements on the item of demotion is steadily growing from 21% in 2006 to 27% in 2010. A more neutral appellation is: age-conscious human resources policies. For a number of years many collective agreements have been requiring the employer to develop age-conscious human resources policies, which must contain measures to retain or increase the number of older employees.

One of the instruments to retain more elderly workers on the labour market is in diminishing the labour costs of these workers and/or in subsidizing their employment. There is a global debate among economists about the effects of age-dependent taxes and also in the Netherlands many studies are done about the most effective (and less costly!!) incentives. The Dutch are still very uncertain about those effects. Over the years there have been several of these kinds of measures in force. Actually there still is in force a regulation that entitles employers to a wage subsidy for the engagement of employees between 56 years of age and the AOW-retirement age (Article 2.2.–2.5 WAA). The employee benefits agency UWV received EUR 67 million for 2013 and 2014 to expand its activities such as network meetings, inspiration days, matching programmes, training courses and other reintegration activities. Finally, a task force is being established to streamline the efforts to rise the effective retirement age. To promote sustainable employability, the tax allowance for training costs has been expanded and agreements have been made with the social partners on the co-financing of sector plans designed to allow companies to retain skilled employees, for 'from work to work' programmes and for cross-sector training schemes. A sum of EUR 300 million has been earmarked for these measures in 2014 and 2015.

Inter alia because the automatic termination of the contract of employment when reaching the retirement age is still largely maintained (*see* paragraph 231), in the Netherlands the number of persons continuing to work after having reached this age, is still low: 13% of the population in the age group 65–69, while the OECD average is 20%. The former government has initiated new legislation to review various aspects of the labour law position of persons over the pensionable age that stay on the labour market (*see* paragraph 52). This is, however, a delicate piece of legislation. On the one hand retired workers indeed require less protection in some fields, as they are not so much dependent on work and income as non-retired workers, but to take away much of the protection would give the retired workers a competitive advantage over other workers.

248. In order to stimulate *partially disabled people* to return to the labour market the generous old Employees Disability Benefits Scheme in 2004 was replaced by a new one which is considerably less generous for partially and non-permanent disabled workers and contains various incentives to stimulate them to return to the labour market in order to use their remaining earning capacities. As a result the influx in this kind of schemes has been reduced (*see* paragraph 165). On the other hand the number of youngsters receiving benefits pursuant to the Young Disabled Persons Benefits Acts has increased significantly. Former governments have taken measures to tighten the criteria. Parts of the Young Disabled Persons Act were integrated into the PW reserving the Young Disabled Persons Benefits Act for handicapped young persons who are fully and permanently incapacitated for work.[273] All these changes necessitate the labour market policies to stimulate the availability and acceptance of jobs that are suitable for partially disabled persons.

After the World War II, the Netherlands, in line with most other Western European nations, adopted a statute that required 2% of the workforce of an enterprise to consist of disabled workers. This Act gradually fell into oblivion. It was replaced by an Act of 1986 and again in 1998 by the Reintegration of Workers with Disabilities Act which offered employers financial incentives to continue the employment or to recruit workers with disabilities and placed a number of responsibilities to reintegrate disabled workers on the employers and on the official services for manpower policies and social security. This Act was abolished in 2006. It was *inter alia* replaced by a regulation that reduced some social security contributions for employers who take on disabled workers of over fifty years. In 2016 the subsidies for disabled workers were again streamlined.[274] Actually the main measures in force are the wage subsidy for disabled workers (with maximum 35% disablement), based on Article 2.6–2.9 WAA as well as a wage subsidy for the re-engagement of disabled workers, based on Article 2.14–2.17 WAA.

Another traditional instrument to provide work for partially disabled workers is the so-called sheltered workplace. Over more than 150 years the Dutch government has provided 'sheltered workplaces' for handicapped persons – and recently – also for long-term unemployed with special difficulties (ex-prisoners, ex-drugs addicts, etc.). A few years ago this service offered about 100,000 jobs, more than 1% of all the jobs in the Netherlands. There were about 100 sheltered workplaces in the Netherlands; 20% of the workers in this field have been posted to 'normal' employers. Employers were encouraged to offer such places by tax advantages. The legal status of those working in this organization was regulated by the Sheltered Workplaces Act (*Wet Sociale Werkvoorziening*). As this services has become increasingly costly – EUR 3 billion yearly – the government decided to close it for new entrants from 2016. From that time on municipalities have to arrange work for people who are only able to work in a sheltered working environment (Article 10b Participatiewet). Municipalities will be able to place people who do not qualify for sheltered employment and whose productivity is less than 80% of the statutory minimum wage with an employer, who will receive a wage cost allowance from the government amounting to the difference between the wage rate set for the employee and the statutory minimum wage. The employer will pay the difference between the statutory minimum wage and the wage under the applicable collective labour agreement. Thirty-five regional public employment services are established to help people with an occupational disability find work with a regular employer. Municipalities had to take the lead in the public employment services, which will be run in association with the employers, trade unions and the UWV. Municipalities have discretion in deciding what support people need and possess a wide range of instruments to assist people who require help in finding and performing work. As it is essential that

273. Act of 2 Jul. 2014, Stb. 2014, 270; Parliamentary Papers 34352.
274. Act of 17 Nov. 2016, Stb. 2016, 444.

employers play an active role in providing regular jobs for people with a handicap and little prospect of employment, agreements have been made with the central employers' associations on the number of jobs that will be provided for people with a handicap in the coming years. Employers in the private sector (including healthcare) have guaranteed to yearly create additional jobs to finally reach a maximum of 100,000 extra jobs in 2026. The public sector employers have guaranteed a total of 25,000 additional jobs from 2024.

A former government was committed to reintroduce a quota system for handicapped persons but on the basis of the Social Agreement, April 2013 (*see* paragraph 285) in which the social partners made the above-mentioned promises, this quota-plan has been put on ice. The legislator has only issued a new Act, the Disablement Quotum Act (*Wet banenafspraak en quotum arbeidsbeperkten*),[275] which may require employers with more than twenty employees to have at least 5% of their staff being handicapped, otherwise a fine of EUR 5,000 for every not realized job will be imposed. The quota would be activated if the agreed number of jobs has not been created, which was evaluated for the first time at the end of 2016, when at least 11,000 additional jobs should have been created in the private sector for people with a handicap. It then was concluded that in the private sector the promised increase in jobs for the partially disabled had indeed been realized, but not so in the public sector. Nevertheless no quota obligation for this sector has been effectuated as yet.[276] Employers are tempted to engage disabled workers in this programme by a wage subsidy based on Article 2.10–2.13 WAA.

249. Women's participation at the Dutch labour force has risen in the recent decades. Actually it stands at about 72%, against male participation at 80% (*see* paragraph 7). Dutch female workers with family responsibilities often work part-time (*see* paragraph 8). Whereas in other countries the increase in female labour force participation was followed by an increase in working hours, the latter step did not occur in the Netherlands. The government policies are to encourage women to work on the labour market and to work there more hours. Former governments believed that financial incentives play a major role in women's decisions concerning employment and used subsidizing childcare and tax instruments to that end. However, evaluations have shown that despite these facilities Dutch mothers still predominantly opted for only part-time working on the labour market.

In the last decades a rise in labour market participation of women was deliberately stimulated by the government through a substantial extension of child care facilities. The money for that purpose was increased from EUR 1 billion in 2005 to EUR 3.7 billion in 2011. Since then the government is trying to reduce this spending. Subsidies to child care have been diminished, and also the present government is committed to reform and introduce savings in the system of schemes for child care. The new and more limited purpose of this policy instrument is to make it financially attractive for single parents receiving social assistance to go to work. The legislators have already stimulated the employment participation of single parents

275. Act of 1 Apr. 2015, Stb. 2015, 154; Parliamentary Papers 33981.
276. Parliamentary Papers 34256.

(mostly women) by limiting the exception of the obligation contained in the unemployment benefit and social assistance schemes to actively search for work.

In order to further enhance women participation in the labour market by tax measures from 2009 the transferable tax credit for breadwinner families is being phased out over a period of fifteen years. So actually this general tax credit for partners without an income has already been reduced to more than two-thirds of that of the primary earners as an incentive to non-working partners to work.

250. The participation rate of *ethnic minorities and immigrants* in the Netherlands is actually about 60%, which is substantially lower than the average participation rate of 76%. The government has taken a number of initiatives to remove obstacles to the accession to and advancement in the labour market for non-western ethnic minorities, particularly in the area of language and schooling, job-hunting strategies and social networks and combating discrimination. However, the results of all these measures up until now are quite meagre. Weak measures of 'affirmative action' applicable to this group have been abolished (*see* paragraph 92). Former governments have always been positive to allow foreign workers from other EU countries and even migrant workers from outside the EU to help overcome shortages in various corners of the labour market although there is a work permits system for extra EU citizens (*see* paragraph 78).

The Netherlands has seen a rash increase of migrant workers since ca. 2000 notably from Central and Eastern EU Member States. Actually their number stands at 400,000, which is 5% of the Dutch labour market. Already in the times of high unemployment (2010–2016) they came to the Netherlands. The reason is that they were prepared to do the many jobs that were despised by the hundred thousands of Dutch unemployed. To a certain extent they were also driving out Dutch candidates for the jobs because thanks to the legal formula of 'posted workers' they were somewhat cheaper for the Dutch employers than Dutch candidates. Now that in recent years the economy of the Netherlands has improved and an increasing number of jobs cannot be filled by Dutch candidates, no decrease of migrant workers may be expected.

In line with EU policies, the Netherlands started some years ago facilitating immigration from outside the EU only for highly skilled workers (earning more than EUR 47,000 a year), for example for the chip-making industry (*see* paragraph 78). Employers may easily obtain a work permit for them, and the taxman allows these immigrants EUR 30,000 tax-free income during at most eight years. The actual government has reduced this to five years.

Ethnic minorities and immigrants may also benefit from a regulation in force that exempts employers from paying wage tax and social security contributions for seasonal workers who – because of working in small part-time jobs (at most six to eight weeks) – are earning less than 30% of the minimum wage.

§7. The Public Employment Services

251. It was only after the beginning of the twentieth century, as from 1902, that various municipal authorities started public labour exchanges/job centres (*arbeidsbeurzen*) in order to assist employers in filling their vacancies and employees in finding a job. In 1930 these facilities were organized on a national scale: the National Employment Service, which was given a quasi-monopoly of intermediary services on the labour market (*see* paragraph 254). In 1940 the National Employment Service was given a highly centralized organization. For long years this placement service has always been a part of the state civil service and was separate from the unemployment benefits administration, which used to be under a strong control of the social partners. It was also separate from the provision of social assistance for employable persons and other clients not entitled to insurance benefits, which is at the charge of local authorities. Since 1990 the employment services and unemployment benefit administration in the Netherlands have undergone a long series of reforms. At first the government decided to divest itself of direct management responsibility for the placement and reintegration of the unemployed and brought its employment services under the responsibility of tripartite boards at central and regional level in the Manpower Services Act (*Arbeidsvoorzieningswet*) 1990. In the mid-1990s, another round of reform reduced tripartite responsibilities again and set the stage for market-type relationships in employment services by encouraging social insurance agencies (five at the time) and local authorities to purchase reintegration programmes for their clientele first from the Public Employment Service and later from private providers (*see* paragraph 253). However, most of these changes were not successful and were reversed by the 2002 SUWI Act (*Wet structuur uitvoering werk en inkomen* – Act on the structure of the administration for work and income), which again changed the institutional set-up of social security, job brokerage and labour reintegration. It merged the main remaining role of the Public Employment Services – placement of workers – with the intake role of the unemployment benefit agencies into a new agency called CWI and brought it back under the sole control of the government. The main aim of the Act was to overcome institutional redundancy and improve preconditions for activating all types of benefit recipients. By way of compensation for their loss of influence the social partners and the municipalities have been given an advisory role via seats in the *Raad voor Werk en Inkomen* (Council for Work and Income), which was consulted by the Minister on all proposed decisions in the field of employment policies. However, this Council was abolished in 2011. Finally, the SUWI Amendment Act of 2007 constitutes the latest link in this chain of structural reforms. By this Act the CWI was merged with the *Uitvoeringsorganisatie Werknemersverzekeringen* (UWV, Employees' social security administration) under the name UWV. Although this is still an independent agency, led by a board of directors, all the members of its supervisory board are nominated by the government. The Ministry (SZW) retains a supervisory role, in particular through the Inspection SZW (*see* paragraph 40). The UWV is funded by an annual subsidy out of the State Budget of EUR 1.7 billion and has ca. 17,000 employees.

Its regional offices apart from their role in the Dutch system of dismissal control (*see* paragraphs 205–209) handle the initial registration of vacancies and the jobless, make a preliminary assessment of jobless' entitlement to benefits; provide free universal job-matching services; and participate in controlling clients' job-search obligations. These regional offices shape the future trajectory of the newly registered clients through profiling (evaluating their distance from the labour market). It refers then the appropriate authority for benefits, i.e., to the UWV (if they are entitled to unemployment or disability insurance benefits) or to municipalities (if entitled to social assistance). Registration with the UWV is a statutory obligation for those entitled to unemployment benefits or social assistance. A website has been created, www.werk.nl, where employees must register to obtain and keep unemployment benefits and where they can consult job offers. Unfortunately there are many complaints that this digital service is not working well. Moreover the UWV is frequently exposed to several forms of fraud.

252. The placement functions of the UWV are performed by the UWV-WERKBEDRIJF. It obtains ca. 0.4 billion a year out of the UWV-budget and has ca. 5,000 employees out of the 17,000 UWV staff. A total of 3,500 of them are working on regional offices, called *Werkpleinen.* Already after four weeks those unemployed who have the largest distance from the labour market have their first personal contact with an UWV official (job-coach); other jobless people only after six months. Other UWV-WERKBEDRIJF officials operate within *Employer-service-points* who are actively focusing on employers in order to harvest vacancies and serve them with candidates. In all these activities the UWV-WERKBEDRIJF may use the various forms of subsidies (*see* paragraphs 244–249) to entice the employers and the unemployed to accept jobs.

Research has revealed that the support of the UWV to flex workers after sickness and for elderly workers is insufficient.

§8. Reintegration Activities

253. Traditionally there are a number of activities to bring the unemployed and the partially handicapped back to the labour market (so-called reintegration): vocational training, job counselling, etc. However the total amount spent on these activities was not high. In the 1990s the Dutch much admired the Swedish model which laid more emphasis and spent more money on reintegration of the unemployed than on granting unemployment benefits. So also in the Netherlands the money for reintegration of unemployed people was substantially raised until EUR 2.5 billion in the year 2002. At the same time it was decided that this money should no longer be spent by the Public Employment Service itself, but could be spent by local authorities and private reintegration firms. The government's expectations were that, by enhancing competition, the effectiveness and efficiency of these services would improve. So the Netherlands has carried out a far-reaching transformation of its Public Employment Service towards the private provision of reintegration services for unemployment benefits as well as social assistance recipients. Since 2000 for unemployment insurance, and since 2002 for social assistance, placement and reintegration services for clients who are not expected to find work within six months are in principle contracted out to private providers. These providers can obtain state money for each worker they manage to reintegrate. The *SUWI Act* provided for the outsourcing of the reintegration activities to private companies. It also required the new social insurance agency (UWV) and (more gradually) the over 300 Dutch municipalities to contract out placement and reintegration measures for most types of clients.

Some 2000 private reintegration firms sprang up to offer courses (for instance, job application training courses) or to assist jobless people in their search for jobs. The Netherlands had become the prototype of a 'reintegration market' characterized by a 'purchaser/provider' split, were private sector and non-private organizations compete for the acquisition of publicly funded tenders to supply re-employment services to the unemployed. Research has revealed that this new approach has not led to better quality and lower costs. Many commercial reintegration businesses are restricting themselves to intake, training for application to vacancies and a search for a job in groups. This often does not match the clients' individual needs. There has been a heavy debate about this mechanism. Independent researchers have claimed that – if one left out all those unemployed who could have found work themselves – about EUR 75,000 of taxpayers' money had been spent on every single successful reintegration support. This conclusion was refuted by the government, which claimed that this reintegration assistance costs only an average of EUR 10,000 a person and that 47% of the people concerned had found work. However the impression remained that the system is too costly and not working well and in the meantime the money spent on reintegration support has been reduced to EUR 1 billion a year.

§9. Private Employment Services

254. In the Netherlands, as in most industrialized countries, private entrepreneurs preceded public authorities in offering 'placement' services to employers and workers. The social partners did not play a substantial role in this field as they did in countries such as France. The private enterprises to service the labour market set–up in the nineteenth century were mostly profit-making services where abuses abounded. This led the ILO to adopt a Convention and subsequently also the Dutch lawmakers to adopt an Act of Parliament on this item in 1930. Profit-making services were prohibited whereas private non-profit oriented services could continue to operate under a licence system. The 1950s and 1960s saw the rise of commercial temporary work agencies and private profit-oriented placement agencies in legal formulas, which escaped the statutory ban as there were many holes in this legislation. According to case law of the HR in the 1960s the 1930 Act did not prohibit profit-oriented enterprises, which serviced only one side of the labour market (either employers or employees). This case law then enabled commercial enterprises for recruitment, job- or head-hunters, outplacement offices, sportsmen-job-brokers etc., to flourish.

A number of commercial firms have specialized in searching for new jobs for redundant workers. Companies which want to make some of their staff redundant, hire the services of these outplacement firms, which are indeed sometimes successful in finding a new job for the redundant worker. So, clauses to provide outplacement services have appeared regularly in individual and collective 'social plans' (*see* paragraph 226) and also in compensation awards made by the judges in dismissal cases.

The Manpower Services Act (*Arbeidsvoorzieningswet*) of 1990 allowed profit-oriented employment agencies to operate on the basis of a licence to which they were entitled provided they observed certain standards of decent behaviour. This act was repealed in 1998 and replaced by the AEIA. This Act, in line with the global process of liberalization of private initiative on the labour market (*see* ILO Convention no. 181), consolidated the system of licences for job placement agencies. However, this licence system was abolished in 2003 by the AEIA Amendment Act, which only maintained a few rules of decent behaviour for the private employment services:

- placement agencies in principle should not charge job seekers for their services, but a Ministerial Decree may allow such charges for certain categories of job seekers or employers;
- no placement services for placement in plants or enterprises hit by a strike, lock-out or sit-in (Article 3 AEIA).

A Ministerial Decree may set further rules for specific categories of job seekers or employers. For sanctions on these provisions *see* paragraph 257.

The AEIA gives the following definition of 'job placement' (*arbeidsbemiddeling*) (Article 1): 'Professional services to either employer, or job seeker, or to both to help them in the search for personnel resp. jobs with the aim of concluding a contract of employment or an appointment in the civil service.' This definition includes outplacement and hiring and selection agencies such as head-hunters, but it excludes 'professional' help in promoting the conclusion of 'work' contracts (not being contracts of employment), for example, for certain professional artists, entertainers and sportsmen. The Act does not cover the publication of data concerning jobs or job seekers via press, radio/TV or other means of communication. Finally, the Dutch definition of 'job placement' does not include temporary work business. Temporary work business is covered by the Dutch notion *ter beschikking stelling van arbeidskrachten* (providing manpower) and is dealt with in a special Chapter of the AEIA (*see* paragraph 255).

§10. Temporary Employment Agencies

255. Temporary agency work (*ter beschikking stelling van arbeidskrachten*) is defined under Dutch law as 'providing for monetary reward a third party with personnel to perform work under supervision and control of that third party, but not under a contract of employment with that third party' (Article 1(1e) AEIA). The temporary work agency contracts the worker and leases him/her to a user firm, in whose business and according to whose instructions the temporary worker must do his work (*see* paragraph 66).

Temporary work agencies existed before World War II, but their number was negligible. In the 1950s that situation started to change considerably, the number of agencies increasing at a rapid rate. Different sectors of industry, in needing for extra workers, offered attractive possibilities for temporary workers. Dutch courts ruled that temporary work agencies were not subject to the then–existing ban on private job placement (*see* paragraph 254).

As the activities of temporary employment agencies had some negative aspects as well, Parliament intervened in 1965 and passed legislation, the Temporary Agency Work Act (*Wet op het ter beschikking stellen van arbeidskrachten*), which after 1970 brought the temporary work agencies under a licence system. They were only allowed to operate provided they observed certain standards of decent behaviour. Among others it was ordered that the wages of the workers to be hired out had to be the same as those of the comparable workers of the user company. In addition assignments of temporary agencies were limited to a maximum period of six months (with exceptional possibilities for prolongation); temporary work was only allowed for really temporary work and temporary work was forbidden in the construction, road haulage and merchant maritime sectors.

Compared to the situation in other EU Member State this was already quite a liberal regime, which subsequently enabled the temporary work agencies to expand dramatically (*see* paragraph 9) in the Netherlands. In the 1990s the major trade union FNV, which had been hostile to temporary work business, became ready to settle for a compromise. In exchange for an improvement of the weak legal status of temporary agency workers it was prepared to endorse the pressures of the industry to a further liberalization of the temporary work business. As this new approach was in line with the government's policies on labour market flexibility and deregulation and also in line with the global process of liberalization of private initiative on the labour market (*see* ILO Convention no. 181), in 1998 the temporary work agencies were freed from most of the legal constraints on their functioning.

This compromise was taken over by the government and laid down in two Acts of Parliament:

- the already mentioned AEIA abolished the system of licences for private temporary work business and repealed the old requirement that temporary agencies were limited to assignments of a maximum period of six months;
- the Flexibility and Security Act (*see* paragraph 193), improved the rights of temporary agency workers.

The AEIA repeats for temporary work agencies the two basic rules it also gives to private employment services:

- to refrain from charging fees or costs to workers (Article 9 AEIA);
- to provide no services to workplaces hit by strikes, lockouts or occupations (Article 10 AEIA).

Finally the AEIA brought the abolition of the licence system which became a further impetus to the growth in numbers of the temporary employment agencies – currently there are thousands of them in the Netherlands. At the same time this has also caused many abuses which have worried Parliament as well as the social partners. The reintroduction of a licence system was considered but finally dismissed. Several other steps were taken. In the first place the introduction of a system of certification by the sector itself. The AEIA supports this by a disposition which provides for the communication of information on administrative fines imposed to firms to the certifying institution (Article 14a AEIA). Then, in 2007, a provision was inserted in the Dutch CC, creating a joint liability for the user company and the temporary work agency for paying the statutory minimum wage and minimum holidays, which, however, would not apply if the agency had a certification (Article 7:692 CC – now replaced by a more general measure, *see* paragraph 132). In the third place the social partners in the industry set up an own inspectorate to monitor the observation of the various working conditions applicable in this industry.

It quickly appeared that these measures were not enough to reduce substantially the many abuses in this industry. So in 2012 the AEIA was further amended to create a mandatory system of registration. Every business in the field of temporary agency work must be registered at the Chamber of Commerce. It is prohibited for user firms to work with employees contracted by non-registered temporary work agencies (Article 7a AEIA).

At the same time the Dutch legislation was purified from the last remaining restrictions on temporary agency work, notably those in the merchant marine. However the Amended AEIA now authorizes the Minister to introduce special requirements or even a licence system for (parts of) sectors in which the good relations at the labour market and the interests of the workers concerned require this (Article 12 AEIA).

The AEIA covers all companies that fall in the definition given at the beginning of this paragraph, so also the so-called payroll-agencies.[277] However, as explained in the next paragraph as from 2020 some special provisions for payroll workers will apply.

256. Traditionally the temporary work agencies were obliged to an equal treatment of the temporary agency worker with the workers of the user firm, but there were many exceptions on these rules. The amendment Act of 2012 brought these provisions in line with the comparable ones in EU Directive 2008/104/EU.[278]

The temporary agency worker has now the same rights as the workers in the user firm (or – if absent there – in the sector) on remuneration, working hours, overtime, breaks, rest periods, holidays and feast days (Article 8(1)(2) AEIA). Also protected in the same way as permanent employees in the user firm are pregnant women, nursing mothers, children and young people. The same rules are applicable about equal

277. Dutch Supreme Court, 4 Nov. 2016, NJ 2017, 370 (Cara 4 Care).

278. M. Houwerzijl, *Regulating Temporary Work in the Netherlands after the Temporary Agency Work Directive*, in *Temporary Agency Work in the European Union and the United States* 125–143 (Roger Blanpain & Frank Hendrickx eds, BCLR 82, 2013).

treatment of men and women, as well as the temporary agency workers are protected against discrimination of sex, race, belief, ideology, disability, age, hetero- or homosexuality (Article 8(3) AEIA). However derogations *in peius* by collective agreement of these provisions are allowed if they are valid for a certain time and include provisions to prevent abuse through chain contracts (Article 8(4) AEIA).

In addition the user firm has to provide the temporary agency worker the same access to collective facilities and services, transportation possibilities, childcare as to permanent workers of his company. Derogations from this are only allowed in collective agreements, and if they are justified by objective grounds. The user firm has to inform the temporary agency worker about a vacant job in its company (Article 8b AEIA).

By virtue of the Labour Market in Balance Act 2019 as from 2020 for employees in payroll enterprises (*see* paragraph 67) the imposed equal rights catalogue is even more complete than for the other temporary agencies workers and it is not possible to deviate from that *in peius* (Article 8a AEIA). The same applies to temporary workers which are leased between companies which belong to the same group of enterprises (=Konzern) (Article 8a(8)).

Traditionally the temporary employment agencies were prohibited to hinder in any form the employee to enter into a contract of employment with the user firm after the expiration of his contract with the temporary work agency. This prohibition was repealed in 1998 but partly revived in 2012. It now contains as only exception: clauses between the agency and the user firm obliging the user firm to compensate the agency for the costs of hiring and training of the worker concerned. Such clauses are allowed (Article 9a AEIA).

Moreover temporary work firms are obliged to provide the temporary workers with information about occupational qualifications and safety rules (Article 11 AEIA).

The possibility of derogating *in peius* from the equal treatment provisions of Article 8 AEIA has stimulated the conclusion of sector collective agreements between the main employers' organizations and the major trade unions in this business. These collective agreements initially contained a set of wage scales which used to offer lower wages than those applicable in the firm in which the temporary agency worker performs his work. However, since 2012 these collective agreements provide for 100% equal remuneration. In addition these collective agreements improve the status of temporary workers according to the principle that the longer the relationship between agency and temporary worker is continued, the more secure the employment relationship. It is a hire and fire system during the seventy-eight weeks, a fixed-term contract system in the following years and finally the possibility of an indefinite employment contract after over six years.

In the Netherlands the public and the policymakers are less negative at temporary work agencies than in other European countries. Recent research has revealed that some of them have also a positive effect because they play a beneficial role in offering jobs to groups with difficulties at the labour market: elderly workers, disabled workers and people from ethnic minorities. This can also be observed in the participation of temporary work agencies in the work plazas (*see* paragraph 252) and in the inclusion of temporary agency work in the definition of 'suitable' work for the unemployment benefits.

Notwithstanding the large approach in working conditions between temporary agency workers and the workers of the user firm, important differences have remained. The most striking ones are:

- in the wage payment obligation (*see* paragraph 130): during twenty-six weeks (in collective agreement: seventy-eight weeks) temporary work agencies may exclude the obligation on the employer to continue to pay the wage if no work is performed (*see* Article 7:691(7)(8) CC);
- temporary work agencies have the possibility during twenty-six weeks (in collective agreements: seventy-eight weeks) to stipulate that the contract of employment is automatically ended when the user firm stops using the employee (Article 7:691(1)(2)(8) CC, *see* paragraph 232);
- for temporary work agencies the statutory restrictions on the successive use of fixed-term contracts (*see* paragraph 230) are less stringent: they do not apply during the first twenty-six week (in collective agreements: seventy-eight weeks); and afterwards the chain of such contracts may extend to four years or six contracts (Article 7:691(1)(8) CC);
- the temporary work agencies may be not obliged to apply in all aspects the same or equivalent terms of the collective agreement and an occupational pension scheme which is applied in the user firm.

All these differences are still so attractive that the business model of the temporary work agencies still flourishes in the Netherlands (*see* paragraph 66).

257. The provisions of the AEIA are, apart from the control by an own inspection service, set up by the social partners in the temporary agency business (*see* paragraph 333), controlled by the Inspection SZW. The statutory provisions are not strengthened by criminal sanctions but by a system of administrative fines and other measures both versus the agencies and the user firms. Workers who are victims of infractions of the rules on placement agencies and temporary work business may enter an action with a court. For their benefit the Act provides that the Inspection SZW (Labour Inspectorate), which notices infractions of the law, will communicate them to the workers, to the employer, the works council and the trade unions concerned (Article 15 AEIA).

Dutch and foreign agencies who are bringing posted workers to work in the Netherlands are now under a number of special obligations by virtue of the Act to implement the EU Directive 2014/67/EU (*see* paragraph 190).

The parties to the main collective agreements in the Temporary Agency Workers business have set up an own body in order to monitor and to fine the non-observation of the collective agreement (*see* paragraphs 44 and 332).

§11. Labour Pools

258. Labour pools may be set up by employers (and are occasionally co-administered by the trade unions) to establish permanent employment contracts in business branches where the volume of production varies throughout the year.

They have existed already for decades in the ports of the Netherlands, but they also exist in other sectors like the engineering industry. The seaport pools of Rotterdam and Amsterdam have been the major example. In this set-up employers borrowed workers from the pool during the periods of labour need, the workers obtained a guaranteed payment by the labour pool and did not lose the connection with the sector during periods of inactivity. The main costs of the labour pools – apart from administration costs – are of course the wages of the workers during the idle periods. In the past a substantial part of the costs of the seaport pools of Rotterdam and Amsterdam was borne by social security agencies. This financial support was increasingly contested in the 1990s (as it was seen as a form of State aid) (*see* paragraph 238) and finally these subsidies were cancelled. This after a certain time has led to a sharp deterioration of the successes of this type of labour pool. Nevertheless new experiments with this type of labour pool have been made in the road transport industry and in the retail trade of major cities like Amsterdam.

Other types of labour pools emerged within the framework of policies to avoid redundancies and to bring back unemployed and partly disabled persons to the labour market:

- 'redundancy pools' were created to maintain an employment relationship with redundant workers. Instead of being dismissed, these workers are taken over from their former employer by such a labour pool and then hired out to other employers. They are also used for temporary jobs with their former employer, and are the first to be rehired when new jobs are made available;
- 'employment integration pools' (*instroom pools*) are set up especially to take on formerly unemployed workers and to hire them out to employers, with the expectation that these workers will be reintegrated into permanent employment after some time. Actually this instrument is under the name 'lease corporations' (*inleenverbanden*), also much used to post handicapped workers to 'normal' employers (*see* paragraph 248).

Both types of labour pool can play a role in preventing and diminishing unemployment. With their help employers may save severance payments and social security agencies may save benefits. Such savings are the driving force behind the establishment of this type of labour pools and they provide the funding for it. Another type of labour pool has been created by the municipalities to hire out long-term unemployed persons (*see* paragraph 245). This kind of labour pool is expecting from the idle workers that they actively look for alternative work and are offering training, reintegration and outplacement support to the idle workers in the labour pool. The trade unions are very much in favour of this instrument but the government is less enthusiastic. It fears that such a tool encourages employers to relegate their elderly and most expensive workers to the labour pool instead of seeking employment for their redundant workers in their own enterprise. Moreover, in the recent banking and financial crisis it became clear, that labour pools are not resistant to a sudden great influx. They are then quickly arriving on the verge of a bankruptcy and would that happen the employees are out of employment anyway.

§12. VOCATIONAL TRAINING OF ADULTS

259. Training is an important instrument to prevent unemployment. Although in the Netherlands as elsewhere it is recognized that education, training and lifelong learning are the best solutions to create employment and to prevent unemployment at the low-wage end of the labour market, this area is not strongly developed in the Netherlands.[279] A recent study of the Council of Europe revealed that the Netherlands devoted 1.4% of its GDP to training of adults, in contrast to Germany (2%) and Sweden (3%).

Over the past years an increase in the participation of employees in training courses can be recorded. Between 1993 and 2000 the percentage of employees taking part in training courses increased from 25% to 40%. In the same period the expenses on employees taking part in training have raised by 40%. However, most of the training refers to maintenance to be able to execute better the present function and only little to retraining for a different function. The Dutch social partners increasingly realize this and deal with employability in their negotiations. In 2000 the Foundation of Labour (*Stichting van de Arbeid*) issued a strong recommendation on lifelong learning to the social partners in the various sectors of the economy. In the 2015 Work and Security Act a new provision was inserted in the Dutch CC obliging the employers to provide their employees with training (*see* paragraph 86).

Vocational training has for a long time been part of the collective agreements in most sectors and enterprises. These clauses give employees specific rights to follow training courses (mostly with continuation of wage payment) and oblige employers to contribute to specific funds to finance training activities. Nowadays, in social plans (*see* paragraphs 226 et seq.) quite often arrangements are made for retraining workers made redundant.

Typical company training schools had become rare in the Netherlands. Only a few large companies, like Tata Steel, had maintained them. Recently they seem to re-emerge in sectors where there is a large labour shortage. The actual government decided in 2019 to create a subsidy of EUR 48 million for small and medium enterprises to set up own vocational training schools in mutual cooperation and in cooperation with public or private vocational education institutions.

Since 2018 retraining scholarships for long-term unemployed (EUR 2,100 a year) are available.[280]

The governmental policy is focusing on the strengthening of cybersecurity and the equipping for sustainable capacities of workers via lifelong learning and development.[281]

In various sectors of the industry employers are obliged to poor money in sector funds on the basis of collective agreements. These sector funds are administrated jointly by employers and unions. Here one sees one of the advantages of the Dutch system on the extension of collective agreements (paragraphs 324 et seq.): in most sectors of the economy employers are legally obliged to contribute to these funds. There are now 130 training funds, covering the majority of the workers in private

279. M.v. Velzen, *Learning on the Fly* (2004).
280. Parliamentary Papers K 30012, nos 41 and 92 and 35074, no. J 212.
281. Parliamentary Papers K 29544, no. 773.

industry. These funds spend EUR 600 million yearly. Short before the banking crisis it was assumed that these funds possessed EUR 1 billion capital, but when this crisis started to hit the Dutch economy the funds had to contribute much to the short-time working schemes (*see* paragraph 133), sometimes even to such an extent that they became almost depleted.

In the Netherlands training of adults in the labour market is primarily regarded by the government as industry's own responsibility. Unlike France there is in the Netherlands no general statutory obligation on employers to set apart money for vocational training. A former government once threatened to refuse to use its power to extend the binding force of collective agreements if the collective agreements are not paying attention to training, but this was never put into effect. The government sees it as its responsibility to contribute financially to these training programmes, set up by various sectors and enterprises. It does so, first of all on the basis of a Decree on the support of sector vocational training (*Bijdrageregeling Bedrijfstaksgewijze Scholing*). Second, in 1997 the government introduced a further tax incentive: a deduction from the company tax for enterprises, which spent money on the training of their adult workers.

The government targets its own activities in the field of training of adults to the unemployed. It does so first of all by way of the Training Framework Scheme (*Kaderregeling Scholing*). This measure provides a national framework by means of which support is given to the vocational training of unemployed workers and workers, whose jobs are under threat and who, without additional training or retraining, cannot be adapted to or maintained in the labour market. Based on submission of a training plan, subsidies granted are 100% for training of unemployed persons and a maximum of 50% for training of employees. Ninety per cent of the training measure programmes last less than one year. Due to cutbacks from EUR 100 million in 1990 to EUR 18 million in 1997, the number of applicants decreased from 72,000 in 1993 to 9,000 in 1996. The evaluation of the Training Framework Scheme shows that it only has little value added for those who work and are threatened with unemployment. The government itself also has set up and finances a number of vocational training centres for Adults (*Centra van Vakopleiding voor Volwassenen*). Since 2003 these centres have been part of Regional Training Centres.

Part of this money can be reclaimed from European funds. So there is money available for training but critics are claiming that the sector funds are not active enough in mobilizing the money available. The realities are that the distribution of training is still very uneven. Poorly educated people, older workers and people with a minor part-time job are far less likely to be eligible for training than other groups. The same goes for workers on temporary contracts. Employers are less interesting in their training than in the training of their hardcore workers.

In an attempt to combat youth employment several municipalities in 2013 introduced a starters-bursary scheme (*see* paragraph 246). Youth between 18 and 27 with a school certificate can themselves look for a trainee place with an employer of their choice. If they find one, they can obtain during six months a starters bursary of EUR 500 a month. The employer must pay an additional EUR 100. The municipalities bear the rest of the costs but are subsidized by the state.

§13. APPRENTICESHIP

260. For many years the Netherlands has had various systems of apprenticeships (*see* paragraph 71). Since the 1970s the Dutch government has supported the system of apprenticeship according to a formula which replaced older ones. Young people who have ended compulsory schooling and are under 18 years old must enter the apprenticeship system. They pick up an apprentice place in an enterprise for four days a week and go to school the fifth day. After two years in this system they may pass an exam and are accorded a certificate. Under this scheme about 450 training courses for a large variety of jobs are offered. The firm pays the salary of the youth and the Ministry pays the school. Subsidies are possible under the PW (Article 10f). The actual government would like to raise the obligatory age for this system to twenty-one, but it is uncertain whether this can be imposed considering the constitutional freedom of occupation (*see* paragraph 85).

The rate of participation of young people in education and training is in the Netherlands with 18% well above the EU average, although the Dutch system has never been as widespread as in Austria, where 40% of the young people concerned are enrolled in such a system.

Employers are cooperating in this scheme by offering apprenticeship places and educating apprentices. They are supported for this by way of a subsidy, which has been changed many times over the years. The actual scheme is the 'subsidy regulation learning by practice' (*subsidieregeling praktijkleren*) which offers a maximum of EUR 2,700 subsidy for a realized training place. Some years ago the financial crisis led to a sharp reduction in the number of places in this system in the construction industry.

The former government wanted to tackle the scarcity of technical personnel, together with the social partners and the education sector. The Technology Pact, which was adopted for this purpose in the spring of 2013, was intended to enhance the cooperation between the education sector and business, improve the quality of technical education and attract more young people to technical professions.

§14. FINANCES

261. The Netherlands, like most EU Member States, is struggling with a too high level of budget deficits (*see* paragraph 5) which appears to be the most important constraint on employment and social policies. All efforts to substantially reduce the deficit in times of sluggish economic growth have mostly negative repercussions on growth and are therefore unlikely to boost employment. This is a constant dilemma for Dutch employment policies.

The operation of the various instruments of active labour market policies cost the government EUR 6 billion in 2002 but have been diminished radically since then.

For a number of years the labour market interventions of the Dutch government have been partly financed with money from the European Social Fund. Unfortunately the Netherlands authorities did not always spent this money in accordance with the rules of the EU. In 2002 the Netherlands was fined EUR 157 million by the European Commission for that abuse.

As in the Netherlands spending on active labour market programmes is still high it would be interesting to know how successful the active labour market policies in the Netherlands of the last twenty-five years have been in reducing unemployment. However, there is no convincing empirical evidence about any of the programmes showing that they have had a substantial effect in reducing unemployment. In particular, the counselling and monitoring has at most a modest effect on employment. The subsidized jobs have been abandoned because of lack of positive effects. There is no evidence of positive effects of training and schooling programmes either.

Part II. Collective Labour Relations

Chapter 1. Overview of Industrial Relations

262. The Netherlands entered modern times with the complete ban on associations, which it had inherited from its French domination in the Napoleonic era (1798–1815). Neither employers nor workers were allowed to unite in order to exert economic pressure (Articles 291–294 and 414–416 of the Dutch Penal Code of those days).

The revolutionary movements all over Europe, 1848, brought the Dutch to adopt a liberal Constitution in which freedom of association was recognized. An Act of Parliament implemented this freedom in 1855. However it lasted until 1872 before the criminal prohibitions on trade unions and employers' associations were abolished.

In the 1860s the first trade unions had been established among diamond workers and typographers. The trade unions of those days had mostly a moderate character; their priority was to cooperate with the employers peacefully. It was not before the 1880s that social unrest became more widespread in the Netherlands. Various anarchist, syndicalist and socialist trade unions were established and there was an increase in strike movements. In 1890, following the Socialist International, the first confederation of that kind of unions was formed (Nationaal Arbeids Secretariaat (NAS)). Employers reacted often to claims and strike movements by dismissing striking workers or lockouts. Sometimes industrial unrest took violent aspects and the police interfered. The bourgeois governments of those days tried to stem the unrest by announcing social reform acts. As the entire social programme of the government moved forward very slowly, social unrest did not disappear and so in 1903 the largest industrial conflict ever erupted with a strike of dockworkers and railway personnel. The government reacted with suppression. New criminal prohibitions on the strike by civil servants and railway personnel were enacted (*see* paragraph 355).

263. Disappointed about the poor results of this chaotic conflict, the social democrat trade unions broke away from the NAS and formed their own confederation in 1906 (Nederlands Verbond van Vakverenigingen (NVV)). Workers with a religious background sought refuge with their religious equals in the Protestant Trade Union Confederation (CNV) and Catholic trade unions movement (KAB, later called NKV). Circa 1900 the first collective agreements were concluded in the printing industry and the diamond cutting industry, mostly at local level. In 1913 the first national collective agreement was concluded after a forceful strike action.

However, the majority of the employers were still reluctant to accept the unions as partners in the negotiation of working conditions.

The revolutionary events in Europe 1917–1918 made employers more prone to conclude collective agreements with the unions and inspired the bourgeois government of the Netherlands to intensify its programme of social and electoral reforms (working time, health and safety, social security). Via the High Council of Labour (*Hoge Raad van Arbeid*) the trade unions acquired a consultative role in this programme, containing *inter alia* a statutory regulation of the collective agreements, which after long years of debates resulted in two acts of Parliament, one in 1927 and another in 1937. The Great Depression of 1929 caused much unemployment and poverty in the Netherlands and incited the government to intervene more directly in the economy than it had done before. However, all this was done without social democrats, who managed to enter the government only in 1939 in the shadow of the looming World War II.

264. After World War II the social democrats formed part of the government (1945–1959) and the actual welfare state was constructed with a large number of statutory protections for the workers: minimum wages, holidays with pay, dismissal control, industrial democracy and social security coverage for the entire population. There was a stringent system of centralized wage bargaining under strict government control on the basis of the Extraordinary Decree on Labour Relations. After around 1960 this system was gradually relaxed to leave increasing room for free collective bargaining, but initially the time was not ripe for complete freedom. The wage provisions of the Extraordinary Decree on Labour Relations were replaced by the WDA of 1970 which established free collective bargaining as a principle but gave the government ample powers to intervene. During the 1970s and 1980s all government interventions in collective bargaining were highly contested: politically, in the courts and also before the ILO. Finally, in 1983 for the private sector and in 1994 for the semi-public sector (healthcare, social services, and so on) the government recognized freedom of collective bargaining as an overriding principle, only to be abandoned in extreme circumstances (*see* paragraphs 281 et seq.).

265. Ever since the Netherlands has seen a new system of free collective bargaining emerging. The remaining state interventions in wage formation in the statute book are of a merely ‘promotional’ nature: the statutes on collective agreements, minimum wage and equal pay m/w. However, the public authorities have continued to intervene directly in the area of civil service wages, since in this area they are the employer. This involves (including education employees) around 15% of the working population. The determination of working conditions and terms of employment in the public sector now increasingly resembles the private sector collective bargaining system.

Recent years have seen mounting criticism of the annual pay rises of top managers as well as on the bonus for such persons. Acts were passed to oblige enterprises and institutions to give information on this issue and even for the (semi-) public sector a wage-cap act could be adopted (*see* paragraph 288).

In contrast to the situation in other countries such as France and Italy, the Netherlands does not have an incomes policy conducted explicitly by the state through state enterprises, since such enterprises are very rare in the Netherlands (and employ less than 3% of the total working population).

266. The Dutch system of collective bargaining has always been characterized by a highly complicated combination of cross-sector and sector-level regulations. The social partners and the state have a tradition of cross-sector collective bargaining going back more than sixty years. There are a number of important institutions at which cross-sector bargaining takes place as a continuing process, including the Labour Foundation and the SER. Although collective bargaining is now free, the Dutch continue to hold egalitarian views on annual pay rises. Politicians and lawyers in the Netherlands are not so reluctant to intervene in the process of collective bargaining as they are in Germany.

The trade unions strove for solidarity-based income development, transgressing the boundaries between sectors and between workers and non-workers. During the 1960s and the 1970s a close link was established between the statutory minimum wage, the level of social security benefits and the wages of civil servants on the one hand and, on the other hand the wage growth in the private sector. Although some of these linkages have formally been broken since the 1980s, harmonious development of all incomes remains a much-valued characteristic of the Dutch social model, which is a strong motive for the government and the social partners to seek agreement on wages and economic developments at cross-sector level. Therefore strong political pressure is put on the private sector unions to moderate their annual pay claims. Sometimes the aforementioned linkages are more or less openly used as bargaining chips, a practice which is of course the more contested the more openly it happens. But the pressure is always there. An example was the pressure by the Dutch government in 2004: it announced that it would continue to extend collective agreements only if these agreements were updated along moderate lines. In 2008 the government promised to renounce of tax increases and offered reduction in social security contributions if, again, the social partners would show moderation in the wage formation.

Unions and employers in the private sector are reacting differently to such pressures, depending on the current circumstances. Sometimes, notably when the Dutch economy is in trouble, they are prepared to bow to pressure by concluding a cross-sector agreement which is then followed in all sectors. Sometimes, notably in periods of economic boom, unions and employers refuse to conclude cross-sector agreements and leave wage formation to the actors in the various sectors of the economy. Even in that case the major employers' and trade union confederations try to harmonize their strategies in the various sectors: the employers clearly from a desire not to be played off against one another; the trade unions because their members include many public sector employees and others who are dependent on social security benefits, giving them grounds to fear what would happen if the various linkages were jeopardized by excessive pay rises in the private sector.

267. So in the course of one century the Netherlands has developed its own brand of industrial relations. Collective Agreements and works councils are highly regulated by statutory law and administrative practices, but trade union rights are largely unregulated by Acts of Parliament whereas the law on strikes is entirely judge-made. The Netherlands has an orderly and legalized system of collective agreements, mostly at the national sector level, but occasionally at the enterprise level. The sectoral collective agreements mostly set minimum standards, allowing enterprises to offer more favourable conditions of employment. They are usually renewed, mostly on a regular basis (every year or two years). The collective agreements are not merely 'gentlemen's agreements' like in the UK, but they are legally binding like in France and Germany. In the Netherlands the courts are actively involved in regulating strikes, as opposed to, for example Belgium, where the courts are staying out of it. The courts adhere to a number of principles to control strike behaviour, such as the peace obligation and the proportionality rule, which unquestionably put limits on the freedom to strike, while at the same time leaving ample room for legal strike action. This strong and effective judicial control of industrial action has been conducive to a low strike record and an orderly system of wage formation through collective bargaining. In the Netherlands collective bargaining, however, is not very developed at enterprise level. One historical reason for this is that the old centralized policy of wage control in the Netherlands did not leave room for collective wage formation at the enterprise level. As a result the Dutch unions did not develop their presence within enterprises, putting emphasis on bargaining at cross-sector and sector levels. The workers' involvement in company affairs largely occurs within the much-legalized system of works' councils. It makes managerial decisions subject to extensive information and consultation of workers' representatives.

268. This entire model of industrial relations – sometimes labelled as the *poldermodel* (*see* paragraph 14) – reflects the Dutch love of equality and consensus. It is a rather harmonious model of collective labour relations which allowed the Dutch economy to benefit from wage moderation and low unemployment. Even in left-wing circles – traditionally opposed to a high degree of union integration in state machinery – there is now support for this system of social dialogue. Certainly, there are critics as well who argue against the perceived benefits of the *poldermodel* on a number of fronts. They argue that extensive consultation prevents speedy reaction to events and slows down the pace of reform. The constant discussion too often means that nothing gets done. The model leads to sclerosis and stagnation. This should be evident in the socio-economic problems that for long years were waiting to be tackled, such as the law on dismissals and on pensions. There is also a view that wage moderation, while creating employment, acts as a negative force on labour productivity: because labour has remained relatively cheap, enterprises have had fewer incentives to look for innovations to save labour costs and enhance productivity. These critics maintain that the Dutch *poldermodel* is now approaching the end of its lifecycle and the government will have to change its policies to promote long-term productivity and economic growth. Some critics of the *poldermodel* stress that it gives too much influence to the trade unions, which represent only 20% of the workforce (*see* paragraph 272).

It should not be forgotten that the *poldermodel* is also a rational product of the fact that the Netherlands is only a small country and therefore that it is not so different from the actual social models in other small countries in the EU, like Belgium, Austria, Denmark and Sweden. In such countries personal relationships are much closer than in large countries which tend to narrow the gap between both sides of industry. A former Main Dutch Employers Confederation (VNO-NCW) president once said: 'In my company I dealt with trade union leaders that I personally knew because I met them frequently. In Germany you are meeting with trade union leaders only once every two years, and if you meet them it is almost immediately a conflict.'

Because of these close relationships many leading personalities in all sections of society prefer making deals instead of open conflicts. Dutch businessmen prefer to safeguard their business interests by making arrangements with their competitors instead of strife. The Netherlands was famous for its many cartels!

Chapter 2. Trade Unions and Employers' Associations

§1. Trade Unions

269. There are hundreds of trade unions in the Netherlands. Their membership varies from close to 1 million in one case to a few hundred in other cases.

The most important trade unions are grouped together in three confederations:

(a) the Confederation of Dutch Trade Unions (FNV), traditionally the most powerful confederation, which was set up in 1976 as a result of a merger of the Social Democrat confederation NVV and the Catholic confederation of trade unions NKV. The trade unions which belong to the FNV have approximately 1,140,000 members;
(b) the Protestant Trade Union Confederation (CNV), a confederation which was and is still largely Protestant inspired and which did not take part in the merger in 1976. The trade unions which belong to this confederation have approximately 280,000 members;
(c) the Confederation for Professionals (VCP) (ex MHP), a confederation of white-collar unions founded in 1972. The trade unions belonging to this confederation have approximately 100,000 members.

In addition to these three confederations there are a small number of independent unions for specific 'occupational categories' like airplane pilots and a few number of small ideological (left-wing or ultra-protestant) unions. Sometimes in a specific sector of the economy such a union may be as influential as or even more influential than the unions belonging to FNV, CNV and VCP. Moreover there are operating a number of unions that must be qualified as 'yellow unions'. All these unions together (outside the three main confederations) may have about 300,000 members.

All three Dutch confederations, FNV, CNV and VCP, are affiliated to the European Trade Union Congress and the global International Trade Union Congress.

Dutch unions have no official links with the political parties, although there is some affinity between the FNV and the Social democrat party on the one hand and between the CNV and the CDA on the other hand.

270. The FNV and the CNV have largely organized their affiliated trade unions within their respective confederations according to the principles of sector-wide trade unionism, i.e., most trade unions try to organize all employees employed in a particular economic sector, such as the building trade, manufacturing industry, public service, education or transport, irrespective of the occupational category of the employees. These unions aim to represent both the manual and the white-collar workers. Their numbers have been drastically reduced in recent years by a process of mergers.

The largest Confederation, the FNV, in recent years even undertook a total merger of all its component trade unions. This attempt was not completely successful but it anyway resulted in the situation that the Confederation FNV is now comprising one major cross-sectoral Trade Union FNV with ca. 1 million members + only a handful of very small sectoral trade unions.

The VCP embraces a great variety of mostly small trade unions.

There is in the Netherlands hardly any competition to attract members among unions belonging to the same confederation. Usually, demarcation disputes between trade unions affiliated to the same confederation are resolved by a special committee within the confederation. Competition does exist, however, among unions, which are affiliated to different confederations or are not affiliated to any confederation at all. On the basis of a gentlemen's agreement between the FNV, the CNV and the VCP, their affiliated trade unions normally refrain from 'poaching' members from the other or from entering into public disputes; they consult one another in a timely way, etc. However, a certain degree of rivalry persists, which occasionally may lead to conflicts. In recent years, for instance, it sometimes happened that the employers could not agree with unions affiliated to FNV and CNV but found a union affiliated to the ex MHP (now VCP) prepared to conclude a collective agreement with them. This irritated the FNV and CNV unions so much that they tried to bar that union from collective bargaining in other sectors of the economy. Although this conflict is over now, recently a new irritation emerged when a CNV-affiliated union signed a collective agreement (Hema) that the FNV had disapproved.

271. Normally, the national unions are run by a general board consisting of full-time officers. The Constitution of Dutch trade unions can certainly be said to be democratic in principle. In theory, members are able to exert every influence on the choice of the leaders and on decision-making. In practice, this influence is limited because of members' apathy and because it is difficult to get a hold over the policies of the leaders.

According to the rulebooks the leaders of the confederations FNV, CNV and VCP have only a limited authority over the behaviour of the affiliated unions. From a moral point their authority is somewhat higher but it should not be overestimated.

The national unions have regional and local sections. Only a few trade unions are organized on enterprise level as in the US and Japan. Because in the years following World War II the emphasis was very much on collective bargaining at national cross-sector level (*see* paragraph 281), collective bargaining at company level was much neglected. In the first decade after World War II this caused no special difficulties, but in the 1960s the lack of union presence in enterprises led to the loss of trade union membership and wildcat strikes. To check this development some unions have established their own plant-based organizations: union members within the larger companies have been organized into special units and some union officials (*bedrijfscontactpersoon*, shop stewards or *Vertrauensleute*) have been appointed to assist these units. However, union activity at company level is still rather limited. This vacuum at enterprise level is being more or less filled by the works councils (Part II, Chapter 6).

272. Union membership in the Netherlands is low. Unionization in the 1970s was about 40%. Since then it gradually dropped to about 20%, judged on a national basis. The Netherlands is now one of the least unionized countries of the EU. Some 18% of Dutch employees belong to unions affiliated to the FNV, the CNV and VCP. A further 2% are members of the other unions.

Rates of unionization vary considerably within the working population. The aforementioned percentages are dealing with both sectors (private and public) together. Unionization in the (semi-)public sector is about 30%; the average unionization in the private sector alone does not exceed 13%. Within the private sector some sectors have a rather high rate of unionization (for instance, construction workers 31% and transport 28%), while others have a low rate (for instance, IT companies 6%, retail 11%, 13% in banking). Unionization is particularly low among employees in the new professions, part-time employees, the flexible labour force, young employees, working women and migrant workers.

Unions are looking for strategies to change this situation, for example by developing new action strategies (such as 'organizing'), opening their ranks for self-employed people (ZZP-ers, not being employers themselves), creating cheap forms of membership, offering special services to their members, such as supplementary social insurance.

273. Dutch unions may be not so weak as their counterparts in for example France, but they certainly are not so strong as their counterparts in for example Belgium or the Nordic countries. The first reason for the relative weakness of the Dutch trade union movement is the rate of unionization. The second reason for this is the pluralist trade union situation in the Netherlands. Although FNV is by far the largest trade union confederation, the other components of the trade union movement are not to be neglected. They are always present with their own agenda on bargaining tables and in consultative bodies and may independently conclude collective agreements if employers cannot reach an agreement with all trade unions concerned. A third reason is the often weak financial position of the Dutch unions; they nowadays even have to rely on sponsorship by the employers' associations, which cannot be good for their independence. Because of this relative weakness but also because of the Dutch character, the Dutch unions are more moderate and prepared to compromise than many of their foreign counterparts.[282] This is not to say that the Dutch unions are powerless and completely under the influence of the employers. As long as the unions behave reasonably they maintain a high standing in public opinion and in the political arena. That is their main power base.

Some critics are even assessing that the Dutch unions have too much power, considering the low rate of unionization. The official answer to this criticism is that it appears from polls that about 80% of workers still have confidence in the unions. Moreover the trade unions are still able to mobilize broad opposition if necessary. For instance on 2 October 2004 they set the country on its feet with a demonstration of 300,000 against the government plans to kill the pre-pension schemes. Critics may counter that such a single demonstration on a sunny autumn Saturday should not be taken as a proof of real strength and is not the same as winning a strike. However, it is contrary to the Dutch mentality to go to the extreme in putting this to test.

---

282. P.T. de Beer & M. Keune, *Dutch Unions in a Time of Crisis*, in *Rough Waters: European Trade Unions in a Time of Crisis, Brussels* 221–244 (S. Lehndorff, H. Dribbush & T. Schulten eds, ETUI, 2017).

§2. EMPLOYERS' ORGANIZATIONS

274. Employers' federations exist in most sectors of the Dutch economy. For those sectors and companies where separate employers' federations do not exist or feel themselves not strong enough to cope with the unions, there is the Cross-industry Employers' Association – *Algemene Werkgevers Vereniging Nederland* (AWVN) to support employers in collective bargaining and manpower policies. In the past, Dutch employers used to organize themselves along ideological lines into Catholic, Protestant and liberal employers' associations. Such divisions were abandoned in the 1990s. At national cross-sector level, almost all major enterprises and all the employers' federations representing large and medium-sized enterprises are now affiliated to VNO-NCW, a merger of the VNO and the Dutch Confederation of Christian Employers (NCW), representing 115,000 large and medium-sized enterprises.

Small and medium-sized enterprises (except those in the agricultural sector) are for the most part members of employers' associations, affiliated to Confederation of Small and Medium Sized Enterprises (MKB-Nederland), a merger of the Dutch Royal Federation of Entrepreneurs and the Dutch Federation of Christian Entrepreneurs, representing about 150,000 medium and small enterprises.

Farmers are federated into LTO-Nederland, a merger of the Royal Committee on Dutch Agriculture, the Dutch Catholic Federation of Agriculturalists and Horticulturalists and the Dutch Christian Federation of Agriculturalists and Horticulturalists, representing 50,000 enterprises in agriculture and horticulture.

VNO-NCW, MKB-Nederland and LTO-Nederland are cooperating within the central RCO. VNO-NCW and MKB-Nederland are both affiliated to the European employers' confederation Business Europe. Since 2012 both organizations cooperate so closely that they share the same premises and much of the supporting staff, conduct preliminary consultations, etc. This, however, to the displeasure of part of the MKB rank and file.

In general, employers' organizations are structured in a democratic way – leaders are elected by members and must report to them on a regular basis. Within certain employers' associations, however, some members may be more influential than others, due to the size of the enterprise they represent.

275. Dutch employers are more union-friendly and inclined to compromise than for instance their German counterparts. The phenomenon of falling membership of employers' organizations in Germany is not matched in the Netherlands. Although there are no official statistics it is assumed that the members of employers' organizations employ 80%–90% of the Dutch labour force. Therefore the percentage of employers covered by a sector collective agreement remains quite constant at about 80% of the labour force, about the same as 10, 20, even 30 years ago. In the Netherlands the grey areas without collective agreements are not expanding as they are in Germany, and the influence of collectively agreed norms and provisions at sector level is not receding as it is in Germany. If in the Netherlands the employers one day started to desert the employers' organizations in the same numbers as they apparently are doing in Germany, this would put a bomb under the Dutch system of industrial relations, given the importance of the extension mechanism and its legal aspects in the Netherlands (*see also* paragraphs 324 et seq.). However, so far Dutch employers seem disinclined to wind up the existing system of industrial relations which guarantees them a quiet labour market. Such an approach would also be strongly rejected by Dutch public opinion and in the political arena.

§3. Trade Union Law

276. In several countries the existence and activities of the social partners are recognized as a fundamental right in the Constitution; in the Netherlands specific trade union law does not exist. Trade union rights are not explicitly mentioned as fundamental rights in the Dutch Constitution. Since 1872, however, it has not been disputed that the general freedom of association enshrined in the Constitution (Article 8) also extends to employers' and employees' organizations.

In the course of time, the Netherlands has signed a number of international documents recognizing trade union rights, such as:

- ILO Conventions 87 and 98.
- European Convention of Human Rights (*see* notably Article 11).
- ESC (*see* notably Articles 5 and 6).

Some of these provisions are directly binding before the Dutch courts and so may be considered as constitutional guarantees for trade union rights in the Netherlands.[283] Moreover the Netherlands is, being an EU Member, now also bound to the Charter of the Fundamental Rights of the EU with its Articles 12 and 28 about trade union rights.

Before World War II and also shortly afterwards there have been a small number of situations in which extremist trade unions have been opposed by the public authorities. At present every union has complete freedom of action and may freely establish its constitution. No legal form is laid down. However, an organization must have 'full legal capacity' in the sense set out in Book 2 of the Dutch CC in order to be able to enter into collective agreements (*see* paragraph 308), to propose lists of candidates for elections of works councils (*see* paragraph 381) or for participation in public law bodies (*see* paragraphs 278 et seq.). Book 2 of the CC, however, greatly facilitates access to 'full legal capacity', so employers' and employees' organizations in the Netherlands have no difficulty in satisfying this requirement. In practice, all employers' organizations and all the major trade unions have acquired this full legal capacity according to common civil law, in contrast with neighbouring EU countries, where unions often stay outside the general law of associations (Germany, Belgium) or governed by a specific trade union law (France, UK). Most of the Dutch unions and all employers' associations are officially registered at the Chamber of Commerce as associations according to the general statutory rules on associations.

283. A. Jaspers, *The Netherlands*, in *Freedom of Association of Workers and Employers in the Countries of the EU* 607–633 (F. Valdés dal Ré ed., Ministerio de Trabajo y Asuntos Sociales: Madrid, 2006).

277. The freedom of an individual worker or employer to join the association of his choice is not laid down in a specific Act of Parliament but follows from the general principles of Dutch law. Certainly, this freedom is not absolute. An association is not compelled to accept an applicant as a member. The executive board of the association can, without giving any reason, refuse an application for membership. In case of refusal the applicant may appeal to the members' meeting and finally even to the judge. In fact this hardly ever happens. The unions are too eager to embrace every new member!

Much more important is the protection of this free trade union choice of the individual workers against infringements of the employers. Since the end of World War I the employers in the Netherlands have come to accept the trade union rights of their workers and no serious cases in this field have been reported. Would such a case occur it is certain that the judges would prohibit any discrimination against workers because of trade union membership on the basis of the general provisions of the Dutch law on employment contracts, making reference to the international guarantees for trade union rights. Because of this the Dutch Parliament has never enacted special statutory provisions to protect trade union rights, apart from a provision which mentions the 'membership of and participation in the activities on behalf of a trade union' in the catalogue of prohibited dismissals (Article 7:670(5) CC, *see* paragraph 198).

In some countries, employees can be obliged to belong to a trade union (the compulsory membership or the 'closed shop'). In the Netherlands an obligation of this type is exceptional: until recently it only existed in the printing industry and among journalists. A statutory provision in Dutch law considers a compulsory membership clause in a collective agreement to be valid as long as the clause refers to all the unions operating in the industry concerned; it is void, however, if one or more unions are excluded (Article 1(3) ACA). Moreover, these types of clauses cannot be extended *erga omnes* to an entire sector of industry (*see* paragraph 325). In case law already years ago the judges required unions, which operate closed shops, to provide for an exception on reasons of 'conscience', but it is questionable whether Dutch courts would currently accept any kind of 'closed shop', seeing the development of the case law of the European Court of Human Rights in this area. Still, as said before, the 'closed shop' is not popular in the Netherlands. Traditionally most unions consider themselves as representing the interests of all workers and not just the interests of their members. Most Dutch workers would dislike unions operating a closed shop, and the unions are reluctant to fill their ranks with unwilling captives.

Pressure to join a union can also be brought upon non-unionized workers by the reservation of more favourable terms of employment exclusively for union members. According to classic legal theory clauses to this effect in collective agreements would presumably be legal, although they cannot be extended *erga omnes* by the Minister of Social Affairs and Employment (*see* paragraph 325). However, this kind of benefit reservation has so far been used very seldom, again, because it would be very unpopular among the workers as appeared each time that trade union leaders suggested such clauses.

The only support that trade unions have acquired is in the way of employers' subsidies. Under most collective agreements employers pay to the unions a certain amount of money a year (in 2018 EUR 20) for each member of the unions, which are party to the collective agreement. Sometimes this money is used by the unions to give their members training facilities or certain bonuses, most of the times this money is used by the unions to finance the costs of their involvement in the process of collective bargaining. This habit, which is now widespread in the Netherlands, is disquieting as it may jeopardize the 'independence' of the Dutch trade union movement.

Several collective agreements contain provisions allowing employees to take part in trade union activities and allowing the trade union to appoint shop stewards within the enterprise, to organize meetings at workplaces, to use the intranet, etc. Such provisions were promoted by a Recommendation of the Foundation of Labour of 1990, issued as an alternative to statutory regulation of this topic, which is lacking in the Netherlands. This Recommendation was repeated and reinforced by a Recommendation of the *Stichting van de Arbeid* on this issue in 1997. It called upon the social partners concluding collective agreements at sector or enterprise level to provide for facilities and legal protection for the active trade union members in the enterprises. In both Recommendations the *Stichting van de Arbeid* emphasized that the presence of trade unions in the enterprise is not meant as a formal bargaining structure inside the enterprise. It is merely there to assist the active members of the unions in performing their tasks.

The EU GDPR (*see* paragraph 107) limits employers and trade union in the way they may process data about trade union membership of workers. Employers may only register the trade union membership of their workers if they have explicitly given their consent for that. Trade unions may not share the lists of their members with third parties without the consent of the employees concerned.

§4. Representativeness

278. As the establishment of employers' and employees' organizations is free in the Netherlands and has effectively led to a multitude of organizations, the problem of their representativeness became evident. It was inevitable that certain rights should be reserved solely for those organizations considered to be representative.

In the Netherlands, the SER undertook the task of laying down criteria for assessing representativeness, a task it achieved by issuing directives. The initial directives adopted in 1954 essentially gave a monopoly to the organizations affiliated to the CNV and the precursors of the FNV. These criteria proved unsatisfactory in the 1970s when the white-collar unions attracted an increasing number of members and became organized in a much more effective way.

During the 1970s, the white-collar unions used social pressure to acquire the places due to them in consultative, administrative and management bodies. Consequently, in 1977, the SER reviewed its 1954 criteria, providing them with greater objectivity. In 2000 the SER issued a formal Regulation on this issue. On that basis it is now possible to lodge an administrative appeal against decisions to admit or reject prospective members of consultative, administrative or management bodies. This administrative appeal, however, is hardly ever used.

All the aforementioned only regards the determination of employers and trade unions, which want to take part in all sorts of administrative, consultative and legal bodies. It is not decisive for collective bargaining on wages and working conditions. For representativeness in the collective bargaining process, *see* paragraphs 311–312.

Chapter 3. The Neo-corporatist System

§1. History

279. In the Netherlands the hostile attitude of the employers vis-à-vis the trade unions faded away after the end of World War I. Stimulated by the government, employers and unions set up various forms of joint consultative bodies, participated in governing boards of social security funds, concluded collective agreements, etc. Between 1918 and 1965 this entire movement was very much stimulated by the social philosophy of the Christian parties, which dominated the Dutch Parliament (*see* paragraph 12). Since the 1880s Social Calvinist and Roman-Catholic thinkers had advocated a reconstruction of economic life along the lines of self-determination of interest groups (in German: *Berufsständische Ordnung*) according to the ideas borrowed from Von Ketteler, Kraetzer, Von Schäffle, Von Vogelsang, Cathrein, Pesch, Weisz, De Mun, Moriseau, Depasse and others. These ideas gained momentum after World War I. The Dutch Parliament supported this movement by instituting the High Council of Labour (1923), issuing an Act on Collective Labour Disputes (1923) and two Acts on collective agreements (1927 and 1937), but also by adapting, in 1922 and 1937, the Dutch Constitution to allow the attribution of lawmaking powers to industrial and professional bodies. In 1933 the Trade Councils Act (*Bedrijfsradenwet*) was brought into the statute book. According to this Act the Crown could in the various sectors of the economy establish Trade Councils (*Bedrijfsraden*), consisting of an equal number of employers' and workers' representatives under an independent chairman. The Act met with much apathy among workers and opposition among employers and the twenty-one Trade Councils that came into existence only possessed the status of being a forum of consultation and cooperation. This process was intensified during World War II. Many captains of industry and trade union leaders came to know and respect each other better in exile, in captivity and in resistance movements. All this led the foundations of new institutional developments after World War II, such as the establishment, by the social partners themselves, of the Foundation of Labour in 1945 and it paved the way for long years of a very centralized wages policy in the Netherlands (paragraphs 281 et seq.). At the same time the idea of self-determination of interest groups in economic life finally seemed to gain the victory. In agriculture and the mining industry Trade Councils were established that exercised special lawmaking powers.

280. In 1950 Parliament passed the Organization of Industry Act – *Wet op de Bedrijfsorganisatie* (OIA), which – besides setting up the Social-Economic Council (*see* paragraphs 290 et seq.) – provided for the set-up of *bedrijfschappen* (joint industrial boards) for each sector of the economy and of *productschappen* (commodity boards) for each chain of products (from producing and manufacturing to selling). The government could grant these boards wide powers to organize such a business sector. The *bedrijfschappen* consisted of an equal number of workers' and employers' representatives and could be attributed advisory as well as lawmaking powers in both economic and social affairs (*see* paragraph 27). In subsequent years about forty of such boards have been established, covering about 15% of the Dutch working population, notably in agriculture, mining, house painting, retail trade, hotel and catering. The Act failed to strike roots in most sectors in which medium size and large enterprises prevail. And even in the sectors where it was materialized the powers of those boards only rarely encompassed labour relations and working conditions. So only in very few cases binding 'orders' containing employees' rights have been issued. One example has been an order of the Joint Industrial Board for the retail sector containing some minimum rules for working times and holidays with pay.

Over the two last decades the government and Parliament considered abolishing the system but it was kept alive after a series of minor amendments modernizing the OIA. Moreover, by a process of mergers and liquidations the number of boards had been reduced to about fourteen. Nevertheless the debate about the wisdom of maintaining this system each time re-emerged, and in 2014 the Dutch Parliament agreed with a complete dismantling of the system per 1 January 2015.[284] Only the top of this Structure, the Social-Economic Council, was maintained. The Organisation of Industry Act was renamed in Act on the Social-Economic Council (ASEC) (*see* paragraphs 290–293).

§2. Wage Formation Policies

281. In the Netherlands the public authorities have been a major socio-economic actor for a long time, especially and very clearly since 1945. This development was shaped by the theories of Keynes, which held sway over Dutch politics for several decades. According to these theories, the public authorities should play a central role in pursuing often conflicting economic objectives, such as maintaining the balance of payments, a sufficient level of investment, a stable price level, full employment, the reasonable redistribution of income and budgetary balance.

Intervention of the government in the economy in general and in wage formation in particular was already emerging before World War II. The AECA of 1937 besides giving the Minister the power to extend *erga omnes* the scope of collective agreements, also gives him the power to declare null and void certain provisions of a collective agreement (Articles 8–9 AECA). However, this competence has almost never been used although these articles are still on the statute book. State intervention in wage formation was vastly strengthened by the Extraordinary Decree on Labour Relations 1945. The Decree instituted a Board of State Mediators whose members were appointed by, but were otherwise independent of, the Minister of Social Affairs. The Board received, *inter alia*, the authority to issue binding rules concerning wages and other conditions of employment. Collective agreements had to be in accordance with these rules and could only be applied after approval by the Board. To ensure compliance with the rulings of the board employers were prohibited – under threat of criminal sanctions – from paying wages other than those approved by the Board. The Board functioned under the 'general directives' of the Minister of Social Affairs, which set the basic guidelines for annual wage changes. These general directives, in turn, represented the general social-economic policy of the Cabinet.

284. Act of 17 Dec. 2014, Stb. 2014, 571.

It is in this context that the public authorities exerted considerable influence, with the 'controlled' wage policy, which was pursued from 1945 to 1958. In practice the system was not as dictatorial as it may seem here. The cooperation of organized labour and management was sought for and achieved by the government; the system could not have operated otherwise. The 'general directives' were issued by the government only after consultation with the Foundation of Labour, a bipartite body consisting of the main workers' and employers' federations (*see* paragraph 290); a special committee of the Foundation was consulted before the Board of State Mediators used its authority in specific cases, i.e., before approving or rejecting the terms of a collective agreement. So, in a way, the system could be described as a system of collective bargaining at national level – with the public authorities as the principal actor. This system of centralized wage determination was deemed necessary to keep labour costs low and preserve competitive Dutch price levels in world markets (*see* paragraphs 1 et seq.). In the first 15 years of its existence the system worked reasonably well. The post-war reconstruction went fairly smoothly with virtually no labour unrest.

The public authorities at that time were made up of a centre-left coalition government comprising Social Democrats and Christian Democrats. In these years almost all political forces were dedicated followers of the economic theory of Keynes, from which they deduced that the government should maintain final responsible for the development of economic growth, employment, monetary policies, prices and wages. Therefore it was as a matter of course that the state developed a tradition of intervention in the process of collective bargaining. This could happen because in the Netherlands nobody saw the freedom of collective bargaining as a fundamental principle. This made the Netherlands so much different from, notably, Germany where industrial relations law since 1949 has been dominated by the principle of bargaining autonomy (*Tarifautonomie*), which the German judiciary had given constitutional status based on Article 9.3 of the German Constitution.

282. After 1958 this rigid wage control system fell into decline for a variety of reasons. The establishment of a European Common Market led to a booming economy, shortages of workers and consequently a 'wage explosion' between 1964 and 1966. The Social Democrats left the government in 1958. After 1958 until 1989, the Netherlands has been ruled by centre-right governments comprising Christian Democrats and liberals, with the only exception of coalitions of Christian democrats and social democrats in 1965–1966 and 1972–1977 (*see* paragraph 12). With the socialists no longer in the government, trade unions were less prepared to restrain themselves. They were increasingly dissatisfied that the centralized wage policy did not leave them much room for bargaining at sectoral and company level. Finally, the general mood of democratization and participation was not conducive to maintaining a stringent government control over wage bargaining.

So, in 1970 new legislation was enacted – the WDA, which replaced large sections of the Extraordinary Decree on Labour Relations 1945. In principle it gave the contracting parties of collective agreements freedom in their wage policy but left the door open for public-authority intervention in this area (Articles 8–11, WDA).

Since then and until the mid-1980s, the government has attempted every year to reach an agreement with employers' and employees' confederations as regards the outlines of wage adjustment, within the broader context of socio-economic policy. This social dialogue should ideally lead to 'central agreements', but they were only rarely achieved. After every failure of this tripartite social dialogue at the highest level, politicians and the media always demanded intervention by the public authorities. The public authorities used their powers to intervene effectively on several occasions between 1970 and 1982. At first, such intervention often led to political and social conflicts (strikes). Legal problems cropped up later when the unions took this intervention before the courts. The courts refused, however, to prohibit public-authority intervention. The problem was even brought before the ILO,[285] which, after a few years, became more critical and, through an expert report by Professor Windmuller, censured this repeated intervention in wage formation. This opinion was issued in 1982, at the very moment when a new centre-right coalition government had come to power. This government, like all centre-right governments in Western Europe, intended to give greater scope to the play of free-market forces. It ruled out state intervention in wage determination and, from an economic point of view, there was no longer any need for this since the Netherlands had a record unemployment level and the unions were consequently in a relatively weak position. Excessive wage increases were no longer to be feared. Dutch policymakers could then adopt the recommendations of the ILO's Windmuller Commission without any problem.

283. In the same year, 1982, the social partners concluded a major agreement (the Wassenaar Agreement) to overcome the recession by reducing working time and repealing the cost of living escalator clauses in collective agreements (*see* paragraph 116). Since 1982 there has been no intervention in wage determination in the private sector. The 1970 WDA, which had left the door open for intervention, was modified on this crucial point in 1986. From then on the public authorities could intervene only in the event of extreme urgency caused by external factors. This new deal was reflected in an amendment of Article 10 of the WDA, which since 1986 has read: 'Our Minister can take general measures concerning wages and other conditions of employment if such measures are, according to his judgment, required in suddenly arising emergency situations, caused by one or more external factors.' Such measures – concerning a wages freeze or wage rises cap – should be temporary (not exceeding six months, this period can be extended with at most another six months) and should be accompanied by the announcement of other relevant measures. Such interventions have not occurred since 1986. The provision in the AECA of 1937 (Article 8), offering the possibility that provisions of a collective agreement are declared null and void by the Minister (*see* paragraph 281), is still on the statute book, but it has not been used in recent decades. Its use would be contested on the ground that it is opposed to the fundamental idea that social partners have the right to free collective bargaining according to several international labour standards applicable to the Netherlands (*see* paragraph 276).

---

285. K. Boonstra, *The ILO and The Netherlands: Different Views Concerning Government Influence on the Relationship Between Workers and Employers* (1996).

284. During the 1960s and the 1970s a close linking of the statutory minimum wage, the level of social security benefits and the wages of civil servants to each other and to the wage growth in the private sector was established – symbols of the very 'solidaristic society' which was a much-desired political aim in that period. Since the 1980s this ambition has been gradually abandoned to give more leeway to differences due to the working of market mechanisms. So the formal linking of the wages of civil servants to the private sector was abolished at the beginning of the 1980s. Also the linking of the statutory minimum wage and the level of social security benefits to wage growth in the private sector was interrupted, but since 1994 this linkage has been restored (*see* paragraph 10). It is still a highly estimated characteristic of the Dutch social model, which is a strong motive for the government and the social partners to seek agreement over wages and economic developments.

The Dutch government remains committed to the principle of wage growth within reasonable and moderate limits, while the social partners carefully monitor the government's socio-economic policy in order to determine their position on wage policy. The harmonious growth of all the kinds of income has almost become an obsessive concern in Dutch policy. This concern also explains why the government feels so involved in the determination of wages in the private sector, although at present it intervenes in the private sector by persuasion and indirect pressure rather than by direct intervention.

285. Each year the government encouraged the conclusion of a cross-sector agreement (*Sociaal Akkoord*) between the large confederations of employers and trade unions about the main items of socio-economic development. Sometimes this succeeds, sometimes it fails.

For instance in 2003 such a *Sociaal Akkoord* could be agreed, providing for a zero wage increase for 2004 and an 'approaching zero' increase for 2005, while leaving scope for negotiating one-off payments in sectors and companies which were performing well. Also in this agreement were: new initiatives to promote youth employment; conversion of subsidized jobs into proper jobs; and additional money to be made available to people living on the social minimum for more than three years; sickness insurance premiums to be reduced by EUR 24.50 in 2004; postponement of the plan to repeal tax breaks for pre-pension and VUT schemes until 2006; dropping of the plan to deduct severance payments from unemployment benefits; scrapping of the plan to take partner's earnings into consideration in awarding employee disability benefits.

In 2009 a *Sociaal Akkoord* could be agreed providing for an almost zero wage increase in exchange for a special commitment of employers to create an additional ten thousands traineeships for youngsters, a specific partial lay-off scheme for business touched by the financial crisis and relaxation of the requirements for recovering to pension funds hit by the financial crisis.

In 2013 a *Sociaal Akkoord* could be agreed on a moderation of initial projects of the government to cut government spending, to recast dismissal protection and unemployment benefits and to reform the pension system (*see* paragraph 195).

The terms of such cross-sector agreements do not have a legal status. They are mere gentlemen's agreements, but the civil relationship between the social partners in the Netherlands guarantees its implementation.

In the past, when a draft *Sociaal Akkoord* seemed possible, it was concluded under the reservation of the consent of the majority of the affiliates to the confederations. In recent years FNV has submitted such draft agreements to the approval of the entire membership of all its affiliates (most recently in the *Sociaal Akkoord* on a new reform of the pension system, 2019).

286. The public authorities have continued to intervene directly in the area of civil servants' wages since in this area they are the employer themselves. This involves (including educational staff) about 15% of the working population.

Traditionally the terms and conditions of employment of civil servants have been set by the government unilaterally. However, since the 1920s the government negotiated them with the trade unions. After 1945 under the then-existing wages policies the yearly adaptation of the wages of civil servants was automatically linked to the average trend in private-sector collective bargaining, which made substantial negotiations particularly for the civil servants superfluous. When finally in the 1980s this automatic linkage was abandoned, independent negotiations on the working conditions and the terms of employment of civil servants re-emerged as a necessity. Ever since, from a procedural perspective, the fixation of working conditions and terms of employment in the public sector increasingly resembles the collective bargaining system in the private sector. In 1995 the rules for the new system of negotiated fixing of working conditions and terms of employment in the public sector were laid down in the Civil Service Act. However, as from the 1 January 2020 the fast majority of the Civil Service Sector shall be brought under exactly the same legal system of collective labour relations as the private sector (*see* paragraph 54).

287. Until the beginning of the 1990s the public authorities have kept control over wage increases for employees of semi-public organizations (hospitals, human services, radio and television, etc.), about 10% of the working population. This control too was subject of criticism by the ILO and was finally abolished in 1994.[286]

In contrast to the situation in other countries such as France and Italy, the Netherlands does not have an income policy conducted explicitly by the public authorities through state enterprises since such enterprises have always been very rare in the Netherlands (actually they employ less than 3% of the total working population). It seemed to become even weaker as a consequence of the trend to privatization, which has already relegated the Dutch Post and Telecom and the Dutch railways to the private sector. However, in contrast, the financial crisis of 2008 brought a new, but only short-lived wave of state entrepreneurship by the acquisition of a major Dutch bank, ABN AMRO and a high state involvement in another one, ING.

288. As has been said before, most statutory instruments for a centralized wage policy were abandoned in the 1980s. One of the consequences has been that the gap between the various levels of income has increased in recent years. This initially has

286. *See* W.G.M. Plessen, *Collectief onderhandelen in de zorgsector* (1996); on pp. 363–371 may be found an English-language description and discussion of government intervention in the fixation of wages and employment conditions in the semi-public sector.

been accepted as a consequence of the prevailing sway of market economics in a globalized society, but recent years have seen mounting criticism on the *excessive pay rises of top managers*. Notably the Dutch Chief Executive Officers (CEOs) of Stock Market companies are earning in average 8.2 million dollars a year, the third-highest in the world. Their salaries are – in average – thirty times the median employee's income in the Netherlands (EUR 37,000 a year).[287]

At first the Dutch government tried to mitigate this development by an Act of Parliament providing for disclosure of executive pay in public service, in semi-public service and in companies operating on the stock market.[288] Moreover in all companies (plus fifty employees) works councils became entitled to be informed about the salaries in the company (*see* paragraph 385).

As far as the private sector is concerned the government confined itself to these regulations. It further relied on the so-called Dutch Corporate Governance Code (*see* paragraph 365). However even in its latest version of 2017 this Code failed to include a cap on the executive pay. It is only provided that companies must publish a report on the remuneration including *inter alia* the pay ratios in the company.[289] In addition to that the legislator recently entrusted the works councils of the larger enterprises (100 + workers) with special powers to discuss with the employer the pay differences in the enterprise and even to usher its opinion in the general meeting of shareholders (*see* paragraphs 379, 385 and 395).[290]

As from 1 January 2015 banks and insurance companies are statutorily prohibited to pay its personnel more than 20% of their salaries in bonuses.[291] This law is actually under some political attack as it is seen as an impediment for financial institutions to instal their seat in the Netherlands.

The Dutch legislator was more energetic concerning the executive pay in public and semi-public institutions. In 2012 the Act on the disclosure of executive pay in public and semi-public service was supplemented with provisions putting a cap on these salaries: Act on the Regulation of Executive Pay – *Wet Normering Topinkomens* (AREP).[292] As from 1 January 2015[293] for all new appointments of top managers in the entire public sector and the vast majority of the semi-public sector there is a salary cap in force of ca. EUR 160,000 yearly remuneration (EUR 194,000 if pensions and costs are included) (Article 2.3 AREP). The Act was on detailed points corrected by an Amendment Act of 2017.[294]

289. Both employers and employees are increasingly interested in *decentralizing collective bargaining*. There is nowadays a strong tendency to give collective agreements, and certainly those on sector level, a more or less framework character. Details should be settled at enterprise level either in agreements with trade unions or in agreements with the works councils. Most of the time details are settled in

287. De Volkskrant, 13 Jul. 2019.
288. Act of 9 Sep. 2006, Stb. 2006, 286.
289. Parliamentary Papers 31083.
290. Act of Parliament 15 Jun. 2018, Stb. 2018, 221; Parliamentary Papers 34494.
291. Act of 28 Jan. 2015, Stb. 2015, 45.
292. Act of 15 Nov. 2012, Stb. 2012, 583; Parliamentary Papers 32600.
293. Act of 30 Dec. 2014, Stb. 2014, 588; Parliamentary Papers 33978.
294. Act of 22 Mar. 2017, Stb. 2017, 151.

agreements with the works councils because the trade unions only seldom have bargaining agents at the level of the enterprises (*see* paragraph 271).

Some companies already prefer to completely circumvent the trade unions and only to negotiate with the works councils (or even with yellow unions). This is a contested phenomenon in present Dutch industrial relations. Moreover the internationalization of companies has a creeping impact on company wages policies. Employers are nowadays less inspired by merely national or even patriotic considerations in the formation of their wages policies. They are now primarily driven by shareholder values of increasingly global dimension.

So actually the main challenge is: how to combine a free system of wage formation by the social partners with:

(a) the necessity to prevent labour costs from rising too much in order not to jeopardize the competitiveness of the Netherlands;
(b) the desirability of keeping in harmony the development of wages in the private sector with those in the (semi-) public sector and with social security benefits.

Both these challenges require a certain amount of centralization of collective bargaining, and this exactly in a period in which industry emphasizes the need for decentralization.

§3. Institutions

290. Due to the long history of centralized wage policy, the practice of institutionalized consultation and cooperation of the social partners is well developed at all levels of the Dutch society.

Employers' and employees' organizations meet regularly and intensively either at sector level or at enterprise level in order to conclude collective agreements and discuss all socio-economic matters relating to the sector or enterprise (placement, vocational training, employee benefits and other social welfare arrangements). In addition representatives of employees' and employers' confederations meet at national level, in some cases on a bipartite basis, and in others on a tripartite basis (with government representatives).

In the Netherlands two forums for social dialogue at national cross-sector level have been created:

- the bipartite *Stichting van de Arbeid* (Foundation of Labour), a private law body which was set up at the end of World War II by representatives of the major employers' and employees' confederations. This Foundation in fact is no more than a board composed on an equal bipartite basis by the leading figures from: on the employees' side, the FNV, CNV and VCP and on the employers' side, VNO-NCW, MKB-Nederland and LTO-Nederland;
- the tripartite SER, a public law body created and regulated by the OIA of 1950 (*see* paragraph 280), now renamed into the ASEC. The confederations of employers' associations and trade unions each hold eleven seats; in addition to these, eleven further seats are reserved for independent members, such as the Chairman

of the Nederlandsche Bank (Dutch Central Bank), the Director of the Dutch Planning Office and some university professors. SER committees also embrace top officials representing ministries which – although formally only observers – play an influential role.

Each member of the SER has a substitute. The employers' and workers' members of the SER are appointed by their organizations, while the independent members are nominated by the government. The SER is financed out of the money of the General Unemployment Fund and thus in fact financed by the Dutch employers (Article 54 ASEC), enabling it to have a considerable secretariat. The *Stichting van de Arbeid* has only limited financial resources and does not therefore have much in the way of offices. Both the SER and the *Stichting van de Arbeid* have their headquarters in the same building (belonging to the SER) in The Hague. Most of the leading personalities of the social partners serve on both bodies.

291. There are obvious differences between the two bodies.

Within the *Stichting van de Arbeid* the social partners are among themselves; they may confer together in camera. In the SER, however, a third party has to be taken into account: the independent members and the governmental observers. The deliberations of the SER, or at least of its plenary sessions, are public. The President of the SER is an independent person, while the *Stichting van de Arbeid* is alternatively chaired by the presidents of the VNO-NCW and the FNV. The *Stichting van de Arbeid* is occasionally used to explore the outlines of cross-sector strategy on working conditions. Within the framework of this body, cross-sector collective negotiations between employers and trade unions may take place. Sometimes this may lead to genuine cross-sector agreements about, for instance, provisions concerning training, career development and employability, labour conditions, etc. Most of the times this results in the adoption of recommendations directed to the social partners that are involved in the sector/enterprise level of the economy. Neither such cross-sector agreements nor these recommendations have a formal legal status but they may more or less influence collective bargaining at sector or enterprise level and even influence case law on employment contracts (*see* paragraph 103).

Moreover, the *Stichting van de Arbeid* is frequently invited by the government to give its opinion on labour law and social security matters. If the government wants to consult the social partners at Cabinet level rather than at civil-servant level, such consultations take the form of a meeting between a delegation of the Cabinet and the *Stichting van de Arbeid.*

Some years ago it had become a custom, that twice a year a roundtable-discussion between the government and social partners took place in the Stichting van de Arbeid. In spring there was a general presentation from the side of the government on the issues of financial, fiscal and budget policies for the next year. In the autumn, after the detailed plans of the government for the next year have been published, there was a discussion about these plans and measures, indirectly in relation to collective bargaining. This is now no longer practised.

292. It is evident from the above that the SER has to leave the initiative to the *Stichting van de Arbeid* as regards consultation about actual working conditions and socio-economic policies on the short-time. The SER is the main player when the other aspects of socio-economic policy have to be discussed. Indeed, the SER prefers to deal with subjects in a more comprehensive socio-economic perspective. This certainly applies to labour market policy, labour law, social security and works councils, but it also includes public expenditure, industrial policy, corporate law, environmental policies, energy, innovation and education. At its height some 300 advices were delivered each year. To that end the SER usually meets *in pleno* once a month. The primary items on the agenda are mostly drafts of advices on various topics. The preparatory work is carried out by permanent commissions assisted by the SER secretariat. Those commissions, just like the Council itself, are of a tripartite composition, i.e., consist of members of workers' and employers' organizations and independent experts. Additionally, ministerial representatives participate, not in an official capacity but as observers of the activities. The ministerial representatives thus maintain the contact between the SER and the various governmental departments, keeping both sides informed on the progress made. The meetings of the SER committees are in private. The final advice of the SER is mostly published in book form and on the Internet. Until 1996 the Cabinet was obliged by statute to consult the SER on all the important social and economic affairs. This obligation was then repealed, but the habit to consult the SER has remained in practice.

293. Notwithstanding all this, the differences between the respective roles of the SER and the *Stichting van de Arbeid* are hard to define properly. This duality is best explained by its historical context: the *Stichting van de Arbeid* was set up in 1945, when the SER did not yet exist, and was recognized by the government as its main partner in the area of wage policy after the war (*see* paragraph 281). When the SER was set up in 1950 it did not oust the *Stichting van de Arbeid* from this role. It should be noted, however, that wage policy since the middle of the 1960s has moved in the direction of deregulation and the scope of action of the *Stichting van de Arbeid* has weakened since then. The *Stichting van de Arbeid* continues, however, to operate because employers' and employees' confederations appreciate this forum where they can meet on an intimate basis, out of the public eye. So the continued coexistence of these two bodies presumably serves best the strategies of the social partners.

It is quite common for representatives of the confederations of trade unions' and employers' organizations in the Foundation of Labour and the Social Economic Council to indulge in lengthy negotiations in order to issue their advice unanimously. They know that a unanimous advice in practice can hardly be ignored by government and Parliament, whereas this impact is missed if they issue divided opinions.

Famous examples of the great influence of the Foundation of Labour and the SER on socio-economic policymaking in the Netherlands were:

– in 1982, in the midst of the worst post-war economic recession, the so-called Wassenaar Agreement was concluded within the framework of the Foundation of Labour, relating to a ADV, an agreement which was obtained in exchange for a moderation of pay rises;

- in 1993, on the eve of the realization of the single market in the EU, a unanimous advice of the Foundation of Labour on the economic aims and strategies to pursue (*Een Nieuwe Koers*), which urged a more decentralized and less standardized model of collective bargaining;
- in 2013 the Sociaal Akkoord on dismissal law and other labour market aspects (*see* paragraph 195).

294. There used to be a number of other institutions in the Netherlands in which representatives of trade unions and employers organizations could meet frequently – consultative bodies in the area of social security and manpower policies, the administrative boards of pension funds, joint industry committees (*see* paragraph 399) and joint sector boards (*see* paragraph 280) – but their number is diminishing as recent years have seen a reduction of the involvement of trade unions and employers' organizations in the area of statutory social security and manpower policies (*see* paragraph 251).

Chapter 4. Collective Bargaining

§1. The System of Collective Agreements

295. Collective agreements appeared in the Netherlands by the end of the nineteenth century, first in the printing industry and among the diamond cutters in Amsterdam. The first nationwide collective agreement was concluded in 1913 in the cigar industry.

Since World War II the Netherlands is characterized by a continuous process of negotiation between the social partners. Most of the collective bargaining is done at national sector level, such as for healthcare (400,000 workers), metallurgy (330,000), hotels/restaurants/pubs (320,000), education (270,000), agriculture (215,000), supermarkets (200,000), engineering (150,000) and road transport (130,000). Those industry-wide agreements cover some 65%–70% of all employees.

Although the absolute number of company-level agreements is rather high, only a minority of the workers (10%–15%) is covered by a collective agreement at the level of the enterprise. Some of these agreements are concluded with large employers, such as Rabo (41,000), ING (30,000), KLM (26,000), Post NL (25,000) and ABN AMRO (22,000). Such agreements are important for the trends in collective bargaining even if those agreements are still of comparatively modest significance in macroeconomic terms. Moreover, their importance varies considerably from sector to sector: in industries dominated by a small number of companies – such as the mineral oil industry, the chemical industry and banking – company collective agreements are the most important type of agreement.

The coverage rate of collective agreements is already since many years stable at ca. 80% of the workers.

This may seem remarkable against the background of the low rate of union membership (*see* paragraph 272). The high number of persons covered by collective agreements is mainly caused by the high degree of organization of the employers (*see* paragraph 275) combined with the active application of the legal tool of extension of the collective agreements *erga omnes* (*see* paragraph 324).

The positive appreciation of collective bargaining at the level of sectors and companies has been justified by the need to protect wages against lower-cost competition. The sector collective agreement is a major instrument by which wages and working conditions are taken 'out of competition'. The Dutch still believe very strongly in the idea that employers should compete on the quality of their products and not on wage costs. Moreover, Dutch employers are still inclined to prefer the rigidities of collective agreements to the social unrest that could result from a breakdown of the system of sector collective bargaining. The fact that without collectively negotiated wage norms at sector level each company has to create its own comprehensive system of employment rules and that this may produce conflicts in many companies is one of the main reasons why Dutch employers still prefer sector collective agreements, even in sectors in which such agreements are rigid and could be avoided because of trade union weakness.

In the Netherlands it is rare for an enterprise to be cumulatively bound by both a sector and a company agreement, as is often the case in France and Italy. Usually,

Dutch enterprises are bound either by one or the other, although supplementary bargaining at enterprise level is gaining ground (*see* paragraph 300). If an employer wants to negotiate a collective agreement at company level he may leave the employers federation and then he is free to negotiate such an agreement with the unions, after the last sector agreement has expired (*see* paragraph 315). However, if there is normally a collective agreement extended *erga omnes* applicable in that sector, such a move does not make much sense (*see* paragraphs 324 et seq.). Large companies sometimes have the privilege to be exempted from the coverage of the sector collective agreement as they have an own company agreement with the unions, but nevertheless remain a member of the employers' federation for the sake of coordinating strategies.

296. In most sectors Collective bargaining is a regular event once every year or two years. In those bargaining rounds the unions and the employers most of the time end up by a renewal of the existing collective agreement. Wages are adapted with a percentage, which tends to be close to the index of price inflation, sometimes a percentage point more, sometimes a percentage point less. Both parties tend to avoid extreme positions, as this would endanger the 'system of linkages' (*see* paragraphs 284 and 289) and therefore would be very much disliked by public opinion in the Netherlands and consequently weaken their status in a collective conflict.

After the centralized governmental wage policies of the 1950s and the 1960s were gradually abandoned in the 1970s/1980s (*see* paragraphs 282 et seq.), the central confederations of trade unions and employers yearly tried to give some guidance to the process of collective bargaining by negotiating 'central recommendations' for the forthcoming bargaining round. However, in most years talks between the confederations failed to reach an agreement on such 'central recommendations' and often such talks were not even started. All-industry collective bargaining between the leading figures of the employer' and employees' confederations has less chances on the issue of pay than on issues like working hours, employment, social security, in which they are more likely to reach 'common conclusions'.

Wage leadership in the Netherlands is not as distinctive as it is, for instance, in Germany. While in Germany the metal industry sector plays a crucial role in determining overall wage levels, in the Netherlands wage leadership is much more diffuse (Philips, the ports, construction, and so on). Nevertheless, although the various collective agreements at sector or enterprise level are concluded independently of one another, there are some links.

In the first place because the trade unions are coordinating internally their strategies. This certainly happens within the FNV, which is party to almost all collective agreements. Also the unions affiliated to CNV and VCP tend to coordinate their approach to each bargaining process as far as possible. Employers, too, are coordinating their strategic positions during collective bargaining in the various sectors and enterprises, through their confederations (VNO-NCW, MKB-Nederland and LTO-Nederland) and the AWVN (*see* paragraph 274). In such cases in which the central organizations try to coordinate the strategies of their affiliated organizations they used to rely on 'resistance funds' that can be called upon by the affiliated organizations in the event of a conflict. However, some years ago VNO-NCW abolished its resistance fund and the strike funds of the trade unions are no longer well filled

(FNV fund: some EUR 20 million?). The result of all this is that although collective bargaining is officially taken place at the levels of occupational sector or enterprise, there has always been a tendency towards some centralization. It is no longer as overwhelming as it was during the period 1945–1960, but it is always lurking around the corner.

297. Since the 1980s both employers and unions became increasingly interested in decentralizing collective bargaining. Sometimes there is even some decentralization to the level of the individual workers. Unilever, in 1999, was the first Dutch company to introduce *à la carte* terms and conditions of employment: within certain parameters employees are able to exchange pay in return for extra days' leave, determine their own weekly working time and decide whether or not to accept payment or compensatory time off in return for overtime working. This policy was much applauded by the smallest Dutch trade union confederation, the VCP-predecessor MHP (white collars), and by some sociologists, who see this model as the future of collective bargaining in an increasingly individualized society. A number of collective agreements (only covering a minority of the employees) nowadays contain this so-called personal choice budget, which the employer can use to sell or buy free time, travel allowances or to finance education and training at an average of EUR 700 a year.[295]

Several employers would like to replace automatic yearly pay increases in the wages scales with new arrangements whereby the payment of the bonus is linked to achieving profit and turnover goals, such as payment by results, performance-related pay and financial participation (*see* paragraph 128). Notably in 1999–2000 there was a drive in the Netherlands for more flexible wage forms. In the Netherlands no legal restrictions on a switch to flexible remuneration exist, apart from the banking sector (*see* paragraph 288). However, the Dutch trade unions have for ideological reasons long resisted this trend. In recent times they seem increasingly prepared to accept some forms of flexible wage systems, but they rejected others. In several sectors the opposition of the unions has been sufficient to put a brake on this development. Moreover the employers themselves were divided on the issue: some disliked flexible wage structures because they are too cumbersome, requiring detailed assessment of their employees. The 'promise' of such pay systems, of course, is that they may result in higher labour productivity. The flipside is that they can often leave employees with too little money in their pockets. Another risk is that employees become excessively money-driven by such systems to the detriment of their health and/or the quality of their work.

298. Of course the collective determination of wages and other employment conditions by way of collective agreements with the trade unions is not a law of the Medes and Persians. In theory companies have the option to avoid collective bargaining with the trade unions and instead fix the wages unilaterally. The industrial relations in the US and the UK show us that unilateral wage formation is a real possibility. Such wage structures can be laid down in company handbooks, which can

295. W. Been & M. Keune, *Chapter 21 The Netherlands*, in *Collective Bargaining in Europe: Towards an Endgame* Vol. II, 455–462 (T. Müller a.o. eds, Bruxelles: ETUI, 2019).

obtain legally binding force by an incorporation clause in the individual contract of employment. In the US and the UK this method is nowadays found more frequently than collective bargaining, although collective bargaining has not disappeared altogether and flourishes in a number of industries. Wage levels set in collective agreements often serve as reference points for wages in companies in which wage setting occurs in unilateral fashion (benchmarking).

In the Netherlands such unilateral wage setting by employers is still very exceptional, although some foreign companies may have already imported this system into the Netherlands. There has been little research on this phenomenon, nor is there much case law. In the Netherlands this development would not be welcomed because it would lead to confusion in terms of working conditions and hinder solidarity. The only notorious phenomenon of unilateral fixation of working conditions is in the praxis of employers fixing higher wages than those in the collective agreements (wage drift).

299. In the Netherlands most of the firms that escape collective bargaining with the unions have wage structures in which they have involved – in one way or another – the works council. Such wage structures derive their legally binding force from incorporation clauses in individual employment contracts. This type of wage setting happened already for many years in a number of plants of MNCs such as Mars Netherlands, which operate in sectors where there are no *erga omnes* extended collective agreements. Notorious recent cases were Jumbo (supermarkets) and Action (retail) which decided to abandon collective bargaining with the unions and concluded company agreements with their works councils.

However, as we shall see in detail, there are many aspects in the Dutch Law on Collective Agreement which can make this alternative difficult to apply. The main difficulty is the lavish application of the extension *erga omnes* of collective agreements in the Netherlands (*see* paragraphs 324 et seq.). Consequently ca. 65%–70% of the labour market companies cannot escape the minimum standards of the sector collective agreement.

Some employers and some politicians would like to strengthen dialogue between employers and works councils, first by introducing the works council as a social partner to genuine collective agreements at enterprise level (*see* paragraph 391) and second by weakening the *erga omnes* mechanism (*see* paragraph 327). They assert that unions are no longer representative of the workforce, as union density in many sectors is so low. Trade unions and labour lawyers are countering that works councils do not have sufficient knowledge of the labour market; that they have to take into account all the interests of the company; that works councils are not allowed to exert pressure on the employer via strikes, etc. Granting full-fledge power to conclude collective agreements to the works councils is seen by most politicians and even by most employers as detrimental to the position of the unions and not compatible with the Dutch poldermodel (*see* paragraph 268). It is therefore likely that in the Netherlands the social partners will struggle to keep alive the many sector collective agreements and to attain more flexibility by other means.

300. Much more widespread is the situation in enterprises which are subject to collective agreements with the unions, where the works councils are charged with the mission to tailor-make open provisions in the collective agreements. There is nowadays the tendency to give collective agreements – and certainly those at sector level – more or less of a framework character. Details should be settled at enterprise level. This supplementary bargaining at company level is slowly gaining ground. Only in a few cases this company bargaining is done by the trade unions as the trade unions seldom have bargaining agents at enterprise level. So this trend has more to do with works councils than with the unions.

Therefore at company level the dialogue between employers and the works council is of much greater significance than bargaining between employers and the unions. One of the most fertile areas of bargaining is the organization of working time, as several Acts of Parliament such as the WTA (*see* paragraphs 110 et seq.), the FWA (*see* paragraph 119), the Work and Care Act (*see* paragraph 125) and collective agreements contain numerous opening clauses which give works councils the legal possibility to make arrangements with the employer on working time, building on and even deviating *in peius* from the standards set in these Acts (*see* paragraph 111) and in the collective agreement.

Nevertheless, there are a couple of legal problems in this field which have not yet been solved. From a strictly formal point of view, the works council does not 'bargain' with the employer, but only gives its 'advice' or 'consent'. The Dutch WCA contains a provision that draws a line between the competences of the trade unions and the works council: if for an enterprise the matter is exhaustedly regulated by a collective agreement, the works council is no longer competent to issue (or withhold) its endorsement of propositions of the employer on that point (*see* paragraph 391). This only leaves room for negotiations on all matters that have not or only poorly been regulated by statute and collective agreement.

Another problem is the binding force in relation to individual employment contracts of agreements with works councils to concretize sector collective agreements. In the Netherlands this binding force is not – unlike in Germany, with the *Betriebsvereinbarung* or works agreement – established by law. It is dependent on auxiliary legal constructions (such as incorporation clauses in individual employment contracts) (*see* paragraphs 323 and 391).

An additional problem is the question of whether the Minister may or should extend *erga omnes* such decentralization clauses in sector collective agreements. The Minister is not prepared to do so with open-ended decentralization clauses (*see* paragraphs 326 et seq.).

All these legal problems and uncertainties have delayed rapid development of this decentralization trend. The trade unions are reluctant to agree to glib solutions to these problems because they fear that this would open the floodgates for employers who would prefer to completely circumvent the trade unions and to negotiate only with the works councils (or even with yellow unions). The trade unions in the Netherlands favour controlled decentralization in which the conditions and the content of company-level bargaining are stipulated by the bargaining parties at sector level through instruments such as opening clauses or delegation clauses. They reject uncontrolled decentralization characterized by a de facto undermining of the existing collectively agreed standards.

301. As already mentioned, the Dutch government has urged the parties to collective agreements to make it possible for employers to obtain permission to deviate from sector agreements (*see* paragraph 327). Such procedures have in fact been created but there has been little research on the recent application of such opening clauses. One may assume that they are incidentally but not widely applied. Once an employee contested the binding force of a simple contract between an employer and a single union which authorized the employer on an ad hoc basis, not via the official opening clauses, to deviate *in peius* from the sector collective agreement. The HR rejected the binding force of this agreement and confirmed the rights of the worker under the collective agreement. This example shows that deviations from collective agreements are regarded by the courts with suspicion. Such deviations must be based on explicit opening clauses in the collective agreement.

302. Also on the flexibility front some companies are experimenting with so-called employability deals: company agreements on employment and competitiveness and in-house bargaining in which the workers' representatives make certain concessions in terms of working time or pay in return for some form of employment guarantee of the kind that can be found in Germany. In the Netherlands such agreements are very rare. The Dutch trade unions seem more prepared to put up with staff reductions than reductions of the existing level of wages and other employment conditions. The rank and file tends to reject deals about reductions in the pay cheque. This became very manifest in 2009 when the unions exceptionally showed themselves prepared to conclude a collective agreement with TNT (former Royal Mail, now Post NL) providing for a 15% wage decrease in exchange for job guarantees; however, the rank and file rejected this agreement. The Dutch law on individual and collective agreements make it quite difficult for employers to unilaterally make reductions on the collectively agreed wages and fringe benefits. Anticipated opening of collective agreements is seldom provided for in the collective agreement itself and presumably hard to obtain from the courts (there are no cases reported!). In recent years some employers in the Netherlands, e.g., the Department stores chain V&D, have tried to obtain direct consent of their own workers with reduction plans. However, unions again and again denounced such activities and it seems difficult for the kind of wage reductions based on such a direct consultation but contested by the trade unions to enforce them when contested in court.[296] The most that seems feasible in Dutch law and practice are deals between the parties to the collective agreement by which employers give employment guarantees for a certain period in exchange for a low wages increase or even a wage standstill. This happened, for instance, some years ago at KLM, when only 1.75% wage increase was agreed in exchange for an eighteen-month employment guarantee. Such deals, however, are exceptional in the Netherlands.

303. Collective bargaining in the Netherlands has indeed seen in recent years more flexibility and decentralization as employers increasingly reject rigidities in collective bargaining. However, this is certainly not the dominant situation. A mixed trend towards centralization and decentralization has been one of the features of the

296. Magistrate Court of Amsterdam 23 February 2015, ECLI:NL:RBAMS:2015:899.

current period. In the end, decentralization may well come to play only a modest role in collective bargaining in the Netherlands. The sector level is still dominant and even the cross-industry level is making itself felt. Wage bargaining at company level is still very secondary. The prevailing situation is that everybody follows trends set by particular wage leaders. If wages are tending to rise 2%, they will rise 2% on average everywhere. If some employees are compensated with bonuses, similar employees will be compensated by bonuses everywhere. All this, of course, is subject to variation according to the economic performance and character of companies. Again, this outcome is very much the result of the political culture of the Netherlands: the Dutch love of 'equal treatment' and for no deviations from general trends, and the fact that 17 million people are living in an open and tolerant society on a very small territory – all this means that trends are followed and that the possibilities for employers to deviate from these trends are limited. However, new trends may emerge, even at a decentralized level. They will be allowed to flourish only if they are accepted at centralized levels; otherwise, after a certain time they will perish. The internationalization of companies is having a creeping impact on company wage policies. Employers are nowadays less inspired by merely social, national or even patriotic considerations in the formation of their wage policies. They are now primarily driven by shareholder value, with an increasingly global dimension. So far, it seems that the social partners at sector level in the Netherlands have been successful in checking the internal erosion of sector collective bargaining. Nor have there been many reports of companies covered by collective agreements actually violating the legally binding norms of a valid collective agreement. Compliance with collective agreements is still the norm in all sectors of the Dutch economy, although there are always minor exceptions.

304. The position of public employees in the process of collective bargaining for a long time has been somewhat different. I have described it in the third edition of this monograph.

The existing pattern of collective labour relations in the public sector will at least formally change as from 1 January 2020, when the overwhelming majority of the public sector will be brought under the same labour law rules as the private sector (*see* paragraph 54). At a material level no important changes are expected.[297]

§2. The Bargaining Process

305. Employers and unions normally meet every one or two years for bargaining relating to the renewal of the collective agreement, since collective agreements are in most cases concluded for one or two years, although there are from time to time agreements concluded for several years. The Act on Collective Agreements (ACA) in practice places only minor restrictions on the parties as far as this issue is concerned (*see* paragraph 314).

297. S. Stiller & K. Boonstra, *Industrial Relations in the Public Sector: The Netherlands* (forthcoming).

The starting point of the annual bargaining round is the existing agreement and the amendments which employers and unions wish to make to it. In the case of economic prosperity, the unions in particular propose a whole series of improvements and employers try to limit or to delay them for as far and as long as possible. If, in contrast, the economic situation is deteriorating, employers attempt to take a backward step and the unions attempt to maintain 'acquired rights' for as long as possible. In recent years often deals could be reached, presented as win-win-solutions. Unions could obtain stabilization or even small improvements in pay, in exchange for conceding to employers more flexibility in wage structures, working hours or types of contract.

The demands to be put forward by the social partners during collective bargaining are established in advance by the various organizations following consultations with their members. Members' influence should not, however, be overestimated; it is the leadership which plays the crucial role. Moreover, the policy of the various unions is also influenced by the confederation to which a union is affiliated (*see* paragraph 296). Nevertheless some trade unions are endeavouring to strengthen the position of the rank and file. In the department of the trade union FNV that organizes cleaning-personnel, members are involved in the bargaining process via a Parliament of regional representative of the workers. In the Netherlands only collective bargaining at all-industry level is institutionalized in bodies like the *Sociaal-Economische Raad* en de *Stichting van de Arbeid* (*see* paragraphs 290 et seq.). At sector level collective bargaining is usually not so much conducted within an institutional framework as it is in Belgium. Only in a few sectors of the economy it is institutionalized within a joint consultative body. In a few other sectors the bargaining process is presided over by an independent chairman.

After the various bargaining sessions attended by the delegations, the social partners normally reach a compromise. This compromise is then passed on to their members. Some trade unions recently started not only to consult their membership but the entire workforce covered by the collective agreement. Every now and then there are some cases reported in which the rank and file rejects the draft for a collective agreement, but this remains exceptional. Once the approval of the rank and file has been obtained, the new collective agreement may be formally concluded.

If the social partners do not reach consensus as regards the new collective agreement, 'war' may be declared in the form of a strike (*see* Part II, *see* paragraph 334). A strike does not, however, always take place. It may be (especially if employees do not feel strong enough to undertake a strike and employers do not effectuate a deterioration of the conditions of employment) that the unions do not call a strike and there is simply a period with employers continue to apply the terms of the old collective agreement. The social partners then resume bargaining a year later.

However, it may sometimes happen that a sector lacks a collective agreement for a number of years because both sides of industry stubbornly fail to reach a compromise.

§3. The Law on Collective Agreements

306. The Netherlands was one of the first countries in the world to have adopted a statutory provision on the impact of the collective agreement on individual contracts of employments. However, this small provision in the 1907 Act on the Contract of Employment left various legal questions unsolved. They were finally tackled, at first in 1927 in the Act on Collective Agreements (ACA) and subsequently in the AECA of 1937. Both Acts are still in force today with only minor amendments.[298]

The Act on Collective Agreements (ACA) of 1927 recognizes the binding force of collective agreements on individual employment contracts. It establishes that any stipulation agreed by an employer and employee contrary to a collective agreement is null and void. Any such stipulation is superseded automatically by the provisions of the collective agreement. In addition the provisions of the collective agreement supplement the contents of those individual contracts of employment on issues about which the individual employment contracts are silent. Not extended collective agreements have these legal effects only for the personnel in enterprises of which the employer is itself a signatory to the collective agreement or is a member of the employers' organization which has concluded the collective agreement (*see* paragraph 323).

The 1937 AECA gives the government the power to extend the binding force of a collective agreement to the personnel of *all* enterprises in a certain sector of the economy. If the Minister has used this power, also the outsider employers and all their workers are legally bound to the collective agreement. The democratic imperative has led the legislators to limit the Minister in this power: he may only extend the collective agreement at the request of the social partners involved and provided the agreement is (without extension) already applicable to a considerable majority of those employed in the relevant sector of the economy.

Finally there is the WDA 1970, which narrowly defines the powers of the Minister of Social Affairs to intervene in the process of wage formation (*see* paragraph 282).

§4. Definition, Form and Publicity of Collective Agreements

307. According to the legal definition, a collective agreement is an agreement concluded between one or more employers or one or more incorporated associations of employers on the one hand and one or more incorporated associations of employees on the other hand, the main or exclusive object of which is to regulate the conditions of employment which must be taken into consideration in individual contracts of employment (Article 1 ACA). A collective agreement must necessarily be in writing (Article 3 ACA).

298. I. Asscher-Vonk, *Collective Agreements in The Netherlands*, in *Collective Bargaining in Europe* 138–159 (Madrid: Ministerio de Trabajo y Asuntos Sociales, 2004).

The parties to a collective agreement must notify the Minister of Social Affairs and Employment in writing of the conclusion, modification or cancellation of a collective agreement, attaching the texts of the agreement or its modification. The Minister confirms as soon as possible the receipt of the notification. A collective agreement or its modification cannot be binding before the day following the sending of the receipt of the notification by the Minister (Article 4 WDA). The HR[299] has confirmed that this notification to the Ministry is a *conditio sine qua non* for any document to be recognized as a collective agreement with all the legal effects that are connected to such recognition. However, this does not mean that a collective agreement, which is not notified to the Minister is deprived of any legal effect. It may produce all effects as far as they can be construed with the general rules of the law on contract.

A public register where collective agreements are kept does not exist in the Netherlands. However many websites nowadays provide access to the texts of collective agreements. The law obliges the parties to the collective agreement to give copies of the agreement to their members (Article 4 ACA). Usually, collective agreements contain the provision that the employer should hand a copy of the agreement to each employee. Moreover, Article 7:655 CC (*see* paragraph 74) contains the provision that the employer shall inform the employee, in writing, of the applicable collective agreement.

If a collective agreement has been declared generally binding (*erga omnes* effect, *see* paragraphs 324 et seq.) this decision has to be published in the *Staatscourant* (Official Gazette) (Article 5 AECA) together with all the provisions that have been declared binding *erga omnes*. Currently that information is easily accessible at www.szw.nl.

§5. Parties to Collective Agreements

308. In the Netherlands almost any association of employers or employees may enter into a collective agreement. No conditions relating to the size, independence or representativeness of the parties to the collective agreement are laid down in statutory law or case law.

The only two legal conditions are:

(a) that the association has full legal capacity (Article 1 ACA);
(b) that the association is explicitly authorized, by its articles of association, to enter into collective agreements (Article 2 ACA).

These two requirements may be readily satisfied by all organizations of employers and employees, even the smallest (*see* paragraph 276). It is sufficient to draft articles of association which correspond to the minimum regulations imposed by the

299. Dutch Supreme Court, 13 Apr. 2001, JAR 2001/82; Dutch Supreme Court, 30 Nov. 2001, JAR 2002/16.

CC on all associations wishing to obtain full legal capacity, to have these articles of association certified before a notary and then to enter the association on the register of associations.

The minimal character of the legal requirements put to the parties to collective agreements was sufficient during the first three decades after World War II when the Dutch trade union landscape was quite homogeneous. However, for a number of years the Netherlands has seen various autonomous trade unions emerge, with a very low membership and often in fact brought into being by employers – the so-called yellow unions (*see* paragraph 269). Some employers have been eager to negotiate with these unions, thus circumventing the traditional trade union movement. This phenomenon is now causing serious concern among labour lawyers who question as to whether the law should put more requirements to the parties on collective agreements (*see* further in paragraph 313).

In the case of an important collective agreement, bargaining is normally conducted by senior trade union leaders; in the case of a less important agreement, bargaining is conducted by the union's district leaders. In a few major enterprises, union delegates from these enterprises may also take part in the negotiations. But it is always in the name and on behalf of the union that bargaining is conducted and agreements are signed.

As far as the employees' side is concerned, only unions, viewed in their formal sense, are entitled to enter into collective agreements, to the exclusion of all other employees' representatives. Under Dutch law works councils are formally not empowered to enter into collective agreements. But this does not prevent them from some forms of collective bargaining (*see* paragraph 391).

309. Collective bargaining in the Netherlands usually has the character of multi-union bargaining. On the employees' side of the bargaining table one normally finds representatives of the unions affiliated to FNV, CNV and VCP, even if such unions have only a few members in that enterprise or business sector. In some enterprises and sectors representatives of autonomous unions also sit on the bargaining table. In most sectors and enterprises the chief employees' spokesman will be the representative of the FNV union as this union usually has the largest membership.

A collective agreement is normally signed by all the unions active in the economic sector or enterprise concerned, or by none of them. Up until now, cases in which collective bargaining has given rise to disagreement between the unions concerned have not been as frequent as, for instance, in France. Until recently 'multi-unionism' was not a problem in the Netherlands as employers did not systematically attempt, as they do in Great Britain, to deal with a single union at the negotiating table. Such a premeditated strategy would be incompatible with traditional Dutch pluralism. In recent years, however, Dutch industrial relations have experienced increasing problems in this field. In a number of cases employers have deliberately circumvented bargaining with the large unions and opted for bargaining with small unions. Or at least the collective agreement was concluded with only the small unions because a deal with the largest union appeared impossible. If such things happen neither the excluded union nor its members are bound by the collective agreement, and they may continue to press for a more favourable collective agreement using methods of collective action. Therefore it stands to reason that the bargaining with circumvention of the largest unions only happens in sectors in which even the large unions are virtually weak because employees' militancy has decreased. Therefore sometimes unions have sought the intervention of the courts in such cases but the courts were not prepared to intervene (*see* paragraphs 311 et seq.).

310. As far as the employer's side is concerned, the legal definition of the collective agreement (*see* paragraph 306) not only recognizes an individual employer to be party to a collective agreement, but also a permanent association of employers and even an ad hoc group of employers. This explains why there are collective agreements at the level of the economic sector (for instance, the construction industry) as well as at the level of the enterprise itself (for instance, Philips, Akzo Nobel and DSM). Sometimes collective agreements at sectoral level are concluded by a number of employers' associations acting together (for instance, in the building industry and the textile industry).

§6. A Right to Collective Bargaining?

311. In the Netherlands unlike the US, France and a few other countries, there is no general legal obligation on employers to bargain with the unions. Collective bargaining is a question of power relations. Only in a few specific cases like collective redundancies, mergers and takeovers is there something similar to an obligation to bargain (*see* paragraphs 360 and 361) and in isolated cases a judge may compel an employer to bargain with the unions.

The absence of a legal obligation to bargain is immaterial for ca. 80% of the Dutch labour market where regular collective negotiations are self-evident and application of the collective agreement is widespread. The great majority of the employers do not dislike collective agreements, as they are for them the key to orderly, stable and predictable labour relations. Take for instance the sector hotels, restaurants and bars, where only 7% of the workforce is unionized. Nevertheless a nationwide collective agreement is yearly negotiated with the unions.

Although cases in which employers deliberately avoid negotiating with any unions (the American phenomenon of 'no union') are rare, there have always been some sectors and enterprises in the Dutch economy where employers avoid dealing with the unions and where the unions cannot impose collective bargaining because of their small membership. It is estimated that this affects 10% to 15% of employees in the private sector. In those enterprises employers either unilaterally establish the conditions of employment or they negotiate them with the works council.

Between 1945 and 1970 trade unions which were not affiliated to the 'official' confederations of those days (the CNV and the precursors of the FNV) were most of the time excluded from the collective bargaining process. During the 1960s, some of these organizations took legal action to obtain support allowing them to take part in collective bargaining. The courts rejected this on the grounds of the principle of the freedom of contract. During the 1970s, the white-collar unions made a major break-through. These unions were finally recognized as partners in collective agreements, more because of major political pressure than because of the size of their membership.

If a union newly becomes a signatory party to the collective agreement then the rights and obligations recognized to the trade unions that were the original signatories, are applied to the newcomer as well. Nevertheless it sometimes happens that unions are refused as a negotiating partner. It is a basic rule of contract law that a party can only join an existing collective agreement if the signatory parties give their consent.

In 1979 the SER rejected the idea of a statutory regulation of the right of participation in the process of collective bargaining and there is consequently no legislation on this issue. This SER opinion confirmed the traditional opinion according to which recognition of the right to participate in collective bargaining should be obtained primarily by force of numbers. According to the SER, only clearly unreasonable cases in which access to collective bargaining is refused to an organization can be brought before the courts. This means that if a certain trade union is refused the access to the bargaining table, the primary way for this trade union is by organizing a successful strike. As an alternative the exclusion of an evidently representative trade union from current collective bargaining may be challenged in court.

In 2007 the HR has ruled that indeed the principle of freedom of contract should in principle also determine cases in this field. However, the larger the interests of an organization to be allowed to participate in the process of collective bargaining are, the heavier weight is required for the arguments justifying a refusal to allow participation to an organization.[300]

312. Ever since some courts have indeed intervened in cases in which organizations have been excluded for inadequate reasons. In other cases organizations have not managed to gain access to the negotiating table by judicial means. For the judges the decisive criterion in these cases is 'representativeness'. To determine the representativeness of a trade union the total number of members in the company/sector represented by the excluded trade union is compared with the number of members in the company/sector represented by each of the negotiating unions (absolute representativeness). In some of the court decisions a trade union had to be admitted to the bargaining table because it was obviously representative for a certain group of workers, which would become subject to the results of the collective bargaining process and which was hardly represented by the others unions (relative representativeness).

In most sectors of the Dutch economy the FNV is certainly the trade union with by far the largest membership. Still there are sectors where a CNV or a VCP trade union or even an autonomous union may outnumber the FNV union.

313. In recent year the question of representativeness has become much more debated because of another actual phenomenon. In the past collective agreements

300. Dutch Supreme Court, 8 Jun. 2007, JAR 2007/162.

used to contain almost exclusively provisions which were favourable to every individual worker. Presently, however, collective agreements sometimes contain provisions, which are not considered by a certain individual as favourable to him/her. For example: provisions in collective agreements, implementing waivers of statutory provisions (*see* paragraphs 34 and 321). Or provisions in actual collective agreements which are less favourable than in an earlier collective agreement. Or redundancy payments in collective agreements which for a certain individual may be less favourable than the usual severance pay granted by the courts. In such cases employees, who are not members of the contracting parties to such a collective agreement take the stand that the collective agreement cannot have binding force on their individual employment relationship. Some lower courts have recognized such claims when they were not convinced of the representativeness of the trade union which had concluded such collective agreements. This has become an increasingly problematic issue in the Dutch law on collective agreements.

The problem was tackled by the legislator for the first time in the 2015 Reform of the law of dismissals, where at two places (Article 7:671a(3) and Article 673(b)(2) CC) it has been required that certain deviations from the statutory rules can only be made in a collective agreement concluded with trade unions which are active on behalf of their members in the enterprise and – including its predecessors – having the status of a legal person for at least two years (*see* paragraph 210). This formula is similar with the formulae used in the law on company enquiries (*see* paragraph 358), on collective dismissals (*see* paragraph 360) and the WCA (*see* paragraph 381). It is only a small hurdle as it does not at all guarantee that such collective agreements are concluded with the main trade unions.

§7. Temporal, Geographical, Personal and Occupational Scope of Collective Agreements

314. Statutory law in the Netherlands has given a very large freedom to the social partners to organize the scope of application of collective agreements – *ratione temporis*, *ratione territorialis* and *ratione personae.* Only a small number of topics are regulated, by statute or by case law, notably as regards the scope *ratione temporis* and even then largely in the form of default (fall-back) rules.

315. As regards the scope of application *ratione temporis*, we have already noted above that collective agreements are generally concluded in the Netherlands for a period of one or two years. Collective agreements containing special provisions (VUT, welfare funds, etc.) are sometimes valid for longer periods. The law provides that a collective agreement shall not be concluded for more than five years. The collective agreement may be prolonged, provided that the parties shall not in any case be bound by the agreement for more than five consecutive years reckoned from the date on which it was agreed to prolong the agreement (Article 18 ACA). If a collective agreement is concluded for a fixed period, unless it contains a provision to the contrary, it shall be deemed to be prolonged for not more than a year at a time of default or denunciation; the period of notice shall be one-twelfth of the period for which the agreement was originally concluded, unless it contains a provision to the contrary. If the period for which a collective agreement is concluded is not fixed in the agreement itself, it shall be deemed to have been concluded for one year, subject to prolongation from year to year, unless it is denounced not less than one month before the end of the year (Article 19 ACA). Notice to terminate a collective agreement shall be communicated to all the parties to the agreement by registered letter or by a notice served by a bailiff (Article 20 ACA). Unless the collective agreement contains a provision to the contrary, denunciation by one of the parties shall cause the agreement to expire with respect to all the parties (Article 21 ACA). The collective agreement comes into force, if not otherwise stipulated, on the fifteenth day after the conclusion of the agreement (Article 7(1) ACA), while Article 4 WDA provides that a collective agreement can come into force not earlier than the day following the sending of the receipt of the notification by the Minister (*see* paragraph 307). Often the date of coming into force is stipulated in the collective agreement itself.

316. Statutory law does not contain any provision concerning retroactive force of the collective agreement and of its after-effects, but case law has given some answers on these items. Collective agreements in principle can have after-effects if they itself provide so,[301] but certain provisions may not be fit for retroactive force, especially provisions that take away existing rights of the employees.

As regards the after-effects the courts have decided that the collective agreement indeed has after-effects for the parties to the individual contracts of employment if they are bound to the collective agreement by membership of the signatory parties or an incorporation clause in their contract of employment.[302] After-effects mean that the conditions in individual contracts of employment remain binding after its expiration as long as they are not changed by individual agreement or by a collective agreement with a minimum character. If the new collective agreement has a standard/maximum character (*see* paragraph 322) and binds only because of extension (*see* paragraph 324), after the expiration even the after-effects of the earlier collective agreement may revive.[303]

317. In the Netherlands, the geographical application of almost all sector agreements covers the whole country. The few exceptions concern, for instance, seaports, in which there are separate collective agreements for each seaport.

318. As regards the personal scope, the rule of the freedom of the social partners prevails. Obviously collective agreements are primarily focusing on contracts of employment. However, the collective agreement may also have relevance for ex-employees.[304]

In addition the collective agreement may also deal with the carrying out of particular jobs and agreements for the performance of particular services (Article 1(2)

301. Dutch Supreme Court, 27 Mar. 1998, NJ 1998, 709.
302. Dutch Supreme Court, 19 Jun. 1987, NJ 1988, 70.
303. Dutch Supreme Court, 8 Apr. 2011, JAR 2011/135.
304. Dutch Supreme Court, 6 Sep. 2013, ECLI:NL:HR:2013:CA0566 (ECN/Omen).

ACA). This means that a number of labour relationships (*see* paragraphs 49 et seq.) may be included in the field of application of a collective agreement, such as 'on-call' contracts, apprenticeship contracts, temporary contracts and home-based work contracts, whether they can be identified as contracts of employment or as contracts for services. For instance, in the collective agreement for the building industry, self-employed workers, if they are not genuine entrepreneurs, are included in the scope of the collective agreement. The collective agreement fixes minimum standards for the remuneration of such persons. This praxis has recently been criticized as being contrary to EU and Dutch competition rules. It seems that the EU is only allowing the application of a collective agreement on bogus self-employed.[305]

On the other hand it also happens that 'atypical' workers are explicitly excluded from the scope of the collective agreement, for instance on-call workers, holiday workers and temporary helps. In the past it even happened that part-time workers were excluded from the scope of collective agreements, but that practice has disappeared as it would violate the Act forbidding discrimination on the ground of working time of 1998 (*see* paragraph 100).

Dutch collective agreements traditionally cover the working conditions of blue-collar employees. For several years, however, a number of collective agreements have also organized the working conditions of white-collar employees. It is rare, however, for collective agreements to lay down pay scales for personnel receiving an annual wage in excess of ca. EUR 80,000. However, in some collective agreements a number of non-pecuniary items of the working conditions of higher-paid employees are regulated. Usually the directors and the managerial staff are excluded from the collective agreements. Their labour conditions are settled in individual negotiations between the employer and the employee.

Because of the fact that Dutch unions are organized in accordance with the principle of sector-wide trade unionism (at least as far as the unions of the same Confederation are concerned, *see* paragraph 270), the boundaries of the field of application *ratione personae* do not raise many problems of rival agreements. Some conflicts may, however, arise: for instance, do the administrative personnel of a shipping company come under the collective agreement for maritime trade or the agreement for the ports sector or even a cross-industry agreement relating to administrative personnel in general? Such questions should be answered unequivocally by the collective agreement itself, but sometimes they give rise to litigation.

319. More frequently litigation is provoked by the fact that either the character of the job or the character of the enterprise or the description of the scope of the collective agreement are not unequivocally pointing to the application of a specific collective agreement. Recent years have seen the phenomenon of employers looking for cheaper collective agreements. One of the strategies is to switch the classification of their business from one sector collective agreement to another, which is considered cheaper. This policy leads occasionally to conflicts and disputes in courts between employer and unions or works councils. In those cases courts must often bring the solution and Dutch courts have developed a number of norms. According

305. CJEU 4 Dec. 2014, C-413/13 (FNV-Kiem); CJEU 4 Jul. 2019; C-377/17 (*Commission v. Germany*).

to the method of interpretation which considers the written text of the collective agreement as decisive (*see* paragraph 331)[306] the courts take the line that not the character of the job should determine the applicable collective agreement, but the character of the enterprise, unless the collective agreement contains a provision to the contrary.[307]

Problems of concurring collective agreements and possible collision may occur in a number of instances.

In the first place, after a merger or transfer of an undertaking two or more collective agreements may be applicable to an employee. For this situation a solution is given in statutory law (Article 14a ACA and Article 2a AECA). These provisions stipulate that the terms and conditions of employment applicable before the merger or transfer of the undertaking remain applicable until a new collective agreement is agreed upon or declared generally binding.

In the second place, there is the case that in an enterprise activities belonging to different branches of industry are performed. For instance, in a department store not only consumer goods are sold, but there is also a cafeteria, a travel agency, etc. To solve this conundrum the courts will apply the criterion of 'what is the principal activity' of the firm?[308]

In the third place, different collective agreements may be applicable because the Ministerial Decree has extended the application of a sector collective agreement to an enterprise which is already bound to a company agreement. In the past such problems could be prevented because the Minister used to make exemptions for such enterprises. If that has not been the case the extended collective agreement prevails, but provisions in the company collective agreement that are more favourable to the workers remain in force, safe if the extended collective agreement has a maximum character.

Finally there is the case of temporary agency workers. Since 2012 the law obliges the agency to apply to these workers more or less the same working conditions as enjoyed by the employees of the user firm. Only under some strict conditions a special collective agreement for temporary agency workers may be applied (Article 8 AEIA, *see* paragraph 256). Moreover another collective agreement may be applicable as well.[309]

§8. Regulatory ('Normative') Content of Collective Agreements

320. In the Netherlands the regulatory content of collective agreements, often called the substantial or normative provisions, covers a wide field: wages, pay supplements, working hours, shift work, overtime, holidays, and terms of notice in case of dismissal, social plans in the case of collective dismissals, etc. Collective agreements also frequently contain rules on health and safety and supplementary

306. Dutch Supreme Court, May 2011, JAR 2011/172.
307. Dutch Supreme Court, 6 Jan. 1995, NJ 1995, 549.
308. Dutch Supreme Court, 31 Jan. 2014, ECLI:NL:HR:2014:215 (Adimec).
309. Dutch Supreme Court, 15 Apr. 2011, JAR 2011/136; Dutch Supreme Court, 25 May 2005; JAR 2005/154.

social security benefits, pensions, etc. They tend to expand into new areas of regulations, such as the financing of crèches and personal arrangements for training. They contain increasingly aspects of flexibility, such as flexible working hours and variable pay forms. On the other hand, issues such as the environment and investments have not usually been the subjects of collective agreements in the Netherlands.

In Dutch law there are no legally protected managerial prerogatives; the scope of a collective agreement does not have to be restricted to terms and conditions of employment in any strict sense. The text of the Dutch Act on collective agreements, defining that the collective agreement has as its 'main or exclusive object … to regulate conditions of employment which must be taken into consideration in individual contracts of employment' (Article 1 ACA) has not curbed the proliferation of the subjects of collective bargaining. This is also borne out by case law of the courts: the question as to whether collective agreements may contain provisions instituting social funds to which individual employers must make a financial contribution has been brought before the courts on a number of occasions. The HR has confirmed this possibility in several judgments.

Collective agreements in the Netherlands also often contain provisions concerning mandatory participation of employees in a specific pension fund or a specific health insurance. Such provisions have given rise to the question of whether they are not violating EU competition law. Although they got their blessing from the CJEU[310] they are focusing scholarly attention to the general question of the relationship between the law of collective bargaining and competition law, which was already touched in the question of whether the collective agreement may contain tariffs for the remuneration of work done by independent contractors (*see* paragraph 318). Similar problems are currently emerging: the relationship between the law of collective agreements and the public procurement law, the law of collective agreements and anti-discrimination law, etc.

Obviously collective agreements cannot be contrary to mandatory provisions, contained either in national or European law. If clauses in a collective agreement are contrary to mandatory provisions, they are null and void. The individual labour contract will not be remodelled by the provision from the collective agreement. Instead the mandatory statutory provisions do apply. For instance if in a collective agreement wages would have been set below the level of the statutory minimum wages, the provision in the collective agreement is null and void and the employee is entitled to the statutory minimum wage. If a collective agreement would contain a clause in violation with the (mandatory) legislation on equal treatment, for instance by awarding less rights to part-time workers, part-time workers can, on the basis of statutory law (*see* paragraph 100), claim equal rights as full-time workers.

All these developments are putting the question: what remains from the autonomy of the social partners to freely agree to the contents of collective agreement? Although this principle is not guaranteed by the Dutch Constitution, it is laid down in ILO Treaties which the Netherlands have ratified (*see* paragraph 276).

310. Court of Justice EC, 21 Sep. 1999 (*Albany* case).

321. In the same vein in the Netherlands there is no relevant demarcation between the rules set out in collective agreements and those set out in law. The issues which may be dealt with in a collective agreement may also be dealt with in law, which is in fact what happens very often: the law often lays down minimum regulations, which are then improved by collective agreement. This is the case in particular in the area of rights to remuneration, paid leave, periods of notice, etc. The question of whether a certain issue should be regulated by statutory law or by collective agreement is much debated in the Netherlands each time a new topic for regulation emerges. Employers and right-wing politicians in general dislike statutory regulation. Unions and left-wing politicians often are in favour. Christian Democrats take a middle position. The end result is that the outcome of the debates varies from case to case, according to the socio-political situation of the moment. There is no general dogmatic line to be drawn.

Collective agreements have played an important role in the development of statutory labour law. Many labour conditions, for instance yearly paid holidays, leave for family reasons and fair dismissal requirements, were first laid down in collective agreements. These and other subjects have found their way in legislation after having matured in collective agreements.

Since the abolition of the wages policies (*see* paragraphs 281 et seq.) collective agreements can contain provisions that are more favourable to the workers than the provisions of the statutes. Sometimes they may also contain deviations from the statutes *in peius*. On a number of places statutory law in the Netherlands gives to parties to the collective agreement the power to agree on provisions which are unfavourable to the workers (*see* paragraph 34). Parliament creates every now and then such provisions as it realizes that sometimes a statutory rule may be too inflexible or too burdensome for specific sectors of the industry. By giving the social partners the chance to deviate *in peius* it is possible for them to find more tailor-made solutions. However, there are also risks to this legal technicality (*see* paragraph 313).

§9. The Mandatory Force of Regulatory Provisions of Collective Agreements

322. The Act on Collective Agreements of 1927 recognizes the binding force of collective agreements on individual employment contracts. It establishes that any stipulation agreed by an employer and an employee contrary to a collective agreement is null and void. The nullity is absolute (thus can be invoked by every interested party)[311] and works *ex tunc*. Any such stipulation is superseded automatically by the corresponding provisions of the collective agreement. In addition the provisions of the collective agreement supplement the contents of those individual contracts of employment (Articles 12 and 13 ACA).

311. Dutch Supreme Court, 27 Mar. 1998, JAR 1998/99.

It is only exceptionally possible for the parties to the individual contract of employment that is reigned by the collective agreement (*see* paragraphs 323 and 324) to deviate from the collective agreement in a termination agreement[312] (*see* paragraph 201).

Moreover, in principle, stipulations in a contract of employment which are more favourable to the workers than the similar clauses in the collective agreement remain valid. Most of the times, the collectively agreed rules have the character of minimum rules – individual employers and employees may agree on terms which are more favourable to the employees. However, this rule is not absolute. Under Dutch law, a collective agreement may contain clauses with a standard/maximum character. And indeed, in a few branches of industry the social partners have given their collective agreement the character of standard/maximum rules, which do not allow for deviations even if these are more favourable to employees. This is notably the case in the semi-public sector (healthcare for instance).

A problem may arise if the contract of employment is more favourable than the collective agreement on one or more points, but less favourable on other aspects. The HR has ruled that in such cases the comparison of the favourability of the individual contract must be made clause-by-clause.[313] So a package comparison is not allowed, unless the collective agreement itself allows it. Some collective agreements indeed give the employees the change to opt between various packages (*see* paragraph 297).

If a new collective agreement replaces a former one the new one usually is more favourable for the worker than the old one. However, it may occur that the new collective agreement is less favourable to the worker than the old one. In those cases the parties to the new collective agreement have normally agreed what should be the fate of the old rules, now replaced by less favourable ones. If they have settled this question the employee must in principle accept the regression, but the courts have to test the fairness of the new rules if they are disputed.[314] If the parties to the collective agreement have not settled this problematic, then the courts will solve this problem along with the rules they have developed on the so-called after-effects of the collective agreement (*see* paragraph 316).

323. The collective agreement is applicable not only to new contracts of employment but also on the contracts of employment in existence at the moment that the collective agreement is concluded, unless the collective agreement contains a provision to the contrary (Article 7 ACA). Such contrary arrangements seldom occur regarding the entire collective agreement, but it may occur regarding some specific clauses.

312. Dutch Supreme Court, 6 Jan. 2017 (Blue Taxi), ECLI:NL:HR:2017:19; Dutch Supreme Court, 9 Jan. 2015, ECLI:NL:HR:2015:39.
313. Dutch Supreme Court, 14 Jan. 2000, JAR 2000/43; Dutch Supreme Court, 24 Apr. 2009, JAR 2009/130.
314. Dutch Supreme Court, 14 Jun. 2002, JAR 2002/165.

As far as the scope of mandatory provisions is concerned, a distinction has to be made between 'ordinary' collective agreements and agreements, which have been rendered generally applicable with *erga omnes* force by an extension order (*see* paragraphs 324 et seq.).

Non-extended collective agreements are binding in principle only for contracts of employment of employees, which are members of a signatory employees' organization and the employer is a member of the employers' organization which has concluded the collective agreement for the occupational sector to which it relates, or is himself a signatory to the collective agreement (Articles 9, 12 and 13 ACA). Cancellation of membership during the original duration of the collective agreement only takes effect after the expiration or a modification of the collective agreement (Article 10 ACA).

However, employers bound by collective agreements are legally obliged to apply their provisions on working conditions for their entire duration to all contracts of employment concluded with non-organized employees, unless the collective agreement contains a provision to the contrary (Article 14 ACA). So the collective agreement may exempt from its application all non-unionized employees. However, in reality Dutch collective agreements almost never make such exemptions. The reality is that the provisions in the collective agreement on working conditions are covering all employees, both unionized and non-unionized employees of the employers which have themselves directly or indirectly (by their membership of the employers' organization) bound to a collective agreement.

However, according to the HR, this Article 14 ACA does not give the non-unionized employees the same claim in court action as unionized employees have (in Articles 12 and 13 ACA), viz. that any stipulation agreed by an employer and employee contrary to a collective agreement is null and void, that any such stipulation is superseded automatically by the corresponding provisions of the collective agreement and that their individual contracts of employment are supplemented by the provisions of the collective agreement. If the collective agreement is not respected by the employer towards the non-unionized employees, it is only the unions which have signed the collective agreement that may invoke this obligation in a court action against an employer (*see* paragraph 332).[315]

That is the theory, but it is only part of the theory. The other part of the theory says that these non-organized employees may successfully secure in court the application of the non-extended collective agreement if this application has been expressly agreed in the individual contract of employment by way of a so-called incorporation clause[316] or if it can be construed as resulting from the general notions of civil law, such as custom and practice (*see* paragraph 31/32). If these constructions (incorporation clause/customs and practice) are a reality, the mandatory force of a non-extended collective agreement can be invoked by employees (whether unionized or not) working for an employer who is party to the collective agreement or member of an employers' association which is party to a collective agreement.

The result of all this is that the mandatory force of the non-extended collective agreement can almost always be claimed by all employees of a bound employer.

---

315. Dutch Supreme Court, 7 Jun. 1957, NJ 1957, 527.
316. Dutch Supreme Court, 25 Jan. 2008, JAR 2008, 55.

All in all, the legal concept of Article 14 ACA is not very convincing, even less because it is interpreted by some courts and scholars as meaning that the non-unionized employee can refuse the application of the collective agreement on him/her. Obviously, employees will never refuse the application of a collective agreement if it is advantageous for them (as it mostly is), but they may refuse it if the collective agreement is disadvantageous for them (as it sometimes may be, *see* paragraph 313). This may create undesirable cherry-picking.

The Dutch Article 14-ACA system is somewhat halfway between the German system of *Tarifgebundenheit* and the French/Belgium system of *extension automatique*, but it is confusing.[317]

§10. Extension *Erga Omnes* of Collective Agreements

324. During the years of the Great Depression prior to World War II, Parliament invested the executive authority (the Minister) with the power to extend the scope of a sectoral collective agreement to all employers in the economic sector concerned, by means of an extension order: the AECA agreements, 1937. When an agreement has been extended to an entire economic sector, all employers and employees in that sector are subject to the collective agreement by virtue of the law, irrespective of whether or not they are unionized, unless the enterprise has obtained an exemption (*see* paragraph 325).

The effect of the extension is that all provisions in contracts of employment that are contrary to the provisions of the collective agreement are null and void; the provision of the collective agreement takes the place of the annihilated provision. However, more favourable provisions in individual or (earlier) collective agreements continue to apply, unless the extended collective agreement has clearly a standard/maximum character.[318]

If the collective agreement has been extended, also non-unionized employees are entitled to take action in court to claim the rights contained in the collective agreement (Article 3 AECA).

This extension is – concerning most of its provisions – also applicable to the so-called posted workers, working in the Netherlands and irrespective of the chosen law (*see* paragraph 190) (Article 2(6) AECA).[319]

Dutch law considers the provisions of a collective agreement that has been extended *erga omnes* as 'objective law',[320] law in the sense of Article 97 of the Act on Judicial Organization, which means that the court must ex officio apply them[321] and that the HR will control them in full.

The Minister grants this extension only at the request of one or several of the employers' and employees' organizations which have signed the collective agreement (Article 4 AECA) and wish to have it respected across the relevant sector.

317. A. van Hoek, *Collective Agreements and Individual Contracts of Employment in Labour Law: The Netherlands*, *EJCL* 248–270 (2004), http://www.ejcl.org/64/art64-15.pdf.
318. Dutch Supreme Court, 8 Apr. 2011, JAR 211/135.
319. Act of 1 Jun. 2016, Stb. 2016, 219.
320. Dutch Supreme Court, 16 Mar. 1962, NJ 1963, 222.
321. Dutch Supreme Court, 27 Sep. 1991, NJ 1991, 788.

Most of the time employers and trade unions make the request for extension in unison, although a request by one of the signatory parties suffices.

The request is publicized in the *Staatscourant* (Official Gazette). Objections may be brought forward. The Minister may consult the *Stichting van de Arbeid* (Foundation of Labour). The Minister can accept a request for extension only if he is convinced that the agreement is already applied to a substantial majority of personnel employed in this occupational sector (Article 2 AECA). Therefore the Minister requires the signatory parties to give him enough in-depth statistical material in order to be able to assess whether this condition is fulfilled. When assessing this majority, the Minister takes account of the number of all employees (whether organized or not) engaged by the employers, which are already bound by the collective agreement, contrasted to the total number of employees in this sector. This method of calculation, which once has been endorsed by the HR[322] enables the collective agreement to be extended, even if the level of trade union organization is fairly low. At the same time this method of calculation makes it possible for a collective agreement to be extended even when it has not been signed by all the major unions.

To give two examples of this: (a) A collective agreement is signed by an employers' association whose members are engaging 70% of the workers in that economic sector, and by the three major trade unions in that sector, who are organizing a totality of only 5% of the workers in that sector. Extension granted. (b) A collective agreement is signed by an employers' association whose members are engaging 70% of the workers in that economic sector, and by only a small CNV union, organizing 1% of the workers in that sector, while the FNV union (4% of the workers in that sector) abstained. Extension granted.

The fact that the quantitative requirement is independent of the unionization rate, but entirely dependent on the employers' organization rate, means that extension practices in the Netherlands would decline dramatically if many employers withdrew from employers' associations, as they did in Germany. However, this is actually not a trend in the Netherlands (*see* paragraph 295).

325. The Extension order will be taken by the Minister for the remaining timespan until the end of the collective agreement, but for two years at most. Only provisions with respect to funds or sectoral committees on dismissals may be extended for a longer duration (Article 2(2) AECA).

The Extension order contains the date that the extension starts as well as the date of expiration of the extension (Articles 4 and 5 AECA). Premature termination is possible by Ministerial Decree (Article 6 AECA). In 2015 the possibility was created that an Extension order of the Minister is prolonged with at most one year if all the parties to this agreement have requested so (Article 4a AECA).[323]

The Extension order cannot have retroactive force (Article 2(3) AECA) nor has it effect after the date set for its expiration.[324] After expiration the provisions in the contracts of employment, as they originally stood or have been altered by an earlier collective agreement to which they were subjected, regain validity. So, in general

322. Dutch Supreme Court, 10 Jun. 1983, NJ 1984, 147.
323. Act of 4 Jun. 2015, Stb. 2015, 233.
324. Dutch Supreme Court, 18 January, NJ 1980, 348.

there is no after-effect of the extended collective agreement. Nevertheless case law[325] has identified a few situations in which a certain after-effect may be justified. For example when a claim, based on an extended collective agreement, has already become effective in the period of extension, the employee does not lose that claim with the expiration of the extension.[326]

The Minister in his Extension order may exclude certain enterprises. In the course of time the ministers have followed various policies in this respect. In the 1990s the Minister embarked on a generous policy. Every enterprise which had already itself concluded a collective agreement with a union, could obtain an exemption of the extension order. This generosity, however, opened the door for abuses as it allowed employers to escape the extension order by negotiating a company collective agreement with a weak union, even with a 'yellow union'. This was seen by the traditional trade union movement and also by the Committee of Social Rights of the ESC as an undermining of the system of collective bargaining. Finally, in 2007 the Minister embarked on a much different policy which leaves very small space for enterprises to obtain an exemption. Currently an exemption is only granted if the application of a sector collective agreement cannot reasonably be required from an enterprise.

The Minister in his Extension order should exclude certain provisions of the collective agreement (Article 2 AECA). The law expressly cites some provisions which may not be extended (in particular, provisions likely to favour union members above other workers (Article 2(5) AECA). The Minister will also exclude provisions in collective agreements from extension which conflict with the law, for instance if provisions in collective agreements would be contrary to equal treatment legislation. Moreover there are a number of other types of provisions which as a rule the Minister will exclude from his Extension order.

326. The government may in theory refuse extension if some of its provisions would be detrimental for the social and economic development. After the demise of the state wage policy in the 1980s (*see* paragraphs 281 et seq.) the ministers have always been reluctant to use this discretionary power. Extension orders were more or less automatically granted if the collective agreement already covered 'an important majority' of the persons employed in that sector (*see* paragraph 324) and provided the text of the collective agreement was not contrary to the law (*see* paragraph 325). Political considerations did not matter. However, in the 1990s the Minister used his power of extension to exercise pressure on the social partners not to neglect the low wages scales. He was only prepared to extend the binding force of collective agreements if the minimum wages contained in the collective agreement were not above the national statutory minimum wage, in order to improve the chances for job seekers in the low pay segment of the labour market (*see* paragraphs 141 and 246). Some years later ministers threatened to refuse the extension of provisions that were not compatible with their policy to eradicate deactivating aspects of the statutory social security schemes. On another occasion ministers wanted to

325. Dutch Supreme Court, 19 Jun. 1987, NJ 1988, 71; Dutch Supreme Court, 2 Apr. 1993, JAR 1993/100.
326. Dutch Supreme Court, 28 Jan. 1994, JAR 1994/47.

require as a sine qua non that collective agreements pay attention to the item of vocational training (*see* paragraph 259). Although those ideas were never put into practice, they brought lawyers to question of whether such (threats of) refusals would constitute an encroachment on the fundamental right to free collective bargaining – the same question I touched already in paragraph 320. This debate has never been closed.

In 1998 the Minister published a set of policy rules for his decision-making in this matter (*Toetsingskader AVV*). The actual version is of 2017.[327] The law sets out procedures for complaints and consultations (Article 4 AECA) on the decision to extend, but no judicial review is possible of the Minister's decision whether or not to extend the terms of a collective agreement.[328] However, a civil law court may check whether the prime condition for an extension order (the important majority) is fulfilled and an administrative court may check the legality of the ministers' decision whether or not to grant an exemption to a certain enterprise.[329]

327. In the Netherlands the mechanism of extension is frequently used. In all the major sectors of industry covered by sector collective agreements, trade unions and employers' organizations together are used to request the Minister, immediately after the conclusion of the sector collective agreement, to give his extension order. Some economists were amazed at this policy of an almost blind granting of extension orders. They claimed that sector agreements, especially those extended *erga omnes* as Dutch sector agreements mostly are, may easily maintain a wage level that is too much above market criteria. However, most Dutch employers see extension as a positive instrument which averts excessive competition and therefore excessive labour market unrest. They believe that individual or enterprise-level wage setting creates more conflict than collective wage setting at sector level. The government favours extension because it guarantees peace on the labour market. Moreover a wide range of extended collective agreements gives it a good excuse to avoid employment legislating and to leave standard setting to the social partners.

The instrument of extending the binding force of collective agreements also came under attack from some lawyers as it is in fact hampering free competition. This claim even reached the CJEU, which threw out this claim as long as the content of the collective agreement is only about working conditions and employment (*see* paragraph 320).

At a certain moment in the 1990s the government considered reforming the system of extension, but it decided later to maintain the instrument as it is contributing to stable social relationships on the labour market. Instead of reforming the system of extension the Dutch government urged the parties to collective agreements to offer expedient procedures for employers to obtain permission to deviate from extended collective agreements. Indeed, such procedures have in fact been created where they did not exist and have been made more transparent and accessible where they already did exist (*see* paragraph 300).[330]

---

327. Latest text in Stcrt. 2017, no. 52963.
328. Dutch Supreme Court, 16 Mar. 1962, NJ 1963, 222.
329. Dutch Council of State, 27 Oct. 2004, WNAR 4606.
330. Parliamentary Papers 29544, 726 and 755.

§11. Contractual Content of Collective Agreements

328. Apart from its regulatory provisions collective agreements often contain various provisions which relate only to the relationship between the signatory parties, for instance on:

- the recognition or even the co-financing by the employer of certain union activities (e.g., the free access to the working place, to intranet, etc. of trade union officials, the training of members etc., *see* paragraph 277);
- the procedure for the renewal of the collective agreement;
- the evaluation or a possible amendment of the current agreement;
- procedures for handling disputes between the signatory parties as regards application of the collective agreement;
- industrial action (the famous no-strike obligation, *see* paragraph 329).

Quite different from the law in the UK, in the Netherlands the obligatory provisions are regarded as normal contractual obligations and as such they are enforceable in court by the signatory parties to the collective agreement. They must be observed in bona fides (Article 6:248 CC) and can be terminated according to the general principles on the law of duration contracts.[331] The HR has ruled that one of the parties cannot easily distract itself from observing the collective agreement, for instance by invoking unexpected circumstances. Non-observation of the collective agreement is only justified if the observation of the collective agreement in the circumstances of the case would be unacceptable according to the criteria of equity and fairness.[332] However, conflicts in this field are usually solved by negotiation; appeals to the courts are a rare exception.

Contractual clauses are not fit for extension *erga omnes*.

As a rule the contractual part of a collective agreement cannot be invoked in court by the parties to the individual contracts of employment covered by the collective agreement. However, it cannot be excluded that certain agreements with a clearly contractual/obligatory character may nevertheless have also a regulatory (normative) character and therefore may also be enforced in court by parties to the individual contract of employment. This for instance can be the case in a collective agreement by which – in exchange for a low wages increase or even a wage reduction – the employer has given guarantees about maintaining the existing level of employment (*see* paragraph 302).

329. Another example of contractual clauses with a regulatory/normative impact is the no-strike or peace obligation clauses. In the Netherlands most collective agreements contain such clauses. They impose on the signatory parties the obligation to respect the provisions of the collective agreement throughout its duration and to refrain from any (threat of) industrial action to change existing conditions within the duration of the collective agreement.

331. Dutch Supreme Court, 10 Jun. 2016, ECLI:NL:HR:2016:1134.
332. Dutch Supreme Court, 25 Feb. 2000, JAR 2000/85; Dutch Supreme Court, 4 Feb. 2005, JAR 2005/51.

Even if the collective agreement does not contain specific no-strike clauses the signatory parties would still be liable to apply this agreement in good faith by virtue of the general law on obligations.

The no-strike obligation is not only seen as binding for the signatory parties of the collective agreement. It also applies to employers and employees who are members of the signatory parties, with the result that they are not authorized to undertake industrial action against one another during the period of validity of the collective agreement (Article 9 ACA). The signatory organizations must exert pressure on their members to respect the collective agreement. It is not quite clear, however, just what kind of pressure is expected from the parties. In any case, the signatory parties need not guarantee the respect of the collective agreement by their members, unless the collective agreement expressly provides for such a guarantee (Article 8 ACA), which is unusual in the Netherlands.

In this context, unions cannot easily support a strike which runs counter to the provisions of the collective agreement. On request of the employers they would be penalized by the courts, which would order them, by summary procedure, to disassociate themselves from the strike under pain of payment of fines (*see* paragraphs 337 et seq.).

The no-strike obligation may be binding on unions and their members only if the unions are signatories to the collective agreement. If this is not the case, the union and its members may start or continue strike action to obtain a more favourable collective agreement.

Peace obligation clauses can be absolute or relative. In case of an absolute peace clause any form of industrial action is a breach of contract; in case of a relative peace clause only industrial action which is directly concerned with matters covered by the collective agreement is ruled out. Whether the peace clause is absolute or relative depends on the text and its interpretation by the courts of the particular clause in the collective agreement.

Most of the existing no-strike obligations contained in collective agreements are of a relative nature. It is therefore possible to organize, during the period of validity of the agreement, other types of strike, for example strikes against the restructuring of a company. There may be some doubt as to whether it is also possible to strike for subjects not included in the collective agreement, for instance for a supplementary bonus and a ruling relating to safety at work. The answer depends very much on whether or not the controversial subject was utterly ignored in the previous bargaining round.

In principle, the no-strike obligation expires when the collective agreement expires or is terminated by agreement, although the text of a no-strike clause may provide that it remains in force for a certain period after the expiration or termination of the collective agreement.

§12. Other Clauses

330. Dutch scholarly writing has identified a third family of clauses in collective agreements, besides the regulatory/normative and the contractual/obligatory clauses. They are called *diagonal clauses*. They appear only in sectoral collective agreements, not in company collective agreements, because in such company agreements these clauses would be contractual clauses.

Diagonal clauses are clauses which are not immediately relevant to the contracts of employment, but impose specific obligations only on one of the parties to the contract of employment, notably the employer.

Examples of such clauses are clauses which:

- give trade unions certain rights on activities inside the enterprise;
- give trade unions right on information or consultation on specific company affairs such as plant closures, takeovers and change of contractor in outsourcing situations;
- charge the employers with a (written) account of the social policy of the enterprise in the preceding year and an outlook on the future social policy;
- oblige employers to donate money to specific funds, for instance for training.

From statute and from case law it may be derived that such clauses are legal, that they can be invoked in court by the parties to the collective agreement and by funds established on the basis of the collective agreement and that they are fit to be extended *erga omnes* by Ministerial Order. However, other aspects of this type of clauses have still to be clarified, such as the question of whether they are binding after the expiration of the collective agreement.

Clauses containing the set-up and the mandatory force of contributions to funds are quite common in the Netherlands, especially to finance training of the employees (*see* paragraph 259) and the costs of the participation of trade unions in the process of collective bargaining (*see* paragraph 277). The Minister is used to extend these clauses if they meet a number of criteria contained in Points 6.2.3.e of the *Toetsingskader*. The courts have confirmed the mandatory character of these clauses[333] and that the funds have an independent right of action against employers that do not pay.[334]

Social plans (*see* paragraphs 226 et seq.) are frequently concluded between trade unions and employers who want to operate collective redundancies. Often they are part and parcel of the regularly collective agreement and then the status of such plans is clear. Often they are concluded on an ad hoc basis and then their status is less clear. The HR has ruled that such plans may be judged as collective agreements, but that is not necessarily so.[335] Sometimes the social plan contains provisions which may be less favourable than an individual employee could claim on another basis. The HR has ruled that also in that case the social plan must be considered as sufficient, although the court cannot shirk an assessment of the reasonableness of its provisions if they are disputed,[336] for instance if they have a discriminatory effect on a worker.[337] The courts will in these cases give attention to

333. Dutch Supreme Court, 19 Mar. 1976, NJ 1976, 407; Dutch Supreme Court, June 1983, NJ 1984, 147 and Dutch Supreme Court, 30 Jan. 1987, NJ 1987, 936.
334. Dutch Supreme Court, 13 Sep. 2002, JAR 2002/248.
335. Dutch Supreme Court, 20 Mar. 1998, JAR 1998/127; Dutch Supreme Court, 26 May 2000, NJ 2000, 473.
336. Dutch Supreme Court, 14 Jun. 2002, JAR 2002/165.
337. Dutch Supreme Court, 19 Apr. 2019, ECLI:NL:HR:2019:647.

the fact whether the trade union that has concluded the social plan, is sufficiently representative (*inter alia* requiring ca. 20%–25% membership of the workforce).

§13. Interpretation

331. The courts will interpret the obligatory (contractual) provisions of the collective agreement (*see* paragraphs 328 et seq.) according to the habitual rules for the interpretation of contracts: the court will not limit itself to a linguistic interpretation of the text, but also take into account the intentions of the parties to the collective agreement and their mutual expectations.[338] However, with regard to the regulatory content of the collective agreements (*see* paragraph 320) the HR has decided that the written text of the collective agreement and its written explanation are decisive. The intentions of the parties to the collective agreement will only be taken into account as far as they have found expression in these texts.[339] The HR rejected the idea, that in cases of doubt the interpretation most favourable to the employee (*in dubio pro operaio*) should be followed.[340]

§14. Enforcement

332. Very much in contrast with, for instance Britain, the Dutch legal system is characterized by the high degree of legal enforceability of the collective agreements. This also explains why in the Netherlands until recently not much attention was paid to the possibility to support collective bargaining by the way of labour clauses in public procurement contracts, as it is customary in British/American labour law (so-called contract compliance) and also endorsed by ILO Convention no. 94.

Normally the enforcement of collective agreements in the Netherlands takes place via the ordinary court system (*see* paragraphs 35 et seq.) and is most clearly visible in the area of the regulatory force of the collective agreement, viz. its normative provisions.

Employers and employees bound by a collective agreement must respect it. If a party to the individual contract of employment covered by a collective agreement does not respect the terms of that collective agreement – intentionally, without premeditation or because of a doubtful interpretation – the other party to the contract of employment may refer the matter to the cantonal judge. The enforcement of the collective agreement takes place almost daily by the courts, which are seized on individual disputes about the contracts of employment. The courts then have to take into account the provisions of the relevant collective agreement.

---

338. Dutch Supreme Court, 13 Mar. 1981, NJ 1981, 635 (Haviltex); Dutch Supreme Court, 18 Oct. 2002, NJ 2003, 258.
339. Dutch Supreme Court, 17 Sep. 1993, NJ 1994, 173; Dutch Supreme Court, 26 May 2000, NJ 2000, 473 and Dutch Supreme Court, 25 Nov. 2016 (Condor), ECLI:NL:HR:2016:2687.
340. Dutch Supreme Court, 11 Apr. 2003, JAR 2003/108.

The normal rules of civil procedure are applicable to cases about collective agreements.

In cases of collective agreements made generally binding by a Ministerial Order both unionized and non-unionized employees may take legal action to claim the rights contained in the collective agreement. In case of a collective agreement which is not made generally binding by a Ministerial Order only the unionized employees of an employer bound to the collective agreement have a clear legal right to claim the rights contained in the collective agreement. Other employees may, however, successfully secure application of a collective agreement before the courts if this application has been expressly agreed in the individual contract of employment or if it can be construed from notions of civil law, such as the presence of an incorporation clause or custom and practice (*see* paragraph 323).

Moreover, signatory organizations of the collective agreement are entitled, because of this status, to initiate action against a member of another signatory organization who has not respected the collective agreement (Articles 9, 15 and 16 ACA). In this procedure the organizations may claim the damages of their members (which they thereupon should hand over to their members) but they can also claim own damages, which often exist in immaterial damages because their authority has been injured by the violation of the collective agreement.[341]

In fact this kind of action is rare. The signatory parties to the collective agreement normally prefer to give legal advice and legal aid in court proceedings to their members. Only in very important cases or when an action by a signatory party appears to be more effective will such a signatory party union sue in its own name.

Trade unions can also avail themselves of the common procedure for organizations to litigate on behalf of its members (Article 3:305a CC). This procedure is seldom used in collective labour law because the use of this procedure is conditional upon several factors: the fact that the interests to be defended should be similar to the own interests of the organization, that there should have been consultation between the parties and that the person concerned raises no objections against the lawsuit. Moreover, such cases can only pertain to publication of the verdict and cannot lead to damages, neither material nor immaterial.

In some branches of industry and in major enterprises, the collective agreement has created specific bodies of conciliation and mediation before which infractions of the collective agreement may be brought. This is not, however, a very current practice in the Netherlands. Moreover it is not always sure that offering this alternative dispute resolution path would bar the parties the access to the court.

Even less usual is the possibility that the collective agreement refers to disputes about its application to arbitration. Moreover, such clauses cannot be extended by a Ministerial Order of extension and cannot bind non-members of the signatory parties.

In recent years in a small number of sectors the parties to the collective agreement have set up own bodies in order to monitor and to fine the non-observation of the collective agreement. This has happened notably in sectors most vulnerable for

341. Dutch Supreme Court, 19 Dec. 1997, NJ 1998, 493; Dutch Supreme Court, 22 Jun. 2018, ECLI:NL:HR:2018:980.

violations of the collective agreement, such as road transport, temporary agencies work, closed bus transport, taxi-business and supermarkets.

333. In the Netherlands the observance of collective agreements is never subject to criminal or administrative sanctions. However, if the collective agreement is extended by a Ministerial Order (*see* paragraph 324) its observance may be monitored by the Inspection SZW (*see* paragraph 40) if this is requested by one of the parties that had requested the extension order or by the above-mentioned monitoring bodies. The Minister informs the petitioners of the result. Finally the Inspection SZW has been charged with an independent mission to control the application of the rules of the collective agreement (be they extended *erga omnes* or not) to the so-called posted workers (*see* paragraph 190) (Article 10 AECA).[342] The works councils have the obligation to further the observance of the provisions concerning labour conditions (Article 28 Works Council Act). In that way, the works council has its own authority to investigate whether labour conditions are observed.

Third parties, for instance the tax authorities, can base their own claims on the labour conditions as shaped by the *erga omnes* extended collective agreement.

Disputes relating to the contractual content of the collective agreement too may be brought before the common law courts but only by the signatory parties to the agreement. However these parties are normally reluctant to bring their differences to the court. In some cases they put the matter before a board of mediation/arbitration, but in most cases they put the problem on a back burner until the next round of collective bargaining. Or they try to resolve it by way of a strike. This, however, enables the common law judge to speak out over the matter if he is asked for an injunction (*see* paragraph 337).

342. Changed by the Act of 1 Jun. 2016, Stb. 2016, 219; Parliamentary Papers 34408; *see also* Ministerial Policy Rules on Art. 10 AECA Stcrt. 2 Jun. 2017, no. 30494.

Chapter 5. Industrial Disputes

§1. Introduction

334. The rather harmonious model of collective labour relations is one of the main characteristics of the Dutch system of industrial relations: employers' and employees' organizations adopt a strategy of conflict avoidance. A climate of industrial peace is predominant. Compared to other countries employees in the Netherlands and their unions only rarely resort to the strike weapon.

The number of working days lost over the years because of strikes used to be one of the lowest in the Western world (Table 19).

Table 19 Days Lost Because of Strikes per 1,000 Employed Persons

	Germany	*Netherlands*	*UK*	*France*	*US*	*Italy*
1950–1959	47.5	19.4	135.9	315.5	550.2	301.5
1960–1969	12.0	16.7	145.7	138.5	382.3	730.5
1970–1979	44.7	35.7	521.6	167.8	457.1	1,041.0
1980–1989	22.9	12.8	292.8	61.7	132.0	433.3
1990–1999	10.5	19.3	25.0	31.2	37.0	110.6

For the recent years the Dutch numbers are as shown in Table 20.

Table 20 Strikes in the Netherlands (per Thousand Employee Persons)

	Working Persons Participating in Strikes	*Number of Strikes*	*Working Days Lost by Strikes*
2001	37,400	16	45,100
2002	38,600	16	245,500
2003	10,800	14	15,000
2004	104,200	12	62,200
2005	29,000	28	41,700
2006	11,300	31	15,800
2007	20,700	20	26,400
2008	51,900	21	126,600
2009	3,600	25	4,600
2010	14,100	21	59,200
2011	47,100	17	22,000
2012		18	219,000

	Working Persons Participating in Strikes	*Number of Strikes*	*Working Days Lost by Strikes*
2013		24	19,000
2014			41,000
2016	11,000		48,000
2017	147,000		306,000
2018			239,000

As one can see, since the turn of the century the strike activity in the Netherlands was quite low, but since the end of the last economic slump (2016) the strike activities are clearly on the rise with 306,000 working days lost in 2017

There have been only seldom lengthy disputes. The last major strike was the one of civil servants in 1983 when the government had decided to a wage freeze and even a wage lowering because of the economic recession. The unions lost this strike and ever since there have been few strikes with a longer duration than one or two months. Most strikes are short work stoppages. They serve to indicate the precise position of the various power relations in a socio-economic and political context, which is continually changing. None of the social partners is actually attempting to destroy the other. When the various parties have established the lie of the land as regards these power relations – which can be fairly readily deduced – a compromise is reached and life continues until there are further doubts about the true nature of power relations.

In large parts of the Dutch economy, especially in small private manufacturing and retail, the trade unions are too weak to organize strikes, venturing to take such action only if the employers make extreme demands. In a number of other sectors, however – such as construction, railways, ports, air travel, hospitals, and lower level civil servants – the Dutch unions are still strong enough to organize strikes more easily. Some of such strikes can seriously disrupt the country. In recent years it often happened that short (one day) strikes were organized to press the government and Parliament to extend social protection (better wages, less workload, stable pensions, more healthcare, etc.).

Notwithstanding the low incidence of collective conflicts, the Netherlands has seen most of the various types of industrial action: strikes in all its forms (general sector strikes, selective strikes, strikes for recognition, sympathy strikes, slowdowns, sit-ins, etc.). The most common form nowadays is a rotating strike (estafette strike) disrupting a sector or an enterprise, organized by the major unions in order to achieve an improvement or to prevent a deterioration of working conditions on the occasion of the renewal of collective agreements.

Also not infrequent are short strikes to obtain a better social plan in case of company restructuring. Sometimes short strikes have been called to object to certain government intentions to intervene in social affairs. Anyway, most strikes arise from genuine disputes of interest. Strikes out of disputes of rights are rare as unions and employees prefer the judicial means of the resolution of disputes of rights. Strikes are sometimes accompanied by picketing, but this is much less violent than in the

UK, for instance. During the last sixty years employers have never resorted to lock-outs. Strikes in state enterprises only seldom occur as such enterprises are very few in the Netherlands. Every now and then there are strikes in the public sector and the semi-public sector, notably on the occasion of the yearly review of working conditions in these sectors.

Over the years the legal position of strikes in the Netherlands has been improved and clarified by case law, but it still has a number of unpredictable aspects.

§2. Historical Development of the Right to Strike and Strike Action in the Private Sector

335. The ban on strike-prone workers' organizations (so-called coalitions) was lifted in the Netherlands in 1872. From that time on, criminal proceedings could not be pursued against people for organizing or taking part in strikes. Therefore it is long ago that strikes were prohibited under penal law. Only in the civil service and the railways strikes were forbidden under penal law (*see* paragraph 355), while until 1979 seafarers on strike at sea could face criminal charges because of 'mutiny'. Of course it is still possible that certain activities are considered as criminal acts even if they are done within the framework of collective action (e.g., lorries blocking a motorway). But there is not such a tradition in the Netherlands.

However, civil law risks were not removed to the same extent: strikers could be dismissed immediately because of 'breach of contract' and even made to pay damages to employers. Between 1918 and 1940 the concept of 'tort' and the summary procedure ('injunctions') entered Dutch civil law. This offered the possibility of initiating civil proceedings against unions inciting strike action. However, these possibilities were hardly used before 1940. In the 1920s the average number of working days lost annually by strikes was more than a million; in the 1930s this average fell to about 400,000. Most of the strikes were organized strikes, i.e., supported by a union.

After 1945, the Netherlands had a controlled wage policy (*see* paragraphs 281 et seq.) and strikes were very quickly seen as strikes against the authorities, which could not be legal by definition. Unions affiliated to the major confederations which were associated with this wage policy felt that strikes would undermine their position; the only strikes, which were organized were wildcat strikes or strikes organized by non-recognized Communist unions and were declared illegal by the courts in every case. So between 1946 and 1960, during the period of central wage policy, the annual average number of working days lost by strikes had dropped even further to about 80,000 working days.

After 1958 when the Social Democrats had left the government, the trade unions distanced themselves further and further from the state-controlled wage policy. In this social context, industrial disputes have become increasingly numerous. This situation led employers to request the courts to place restrictions on the freedom to strike. In 1960, the HR gave its famous *Panhonlibco* ruling,[343] holding that strikes should, in principle, be considered as a 'breach of contract' by employees against

343. Dutch Supreme Court, 15 Jan. 1960, NJ 1960, 84.

their employers, and that unions inciting employees to take such action were committing a tort. The HR left only a small opening for legal strikes, i.e., when 'the circumstances ... are such that, in the prevailing legal opinion, it is not reasonably possible to request employees to continue to carry on with their work'. The HR did not specify under what circumstances such lawful stoppage of work would be justified. This HR ruling was widely criticized – the space which it left for strikes, was considered to be too small. The government requested the opinion of the SER and in 1969 introduced a Bill to regulate the right to strike. This Bill provoked further criticism and was finally withdrawn in 1980. In the meantime, in 1972, the Amsterdam Court of Appeal had already changed the framework used up until then in case law by a ruling that a strike is legal in principle unless the circumstances of the case made it illegal. This decision laid the foundations for a renewal of case law on strikes during the period until 1986.

This erosion of the *Panhonlibco* doctrine did not, however, guarantee an unfettered freedom to strike. In some cases, for instance, the judges considered a strike to be unlawful because the unions had not exhausted all possibilities of collective bargaining or, in other words, because the strike was not used as the 'ultimate weapon'.

Following ratification of the ESC by the Netherlands in 1980, this Charter backed up the new tendency of Dutch case law.[344] In a landmark ruling of 1986, the HR finally stated that the provisions of the ESC, which recognized the right to strike in Article 6(4), were directly applicable in the Netherlands and that, for these reasons, the right to strike should be recognized in principle.[345]

In the Netherlands the right to strike is not mentioned in the Constitution or in statutory law. All strike law is the result of case law of the courts and therefore very casuistic. And although the right to strike is secured by this case law it is not an absolute right. The HR has put various conditions on it.

§3. Definition/Concept of the Legal Strike

336. According to this HR ruling of 1986, strikes are illegal when major procedural rules have been disregarded. This includes cases in which:

- a strike is organized before any substantial bargaining has taken place;
- no minimum safety precautions have been taken;
- the strike conflicts with the no-strike obligations set out in the collective agreement (*see* paragraph 329).

344. *See* L.A.J. Schut, *Internationale normen in het Nederlandse stakingsrecht*, Den Haag, 1996; on pp. 215–223 may be found an English-language description and discussion on international legal norms in the Dutch law on the right to strike.
345. Dutch Supreme Court, 30 May 1986, NJ 1986, 688.

In a later judgment[346] the HR affirmed that it wants to consider the strike as *ultimum remedium*, although it emphasized that this idea should be applied by the courts with reticence.

Strikes are also illegal when, after evaluating all the specific conditions and circumstances of the strike, as well as their internal links and interdependence, it must be concluded that the unions should not reasonably have taken such extreme action.

This mainly includes cases in which the damages caused by the strike are excessive in respect to the interests at stake. In later judgments the HR affirmed that a strike can only be justified if it does not disproportionately encroach on the rights of others.[347] The proportionality test, described in the last phrase is an important means for all Dutch courts to balance the right to strike against other constitutional values, public goods and economic rights.

For all these reasons the Dutch Trade Union Confederation FNV has protested to the European Committee of Social Rights, which oversees the application of the ESC, against the application of the principle of proportionality by the Dutch courts. In response this committee has given the opinion that the judicial practices in the Netherlands by their nature restrict the right to strike and that they go beyond the restrictions admissible under Article 31 of the Charter. The Dutch government has passed this opinion to the judiciary and judges have taken it into account. On the other hand it should be recalled that the application of the principle of proportionality seems to be well in line with the judgment of the CJEU in the *Laval* case, 2007.

In 2015, finally, the HR in its Amsta-judgment formulated a modernized version of the criteria on which the legality of strikes should be measured. All collective actions of workers are henceforward under the protection of Article 6 ESC if the action can reasonably contribute to the effective exercise of the right to collective bargaining. A limitation of the right to conduct such an action must take place on the basis of Article G ESC and must be an urgent public necessity, to be judged on the merits of the case. As regards the fulfilment of the last-mentioned condition the one who wants to limit an action has an enhanced duty to postulate and the court has an enhanced duty to motivate.

In this judgment the HR called the question of whether major procedural rules were respected no longer an independent condition for the legality of a collective action. Such rules are no more than 'points of view' that must be taken into account when analysing whether the action must be limited or forbidden.[348]

It is however doubtful how much the lower courts are already following this rather permissive Amsta-judgment. Sometimes the lower court judges are producing innovative rulings to limit strike activities. For instance the District Court of Roermond stopped an industrial action at VDL Nedcar as this action would jeopardize the future of this plant.

346. Dutch Supreme Court, 28 Jan. 2000, JAR 2000/64.
347. Dutch Supreme Court, 21 Mar. 1997, NJ 1997, 437.
348. Dutch Supreme Court, 19 Jun. 2015, ECLI:NL:HR:2015:1687.

§4. Judicial Methods and Procedures

337. Dutch society as a whole generally feels ill at ease when an industrial dispute arises, and attempts are then made to make it last as short as possible. It is often the case that, when a strike is called, employers initiate summary proceedings with a judge of the District Court. In their request, they ask the judge to prohibit the unions from organizing or supporting the strike, under penalty of a fine. The courts have no problems in accepting such requests. Different from the situation in Belgium, Dutch unions are incorporated associations (have full civil personality, *see* paragraph 276) and can therefore be summoned in court. The courts will consider the case on the basis of the rules given by the HR (*see* paragraph 336). If the strike is considered within the limits set by the HR, the trade unions can go ahead with the strike. The unions are not committing a tort and are not responsible for the damage caused by the strike. If the court rules that the strike is illegal the ruling will request the unions to immediately stop supporting the strike (verbally and in writing, and especially in financial terms: the use of the strike fund). Failure to observe this order attracts a fine and the union may in principle be ordered to pay damages to the employer or to third parties. In the Netherlands, however, unions normally abide closely by the decisions of the courts. If they lose in court the unions always withdraw their support from strikes; they are therefore never forced to pay a fine. There are only a few examples in which employers have claimed damages from the unions. It is the end of the strike which is sought and not damage to the opposing party. So in practice a (conditional) acceptance of the employers' request by the court means that unions withdraw their support for the strike. The social partners then meet around the negotiating table in order to find a compromise.

Sometimes the unions lodge an appeal against the judgment prohibiting the strike, but this procedure leads to a Court of Appeal judgment, which normally takes several months; by that time, the strike is long over and the appeal judgment is of no significance, other than for the development of case law. Appeals to the HR take place only rarely.

If, in contrast, the court authorizes the industrial action, this is an incentive for the employers to return to the negotiating table to find a compromise as quickly as possible. If a compromise cannot easily be reached, the strike might continue amidst considerable political and media concern and the pressure to settle the dispute is mounting.

338. Although there are few strikes in the Netherlands, the general public is seldom very sympathetic to strikes. Recent times have seen third-party lawsuits, for instance patients' organizations against a strike of hospital staff and commuters' organizations against a strike of railway personnel. The judges will hear those claims but are still reluctant to endorse them.

When the trade unions refrain from strike action, the workers will usually follow their example. Also there are not many wildcat strikes. All this because of the legal position of the individual employee, which is weak if he has no support of the unions. In the case of an organized strike, there are few reasons and opportunities for employers to take summary action against individual employees. In theory such actions are possible in the case of wildcat strikes, but in reality this is rather cumbersome.

In the past, employees ran the risk of having an 'order to resume work' enforced against them, under penalty of a fine or a lodging of security, but these actions have been abolished by law since 1979 (Article 7:659(2) CC, *see* paragraph 80).

§5. Various Kinds of Strikes

339. In a number of countries a distinction is made between 'disputes of right' and 'disputes of interest'. In the Netherlands most strikes are due to genuine disputes of interest. Strikes arising from disputes of rights are not very common in the Netherlands as:

- the rights of Dutch employees have been strongly enshrined in law;
- the courts may deal in full with labour law disputes without being subject to any restrictions;
- the existence of summary proceedings and of legal aid have greatly facilitated employees' access to this 'legal channel';
- unions may also take action in the courts in the event of disputes relating to interpretation of a collective agreement (*see* paragraph 331).

Consequently unions and employees alike prefer judicial means of resolving disputes of rights. As strikes arising from disputes of rights are not very common in the Netherlands, it is not quite evident whether such strikes are *per definitionem* illegal. In the scarce case law on strikes out of disputes of rights the courts have only seldom taken such a dogmatic stand.

340. In the Netherlands most collective agreements contain no-strike clauses (*see* paragraph 329). Strikes in conflict with the peace obligation are in principle illegal. However, the peace obligation, if not otherwise stipulated, is only relative, so that in principle there can be legal strike action on items not regulated by the collective agreement.[349]

341. Strikes organized by trade unions with the aim of obtaining recognition of the employers are in principle legal. The same applies to strikes in order to obtain a better social plan.

342. The HR, although asserting that political strikes were not protected under the ESC, nevertheless is prepared to recognize in principle the legality of political strikes if they are related to the working conditions and social security of the employees.[350]

349. Dutch Supreme Court, 19 Apr. 1996, JAR 1996/115.
350. Dutch Supreme Court, 30 May 1986, NJ 1986, 688; Court of Appeal of Amsterdam, 4 May 2010; JAR 2010/140.

343. The legality of unofficial (wildcat) strikes is measured against the same criteria as that of official strikes. Although 30% of the strikes in the Netherlands commence as wildcat strikes, they are mostly swiftly extinguished or taken over by the trade unions, because the individual employee's legal and material position is weak without trade union support. Indeed, recent years have seen more strikes called by autonomous/spontaneously emerged workers groups (nurses, 2014; education, 2017) which were later taken over by the official unions.

344. In the Netherlands secondary action (sympathy or solidarity action) plays a very limited role in industrial relations. Therefore there was not much actual case law concerning these actions in the Netherlands. However, in a recent case about a declaration as 'contaminated' by the trade union of certain work hit by a strike action (with the result that other workers were called not handle that 'contaminated' work), the HR restated its position. Such a secondary action is covered by the right to strike under Article 6 ESC and therefore in principle legal when it can contribute to the purpose of the primary action which is aimed at collective bargaining[351] (for international solidarity action *see* paragraph 351).

§6. Strikes in Essential Services

345. There are no legal provisions in the Netherlands in this area. In 1980 the government proposed to make the social partners responsible for regulating this issue, through a code of practice on strikes, but this idea was never realized.

In the Amsta-judgment (*see* paragraph 336) the HR observed that a collective action is easily unlawful if the action is damaging persons with a specific vulnerability, such as youth, handicapped and elderly persons and other people in need for special care when they are exposed to the danger that their health may be harmed.[352] The courts assess the legality of a strike by taking account of the fact that certain occupational sectors require a minimum service or safety measures in the event of strikes, and that employees in some essential services cannot strike without alternative arrangements being made.

As mentioned above (*see* paragraph 338), the courts have accepted to hear cases against unions brought by customers' organizations if a strike threatens public interests (e.g., a bus drivers' strike).

§7. Legal Effects of Strikes

346. If strikes are legal, this legality has consequences for the legal position of the unions organizing them and for individual striking employees:

- The unions are not committing a tort and are not responsible for the damage caused by the strike.

351. Dutch Supreme Court, 27 Oct. 2014, ECLI:NL:HR:2014:3077 (Enerco).
352. Dutch Supreme Court, 19 Jun. 2015, ECLI:NL:HR:2015:1687.

- Striking employees are not committing a 'breach of contract' and their employers cannot legitimately take disciplinary action, such as dismissal and demotion, against striking employees. This because the prevailing legal doctrine considers the strike as a 'suspension' of the contract of employment. If such sanctions are taken by the employer the courts may overturn these sanctions and order the employer to re-employ the employee in his former position and to reinstate his rights.[353]
- For the same reason no action for damages can be taken against workers who go on a legal strike.

However, employees participating in a strike forfeit their right to remuneration and they are not entitled to social security benefits instead of wages. Only in union-supported strikes will the members of a union be provided with a small strike pay from union strike funds.

Most strikes end fairly quickly in the Netherlands and in some cases employers pay wages for the days on which employees have been on strike because they consider it too much of a hassle to correct the often automatic wage administration.

347. If a strike is considered unlawful, the unions supporting a strike are committing a tort or a breach of contract and they may be held responsible for the damages caused by the strike. However, in Dutch reality such actions did seldom occur. The Netherlands unions normally abide closely by legal decisions and stop their support immediately after such a court ruling. For this reason it is uncertain to what extent unions may be held responsible for damages caused after they should have withdrawn their support but did not. There is no actual case law on this matter.

As long as a collective action has not been declared illegal by a court the employees may assume that the action is legal, unless it manifestly is not.[354] Employers may take disciplinary action against individual strikers who continue to participate in a strike that has been declared illegal by a court, provided the disciplinary action is not disproportionate. It is not certain whether the employer or third parties may take action for compensation of damages against employees participating in an illegal strike. There is no actual case law on this matter.

§8. Other Types of Industrial Action

348. The recognition in principle of the right to collective action in Dutch case law is not narrowly limited to the specific form of the strike. Also other forms of collective action can be justified under it, but not all.

A go-slow or a work-to-rule action may be held legal by the Dutch courts if they would assess that a strike would be legal under the same circumstances. The same applies to actions in which for instance public transport workers allow passengers

353. Dutch Supreme Court, 22 Apr. 1988, NJ 1989, 952.
354. *Ibid.*

to travel without paying. According to the HR[355] in these cases the employers do not have to pay all employees their full wages. It is not exactly certain, however, how much employers must pay and to whom payment must be made. There is no case law on this matter.

349. The occupation of a factory in the form of a sit-in or a work-in emerged as a new form of industrial action in the 1970s. Workers have resorted to it occasionally, especially in the event of the closure of an enterprise or a collective dismissal. According to the HR a sit-in was not covered by the right to strike as laid down in Article 6 ESC. Its legality was to be judged on the basis of Article 6:162 Dutch CC (tort). A sit-in is illegal if it has a too far-reaching character, while its purpose can be attained by way of litigation before the courts.[356] A trade union organizing it could have to pay damages.[357] All this may now be different under the Amsta-ruling of the HR (*see* paragraph 336). Anyhow, most of the times employers involved in such actions have preferred to resolve matters by negotiation. Sit-ins may also entail criminal proceedings in the case of serious crime, but if such crimes are absent the police often prefers not to intervene.

350. A picket may also in principle entail action by the police. In practice, the police prefers not to interfere in an industrial dispute as long as it does not result in serious crimes, something which is very rare in the Netherlands. Obstructing roads or entrances is not allowed by case law while peaceful picketing is allowed. Employers may request a summary court judgment ruling that the picket is illegal and subject to the penalty of a fine. In the majority of the adjudicated cases, the courts considered pickets to be illegal.[358]

351. International solidarity actions, often in the form of a boycott, have been brought to Dutch courts several times.[359] Most of them were connected to international actions organized by the International Transport Workers Federation against ships under flags of convenience.[360] In fact the leading Dutch court case on the right to strike in the 1960s was exactly pronounced in the case of an international boycott: in 1960 the HR[361] considered illegal a sympathy action of Dutch dockworkers in support of the ITF-boycott of the ships of convenience (*Panhonlibco*). According to the doctrine based on the *Panhonlibco* decision, industrial action, and thus above all secondary action, is generally illegal. Actions were considered legal only if those

355. Dutch Supreme Court, 30 May 1986, NJ 1986, 688; Court of Appeal of Amsterdam, 9 Jan. 2003, JAR 2003/34.
356. Dutch Supreme Court, 19 Apr. 1991, NJ 1991, 690.
357. Dutch Supreme Court, 12 Dec. 1997, JAR 1998/38.
358. Dutch Supreme Court, 7 Nov. 1986, NJ 1987, 226.
359. *See* the contributions of A.T.J.M. Jacobs J.H. Even & F. Dorssemont (eds), *Cross-Border Collective Actions in Europe: A Legal Challenge* 179–191 and 355–402 (2007).
360. L.F.D. ter Kuile, *International Issues on Collective Agreements of Seafarers, Liber Amicorum Erades* 92–103 (1983).
361. *See* Dutch Supreme Court, 15 Jan. 1960, NJ, 1960, 84.

taking action were able to prove that under prevailing conditions it was unreasonable to require them to continue work (*see* paragraph 335). The HR did not, however, specify under what type of conditions the requirement of the employees to continue work may be considered unreasonable.

When in 1962 the Dutch trade union of seamen urged its members not to perform longshoremen's work in the port of New York out of solidarity with the dock workers on strike, the Dutch courts considered this as a tort (incitement of breach of contract of employment).[362] In 1972 the President of the Rotterdam District Court ruled illegal a boycott of a Chilean ship that was earlier boycotted in France.[363]

Also some cases related to strikes on board of the ships sailing under a flag of convenience, moored in the Dutch ports, have been tested on their legality by Dutch courts. From this case law it has become clear that Dutch law is not in principle hostile to the application of foreign strike law on collective actions on board of foreign ships, moored in Dutch ports. Most cases, however, are approached more on a pragmatic than on a dogmatic basis.

The last reported case is about a solidarity action of KLM pilots with a strike of pilots of Northwest Airlines (sister-company of KLM) in 1998. In summary proceedings (injunction) the President of the District Court of Amsterdam declared this secondary/sympathy action illegal.[364] However, in the light of recent case law of the HR on secondary action (*see* paragraph 344) this way of thinking may now be out of date.

§9. The Lock-Out

352. In the Netherlands lockouts sometimes occurred in the first part of the twentieth century, but they are not reported since the beginning of the 1950s. Lockouts are not regulated by statute and their legal status is uncertain because there is no modern case law.

Lockout is in some cases taken to mean the dismissal of all striking employees. In Dutch law this is only legally possible in case a court has declared a strike to be illegal and the strikers continued the strike (*see* paragraph 347). And even then this kind of lockout might be disproportionate. In recent history in the Netherlands there have been no such cases or court verdicts on them.

Lockout may also be taken to mean: the laying off of non-striking employees because of a strike. The employer cannot easily give this laying off the form of a dismissal of the non-striking workers, as under Dutch law summary dismissal (*see* paragraph 222 et seq.) cannot be used for this purpose (because non-strikers are not breaching their contracts!), an ordinary dismissal is not possible without a prior authorization of the UWV or a court (*see* paragraph 202) and no unilateral reduction of working time is legal (*see* paragraph 173).

---

362. President District Court of Rotterdam, 2 Oct. 1962, Sociaal Maandblad Arbeid 1962, p. 798; affirmed by the Court of Appeal in The Hague, 21 Dec. 1962, Sociaal Maandblad Arbeid 1963, p. 229.

363. President District Court of Rotterdam, 24 Oct. 1972, NJ 1972, 457; A. Kortes Altes, *Seamen's Strikes and Supporting Boycotts, Liber Amicorum Erades* 115 (1983).

364. President District Court of Amsterdam, 26 Aug. 1998, JAR 1998/195.

The employer may consider laying off his non-striking workers in the form of an interruption of the payment of wages, but difficulties may arise as regards the Dutch law on the obligation to pay wages (Article 7:628 CC, *see* paragraphs 147 and 148). It is not very clear whether employers are liable to continue to pay wages to non-striking workers who cannot work as a consequence of a strike. The HR case law once ruled[365] that the answer to this question depends on the nature of the industrial dispute. In the case of a strike organized to obtain improved working conditions for the majority of employees, employers are not liable to pay the wages of those who wish to work but are prevented from doing so because of the strike. In the case, however, of a wildcat protest action of short duration, in which only a few employees take part, employers are liable to pay the wages of the non-striking employees, who cannot work because of the strike. In practice this doctrine leaves open many questions. The borderline between the two categories is not quite sharp. What about an organized protest strike? What about a wildcat strike concerning conditions of employment? It is sometimes difficult to decide whether these kinds of actions belong to the first category or to the second.

If there is no right to payment of wages, non-striking employees may possibly request unemployment benefit or public assistance. In principle this will be refused, but in problematic cases exceptions can be made.

None of these questions has been dealt with in depth because the lockout has not been used in the Netherlands since the 1950s and employers prefer to continue to pay non-strikers (as long as it is not an organized strategy and they are genuine non-strikers) because they are considered as their allies.

353. Dutch law prohibits public employment referral services from referring workers to job vacancies resulting from a strike (Article 27 SUWI Act, *see* paragraph 251) and it prohibits private employment agencies or temporary employment companies from supplying workers as replacements for strikers (Article 10 AEIA, *see* paragraph 255).[366] In recent years the practice has appeared that companies hit by strikes have resort to use of personnel of other companies (not being temporary employment agencies) or to the use of personnel from sister companies belonging to the same group to replace striking workers by way of temporary outsourcing. The Dutch trade unions maintain that these practices are illegal. However the HR has recently judged that the norm of Article 10 AEIA is a restrictive one and applies only to workers leased by companies on which the AEIA is applicable, not to the deployment of own personnel from the employer or from another enterprise of the group.[367]

In rare cases Dutch employers have used various forms of anti-strike premiums. The HR confirmed the illegality of a condition in a contract of employment which

365. Dutch Supreme Court, 7 May 1976, NJ 1977, 55.
366. Sections 3 and 10 of the Allocation of Employees by Intermediaries Act.
367. Dutch Supreme Court, 19 Jul. 2019, ECLI:NL:HR:2019:1245; Court of Appeal Amsterdam, 24 Jan. 2008, JAR 2008/105.

made a profit-sharing scheme dependent on the worker not having participated in a strike. The HR considered such a clause as an illegal means of pressure against the use of the right to strike.[368]

§10. Dispute-Settlement Mechanisms

354. As we have seen (*see* paragraph 337) the settlement of collective labour disputes in the Netherlands is mainly in the hands of the courts. Conciliation and mediation in such disputes only plays a very minor role.

For the first time in 1897 the Dutch legislator started to promote conciliation and mediation in collective labour disputes when it created Chambers of Labour with *inter alia* this function (*Wet op de Kamers van Arbeid*). These Chambers were not very successful and after World War I the Act was replaced by the Labour Disputes Act (*Arbeidsgeschillenwet*) of 1923, which provided for a State conciliator in each of four geographical areas of the Netherlands to help settle labour disputes. The state conciliators were appointed by, but independent of, the Minister of Social Affairs. Although the Act was never formally withdrawn, it virtually ceased to exist, as in 1945 the tasks of the conciliators were fundamentally altered by the Extraordinary Decree on Labour Relations (*see* paragraph 281).

After World War II no formal machinery was established to promote the settlement of labour conflicts. The prevailing climate of industrial peace seemed to make such a move unnecessary. Whenever an industrial dispute did arise, it was resolved either by the parties themselves or with the help of ad hoc mediation.

A Bill introduced in 1969 containing new regulations on dispute-settlement mechanisms was never enacted and was withdrawn in 1986. Meanwhile, the idea of self-regulation of strike action by representatives of employers' and employees' confederations in the *Stichting van de Arbeid* has proved attractive to some people but has never been put into practice.

Arbitration is seldom used as a means of resolving industrial disputes. Mediation and conciliation may occur on an occasional basis if industrial conflict lasts for a long time. However, all this takes place on a strictly voluntary basis.

Collective agreements in some cases contain provisions relating to the procedures to be followed in the event of an industrial dispute, but these provisions are very rarely used. Industrial disputes of longer duration are sometimes mediated on an ad hoc basis by a conciliator who is a high-level personality.

Statutory mediation machinery is offered in the field of workers' participation in the enterprise (*see* paragraph 399) as well as in the public service, for which a consultation and arbitration commission was set up in 1985 (*see* paragraph 355).

In summary: the role of conciliation, mediation and arbitration in resolving collective labour disputes is quite small in the Netherlands.[369]

---

368. Dutch Supreme Court, 24 Sep. 1999, JAR 1999/214.

369. *See* A.F.M. Brenninkmeijer & L.C.J. Sprengers, *Collective Labour Law Disputes in the Public and Private Sector*, in *Effective Resolution of Collective Labour Disputes* 3–14 A.F.M. Brenninkmeijer, L.C.J. Sprengers, A.J. de Roo & R.W. Jagtenberg, Groningen, 2006); J.A. de Roo & R. Jagtenberg,

§11. STRIKES IN THE PUBLIC SERVICE

355. After a protracted all-out strike which shocked the nation, public servants and railways personnel were prohibited from striking in 1903 and subject to criminal proceedings in that event. This prohibition was a dead letter since the 1960s and finally was abolished in 1979, but the government did not wish to grant an unfettered right to strike to public servants and consequently announced a Bill to regulate public servants' right to strike. This idea was never put into practice and there is no statute on this matter.

Public servants' unions organizing a strike could still be brought before the courts and could incur a prohibition accompanied by a fine imposed upon them. Public servants themselves could be disciplined by demotion, dismissal, etc.

The courts have been prepared to condone public servant strikes, but a limited number of civil servants, such as the military and prison guards will certainly not be allowed to strike for a substantial period. But what exactly is allowed and to whom? In some cases the courts have already ruled that a strike by public servants is legal; in other cases, for instance in the case of police personnel, one time a strike action was prohibited, another time it was condoned.

Finally mention should be made of the special procedure for settling disputes at the central government sector established in 1985. In that year the Advisory and Arbitration Committee (AAC) was appointed. If one of the negotiating parties considers that consultations are unlikely to culminate in an agreement, the point at issue can be submitted to the AAC. The committee's advice may be requested by the chairperson or by the (majority of the negotiating) staff federations. For arbitration all of the participants have to subscribe the request, but this almost never happens.

Settling Labour Disputes in Europe, Kluwer, Deventer, 1994; on pp. 209–263 one finds an English-language description and discussion of the settlement of labour disputes in the Netherlands.

Chapter 6. Employee Participation in the Enterprise

§1. Introduction

356. The oldest trade unions in the Netherlands emerged in the 1860s. They first had a moderate character, but when later trade unions assumed a more militant nature they were regarded by the employers with scepticism and hostility. Some employers found that they could better organize communication directly with the workers of their enterprises. So the first works councils in the Netherlands were established around 1880 by two social progressive employers. These works councils were called *kernen* (= nucleus, after Le Noyau in the Paris enterprise of Leclaire in the 19th century). After 1900 these pioneer employers were followed by other employers out of a strategy to contain the growing attractiveness of the trade unions. This prompted notably the radical and social democrat trade unions to a hostile attitude to the idea of works councils. Around 1922 there were over 100 works councils. They were predominantly involved in social affairs and not allowed to discuss economic questions. In 1923 the still oppositional social democrats, having studied the German concept of *Betriebsräte*, spoke out in favour of industrial democracy at the level of the enterprise, but the ruling Christian democrat parties preferred to lay emphasis on industrial democracy at sectoral level (*see* paragraph 279). Therefore workers' representation at enterprise level was very much neglected by the lawmakers. Although in 1945 a Royal Decree had established works councils in the entire mining industry (privately as well as state owned) and Parliament had passed the first WCA in 1950, the works councils were only slow to grow. During the 1950s theorists in all political corners began to write about the subject of industrial democracy in the enterprise. It was finally in the 1960s that the general trend to more democratization in society was also focused on the enterprise level. Many scholars, trade unionists and politicians referred to the set-up of *Mitbestimmung* in Germany. Some even pointed at the Yugoslav model of workers control of enterprises. A State Commission (Commissie-Verdam) advised a number of legal props to enhance employee participation in the enterprise, e.g., by modernizing the works councils legislation and workers influence of the management structure of the enterprise. Parliament followed to a large extent the proposals of the Commissie-Verdam when it adopted in 1970/1971 four statutes to strengthen employee participation. These included:

- an act on the annual accounts of the company;
- an act on company enquiries (*see* paragraphs 358 et seq.);
- an act on the management structure of major enterprises (*see* paragraphs 364 et seq.);
- a new WCA of 1970 (*see* paragraphs 370 et seq.).

The Acts on the annual accounts and on company enquiries have been consolidated. The Act on the management structure of major enterprises has been changed substantially by an Act of 2004 (*see* paragraphs 367 et seq.). The WCA of 1970 was heavily amended by an Act of 1979 and has been amended several times since then (*see* paragraph 370).

357. The result of this legislation was that the employee's participation in the enterprise has notably been channelled through the systems of works councils. As a consequence in the Netherlands there is not a single line of workers' representation as there is in the US, on the British Isles and Scandinavia, but, as in most continental European countries, there is in fact a plurality of employees' representatives: trade unions and works councils. However, unlike France, Belgium and Italy, and more like Germany, at company level the key social partner of management is, in most cases, the works council and not the trade union.

In the Netherlands the trade union movement benefited less from the drive to expand industrial democracy at enterprise level. Union delegates on the shop-floor are only recognized in a number of collective agreements. Legal regulations on this issue have never passed the preparatory stage and were withdrawn in 1991 (*see* paragraph 277). The only statutory rights secured for the trade unions were those included in the Act on company enquiries (*see* paragraph 358) and in the Act on the notification of collective dismissals (*see* paragraph 360). In addition the trade unions were to play a role in the rules of conduct to be observed in cases of merger or transfer of enterprises (*see* paragraph 361).

The attitude of the unions towards works councils has been hesitant, although they have shown increasing interest. A kind of unofficial division of tasks between unions and works councils has emerged:

(a) collective bargaining about terms and conditions of employment remained the monopoly of the unions; the works councils obtained some advisory and co-decision-making powers with regard to the social policy of the enterprise;
(b) the conditions of employment fixed at sectoral level by collective agreements are often tailor-made at the level of the enterprise in cooperation between employer and works council.

Some factors have made the acceptance of works councils easier for unions, in particular, the fact that unions may themselves present a list of candidates for the election of works councils (*see* paragraph 381) and the fact that legislators have deliberately denied works councils any power over matters which are exhaustively regulated by collective agreement (*see* paragraph 391).

§2. Union Participation Rights

I. Involvement in the Law on Company Enquiries

358. In 1971 Dutch company law was amended to give the judiciary the power of investigation into the policy and daily management of an enterprise. Such an enquiry can be ordered by the Court of Appeal of Amsterdam (Companies Bench, *see* paragraph 38). Applications for such enquiries to be held can be filed by the trade unions, the shareholders, the management board, the supervisory board, the receiver (in case of bankruptcy) or by the public prosecutor of the Amsterdam Court of Appeal (Article 2:345–347 CC). Quite remarkably the works councils do not have this right.

The right to file an application for such a company enquiry is vested in a trade union which has among its members persons working for the enterprise and has had full legal capacity for at least two years, provided its object under its articles is to promote the interests of its members as employees and it is active in such capacity in the sector of business or in the enterprise (Article 2:347 CC).

The applicants and the public prosecutor have no *locus standi* if they have not given advance notice of their objection against the policy or conduct of business to the management and the supervisory board. Unions must also have given the works council connected with the enterprise an opportunity to express its views (Article 2:349 CC).

An application for an enquiry is allowed by the Court of Appeal of Amsterdam (Companies Bench) only if there appear well-founded reasons to doubt the correctness of the managerial policy (Article 2:350 CC). In that case, the court appoints one or more persons to conduct an enquiry into the policy and management of the enterprise. Investigators are entitled to examine the books and records of the legal person and the directors, the members of the supervisory board and the employees of the legal person shall, on request, be obliged to provide the investors all such information as shall be necessary for the implementation of the enquiry (Article 2:350 and 2:351 CC).

If 'misconduct' (incorrect management) is established by the investigators, the court may take any necessary measure, such as the suspension or annulment of decisions of the management board, the supervisory council or the meeting of shareholders, the suspension or dismissal of one or more directors or members of the supervisory board, the temporary appointment of one or more directors or members of the supervisory board, the temporary derogation from the articles of the company and even the winding up of the legal person (Article 2:355–358 CC).

Appeals in Cassation to the HR may be instituted against orders of the Court of Appeal of Amsterdam (Companies Bench) (Article 2:359 CC).

359. In practice, unions use this right to apply for an enquiry rarely. First, because the criteria adopted by the Court of Appeal of Amsterdam (Companies Bench) as regards 'misconduct' requires a kind of management that has violated all the fundamental principles of a responsible management. This is hard to prove. Fortunately the court differentiates between social management and economic management. Even if there had not been economic 'misconduct' there might have been 'social misconduct' when important procedural rules had been violated and negotiations with the unions and the works council had left much to be desired. In practice, it seems that it is easier to prove 'social misconduct' than 'economic misconduct'.

Second, a request for an enquiry is a risky undertaking since an applicant whose application has been dismissed may be ordered to pay damages to the legal person if the request was not made on reasonable grounds (Article 2:350 CC). Although the court has been prepared not to apply this possibility quickly, it always remains a risk.

Finally there is the time factor. The enquiry procedure takes a considerable amount of time. In the case of the closure of the production unit of Ford Netherlands at Amsterdam in 1981, the ruling – which rejected the unions' application –

was given only after closure of the enterprise. However, this problem can now be remedied: the applicants may apply that the Court of Appeal of Amsterdam (Companies Bench) order an immediate remedy for the duration of the proceedings at most (Article 2:249a CC), for instance a temporary prohibition of certain managerial decisions to be executed.

II. Collective Dismissals

360. Dutch unions have a statutory right on information and consultation in the case of collective dismissals. This is laid down in the NCDA, which implements the EC Directive on collective dismissals. If an employer makes twenty or more employees redundant within three months, that employer is obliged to notify this collective dismissal to *inter alia* the trade unions. Implementing the collective dismissal is forbidden during a 'waiting period' of one month (*see* paragraph 224). The trade unions can use this period to negotiate a 'social plan' with the employer (*see* paragraphs 226 and 330). When such consultation with the unions has been carried out in good time with favourable results and the other requirements laid down by the NCDA have been met, collective dismissals by the employer can take place immediately.

Entitled to notification are unions which are active on behalf of their members in the enterprise having the status of a legal person for at least two years, but only insofar as they have been known as such to the employer.

In bankruptcy situations this information and consultation must be provided by the receiver (*see* paragraphs 228 and 390).

The duties imposed by Dutch law and by collective bargaining on employers to inform and to consult the trade unions and the works councils enable the workers' representatives to exert pressure on the employer to research all possible alternatives for a collective dismissal and, if dismissals are unavoidable, to provide for severance pay, retraining or other help to find another job.

If the employer does not bow to such pressures the works councils have some possibilities to hinder the employer in proceeding with the collective dismissal (*see* paragraph 387). The trade unions may ask for a judicial enquiry (*see* paragraph 358) or have recourse to (the threat of) collective action (strikes, sit-ins, etc.). The Netherlands has seen in the past decades a few actions of this type, such as those at Akzo, Ford Nederland, Batco and Heineken. These actions have had various results. Sometimes they have delayed the closure of a plant or increased the amount of compensation paid to redundant workers. Occasionally they have resulted in short-term government subsidies to enterprises (*see* paragraph 238). Such collective actions have met with different judgments when they were contested in court. Some actions were declared unlawful, but others were tolerated. Much depended on the type of the action and the circumstances of the case. Strikes are lawful in principle (*see* paragraph 341), but sit-ins are more dubious (*see* paragraph 349).

III. The Merger Code

361. A final information and consultation measure to the benefit of the trade unions, the Merger Code, relates to mergers and takeovers. It requires employers to inform the trade unions concerned whenever they are involved in merger/takeover negotiations and before an agreement is reached. These rules are not set out in an Act of Parliament but in a document of 1970, amended in 1975, 2000 and 2015 issued by the SER (*see* paragraphs 290 et seq.), the so-called *SER-Besluit Fusiegedragsregels 2015* (Merger Code).

The Merger Code applies to any transfer of the control, directly or indirectly, over an enterprise or part of it, as well as to the construction of a combination of enterprises ('group' or (German) 'Konzern' (Article 1(1)(e)). It consequently relates both to mergers by transfer of shares and to legal mergers or mergers by sale, etc. The Merger Code is also applicable when a merger takes place on the basis of a takeover bid (Article 5 Merger Code) and a gradual process of buying shares (Article 6 Merger Code). And also in case of a business transfer involving a bankruptcy-related assets transaction.

Its scope of application is limited, however, to mergers concerning an enterprise or group of enterprises in the Netherlands employing at least fifty employees. The Merger Code initially related solely to the market sector, but in 2015 this limitation was lifted when the scope of the Code was equated with that of the WCA (*see* paragraph 373) (Article 1(1)(a) Merger Code).

Before merger negotiations are publicly announced and an agreement is concluded, the employers concerned must immediately notify the trade unions concerned and the Secretariat of the SER (Articles 3, 4 and 8 Merger Code). The trade unions must be informed of the reasons and effects of the merger and must be allowed to give their opinion on the merger from the point of view of employees' interests. This consultation is about the social consequences of the merger for the workers concerned and the measures taken to cope with them (Article 4 Merger Code). The trade unions must observe the confidentiality of these information (Article 7 Merger Code).

Because the 'Merger Code' is not an Act of Parliament, the courts cannot enforce its observance. There is, however, a Dispute Committee, which supervises the observance of the Code (Articles 9–33 Merger Code). This Dispute Committee comprises representatives of the representative organizations of employees and employers as well as independent members. As the only sanction against failure to observe the code, the Dispute Committee may issue a decision about the non-observance of the Code (public statement) (Article 32 Merger Code).

The Merger Code does not operate well in the case of a genuine struggle to take over a company. Under the pressure of time, vital decisions may be taken as to the future of the enterprise, such as a merger with a third party or the establishment of a protective legal fence (only recently done by KPN against the acquisition by American Movil, *see* paragraph 366), which do not always allow the compulsory information and consultation within due time.

362. The Merger Code is also applicable to any foreign enterprise which is directly involved in a merger with a Dutch enterprise, whatever its nationality or place of establishment. The result is that, in the case of a merger, the foreign partner, in the same way as the Dutch partner, is required to participate in the process of information and consultation as regards the Dutch unions. It is taken for granted that the Dutch partner will inform its foreign partner of its specific obligations. If this is not the case, no rigorous action is taken against the foreign partner in respect of any infraction of the Merger Code (bearing in mind that the code sets out only symbolic sanctions!).

The Code nevertheless makes a very important exception for mergers 'which do not come within Dutch legal jurisdiction' (Article 2(3d) Merger Code). This exception relates to mergers between two or several groups of foreign companies whose actual management takes place outside Dutch territory, although they include Dutch establishments employing more than fifty employees. This exception is narrowly construed. A full merger between the Péchiney group and the American National Can group would not come within the scope of application of the Merger Code, although both these groups have major subsidiaries in the Netherlands. However, mergers involving 'solely or principally' the Dutch subsidiaries of a foreign group would be subject to the Merger Code, which means that a merger of Péchiney Holland and American National Can Holland would be governed by the Merger Code. The notion of 'solely or principally' is interpreted on the basis of the number of employees involved.

A Dutch enterprise or a Dutch financial group wishing to take over a foreign enterprise would have to respect the Merger Code, if it could be expected that this takeover would have major consequences for Dutch personnel: for instance, because of the size of the foreign enterprise or the harmonization of activities or markets.

363. In a number of sector or enterprise collective agreements the trade unions have acquired for themselves information and consultation rights. Such agreements often oblige the employers to inform and consult the trade unions in case of restructuring the enterprise, outsourcing, offshoring, collective dismissal, mergers and the like. Those provisions often require the employer to negotiate in those cases with the trade unions a so-called social plan. Those provisions are not to be disregarded because the trade unions may enforce these rights via the courts (as collective agreements are generally binding in the Netherlands, *see* paragraphs 328 et seq.). If a social plan is properly concluded and communicated to the Ministry of Social Affairs it is regarded as a collective agreement and has binding force as such (*see* paragraph 307). If no agreement is reached about a social plan the trade union may call a strike (*see* paragraph 341).

§3. Workers' Influence on the Composition of the Top-Level Management of Major Companies

364. In the Netherlands, like in Germany, in the course of time the major enterprises have taken the legal form of a limited company under a two-tier structure: a managing board which is responsible for day-to-day affairs and a supervisory board, which supervises and advises the managing board. According to traditional Dutch company law, the ultimate power in a company was vested in the general meeting of shareholders. It was the shareholders' meeting which drew up the articles of association, appointed and dismissed the members of the managing board and the supervisory board, ratified the annual balance sheet and profit and loss account, could modify the capital structure of the company, etc.

When in the Netherlands in the 1960s discussions about industrial democracy started, opinion was divided. Some unions wanted a system in which the works council should be authorized directly to appoint some of the members of the supervisory board, on the same lines as in Germany, while other unions were afraid that worker representation would entangle them too much in the capitalist system. The employers opposed any direct influence of workers representatives in the board rooms of the companies. Opinion was still divided when the government asked the Social Economic Council to draft a proposal for legislation in 1969. At the decisive session of the Social Economic Council, a compromise was introduced quite suddenly and – to everyone's surprise – accepted. In the major companies the ultimate power should shift to the supervisory board, which henceforward was to be composed by members who all enjoy the confidence of both labour and capital. The philosophy behind this compromise was that the supervisory board should not be composed of persons representing a particular interest. It reflected the feeling which we have already mentioned that in the Netherlands 'consultation' and consensus building as means of conflict resolution are more highly thought of than an overt clash of interests.

365. This compromise was adopted by the government in the Bill which became the Structure Act of 1971. This Structure Act amended the provisions of company law in the Dutch CC to allow employees to have some influence over the composition of the top level of management of major enterprises. The competence to nominate the members of the management board and to approve its main decisions was given to the supervisory board. All vacant positions in this supervisory board should be filled by the Board itself (co-optation), but both the shareholders' assembly and the works council were given a qualified power to veto any nomination in the supervisory board.

The Dutch 1971-solution for the composition of the supervisory board was certainly original, but – because the veto-power was very much 'qualified' – it has not given works councils the feeling that they could really influence the composition of the supervisory board in its totality. In most large companies it became the custom, that the works council proposed an extern workers-friendly personality for the role of 'social' member of the supervisory board. Those persons normally saw themselves not as representatives of the workers but only as a board member which should pay special attention to the social aspects of management. This system has certainly contributed to an improvement of the quality of the supervisory boards, but at the same time it has given the shareholders' side the impression that it had created an amalgamated power of management and supervisory board, which had become virtually uncontrollable. The system had in fact helped the managers of Dutch companies to entrench their companies against hostile takeovers. Observers considered Dutch company law as very friendly towards all sorts of legal constructions which favour the private interest of company managers. So the Dutch model became heavily contested in the 1990s during the Dutch version of the international debate about 'corporate governance'.[370] In the meantime a tendency to strengthen the powers of the general assembly of shareholders and consequently to limit the powers of the supervisory board gained support. A committee set up to come forward with changes in company governance proposed important amendments and subsequently a new compromise about the composition of the supervisory council was reached in the Socio-Economic Council in 2002.

Finally in 2004 the Dutch Parliament gave back the power to adopt de annual account to the meeting of the shareholders (Article 2:101 CC) and replaced the existing system of the nomination and composition of the supervisory board by a model somewhat comparable with that of the German *Mitbestimmungsmodel* of the *Drittelbeteiligungsgesetz* 2004.

366. This Structure Act 2004, which is still in force today, is applicable to major enterprises, driven as public limited companies or partnerships, cooperatives and mutual guarantee companies (a) whose paid-up capital, including reserves, is at least EUR 13 million, (b) employ at least 100 employees in the Netherlands and (c) have established a works council (Article 2:262 CC). Such companies must establish a supervisory board, which has the legal powers to appoint the members of the management board (safe in case of the natural person being the only shareholder (Article 2:265a CC)) and to approve major management decisions (Article 2:274 CC). All the members of the supervisory board are again – as before 1971! – appointed by the shareholders (Article 2:158(4) CC. However, the works council may propose candidates for – depending on the size of the Board – between 20% and 33.3% of the seats in the supervisory board. The sitting members of the supervisory board may turn down such proposals, solely on the basis of the prediction that the candidate will not be suitable to carry out the functions of a member of the supervisory board, or the fact that the supervisory board will not be duly constituted if the intended appointment actually takes place. The shareholders are not obliged to appoint the works councils' candidates and they may dismiss them with a simple majority of more than 50%) (Article 2: 268 CC). Since 2004 there has been only one case reported in which either the supervisory board or the meeting of shareholders has rejected a candidate who has been proposed by the works council.

367. So, at first sight and formally speaking, the Structure Act 2004 has turned back the clock quite dramatically. However, the reality as described above, that in all major enterprises an extern workers-friendly candidate of the works council is smoothly accepted as the 'social' member of the supervisory board, has been continued. Although in 2007 the Socio-Economic Council was still satisfied with the present way the top of big business in the Netherlands is put in place, nevertheless during the financial crisis of 2007–2008 a number of observers remarked that the changes in the Structure Act 2004 have given the shareholders too much power in Dutch corporate governance. However nothing has been changed since then on this point.

370. R. Kleipool a.o., *Corporate Governance in The Netherlands* (2018).

368. In the Structure Act the participation model is structured 'upwards': it is enough for the parent company to respect the model for its subsidiaries to be exempted (Article 2:153 CC). This parent company, however, does not necessarily represent the highest management level of the group. In MNCs it is often merely the highest level of the group's Dutch establishments. Above it, there is generally an international holding company which – even if it has its seat in the Netherlands – normally falls outside the scope of the aforementioned model of participation, simply because it normally fails to have 100 employees. Already for this reason Dutch MNCs such as Philips and Akzo Nobel have been able to keep the registered offices of their holding companies in the Netherlands without their holding company being confronted with the Dutch rules on the supervisory boards.

MNCs, which have most of their employees employed outside the Netherlands, are served by another exception. They may give their supervisory boards a much 'lighter' stature in the sense that it only has the power to control the major decisions of the management but not the power to appoint management (Article 2:155 CC).

369. The rules on workers' influence on the composition of the top-level management of major companies were initially designed to serve the only applicable structure-model in the Netherlands, namely the dualist or two-tier-model: the company is governed by a board of directors, who are working under a supervisory board (*see* paragraph 364). In the UK and other EU Member States a formally different structure-model is applied, viz. the monist or one-tier-model: the company is governed by a board of directors, some of them are directly in charge of the daily management of the company, others play a more distanced role. In 2011 the Dutch lawmakers decided, that henceforward Dutch companies may opt out of the dualist model and opt for the monist model (Article 2:239a CC). At the same time it was provided, that the works council in an enterprise governed according to the monist model must have *mutatis mutandis* the same rights on workers' influence, which then are directed towards the nomination of the non-executive members of the board of directors (Article 2:274a CC).

§4. Works Councils

I. Legal History

370. The first statute relating to works councils was the WCA of 1950. This was a weak piece of legislation which was not very helpful to further the development of works councils. The democratization movement of the 1960s resulted in a new and more supportive enactment: the WCA of 1970. This Act considerably extended the scope and the powers of works councils. Under this Act employers with 100 or more employees were required to set up works councils. The Act gave the works councils, *inter alia*, a right to information, a right to prior consultation (advice) on important economic and social company decisions as well as a right to co-determination (consent) of certain specified social issues. Moreover the legal protection of the members of the works council was increased and penalties were established to cover cases of non-observance.

Many people, however, were not satisfied with this Act as the works council was still presided over by the CEO of the company. And because the Act did not cover companies below 100 employees.

The ever-increasing trend towards democracy led in 1979 to a major amendment of the Act, through which the works council became a real employees' committee (the employer being no longer its chairman) and the powers, possibilities of appeal and legal protection of works councils' members were again extended.

In 1982 the scope of the WCA was greatly extended by rules on employee participation in small and medium-sized enterprises. In 1990 the WCA was again amended to simplify the procedures of judicial review and to harmonize them with those of the Health and Safety Act. In 1998, the scope of the Act was again extended and a few new powers and facilities attributed.

Initially the public service was left outside the system of works councils. For civil servants of the state, since 1982 departmental committees have been set up to serve as participation centres organized in accordance with the various regulations covering public servants. In 1994 however this special system was abolished and the public sector was brought under the WCA.[371]

In 2004 the Act was tested against the EC General Framework Directive on information and consultation. The transposition of this Directive was not very cumbersome for the Netherlands, because most of its provisions had already been realized by the WCA. The implementation of this Directive therefore led only to a few very minor adaptations.

A somewhat more comprehensive overhaul of the provisions of the WCA was proposed by the government in 2004, but this Bill did not receive much enthusiasm in Parliament and was withdrawn in 2005. In 2013 an amendment Act was adopted which brought only minor changes in the existing rules. Also in the following years other minor changes have been made in the WCA.

Today only in education (both public and private) specific participation regulations apply in order to include the participation of parents, pupils and students. Because of the constitutional guaranteed freedom of education, these regulations are to some extent less strict than those in the economic sector. These are laid down in acts on industrial democracy in primary and secondary education of 2006, higher and scientific education of 1998 and vocational education of 2009. In 2017 these Acts were modernized.[372]

II. The Duty to Establish a Works Council

371. The WCA obliges all types of entrepreneurs carrying on an enterprise in which normally at least fifty persons are working to set up a full-fledged works council (Article 2 WCA).

371. L.C.J. Sprengers, *De Wet op de ondernemingsraden bij de overheid* (1998). On pp. 739–748 is found an English-language description of the backgrounds of the introduction of the Works Councils Act in the public sector as part of the ongoing process to bring the public sector labour laws more in line with those customary in the private sector.

372. Act of 15 Jun. 2016, Stb. 2016, 273; Parliamentary Papers 34251.

In enterprises in which there are normally at least ten and fewer than fifty persons working the entrepreneur may establish and maintain a works council (Article 5a(2) WCA). If he has not established a works council, the entrepreneur may set up an ERB (Article 35c(1) WCA). An ERB must be set up at the request of the majority of the persons working in the enterprise (Article 35c(2) WCA). Such an ERB will have almost the same rights to information, but has fewer facilities and powers of consultation and co-determination (Article 35(c) WCA).

If neither a works council nor an ERB has been established the entrepreneur shall give the persons working in the enterprise an opportunity of meeting with him at least twice each calendar year. He shall also convene a meeting with the persons working in these types of enterprises when at least one-quarter of them submits a request to this effect together with a statement of the reasons for making the request (Article 35(b) WCA).

Finally, in enterprises in which there are normally fewer than ten persons working and for which no works council has been established, the entrepreneur may set up an ERB if he so wishes. That body may have even more limited facilities and powers than its equivalent in an enterprise with more than ten employees (Article 35(d) WCA).

Over the years research has established that constantly in ca. 25% of all enterprises which legally should have a works council, such a works council is lacking. Apparently in those companies nobody is trying to enforce the establishment of a works council although this is possible (*see* paragraph 398).

372. Any entrepreneur who is under an obligation to establish a works council shall, insofar as necessary, establish by provisional Rules of Procedure provisions that properly fall under the powers of the works council until such time as the works council exercises these powers itself. The views of the trade unions mentioned in Article 9 WCA (*see* paragraph 381) shall be sought with regard to the said provisional Rules of Procedure (Article 48 WCA).

III. Notions, Definitions and the Structure of a System of Works Councils

373. According to the WCA an enterprise is ‘any organization operating in the society as an independent entity in which work is performed on the basis of a contract of employment or public law appointment’ (Article 1(1c) WCA). So the term ‘enterprise’ does not refer solely to commercial enterprises. The WCA covers profit-making business and non-profit organizations alike. Even organizations, which are not conventionally considered to be ‘enterprises’ must organize a works council, for instance hospitals, welfare organizations and even religious societies like the Salvation Army. As we have seen already also the public service is brought under the WCA and therefore covered by the notion of ‘enterprise’ which in the ambit of the WCA has completely lost any commercial connotation.

Only very limited sectors of the Dutch society are excluded from the scope of the WCA. This concerns more especially educational institutions for which special arrangements of industrial democracy are issued (*see* paragraph 370). In addition are exempted the Ministry of Defence, the National Ombudsman, the judicial officers of the HR, the Members of the Council of State and of the Netherlands Court of Audit (Article 53–53c WCA).

Furthermore the concept of 'enterprise' as defined above is reflecting actual situations of independent presentation in society. It may be but is not necessarily identical with the legal concept of 'company' which is used in company law. In that domain 'company' is always taken formally to mean the employer as a physical or legal person.

However, the English notions of 'enterprise', 'company', 'plant' and 'establishment', the French notions of *entreprise* and *établissement* and the German notions of *Betrieb* and *Unternehmen* are not consequently defined under Dutch law. Their Dutch equivalents – *bedrijf* and *onderneming* – are often mixed up.

If a plant or an establishment is not an independent entity within the enterprise – such as a ship, a service station or a building site – it is often described in Dutch law as 'part of the enterprise'.

374. An entrepreneur who carries on two or more enterprises in which in totality normally at least fifty persons are working shall establish a Joint works council for all or a number of these enterprises if this is in the interests of the proper implementation of the WCA within the enterprise. Such enterprises are considered to be one enterprise for the functioning of the Act. The same applies for a group (= Konzern) of entrepreneurs which carries on two or more enterprises in which in totality normally at least fifty persons are working. Those entrepreneurs must nominate one of them as the entrepreneur in the sense of this Act (Article 3 WCA). However if this is in the interests of the proper implementation of the WCA the entrepreneur must establish for a part of the enterprise a separate works council. The part of the enterprise for which a separate works council is established is considered to be an enterprise for the functioning of the Act (Article 4 WCA).

Any entrepreneur who has established two or more works councils shall also establish a Central Works Council for the totality of these enterprises if this is in the interests of the proper implementation of the WCA in respect of those enterprises (Article 33(1) WCA). With the same reasoning entrepreneurs with a vast number of works councils shall establish a *Groepsondernemingsraad* (Group Works Council) for a number of these enterprises. This intermediate level between the upper level of the Central Works Council and the basic level of the various local works councils is notably created in enterprises that consist of several 'divisions' (Article 33(2) WCA). Nota bene, the remarkable notion of 'group' in this provision of the WCA. In English-speaking areas 'group' normally means the totality of all the enterprises depending on a holding company (the German notion of *Konzern*). This is also followed in the Dutch texts of company law, notably in the Structure Act (*see* paragraphs 365 et seq.) and also in Articles 2 and 33(3) WCA. However, in Article 33(2) about the Groups Works Council the notion 'group' means: a division of a *Konzern*. It should also be noticed that there are no rules about information and consultation for persons working in joint ventures set up by various groups (*Konzern*).[373]

373. Dutch Supreme Court, 14 Mar. 2008, JAR 2008/112; ILLR Vol. 28, p. 374.

The Central Works Council and the Groups Works Councils are made up of members elected by the relevant works councils from among the members of each of these works councils (Article 34 WCA).

The 'Central Works Council' and the 'group(divisional) works council' shall only deal with matters of common interest for all or most of the enterprises for which they have been established, regardless of whether individual works councils may exercise powers in relation to such matters. If, however, individual works councils have powers in relation to such matters of common interest, they are transferred to the Central Works Council or Group Works Council. The Group Works Council shall not deal with matters that are dealt with by the Central Works Council (Article 35WCA). Still, these competence rules are not very clear. Sometimes there have been disputes about the distribution of competences and a case has been reported in which a works council has taken legal action against the Central Works Council!

As a result of all these provisions a complicated network of participatory bodies has emerged in major financial groups, large department stores, etc. They often maintain an entire network of works councils: works councils on a local (plant) basis; works councils for all plants with interrelated products (division) as well as a central works council for the entire group on a national scale. On top of that there may even be a European Works Council (*see* paragraphs 402 et seq.).

If exceptional circumstances prevent the proper implementation of the Act within a given enterprise, the Social-Economic Council may, at the request of the entrepreneur, grant him an exemption, provided he has taken steps to ensure compliance with the requirements of EC Framework Directive on information and consultation, 2001 (Article 5 WCA).

Finally there are some provisions about works councils which the entrepreneurs have merely set up/maintained on the basis of a collective agreement or at his own discretion (Article 5a WCA).

375. As the works council may set up committees (Article 15(3) WCA, *see* paragraph 383), it may establish committees for parts of the enterprise to deal with matters concerning the said parts of the enterprise, notably if a particular site is not large enough or independent enough for the establishment of a separate works council. Then the works council may establish a committee for this site which is responsible for consultation with the local manager.

376. The WCA at first sight does not contain exceptions to accommodate MNCs.[374] Multinational enterprises are subject to the WCA and therefore have to establish works councils and even a central works council for their subsidiaries in the Netherlands if they fit in the criteria of the WCA.

However, the Dutch WCA cannot impose on multinationals to establish works councils for their enterprises outside the Netherlands. Nor can it impose on MNCs the establishment of a central works council which is representative for all the enterprises of the multinational, in the Netherlands as well as in other countries.

374. M. Meyer, *The Position of Dutch Works Councils in Multinational Corporations* (2018).

Yet, implementing a EU Directive, the Netherlands has adopted an Act which obliges multinational enterprises, which meet the requirements of this directive, to establish a European Works Council (*see* paragraph 402).

IV. Statutory and 'Autonomous' Arrangements

377. The WCA gives a general framework for the operation of the works council. However, this framework has been made flexible as the Act authorizes on several points deviations from the statutory provisions. Such deviations as well as further arrangements for the operation of the works council must be laid down in the standing orders of the works council (Articles 8 and 14 WCA). The works council is largely autonomous in determining its standing orders, but the WCA has given some minimum provisions. The standing orders must include the arrangements to notify the entrepreneur and the other persons working in the enterprise on the agenda of its meetings and to make available to them the minutes of its meetings. Prior to approving its standard orders the works council shall give the entrepreneur an opportunity to express his views. For some issues the works council needs the consent of the employer (e.g., on a larger number of members of the works council than provided for in the WCA (*see* paragraph 378)). More in general the employer may oppose terms of the standing orders as contrary to or hindering the proper implementation of the WCA; he can submit such a difference to the court (*see* paragraph 398). The works council may conclude written agreements with the employer on further details of its functioning or enlargement of its facilities and powers (Article 32 WCA, *see* paragraph 391).

V. Composition of the Works Council and Contact with the Employer

378. The works council is composed solely of workers' representatives. Their number varies from three to twenty-five according to the number of employees in the enterprise concerned. The exact number may deviate from the statutory standard (*see* paragraph 377). The works council may also nominate deputy-members (Article 9 WCA). The works council elects its own chairperson and vice-chairperson(s) from its number (Article 7 WCA). The employer is obliged to provide for secretarial support.

379. The law obliges the employer and the works council to meet within fourteen days after either party have submitted a motivated request for a consultation meeting to be held and have stated the reasons for desiring such a meeting. These 'consultation meetings' shall deal with matters relating to the enterprise concerning which either the entrepreneur or the works council considers such a meeting desirable or which are required by the WCA. In enterprises of 100 or more employees at least one time a year the consultation meeting must deal with the employment conditions arrangements and the salaries meant in Article 31d WCA (*see* paragraphs 288 and 385).[375]

The works council may submit proposals to the entrepreneur regarding these matters both inside and outside the consultation meetings (Article 23 WCA). Unless the entrepreneur and the works council jointly agree otherwise, the consultation meeting shall be chaired alternately by the manager of the enterprise and the chairman of the works council or their deputies (Article 23a(2) WCA). At least twice a year, the general operation of the enterprise shall be discussed in consultation meetings. The entrepreneur shall inform the said meetings about any decisions he is considering relating to the matters mentioned in Articles 25 and 27 WCA (*see* paragraphs 386 and 391), in the presence of a representative of the supervisory board, if such a board exists (Article 24 WCA).

VI. The Electoral System and the Relationship Between Unions and Works Councils

380. The works council is elected in free and secret elections by all employees in the enterprise, with the exception, however, of the manager of the enterprise. The works council is thus representative of all personnel in the enterprise.

Elections must be held every three years (Article 12). The WCA does not provide for – as in Belgium – a nationally harmonized date for the elections. A few years ago a proposal of the government to harmonize the dates and times of works councils' elections across all sectors was withdrawn.

Any person who has been working in the enterprise for at least six months is eligible to vote. In order to be eligible to stand for election as a member of the works council, a person must have worked in the enterprise for at least one year (Article 6 WCA). Research has shown that today many employees are no longer interested in the activities of works councils. Often works councils are not able to fill their vacancies as not enough candidates have presented themselves to stand for seats in the works councils.

Temporary agency workers are eligible to vote and to stand for the works council of the temporary agency, but also for that of the user firm if they have an employment record of at least two years duration with that firm (Article 1(3)(a) WCA).

381. Unions are not authorized to make appointments, but they may present lists containing their own candidates. Any trade union whose membership includes persons working in the enterprise who are eligible to vote, whose aim according to its Articles of Association is to protect the interest of its members and which operates as such in the relevant enterprise or industrial sector, and which moreover has had full legal competence for at least two years, may submit a list of candidates, provided that it has consulted its members in the enterprise on the composition of the list of candidates.

375. Act of 15 Jun. 2018, Stb. 2018, 221; Parliamentary Papers 34494.

This right is not exclusive though, as slates of candidates may also be submitted by every employee or group of employees, not being member(s) of the trade unions which have presented a list of candidates (Article 9 WCA).

Union members are overrepresented on works councils in general. According to a recent survey about 65% of the membership of such councils was unionized, whereas the unionization of the total workforce in the Netherlands is in average not higher than about 20%.

It is difficult to give an overall picture of the factual relationship between the works councils and the unions. On the one hand, there are many works councils which operate quite effectively with the support of the unions. At the same time works councils have sometimes proven to be ready to take an independent position (for instance, during strikes) which has brought them into conflict with the unions.

Generally speaking the Dutch trade unions have less influence on works councils than their German counterparts.

382. The entrepreneur must ensure that no person working in the enterprise whose name appears or has appeared on a slide of candidates or who is or has been a member of the works council or one of its committees is placed at any disadvantage with respect to his or her position in the enterprise on the grounds of his/her candidature/membership (Article 21 WCA).

Members, old members and candidate members of the works councils, ERBs, members and former members of committees of the works councils or ERBs, etc. in principle cannot be dismissed (Article 7:670(4)(10-13) CC; *see* paragraphs 198 et seq.). However the court may rescind the employment contracts with these persons if the request for rescission has no relationship with these functions or must be in the interest of these persons (Article 7:671b(6) CC). A member of the works council or its committees may be barred from taking part in the works council's activities only by the court and at the request of the works council or the entrepreneur and for the sole reason that the member of the works council is seriously hindering the work of the works council or the consultation meetings between the works council and the entrepreneur (Articles 13 and 15(5) WCA).

VII. Organization, Facilities and Prerogatives, Confidentiality

383. The works council may set up any committees which it may reasonably be deemed to require in order to perform its duties. For instance standing committees to deal with any matters it may specify, such as a standing committee monitoring the safety, health and welfare of employees in the enterprise. Ad hoc committees may also be set up to prepare certain subjects for its subsequent consideration. Standing committees must include a majority of works council members; committees set up for parts of the enterprise (*see* paragraph 375) as well as ad hoc committees should each have at least one member who is a member of the works council (Article 15 WCA).

The WCA gives the works council a wide variety of general facilities and prerogatives.

Works councils possess the right to:

- invite and consult experts (Articles 16 and 22 WCA);
- use certain facilities belonging to the enterprise, such as a meeting place (Article 17 WCA);
- meet in mutual consultation and to consult with other persons during working hours and with full pay (Article 18(1) WCA);
- attend a minimum of paid days of training every year (Article 18(2) WCA). The costs of this training are borne by the entrepreneur (Article 22(3) WCA).

The normal operating costs of the works council and its committees are borne by the entrepreneur. The costs of legal proceedings and consultation of experts are borne by the entrepreneur if he has been notified in advance that the said costs will be incurred (Article 22 WCA).

In the event of a dispute, the matter may be resolved by the District Court (*see* paragraph 398).

Some of the rights mentioned above are modified in respect of small and medium-sized enterprises (Article 35(b-d) WCA).

384. Members of the works council and of its committees as well as any experts consulted and the secretary of the works council have to treat all business and industrial secrets which may come to their knowledge in the said capacity in strict confidence and also in all matters with respect to which the entrepreneur, the works council or the relevant works council committee has imposed an obligation of confidentiality, or whose confidential nature they may be expected to understand. However, all the said persons as well as the works council as a whole may request the court to lift any obligation to confidentiality imposed, on the grounds that, in considering the interests of those involved, the entrepreneur's decision to impose confidentiality was unreasonable (Article 20 WCA). In future the application and interpretation of this Article will certainly be influenced by the new Act[376] on the protection of trade secrets, adopted in 2018 to implement EU Directive 2016/943/EU, although Article 3(1)(c) of this Act clearly states that the legitimate exercise of the right on information of workers and workers' representatives cannot be qualified as illegal acquisition of trade secrets.

VIII. General Powers/Rights to Information

385. The works council has, in the first place, a certain number of general powers needed for an effective operation.

First, works councils have a right to information from the employer. The law describes in detail what is understood by this right to information. The works council is entitled to raise all issues as it sees fit with the employer and demand information about these issues. The entrepreneur must provide the works council in a timely fashion with all the information and data such as they may reasonably be deemed to require in order to perform its duties. This includes, *inter alia*, basic data about the legal form of the enterprise, the group (= *Konzern*) to which it may

376. Act of 17 Oct. 2018, Stb. 2018, 369.

belong, names and addresses of the members of the Board, etc. In multinational enterprises the local management must also provide basic information about the (ties with) sister companies abroad (Article 31(2)(d)WCA). Then general information concerning the activities and financial results of the enterprise relating to the preceding period and the expectations with respect to the activities and the financial results of the enterprise in the coming period, in particular with reference to matters where consultation is required. In addition annual information on employment and prior information on changes, which affect the workforce and about any intention to commission an outside expert to make recommendations on matters where the endorsement of the works council is required (*see* paragraph 391) (Article 31a, 31b and 31c WCA). In enterprises that normally have at least 100 employees, the employer must also give information to the works council about the salaries of the various groups of employees, as well as on that of the top management and members of the supervisory board (Article 31d and 31e WCA).[377]

IX. Economic Powers

386. The entrepreneur has to inform and consult the works council on any decision it proposes to make concerning:

(a) transfer of control of the enterprise or any part thereof;
(b) establishment, takeover or relinquishment of control of another enterprise, or entering into, making a major modification to or severing a continuing collaboration with another enterprise, including the entering into, the effectuation of major changes to or severing of an important financial holding on account of or for the benefit of such an enterprise;
(c) termination of operations of the enterprise or a significant part thereof;
(d) any significant reduction, expansion or other change in the activities of the enterprise;
(e) major changes in the organization of the enterprise or in the distribution of powers within the enterprise;[378]
(f) any change in the location of the operations of the enterprise;
(g) recruitment or borrowing of labour on a group basis;
(h) making major capital investments on behalf of the enterprise;
(i) taking out major loans for the enterprise;
(j) granting of a substantial credit to or giving security for substantial debts of another entrepreneur, unless this is normal practice and part of the activities of the enterprise;
(k) the introduction or alteration of an important technological provision;

377. Act of 14 Jun. 2006, Stb. 286; Parliamentary Papers 28163.
378. *See* for instance Dutch Supreme Council, 6 Jun. 2001, JAR 2001/128, ILLL Vol. 21, p. 493, about the question: is the decision of the management to ask for judicial leave to defer payments of debts such a major change in the organization of the company?.

(l) taking an important measure regarding the management of the natural environment by the enterprise, including the taking or changing of policy-related, organizational or administrative measures relating to the natural environment;
(m) bearing the financial risk connected to the statutory disability benefits scheme for employees;
(n) the commissioning of an expert from outside the enterprise to advise on any of the matters referred to above and formulating his terms of reference.

The entrepreneur must submit the proposed decision in writing to the works council and ask its advice at a time when it can still significantly affect the decision to be taken. The works council shall be furnished with a summary of the grounds for the decision, its expected consequences for persons working in the enterprise and the measures proposed for dealing with such consequences. The works council shall not render its advice on a proposed decision until the matter has been considered at least once in a consultation meeting with the entrepreneur. If the decision is taken the entrepreneur shall, as soon as possible, send the works council written notification of the decision. Unless the entrepreneur's decision accords with the advice of the works council, the entrepreneur shall postpone implementation of the decision until one month after the day upon which the works council was notified of the decision. This obligation lapses if the works council gives notice to that effect (Article 25 WCA).

387. Within that month the works council may lodge an appeal with the Court of Appeal of Amsterdam (Companies Bench) against a decision by the entrepreneur on the topics mentioned in paragraph 386 if the decision does not accord with the advice of the works council. Appeals may be lodged only on the grounds that the entrepreneur, in weighing the interests involved, could not in all fairness have arrived at the said decision (Article 26 WCA). This means that the entrepreneur in the decision-making process must take into account all justified interests related to the enterprise. This is a marginal control of the courts. It leaves much policy liberty to the entrepreneur.[379]

The court deals with the petition with the utmost urgency. If the court considers the disputed decision of management incorrect, the entrepreneur may be ordered to rescind the decision in whole or in part and to reverse specified consequences of the decision. Or he may be prohibited from performing certain actions in implementation of the decision or parts thereof. If necessary without delay the court may take provisional measures. Appeals against a decree of the court may be lodged with the HR (Article 26 WCA).

388. Research has revealed that yearly less than fifty requests in this field are being filed with the court of which more than 60% are withdrawn before the court hears the case, mostly because in these cases a settlement between the parties concerned (entrepreneur and works council) could be reached. Of the other 40% about one-third seems to be well founded, often on account of procedural mistakes made by the employer vis-à-vis the works council.

379. Dutch Supreme Court, 18 May 2018, ECLI:NL:HR:2018:725.

Practice shows that the court avoids any intervention as regards economic choices made by employers. It does not want to interfere with the laws of the marketplace. The investigation by the court of decisions taken by entrepreneurs consequently concentrates on procedural aspects, for instance if the entrepreneur has failed to duly inform and consult the works council. Several works councils have won their cases because of such procedural mistakes. Also a decision of the entrepreneur in violation of earlier agreements with the works council may easily be dismissed by the court. Thus an entrepreneur was prohibited from closing part of an enterprise as he had previously given his agreement to its continued existence. A decision will also be overturned if it does not give sufficient explanation for its deviation from the opinion of the works council. In the court's case law in these cases scholars have discerned a bunch of 'principles for social corporate governance': the case law of the court encourages management to work correctly with works councils, thereby giving the maximum opportunity for employee participation through the works council. The statutory provisions on the powers of the works council are helpful to stimulate the employer to offer transparency in decision-making and to seek an agreement with the representatives of its workforce, notably on the social consequences of his decisions. However, the judges are very reluctant to challenge the economic rationale of managerial decisions.

A good example was the case of the Amsterdam plant of the British American Tobacco Company (Batco). In 1981 the Court of Amsterdam (Companies Bench) turned down the decision of management to close down the plant, simply because the management had grossly neglected all the participation rules to be followed in such case. The plant stayed open for another ten years. In 1991 the management again decided to close the Amsterdam plant, and to concentrate its production in Brussels. This time all the participation procedures were correctly followed. Nevertheless the works council challenged this decision because apparently the Amsterdam plant was still a profitable business, so why close it down? However, this time the Court of Appeal of Amsterdam (Companies Bench) upheld the decision as it was apparently based on management strategies that were not unreasonable.

So at the end of the day management in the Netherlands is still free to take the economic decisions as it pleases, provided these decisions are taken according to the procedures for information/consultation, laid down by statute, and the social consequences are duly taken into account.

389. As paragraph 376 shows, the Dutch rules on workers participation are also applicable to multinationals with plants in the Netherlands. However, sometimes special adaptations have been made for these multinationals. The advice of the works council can be omitted if the proposed decisions on the second and the last topics mentioned in the list in paragraph 386 are dealing with enterprises abroad and cannot reasonably be expected to have an impact on the third to sixth topics in that list effecting the Dutch subsidiaries of the entrepreneur (Article 25(1) WCA). And even if these decisions have that impact, the obligation to inform and consult the works council does not concern foreign partners in a multinational or in an international merger or transfer or bankruptcy. In such situations the scope of application of the WCA is limited solely to the plants in the Netherlands. Then only the local management of the subsidiaries established in the Netherlands is concerned by this obligation of information and consultation. This situation harms the effectiveness of the workers' involvement in multinational enterprises, which have the real centre of decision-making outside the Netherlands and whose local managers are merely 'puppets on a string'. Consequently, the Dutch system of industrial democracy by way of works councils, although in theory quite strong, is in practice gradually weakened by the internationalization of business.

This type of problems with worker participation can only be solved by participation on a transnational level. In fact the European works council is the only forum for that (*see* paragraph 402). However, the concept of European works councils is still too weak to make up for the degradation of the quality of workers democracy in the Netherlands as a result of the internationalization of business.

390. In a bankruptcy the normal rules on employee participation must be observed by the receiver, given that within the meaning of the WCA the receiver is classed as the entrepreneur. The HR has affirmed[380] that decisions taken by the receiver regarding dismissals, closure of the enterprise, sale of company assets, etc., must be submitted to the works council for its opinion in accordance with Article 25 WCA. However, the rules of the WCA are not in all aspects compatible with those of the BA and therefore cannot be applied to the full in bankruptcy cases. In reality there exist almost no known case law on instances of a receiver having been censured by the court for having taken a decision at which the receiver could not in all fairness have arrived. Presumably works councils are feeling that they stand little chance in those cases, even if the receiver has not duly respected the works council's rights on information and consultation.

X. Social Powers

391. The entrepreneur needs the consent of the works council for any proposed decision for adoption, amendment or repeal of any arrangement pertaining to:

(a) a pension contract, insurance, profit-sharing scheme or savings scheme;
(b) hours of work, rest periods and holidays;
(c) pay or job-grading systems;
(d) health and safety at work, absenteeism because of illness or reintegration;
(e) recruitment, dismissal or promotion policy;
(f) staff training;
(g) staff appraisals;
(h) social welfare services for the undertaking;
(i) shop coordination meetings;
(j) grievances procedures;
(k) the handling and protection of personal information of persons working in the enterprise;
(l) measures aimed at or suitable for monitoring or checking the attendance, behaviour or performance of persons working in the enterprise;

380. Dutch Supreme Court, 2 Jun. 2017, ECLI:NL:HR:2017:982.

(m) a procedure for handling suspects of abuses in the sense of the Whistleblowers Protection Act (*see* paragraph 83).

The consent of the works council is required only insofar as these arrangements, schemes, etc., relate to all the persons working in the enterprise or any group thereof. In other words the works council shall not be involved in individual decisions. This is a very remarkable difference with the works councils in Germany, which are explicitly involved in individual cases.

There is a further very important limitation to these social powers of the works council: the entrepreneur does not need to seek the works council's consent for these matters if and insofar as the relevant matter has already exhaustively been regulated for the enterprise in a collective agreement or an administrative regulation or a mandatory pension fund (Article 27(3) WCA and Article 32(3) Work and Care Act, *see* paragraph 155). This rule enshrines the priority of collective bargaining with the trade unions above negotiations with the works councils. In practice, however, it often occurs that the collective agreement with the trade unions has not settled a matter exhaustively but only rudimentarily. In those cases the employer must seek the consent of the works council on its concrete implementation.

One of the most fertile areas of bargaining by the works councils is the organization of working time and leave arrangements, as both the WTA and the Work and Care Act as well as collective agreements contain numerous opening clauses which give works councils the legal possibility to make arrangements with the employer on working time, deviating from the standards set in statutes and collective agreements (*see* paragraph 299).

However, it should be noted that the Dutch legislator has only in one case explicitly provided that works councils may enter into formal contracts with the employer, viz. with respect to additional competences (Article 32(2) WCA (*see* paragraph 397)). Although sociologists may consider the activities of the Dutch works councils as a kind of negotiation/collective bargaining leading to agreements, lawyers will emphasize that the statute uses the more neutral and somewhat vague word *instemming* (consent). In contrast with the German labour law, which explicitly provides for the *Betriebsvereinbarung* with specific legal effects, the Dutch legislator has renounced of regulating the contractual relationship between employer and employee. Perhaps the terms like negotiation and agreements are avoided because the WCA sees the works council not only as a body to ensure the proper consultation and representation of the persons working in the enterprise but also as a body serving the interests of the proper functioning of the enterprise with respect to all its objectives (Article 2(1) WCA).

On the other hand: in some parts of Dutch labour law a competence is given to the works council and the employer together to derogate from specific statutory provisions (*see* paragraph 28). It must be assumed that if such competences have been used the contents of this agreed derogation are made in writing and have direct effect on the contracts of employment of the workers concerned. Other types of contracts between the employer and the works council can be based on the general law on contracts. They have the effects of all contracts based on that general law (so:

legally binding both sides) but are not – like collective agreements – directly binding the employees. It may, however, been possible to construe under certain conditions a binding effect, for instance when the individual contract of employment contains a reference to such documents (incorporation) or on the basis of custom and practices (*see* paragraph 298). The contractual relationship between employer and works council is a still much-debated item among Dutch labour law specialists.

392. If the entrepreneur does not obtain the works council's consent on these issues, he may put the case before the District Court to rule on the matter. The WCA states explicitly that the court shall only grant permission for the decision to be implemented if the works council's refusal to agree with the decision is unreasonable or if the entrepreneur's proposed decision is required for important organizational, economic or social reasons relating to the enterprise (Article 27(4) WCA). Appeal against the decision of the District Court is possible, first to the Court of Appeal with further appeal to the HR (*see* paragraph 398). An entrepreneur's decision on the above-mentioned issues taken without either the works council's consent or a Court's approval is null and void if the works council has invoked its nullity in writing within one month. The works council may request the court to order the entrepreneur to refrain from any action which would involve implementing or applying an invalid decision. The entrepreneur may request the court to declare that the works council's appeal against a decision on the grounds of invalidity is unfounded (Article 27(5) and (6) WCA).

XI. Other Tasks

393. In addition the works council has the task of ensuring due observation of any regulations applying to the enterprise regarding terms of employment and issues of working conditions and working and resting hours of persons working in the enterprise. The works council shall also promote the consultative coordination of work activities and the transfer of responsibilities within the enterprise in order that the persons working in the enterprise may be as involved as possible in regulating work in the part of the enterprise in which they work. Moreover the works council shall guard against discrimination in general within the enterprise, and in particular promote the equal treatment of man and women and the employment of disabled persons and minorities in the enterprise. Finally the works council must promote care for the natural environment (Article 28 WCA).

394. Works councils have the right to information and consultation relating to all matters affecting employees' health, safety and welfare.[381] All company arrangements pertaining to health and safety at work, absenteeism because of illness and reintegration require the consent of the works council (Article 27(1)(d) WCA, *see* no. 382). The works council must be involved in the implementation of health and

381. *See* J. Popma, *Het Arbo-Effect van medezeggenschap*, Alphen a/d Rijn, 2003; on pp. 313–317 we find an English-language description and discussion of the history of occupational health and safety regulations in the Netherlands, with special focus on workers' participation.

safety policies in the enterprise, such as the risk assessment and evaluation and the assistance of health and safety professionals. They may accompany officials from the Inspectorate SZW during their visits to the enterprise and may speak to them confidentially (Article 12 HSA, *see* paragraph 161) and must have access to the company doctor (Article 14 HSA, *see* paragraph 163). The nomination of HSA prevention assistants, their position in the work organization and their tasks must have the consent of the works council (Article 13 HSA, *see* paragraph 162).[382] In many enterprises the works council has established a standing committee for health and safety matters. Such a committee however is not compulsory.

395. If the employer establishes an institution for the benefit of his employees, for instance a welfare fund, the works council is entitled to appoint at least half of the board members (Article 29 WCA). The works council has also acquired the right to speak on the general assembly of the shareholders of a company about some important items. One of them may be the remuneration of the top executives of the company (Article 2:135 CC).[383]

The works council has a right to consultation when a director of the enterprise should be appointed or dismissed. It does not, however, have recourse against the appointment of a director (Article 30 WCA). The term 'director' here must be construed strictly as referring to the individual who, alone or jointly with others, exercises the highest direct authority in managing work within an enterprise (Article 1(1)(e)). It does not necessarily mean: one or all the members of the board of directors. In major enterprises covered by the Structure Act the works council can influence the composition of the supervisory board (*see* paragraphs 364 et seq.). Finally on the basis of a number of Articles in Book 2 CC the works council has the right to obtain information and to present its opinion to the general meeting of shareholders concerning essential decisions subject to the permission of the general meeting of shareholders, projects to nominate and sack members of the board of directors and the supervisory board of enterprises that are not covered by the Structure Act (Article 2:107a, 2:134a, 2:144a and 2:135 CC).

396. It should be recalled that the various facilities and powers, as they were described in the preceding paragraphs, are applicable to the works councils in enterprises with at least 50 employees. In enterprises with less than 50 employees there must be or may be works councils or ERBs (*see* paragraph 371), but those councils and bodies have more limited facilities and powers than the works councils in enterprises with more than fifty employees (*see* Article 35b, 35c and 35d WCA).

397. The powers of the works council may be extended in a collective agreement with the unions or in an agreement between the employer and the works council (Article 32 WCA). On these wider competences the same priority for collective bargaining (*see* paragraph 391) and the further procedural rules of the standard powers of the works council are applicable (Article 32(3)(4) WCA).

382. Act of 8 Feb. 2017, Stb. 2017, 22.
383. Act of 30 Jun. 2010, Stb. 210, 250; Parliamentary Papers 31877.

XII. Dispute Resolution

398. Any party with a legitimate interest may petition the District Court to rule that the entrepreneur or the works council must comply with all requirements stipulated in the WCA relating to the establishment and operation of a works council, the drawing up of provisional or definitive Rules of Procedure for the Works Council, the nomination of candidates for and the election of members to the works council, and also relating to the publishing of the agendas and minutes of its meetings, insofar as the entrepreneur or the works council are responsible for such matters. Appeals may be brought before the Court of Appeal with a further appeal to the HR (Article 36 WCA).

399. The WCA regulates the composition, appointment and powers of 'joint sectoral committees' (*bedrijfscommissies*). Those committees have been set up by the SER for two segments of the economy, the private sector and the (semi-)public sector. They are standing committees, composed of an equal number of representatives of employers and unions. These joint industry committees have mediation and advisory powers as regards disputes arising between works councils and the employers in the sector (Articles 37–46 WCA).

XIII. Special Provisions for Works Councils in the Public Sector

400. Finally the Act contains special provisions for works councils in the public sector. One of its main topics is the rule saying that in applying Article 23(2) of the Act (*see* paragraph 379) 'matters relating to the enterprise' shall not include the establishment of tasks of public bodies or parts thereof by public law, nor policy relating to or the implementation of the said tasks, except insofar as the same have consequences for the activities of the employees (Article 46d(1)(b) WCA). This means, for example, that the works council of a municipality may not use its competences under the WCA to challenge the decision of a Municipal Council to seek a merger with another municipality. It may only challenge certain personal consequences of such a decision.[384]

XIV. Evaluation

401. Although the Dutch system of works council resembles to a large extent the German system of works councils, it may be useful to highlight here a number of specific differences in the law and practice of works councils in both countries.

The German trade unions have a firm grip on many works councils. The overwhelming majority of German works councils see their activities within the context of the overall objectives formulated by the trade unions. Consequently, the German unions have accepted a clear negotiating role for works councils in Germany in the

384. Dutch Supreme Court, 26 Jan. 2000, JAR 2000/30; Dutch Supreme Court, 22 Mar. 2019, ECLI:NL:HR:2019:397.

conclusion of *Betriebsvereinbarungen* or works agreements of a mandatory character. In the Netherlands, for a variety of reasons, the trade unions have much less influence on works councils. The trade unions have always been reluctant to agree to a clear bargaining role for the works councils, which indeed is lacking in the law (*see* paragraph 391). Company pacts on employment and competitiveness (*Bündnis für Arbeit*) and in-house bargaining in which the employees make certain concessions in terms of working time or pay in return for some form of employment guarantee of the kind found in Germany are almost completely unknown in the Netherlands (*see* paragraph 302).

German works councils are also involved in individual personnel matters (such as hiring and firing), while Dutch works councils are not. In the Netherlands there is no direct representation of the workers on the supervisory boards of large enterprises as there is in Germany. By way of compensation Dutch works councils have a somewhat stronger influence on economic decision-making: for example, they may temporarily halt economic decisions by appealing to a specialized court (*see* paragraph 387).

§5. European Works Councils C.A.

402. Following the adoption at EU level of the Directive on European Works Councils, the Dutch Parliament adopted, in 1997, the European Works Councils Act (EWCA) to implement the EU rules. This Act was amended in 2012 to implement the Recast EU European Works Councils Directive.[385] The Dutch Act scrupulously follows the model for the introduction of European works councils as laid down in the EU Directive. All multinationals, seated in the Netherlands, with at least two plants in the various EU Member States, in each of which at least 150 employees are working, and have at least 1,000 employees altogether working in the EU Member States, must establish a European works council or an equivalent system of information and consultation (Article 1(1)(c) EWCA).

The establishment of such a European works council has to be negotiated by a 'special negotiating body' (SNB). According to Dutch law the members of this SNB, representing the plants in the Netherlands, are chosen by the works councils implicated by the establishment of the European works council (Article 10 EWCA).

The employer and the SNB are free in the set-up of the European works council. However, if the employer refuses negotiations with the SNB or does not, within three years, reach an agreement with that SNB about the set-up of a European works council, then the European works council must be set up according to the rules of a standard model.

This standard model in the Dutch EWCA is very much the same as the one set out in the EU Directive, but it goes a little bit beyond that on one point by ordering information and consultation also on the care of the environment (Article 19(1)(b) EWCA).

385. *See* the Monograph of J. Cremers, European Works Councils in the Netherlands, in Blanpain, *International Encyclopedia for Industrial Relations*, Kluwer, Deventer, 2018.

All the aforementioned is not applicable to European works councils at multinationals in the Netherlands set up before 22 September 1997. However, only very few European works councils at Dutch multinationals had been set up at that time. Actually about 350 Dutch enterprises are represented in a European works council out of the about 800 Dutch enterprises which fall within the scope of the EU directive.

The EC Directive 2001/86/EC on workers participation in the European Company and Directive 2003/72/EC on workers participation in the European cooperative company have been implemented in the Netherlands by the Act on the involvement of employees in European legal persons,[386] which scrupulously follows the provisions of both directives. Finally there is the EU Directive 2005/56/EC on cross-national mergers, which is – after earlier criticism of the CJEU[387] – implemented by a new text of Article 2:333k CC.[388] This new provision must ensure that, in case of the emergence of a new company with legal seat in the Netherlands, the workers of its plants in other EU countries have the same participation rights as the workers in the Dutch plants.[389]

§6. Other Forms and Aspects of Workers' Participation

403. Workers' cooperatives have been established in the Netherlands various times, notably in the mid-nineteenth century. The latest scientific research on these companies dates back to 1979. It revealed that there have been some grosses of such cooperatives in the Netherlands. Some have been successful, some have been a failure, but most of them were never flourishing. All experienced problems in the field of financing, taxes and social organization. Even although there is a specific legislation on cooperatives in the Netherlands, it apparently is not well suited for workers' cooperatives. The only thing the Dutch legislator ever has done to better accommodate workers cooperatives was an amendment of the statutory schemes for social security of employees, which were extended to cover the workers in these kinds of workers' cooperatives (*see* section 4 UBA).

404. In the Netherlands many enterprises have settled practices of quality circles, autonomous or semi-autonomous teams and other management-led practices of employee involvement. Such forms of direct participation are not regulated by the law. The only statutory rule in this field is that all company arrangements pertaining to shop-floor consultations require the endorsement of the works council (Article 27(1)(i) WCA, *see* paragraph 391).

405. In the Netherlands many enterprises have settled practices of profit-sharing schemes. Fourteen per cent of the collective agreements contain provisions in this area. There is however a tendency to convert profit-sharing schemes, which do not

386. Act of 17 Mar. 2005, Stb. 2005, 166.
387. CJEU 20 Jun. 2013, C-635/11.
388. Act of 11 Feb. 2015, Stb. 2015, 84.
389. R. van het Kaar, *Chapter The Netherlands*, in *Exercising Voice Across Borders – Workers' Rights under the EU Cross-Border Merger Directive* (J. Cremers & S. Vitols eds, Brussels: ETUI, 2019).

reflect the individual performances of the employees, into individual bonuses for performances (*see* paragraph 128). The only statutory rule in this field – apart from one for the financial institutions (*see* paragraph 288) – is, that all company arrangements pertaining to profit-sharing schemes require the consent of the works council (Article 27(1)(a) WCA, *see* paragraph 391).

406. Employee share-ownership schemes are not widespread in the Netherlands. This form of participation is not regulated by the law as it is in France, nor is it encouraged by the government by way of tax concessions as it is in Belgium. It also plays a much weaker role in the process of privatization of public enterprises than it does, for example, in France.

Selected Bibliography

Written in English

E.G.v. Arkel & C.J. Loonstra, 'The Netherlands'. In *International Labor and Employment Laws*, Vol. II, edited by William L. Keller. Washington DC: BNA, 2001, pp. 9-1–9-75, and Supplement 2002, pp. 9-1–9-11.

E.G.v. Arkel, *A Just Cause for Dismissal in the US and The Netherlands*, Den Haag, 2007.

I. Asscher-Vonk, *Collective Agreements in The Netherlands, in Collective Bargaining in Europa*, Ministerio de Trabajo y Asuntos Sociales, Madrid, 2004, pp. 138–159.

W.M. Been & De Beer P.T., Case study report *The Regulation of Employment Conditions of Labour Migrants in the Temporary Work Agencies Sector: The Cases of the Netherlands and the U.K.*, UvA, Amsterdam, 2018.

W. Been & M. Keune, 'Chapter 21 The Netherlands'. In *Collective Bargaining in Europe: Towards an Endgame*, Vol. II, edited by T. Müller a.o. ETUI: Bruxelles, 2019, pp. 455–462.

R. Beltzer, *The Transfer of Undertakings and the Importance of Taking over Personnel – A Vicious Circle, IntJCompLLIR* 2007, http://dare.uva.nl/document/224144.

L. van den Berg & S.S.M. Peters, *Study on the Protection of Workers' Rights in Subcontracting Processes – The Netherlands, Core Report and Survey Report,* published in Yves Jorens, Saskia Peters & Mijke Houwerzijl, *Study on the Protection of Workers' Rights in Subcontracting Processes in the European Union: Final Study* (p. 192) (research commissioned by the European Commission), June 2012, http://ec.europa.eu/social/keyDocuments.jsp?advSearchKey=subcontracting+&mode=advancedSubmit&langId=en&search=Search).

K. Boonstra, *The ILO and The Netherlands: Different Views Concerning Government Influence on the Relationship Between Workers and Employers*, Leiden, 1996.

W. Bouwens, National Report on The Netherlands for the VII World Congress of Labour Law and Social Security, theme I, 2003.

A.F.M. Brenninkmeijer & L.C.J. Sprengers, 'Collective Labour Law Disputes in the Public and Private Sector'. In *Effective Resolution of Collective Labour Disputes*, edited by A.F.M. Brenninkmeijer, L.C.J. Sprengers, A.J. de Roo & R.W. Jagtenberg. Groningen, 2006, pp. 3–14.

Selected Bibliography

J. Cremers, *European Works Councils in the Netherlands, in Blanpain, International Encyclopedia of Industrial Relations*, Kluwer, Deventer, 2018.

A. Deelen, E. Jongen & J. Visser, *Employment Protection Legislation: Lessons from Theoretical and Empirical Studies for the Dutch Case*, The Hague, 2006.

L. Delsen, *Exit Polder Model? Socioeconomic Changes in The Netherlands*, Praeger Publishers, Westport, USA, 2002.

European Foundation for the Improvement of Living and Working Conditions, *European Employment and Industrial Relations Glossary*: The Netherlands, Dublin, 1997.

J.H. Even, 'Striking the Tight Balance with Regard to Posted Workers'. In *Balanceren met detacheren*, edited by J.H. Even. Boom, Den Haag, 2018, pp. 69–135.

F.B.J. Grapperhaus & L.G. Verburg, *Employment Law and Works Councils of the Netherlands*, Allen & Overy Legal Practice, Kluwer Law International, The Hague/London/New York 2002.

F.B.J. Grapperhaus, *The End of the Affair*, Deventer, 2006.

G.J.J. Heerma van Voss, 'The Concept of "Employee": The Position in The Netherlands'. In *Restatement of Labour Law in Europe*, Vol. I, edited by B. Waas/ G.J.J. Heerma van Voss. Oxford-Portland: Hart Publishing, 2017, pp. 477–503.

G.J.J. Heerma van Voss, 'Atypical Employment Relationships: The Position in The Netherlands'. In *Restatement of Labour Law in Europe*, Vol. II, edited by B. Waas & G.J.J. Heerma van Voss. Oxford-Portland: Hart Publishing, forthcoming.

G.J.J. Heerma van Voss, 'Dismissal Protection: The Position in The Netherlands'. In *Restatement of Labour Law in Europe*, Vol. III, edited by B. Waas & G.J.J. Heerma van Voss. Oxford-Portland: Hart Publishing, forthcoming.

P.F.v.d. Heijden, 'Post-Industrial Labour Law in The Netherland'. In *Labour Law in the Post-Industrial Era*, edited by W. Wedderburn. Aldershot, 1994.

A. van Hoek, 'Collective Agreements and Individual Contracts of Employment in Labour Law: The Netherlands', *EJCL* 2004, pp. 248–270, http://www.ejcl.org/64/art64-15.pdf.

M.S. Houwerzijl & S.S.M. Peters, *Liability in Subcontracting Processes in the European Construction Sector – Netherlands* (research commissioned by the European Foundation for the Improvement of Living and Working Conditions (Eurofound)), January 2009, http://www.eurofound.europa.eu/publications/htmlfiles/ef08877.htm.

M.S. Houwerzijl, 'The Dutch Understanding of Posting of Workers in the Context of Free Services Provision and Enlargement: A Neutral Approach?'. In *Cross-Border Services, Posting of Workers, and Multilevel Governance*, edited by Stein Evju. Institutt for Privatretts Skriftserie 193/2013, Oslo, Privatrettsfondet, 2013.

H. Houwing, *A Dutch Approach to Flexicurity? Negotiated Change in the Organisation of Temporary Work*, Amsterdam, 2010.

A.T.J.M. Jacobs, *Labour Law and Social Security in The Netherlands*, Bookworld, 's-Hertogenbosch, 1997.

A.T.J.M. Jacobs, 'Chapter The Netherlands'. In *The Regulation of Working Conditions in the Member States of the European Union*, Vol. 2, European Commission, Brussels, 1998, pp. 145–170.

A.T.J.M. Jacobs (ed.), 'Employee Rights in Bankruptcy', *Bulletin of Comparative Labour Relations*, Deventer, 2002, p. 69.

A.T.J.M. Jacobs, 'The Netherlands'. In *Collective Bargaining and Wages in Comparative Perspective, Bulletin of Comparative Labour Relations*, edited by R. Blanpain, T. Blanke & E. Rose, no. 56, Kluwer, Law International, 2005, pp. 89–115.

A.T.J.M. Jacobs, 'Chapter 20 – Labour Law and Social Security'. in *Introduction to Dutch Law*, edited by J. Chorus et al. Wolters Kluwer, 2016, pp. 503–535.

A. Jaspers & F. Pennings, 'Occupational Health and Safety in The Netherlands'. In *Health and Safety at Work: European and Comparative Perspective*, edited by E. Ales. Wolters/Kluwer Law and Business, Deventer, 2013, pp. 329–374.

A. Jaspers, 'Report on The Netherlands'. In *The Situation of Workers and Employers in Restructuring in the EU*, edited by C. Sachs-Durand. Strasbourg, 2014, pp. 155–172, 225–241 and 293–309.

R. van het Kaar, 'Chapter The Netherlands'. In *Exercising Voice Across Borders: Workers' Rights under the EU Cross-Border Merger Directive*, edited by J. Cremers & S. Vitols. ETUI: Brussels, 2019.

M. Keune (ed.) *The Polder Model, Still a Dutch Miracle*, Amsterdam University Press, Amsterdam, 2015.

R. Kleipool a.o., *Corporate Governance in The Netherlands*, The Hague, 2018.

R. Knegt (ed.), *The Employment Contract as an Exclusionary Device*, Antwerp, 2008.

C. Loonstra & J. Quist. 'The Dutch Supreme Court versus the Lower Courts: Summary Dismissal and the Catalogue of Viewpoints'. In *The Legitimacy of the Highest Courts' Ruling*, edited by N. Buls et al. The Hague, 2009, pp. 343–368.

M. Meyer, *The Position of Dutch Works Councils in Multinational Corporations*, Maastricht, 2018.

T. van Peijpe, *Employment Protection under Strain (Sweden, Denmark, The Netherlands)*, Kluwer Law International, The Hague, 1998.

A. de Roo & R. Jagtenberg, *Settling Labour Disputes in Europe*, Ph.D. Erasmus University, Rotterdam, 1994, pp. 209–263.

T. Schilf, *Employment Protection in Dutch Collective Labour Agreements*, Amsterdam, 2007.

M.v. Velzen, *Learning on the Fly*, Ph.D. University of Amsterdam, Amsterdam, 2004.

J. Visser, 'Two Cheers for Corporatism, One for the Market: Industrial Relations, Wage Moderation and Job Growth in The Netherlands', *British Journal of Industrial Relations*, 1998, pp. 269–292.

J.P. Windmuller, *Labor Relations in The Netherlands*, Ithaca NY, 1969.

Written in Dutch

H.L. Bakels, *Schets van het Nederlands arbeidsrecht,* Kluwer, Deventer, 2019.

W.H.A.C.M. Bouwens (et al.), Van der Grinten, *Arbeidsovereenkomstenrecht*, Kluwer, Deventer, 2018.

R. Houweling (ed.), Arbeidsrechtelijke themata (Vol. I and Vol. II), Boom, Den Haag, 2018.

A.T.J.M. Jacobs, *Sociaal Recht*, 2e druk, Paris, Zutphen, 2010.

Selected Bibliography

A.T.J.M. Jacobs, *Collectief Arbeidsrecht*, 4e druk, Kluwer, Deventer, 2017.
J.P. Windmuller, C. de Galan & A.F. van Zweeden, *Arbeidsverhoudingen in Nederland*, Utrecht, 7e druk 1990.

Index

The numbers here refer to paragraph numbers.

Index

www.ingramcontent.com/pod-product-compliance
Lightning Source LLC
Chambersburg PA
CBHW071422230926
51846CB00001B/105